GUIDE TO WESTERN CANADA

Guide to
Western Canada

All you need to know for four seasons' travel in:
British Columbia ● Alberta ● Saskatchewan
Manitoba ● Yukon and Northwest Territories

by
Frederick Pratson

A Voyager Book

Chester, Connecticut 06412

Photographs courtesy of the tourism services of British Columbia, Alberta, Saskatchewan, Manitoba, Yukon, and Northwest Territories and the federal tourism promotion department of the government of Canada.

Library of Congress Cataloging-in-Publication Data

Pratson, Frederick John.
    Guide to western Canada / by Frederick Pratson. — 1st ed.
      p.   cm.
    "A Voyager book."
    Includes index.
    ISBN 0-87106-762-5 (pbk.)
    1. Canada, Western—Description and travel—Guide-books.
I. Title.
F1060.4.P72 1987
917.12′043—dc 19   87-19822
                                                                       CIP

Manufactured in the United States of America

First Edition/First Printing

Contents

1. The Special Allure of Western Canada.. 1
2. General Information... 16
3. Canada for Non-Canadians... 38
4. Touring British Columbia... 56
5. Vancouver: Camelot by the Pacific.. 95
6. Victoria: England by the Pacific... 148
7. Touring Alberta.. 197
8. Touring Saskatchewan... 260
9. Touring Manitoba... 297
10. Exploring the Yukon and the Northwest Territories............... 327

Index.. 359

Maps

Western Canada... 2
British Columbia.. 58
Metro Vancouver.. 106
Vancouver Centre City.. 107
Metro Victoria.. 156
Alberta.. 198
Metro Calgary... 213
Saskatchewan.. 262
Manitoba.. 298
Metro Winnipeg... 309
Yukon and Northwest Territories... 328

I am especially pleased to dedicate *Guide to Western Canada* to three exceptional people, who are tourism specialists at the Canadian Consulate in Boston, Massachusetts: Ralph Johansen, Janet Aiton, and Linda Schmidtke.

Over many years Ralph, Janet, and Linda have been invaluable to me with regard to my many forays in Canada and my subsequent writings. I consider them friends, actually members of my extended family.

I also dedicate this edition to the memory of Sam McKelvey, who passed away in Cairo, Egypt, while serving Canada. Sam was a beloved member of the Society of American Travel Writers and one of the finest and most able tourism specialists the Canadian federal government ever fielded to promote its interests in other countries. For a number of years Sam was truly "Mr. Canada" in New York City.

Preface

During the early 1970s, when I was doing research for my book *Guide to Atlantic Canada*, which was later expanded into *Guide to Eastern Canada*, I stood on the steep cliffs overlooking the open Atlantic at the edge of Cape Spear in Newfoundland, the easternmost point of land in Canada. I turned, faced west, and had all of Canada before me. I looked forward to one day doing the same thing at the edge of the Pacific Ocean in British Columbia, where I would have all of Canada to the east of me. In 1987, while researching this book, on a foggy, rainy winter's day on Vancouver Island, I did just that.

Over the years, traveling over so much of Canada, getting to know the people, their history and ways, their landscape, I often thought of myself as the early explorer Sir Alexander Mackenzie, who is to Canadians what Lewis and Clark are to Americans. However, the major differences between me and Mackenzie are that he traveled in unknown, hazardous territory and lived off the land, while I had the comforts of fancy hotels, gourmet cuisine, and jet transportation. On the other hand, there were many times, when alone in some wilderness area, far from human habitation, I felt the presence of Sir Alex by my side, prompting me to continue. In addition to the research and travel, one of the major obstacles for me to overcome was to write this book, word after word, page after page. In this regard, I really did feel kin to Mackenzie as he moved step after step over the rugged, uncharted terrain of Western Canada. He did it in fact. I did it in spirit and on paper.

Many people over the years have asked me why I write about Canada. I simply say that I love the country, in its nobility and occasional absurdity, as I do my own, and that I consider myself Canadian in the spirit of its explorers and sometimes regret that I wasn't born several generations ago when I too could have been among the first to trek over the magnificent landscape that became the nation of Canada.

How to Use This Guide

Chapter 1 of this guide tells why Western Canada is a special region of North America to visit. It provides some basic information on history, geography, weather, and other general aspects of the region that will help you appreciate Western Canada more.

Chapter 2 provides general information for all travelers to Western Canada—the "nuts and bolts" of how to get there, sources of information, and so on. Chapter 3 will orient non-Canadians to Canada, in terms of history and regulations involving customs.

Chapters 4 through 10 describe touring the provinces and territories of Western Canada, focusing on major cities and what they offer and on the national parks of this region. There is a great deal of specific information in these chapters regarding attractions, accommodations, dining, transportation, sports, shopping, and entertainment. If you require more specific information that is not contained in this guide, refer to the lists of government tourism agencies and the material on how to contact them. Although this guide perhaps is a bit more comprehensive than others, it is not an encyclopedia for travelers. All of the listed government tourism agencies will provide the information you need free of charge, either over the phone or through the mails. They will also send you maps and brochures free of charge. If you use this guide in conjunction with information provided by these agencies, you'll have everything you need to know.

This guide has been designed for easy use while planning your trip prior to departure and while en route through your travels. It is also a handy source of good ideas for future vacations in Western Canada. The region is so vast that you cannot visit it all on one trip, unless you have unlimited time. But its allure is so powerful that you will want to come back again, many times.

There is also a substantial amount of information in the major city sections for the business traveler and for the convention/meeting planner—everything from prime exhibition space to the best executive hotels.

Acknowledgements

I take this opportunity to thank the following individuals and their organizations who supplied information and/or manuscript checking. Elvira Quarin of the Greater Vancouver Convention and Visitors Bureau. Laverne Barnes, Wendy Copeland, Cathy Wilson, Benita Jekubik, and Kathy Ferguson of Tourism British Columbia. Joyce Brookbank and Tracy Weisgarber, Tourism Association of Vancouver Island. Moira Fitzpatrick, Four Seasons Hotel in Vancouver. Also in British Columbia: Don Foxyord and Marilyn McKil, Rocky Mountain; Verne Parnell, the Sunshine Coast; Greg Meredith and Lori Loset, North by Northwest; Linda Scarfo, Peace River Alaska Highway; Deanna Merrick and Rosemary Eaton, the Okanagan/Similkameen; Eva St. Amand, High Country; John Dennings and Kelly Hasewgawa, Southwestern B.C.; Roy Shields and Kelly Sallis, Kootenay Country; Gordon Finlay and Linda Williamson, Caribbo; Kevin Walker and Jill Whitmore of the Oak Bay Beach Hotel in Victoria; Ernie Pshebnisky of the British Columbia Convention Centre and Ron Davis and Bill Bouchard of the British Columbia Ferry Corporation.

Also: Steve Pisni representing Air Canada in the eastern United States; Kevin Shackell of Yukon Tourism; Harvey Dryden and Gerard Makuch of Saskatchewan Tourism; Marla J. Daniels of Edmonton Tourism; Gerry Krisch of Travel Alberta; Hap Freeman of Calgary Tourism; Dan Cherney of Travel Alberta; Jim Waters of the XV Olympic Winter Games Organizing Committee; Carole Wakabayashi of the Saskatoon Visitor and Convention Bureau; C. Michalenko of the Regina Convention and Visitors Bureau; Robert Bridge and Joyce Meyer of Travel Manitoba; Cheryl Grant-Gamble and Frona Scott of TravelArctic (Northwest Territories); Kate MacGregor of the Department of Regional Industrial Expansion, Government of Canada; and Diane Houston of (Ottawa) Canada's Capital Visitor's and Convention Bureau.

Finally, but hardly least of all, I wish to thank Pierre Turcotte, Ralph Johansen, Janet Aiton, and Linda Schmidtke of the Canadian Consulate in Boston for their assistance, enthusiasm, and friendship.

CHAPTER 1

The Special Allure of Western Canada

To say that Western Canada is one of the most magnificent regions in North America is not a trite superlative but an understatement. Within this vast region are some of the highest mountains on the North American continent, sprawling glaciers and giant trees, scores of wild rivers and thousands of unnamed lakes, moody seacoasts rich with Indian legends and with the varied species that live therein, sprawling prairies thick with golden wheat and the mysterious Arctic region itself inhabited by the "first people" of the Western Hemisphere, cosmopolitan cities offering the best of the modern world and quaint towns that bespeak of bygone times and values, major expositions and international sports events, ethnic festivals and cowboy rodeos, magnificent resorts and charming inns. In Western Canada you can go helicopter skiing, white-water rafting, trail riding; play golf surrounded by the Rocky Mountains; canoe, windsurf, hunt, fish; photograph the beauty all around you; hike, camp; ride on top of a glacier; attend plays, opera, and symphony; stay at some of the finest hotels in the world and dine at superior gourmet restaurants; see unusual exhibits of art and science; thrill to the sight of orcas (killer whales), eagles, bears, moose, caribou, elk, mountain sheep. Western Canada is an untamed wilderness that offers the utmost in human civilization as well. Here you can explore and partake of both.

Although most travelers have had some knowledge of Western

1

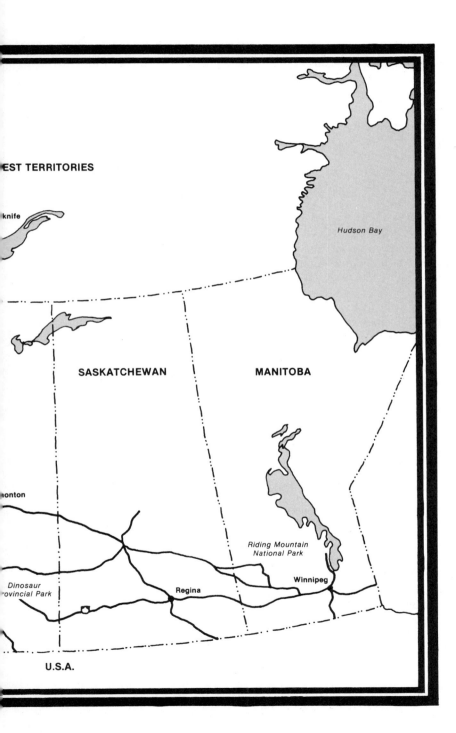

ST TERRITORIES

knife

Hudson Bay

SASKATCHEWAN

MANITOBA

onton

Riding Mountain
National Park

Dinosaur
ovincial Park

Regina

Winnipeg

U.S.A.

Canada, if only through brushes with it in geography lessons, it was not until 1986, because of all the hoopla promoting Expo in Vancouver, that people began to perceive the true allure of this region and consider it a prime destination for their vacations. Expo, the barrage of television and print advertising from Canadian tourism, and a genuine fear of travel to other foreign places brought people to Western Canada in droves. When they returned home, raving about their fabulous Western Canada experiences, a geometric progression, attracting more people, was set in motion. At the same time, thousands of others who wanted to come were left disappointed because every kind of accommodation and transportation service was booked solid, but the allure was so powerful that many of the denied in 1986 planned on making Western Canada their main vacation destination in the years to come. The great crowds brought into the region by Expo have thinned out. Now there's a less frenetic pace to all aspects of travel in Western Canada. The best of the region remains. Its natural attributes are as awesome as ever. Its cities, such as Vancouver (Expo) and Calgary (site of the 1988 Winter Olympic Games), are even better and more exciting than before. And the proud people of Western Canada, representing every ethnic and racial group on Earth, are eager to make a new batch of friends—warmly welcoming you and your family to their Promised Land.

When you travel through Western Canada, may there be more sunny days than stormy ones; but even in the mist, when a snow-capped mountain peak suddenly appears breaking through a cloud, you know you are where you have always wanted to be.

Geography

Western Canada forms its southern border with the United States (the U.S. northern border) at the 49th parallel, all the way from just south of the city of Vancouver to the western border of Ontario. The southeastern section of Vancouver Island, facing the Pacific Ocean, with the capital city of Victoria at its tip, dips below the 49th parallel and near the 48th. This section of Vancouver Island is in the area of the Strait of Juan de Fuca and the San Juan Islands, and it is pointed toward Seattle, Washington. Along the 49th parallel, from west to east, are the provinces of British Columbia, Alberta, Saskatchewan, and Manitoba. South of the border, from west to east, are the states of Washington, Idaho,

Montana, North Dakota, and Minnesota. To the north of British Columbia is the Yukon Territory, which borders eastern Alaska and western Northwest Territories. The Yukon also has a small coast along Mackenzie Bay, which is part of the Beaufort Sea and thence the Arctic Ocean. The Northwest Territories span much of northern Canada, from the Yukon to Davis Strait, which separates Canada from Greenland.

Looking at the impressive, varied topography of Western Canada, from west to east, the Pacific coastline of British Columbia is indented with long fjords and broken into hundreds of islands, the largest of which are Vancouver Island and the Queen Charlotte Islands. Queen Charlotte Strait and the Strait of Georgia separate Vancouver Island from mainland British Columbia. Most of the population in the province live in the extreme southwest part of British Columbia. The Fraser River, a great waterway of Canada, flows through the province and empties into the Strait of Georgia at the city of Vancouver. British Columbia is essentially a province of mountain ranges: Vancouver Island Ranges, Coast Mountains, Columbia Mountains, Monashee Mountains, Selkirk Mountains, Purcell Mountains, Rocky Mountains. The Japan Current helps to create a mild climate along the Pacific Coast. The Coast Mountains trap most of the storms moving east, and a great deal of rain is dumped along the coast, making for extremely lush forests of giant trees and for a relatively long growing season. As a result, this area supports thriving lumber and agricultural and allied industries, with much of the product exported to other countries. The fisheries are also vital to the economic life of the province, especially the catching and processing of salmon. However, just east of the Coast Mountains, the landscape is very arid, almost similar to that of the southwestern United States. This area is also one of the most productive agricultural areas in the province because of intensive use of irrigation.

North central British Columbia is a rugged plateau with many lakes and dense forests. The cordillera (mountain ranges) continues through much of the Yukon and through Alaska. Mount Logan (19,850 feet) in the Yukon is Canada's highest mountain. The famous gold fields of the Klondike are also in the Yukon. Mining is a major economic activity in both the Yukon and British Columbia. The western section of the Northwest Territories is primarily tundra, with many lakes, such as Great Bear Lake and Great Slave Lake, two of the largest in North America. The Mackenzie River, running north from Great Slave Lake to Beaufort Sea, is one of Canada's important waterways.

The border of British Columbia and Alberta is formed by the impressive Rocky Mountains. Here is also the Great (Continental) Divide, where rivers and streams on the west side flow toward the Pacific and those on the east side flow toward the Atlantic. Recreation (national parks, resorts, skiing, trail riding, hiking, and so on), mining, and forestry are the chief economic activities in the Rockies. The Rockies form only the western edge of Alberta; the rest of the province is flat or rolling terrain, known as the Interior Plains.

The Interior Plains stretch across the rest of Western Canada—Saskatchewan and Manitoba—to the Ontario border. Much of the land is devoted to growing wheat and other grains and to raising beef cattle. Alberta has large deposits of oil, oil-bearing materials (tar sands), and natural gas. Because of its high volume of petroleum production, this province is often referred to as the "Texas of Canada." Saskatchewan is one of the world's leading producers of potash, used as fertilizer in agriculture.

Located in the interior of Manitoba is Lake Winnipeg, which is almost 2,000 square miles larger than Lake Ontario, one of the Great Lakes. The northeastern portion of this province also has shoreline on Hudson Bay, the largest inland sea in the Western Hemisphere. The Churchill River, a favorite haunt of naturalists and explorers, flows through northeastern Manitoba into Hudson Bay, where there is a major habitat for polar bears.

Northern Alberta, Saskatchewan, and Manitoba are primarily wilderness areas of countless lakes but nevertheless attractive to the serious angler. All the major cities and towns and transportation routes in these three provinces are located in the south, where the land is finer for agriculture and the winter climate less severe.

History

In 1885 two significant events took place in Western Canada—the completion of the country's transcontinental railroad and the Battle of Batoche. On November 7 of that year, at Craigellachie, within the rugged Monashee Mountains region, near the Eagle River, the last spike of the Canadian Pacific Railroad was driven into place. Almost the entire breadth of Canada was at last linked, from coast to coast, by a modern transportation system that would greatly increase the human settlement and economic progress of a vast area of North America. The completion of this railroad was one of the great accomplishments of the nineteenth century: in its time, similar in complexity, effort, and investment to what it took to land humans on the moon in ours, and just as important in the synergism of progress it set in motion.

Prior to the completion of the railroad, Canada was a confederation of seven provinces: Ontario, Quebec, New Brunswick, Nova Scotia, Prince Edward Island, Manitoba, and British Columbia. British Columbia joined confederation on the strict stipulation that it be connected to the rest of the country by rail; otherwise, it would, considering several possibilities of destiny, remain a colony of Great Britain, join the United States, or become independent. At that time, Canada was fortunate to have Sir John A. Macdonald as its first prime minister under the British North America Act, the instrument that created confederation and the beginnings of the Canadian nation. Macdonald goaded Parliament into moving ahead with this monumental transcontinental venture in order to keep British Columbia in confederation and, as a result, forge a new country from ocean to ocean.

Building the transcontinental used the sweat and muscle of thousands of workers. The hazards of harsh weather, rugged terrain, bad food, and poor medical care killed off or injured many of them. Great numbers of men from China were brought in to work as coolies at this task. In addition to the usual hardships everyone suffered, the Chinese had to endure bigotry, lower wages and poorer working conditions than their coworkers, and cruel separations from their families. These workers, Caucasian and Asian, built track across prairies and muskeg and blasted the line through range after range of mountains.

While the line was being built, the railroad ran out of money, but thanks to Lord Revelstoke, top man at London's prestigious investment-banking firm of Barings, necessary funds were injected into the project to bring about a successful conclusion and thereafter profits for those who had vision. Both a small town and a mountain are named in the honor of Lord Revelstoke near the spot where the last spike was hammered down. And when that day finally came— November 7, 1885—British Columbia was no longer isolated by land from Eastern Canada.

The contemporary settlement and economic development of Western Canada began in earnest, and Canada as such evolved from fractious enclaves hugging the shores of the Atlantic and the Great Lakes into what would rapidly become the second-largest nation in the world. Once the means of transcontinental transportation were set in place, tens of thousands of settlers—native-born North Americans; immigrants from eastern Europe, Germany, Scandinavia, and other countries; and canny investors—headed west for a new life of what they hoped would hold better possibilities. Small towns, such as Winnipeg, and police garrison posts, such as Calgary, became cities of consequence. Alberta and Saskatchewan became provinces in confederation with the seven others in 1905. Victoria and Vancouver assumed separate thrones as queen cities of Canada on the sparkling Pacific.

Also in 1885, at Batoche, fifty-five miles northeast of the city of Saskatoon in Saskatchewan, the last decisive battle of the Northwest Rebellion (also known as the Riel, Red River, or Métis Rebellion) took place. Louis Riel was the leader of the Red River (Manitoba) métis, people of mixed French and Amerindian blood whose lands were stolen from them by unscrupulous speculators and naive settlers. Riel, one of the most charismatic figures in Canadian history, wanted his people to have permanent ownership rights to lands of their own and to preserve their culture. He was prepared to fight the forces of Canada to secure his goals, and he and his people did so—first with common sense and a belief in the efficacy of democracy and then, feeling betrayed, with a fierce vengeance. His establishment of a provisional government led to the creation of Manitoba as a province of Canada in 1869.

The downfall of Riel began at Duck Lake, Saskatchewan, where a Northwest Mounted Policeman was killed. This murder caused a sensation in Eastern Canada, and the federal government sent troops to subdue Riel, who was held accountable, and his forces. The métis figured they would get no justice and, using what we now term "guerrilla" tactics, fought a series of battles with the professional soldiers. The métis made their last stand at Batoche. Because the métis were well dug in, this battle lasted for four long days. However, Riel had no alternative but to surrender, after which he was taken to Regina, where he was put on trial. Riel was found guilty and then was hanged. His execution pleased an agitated public opinion in the East, but it also became a dominant part of the folklore of Canada because enough people believed and continue to believe that Louis Riel was murdered by an example of the Canadian justice system that preferred expediency to truth.

With the defeat of the métis and death of Riel, the broad, fertile lands of Manitoba and Saskatchewan were now open to all comers, and come they did. The newcomers were the winners, and the losers were, as in the United States, those of Amerindian and mixed blood.

The history of Canada was shaped by a number of other important events. In 1670 the Hudson's Bay Company was founded in London, England, where it continues to have a headquarters. Its purpose as a trading company was not to develop a nation in the political sense, but to use its leverage to make as much money as possible for British investors through the North American fur trade. In time, because of its strategically located trading posts throughout the North and West, Hudson's Bay controlled much of the territory of what is Canada today, thus becoming an empire unto itself. Hudson's Bay investors hired tough, canny Scots to operate these far-flung outposts of commerce, and they did their deals with the native peoples, trappers, and mountain men exceedingly well. Some Montréal Scots, seeing no need to share hard-earned proceeds with a far-off gentry, started a trading company of their own, the North West Company. For many decades, these two companies were in savage competition with each other for turf, product, and profit. Their enterprises ranged from the Arctic down to what are now the states of Washington and Oregon. Eventually, Hudson's Bay won, absorbing the operations of the North West Company, not unlike today's corporate mergers. In 1868, however, Britain's Parliament made Hudson's Bay turn over its immense holdings of territory to the relatively new government of Canada, although the company continued with its business dealings throughout much of these lands. Today, Hudson's Bay Company is familiar to all Canadians and to visitors as a chain of excellent department stores, known as the Bay. On the other hand, if you travel to the remote reaches of northern Canada, there's a good chance you'll make a stop for supplies at a Hudson's Bay Company trading post, because there's usually nothing else around for hundreds of miles, and you'll experience a bit of the heritage that has gone on unbroken and with distinction since the seventeenth century.

To adventurous souls in the nineteenth century, the big news coming out of Western Canada was not a railroad but the discovery of gold—and "gold fever" was the great contagious disease of that age. The coast of British Columbia and the interior regions of the Yukon were flooded by thousands of men with wild dreams of

9

fabulous wealth spurring them on. The sandbars of the lower Fraser River and the Klondike became famous; their immortality in folklore continues. Some would find gold, strike it rich, and go on to live like kings. Some would strike it rich by bilking those who sought gold, and they, too, would take on the lifestyles of royalty. Many, however, would "lose their shirts" and their health in the quest. Still others, wearing ragged clothes with pockets empty of cash, would die on the trails, in the mines, and at the panning streams. These risk-takers, whether successful or not, infused Western Canada with a bullish spirit that anything is possible with a lot of pluck—in contrast to the East, where proper establishment credentials counted for more than the magic of individual potential. Much of this individualistic, entrepreneurial spirit still exists in Western Canada and motivates its people, whether progeny of several generations or the most recent immigrant.

Western Canada is different from the western United States in a very fundamental way: It was not as wild in the gun-shooting, Indian-chasing sense. Law and order came to Western Canada in tough, disciplined men wearing the red tunics and blue pants of the Northwest Mounted Police—the world-famous and legendary Mounties, established in 1874. This glowing legend contains more truth than falsehood. The Mounties came to Western Canada as the federal government's strong arm and to provide assistance to provincial and territorial governments that had scant other such law-enforcement services. The Mounties protected the rights of both Indians and white settlers in a fair and just manner, not every time, but often enough to win respect. They stopped whiskey traders from exploiting the Indians. After the battle of the Little Bighorn, thousands of U.S. Indians, including Sitting Bull, knowing that their victory was an advent to killing and terror from forthcoming waves of U.S. soldiers, moved across the border into lower Alberta, seeking refuge ensured by a shield of compassion and resolve provided by the Mounties. One Mountie legend says that "a Mountie always gets his man." In case after case, the Mounties have kept after a law breaker, often under extremely harsh weather and terrain conditions, until they got him or her, preferably alive. Their record in this regard isn't 100 percent, but it and the quality of men and women themselves have been good enough to serve as a

The Royal Canadian Mounted Police are a force of legend and distin- ▶ **guished public service. The Mounties opened and made decent Western Canada for all people.**

prevention to crime. Today's Mounties are officially known as the Royal Canadian Mounted Police, or RCMP. Their major training center is at Regina, Saskatchewan.

The early history of Western Canada is replete with the names of immortal explorers. Some historians speculate that Sir Francis Drake could have seen the coast of British Columbia from his ship in the sixteenth century, but they are sure that Captain James Cook landed on what would be later called Vancouver Island in 1778. Captain George Vancouver, from whom the island and the chief city of the province derive their name, mapped the British Columbia coast from 1792 to 1794, to strengthen British claims to this North American territory. Around the same time, in 1793, Sir Alexander Mackenzie, a Scot working for the North West Company, reached the Pacific after crossing much of the continent. He accomplished this amazing feat, including extremely difficult crossings of the Rockies and other mountain ranges of British Columbia, about thirteen years before Lewis and Clark stood at the shores of the Pacific. He was also the intrepid explorer of the 1,120-mile-long river bearing his name that runs north, through the Northwest Territories and near western Alaska, from Great Slave Lake to Mackenzie Bay and Beaufort Sea above the Arctic Circle. Western Canada also saw the likes of countless trading company explorers, trappers, mountain men, French Jesuit priests, and others who were keen on adventure and bringing new geographical prizes home to their patrons. Much of the northern portions of Western Canada has yet to be explored and experienced in ways similar to those who trekked through in times far removed from ours.

The human history of Canada began thousands of years ago, when nomadic, tribal peoples crossed the then-existing land bridge between what is now Soviet Siberia and Alaska. No one knows for sure what climatic changes and food shortages caused this migration, but enough people did come over to spread throughout the Western Hemisphere. Some created impressive civilizations, such as in Mexico, Peru, Ecuador, and in Western Canada, particularly along coastal British Columbia. Today the progeny of these ancient peoples continue to live and develop their cultures in Western Canada—the Inuit (Eskimos, as most whites call them) in the Arctic areas (Northwest Territories); the coastal tribes of British Columbia (also inland tribes), the Yukon, and Alaska; and the plains tribes of Alberta, Saskatchewan, and Manitoba. The land that was new, strange, and amazing to white explorers and settlers was a familiar and long-standing home to these native peoples. Despite frequent contention among themselves, they lived in harmony with this magnificent nature, taking from it only what they needed, occasionally a little more, but never exploiting what they considered a gift from God out of insatiable avarice. The sons and daughters of the "first people," living in Western Canada today, continue to pursue the same pragmatic and spiritual values of their ancestors. The perception of human existence gained through their eyes can be one of the most rewarding experiences of your trip to Western Canada.

The Great Cities of Western Canada

It is hard to believe that one hundred years ago the great cities of Western Canada—Vancouver, Victoria, Calgary, Edmonton, Saskatoon, Regina, Winnipeg—were little more than trading posts, frontier police garrisons, or logging towns. When you see their gleaming, impressive skylines today, all the marks of a progressive, contemporary society are there. You see commercial and industrial activities of all kinds, a wide variety of cultural and entertainment attractions, fine universities and medical centers, and wonderful hotels and restaurants. You see a broad diversity of people representing just about all ethnic, racial, and religious groups inhabiting this planet. In the cities of Eastern Canada great emphasis is placed on the two founding cultures—French and British. In Western Canadian cities, however, the second most important culture, after English, might be Ukrainian or Chinese.

Although Western Canadian cities can't boast of long, dramatic histories, except in the case of Amerindian tribes, a dynamic "We can do it!" spirit is here that is often lacking in more established areas. These cities have had their boom-and-bust times, particularly in the commodities they produce and ship—oil, minerals, lumber, fish, grain. Regardless, they have always bounced back bigger and better than before. Look at Vancouver, with its blockbuster Expo 86! It recorded 22 million visitors. Look at Edmonton, with a shopping mall that rivals Disney World in style and substance!

The quality of urban life the people here have created and continue to refine is the envy of cities centuries old. Here, there is always a sense of anticipation, of becoming, of something new

Calgary, site of the 1988 Winter Olympic Games, is one of the great cities ▶ of Western Canada; here, oil and cattle are king.

around the bend. On a more mundane but nonetheless important level, Western Canadian cities are about as immaculately clean as cities can be. They are also crime-free, not completely, but enough so that most people are not afraid of the risk and live a normal and even a contented life. And they are on the threshold of the great Canadian wilderness, where a person can travel hundreds of miles over a rugged, magnificent landscape and meet hardly another soul. After you've visited some of the great cities of Western Canada and toured their countryside, you won't return home wondering when you'll be back for another visit. You will, most likely, be planning on how to make things work out so that you can return to stay for good.

CHAPTER 2

General Information

Free Information for U.S. Travelers

The tourism section of the Canadian Consulate General near you is one of your best resources for free information and advice on almost any aspect of travel to and within Canada. Consulate offices have brochures and maps from every province and major city and will provide these materials on request by phone or through the mails. Consulate offices are open during ordinary business hours, Monday through Friday, but are closed on the national holidays in the countries in which they are located and on Canadian national holidays, such as Victoria Day, Canada Day, Canadian Thanksgiving Day, and Boxing Day.

400 S. Omni International
ATLANTA, GA 30303
(404) 577–7445

Suite 400, Three Copley Place
BOSTON, MA 02116
(617) 536–1730

One Marine Midland Centre
Suite 3550
BUFFALO, NY 14203
(716) 852–7369

310 South Michigan Avenue
12th Floor

CHICAGO, IL 60604
(312) 427–1888

55 Public Square
Suite 1038
CLEVELAND, OH 44113
(216) 771–1684

St. Paul Tower, 17th Floor
750 N. St. Paul
DALLAS, TX 75201
(214) 922–9814

1900 First Federal Building
1001 Woodward Avenue

DETROIT, MI 48226
(313) 963–8686

300 South Grand Ave.
LOS ANGELES, CA 90014
(213) 687–7432

701 Fourth Ave., South
9th Floor
MINNEAPOLIS, MN 55415
(612) 332–4314

Room 1030
EXXON Building
1251 Avenue of the Americas
NEW YORK, NY 10020
(212) 757–4917

Suite 1160
Alcoa Building
One Maritime Plaza
SAN FRANCISCO, CA 94111
(415) 981–8515

412 Plaza 600
Sixth and Stewart
SEATTLE, WA 98101
(206) 223–1777

1211 Connecticut Ave., N.W.
Suite 300
WASHINGTON, DC 20036
(202) 735–1400

Provincial and Major City Tourism Offices

The following provincial and city tourism agencies will also supply you with free information and advice on travel in their areas:

BRITISH COLUMBIA
Ministry of Tourism,
  Recreation and Culture
Parliament Buildings
Victoria, British Columbia
  V8V 1X4
(604) 387-1642

Vancouver Travel Info Centre
562 Burrard Street
Vancouver, British Columbia
Canada V6C 2J6
(604) 683–2000

Tourism Victoria
812 Wharf Street
Victoria, British Columbia
Canada V8W 1T3
(604) 382–2127

ALBERTA
Travel Alberta
10025 Jasper Avenue, 15th
  Floor
Edmonton, Alberta
Canada T5J 3Z3
(800) 661–8888 (continental
  United States)

Calgary Tourist & Convention
  Association
237–8th Ave., S.E.
Calgary, Alberta
Canada T3C 0K8
(403) 263–8510

Edmonton Convention Bureau
9797 Jasper Ave.
Suite 104

17

Edmonton, Alberta
Canada T5J 3H1
(403) 426–4715

SASKATCHEWAN
Tourism Saskatchewan
2103 11th Avenue
Regina, Saskatchewan
Canada S4P 3V7
(800) 667–7191 (continental
United States)

Regina Tourist & Convention
Bureau
Highway 1, East
Regina, Saskatchewan
Canada S4P 3H1
(306) 789–5099

Saskatoon Tourist &
Convention Bureau
601 Spadina Crescent East
Saskatoon, Saskatchewan
Canada S7K 3G5
(306) 242–1206

MANITOBA
Travel Manitoba

Department 6020
155 Carlton Street, 7th Floor
Winnipeg, Manitoba
Canada R3C 3H8
(800) 665–0040

Winnipeg Convention &
Visitors Bureau
232-375 York Avenue
Winnipeg, Manitoba
Canada R3C 3J3
(204) 943–1970

YUKON
Tourism Yukon
P.O. Box 2703
Whitehorse, Yukon
Canada Y1A 2C6
(403) 667–5430

NORTHWEST TERRITORIES
Travel Arctic
Yellowknife
Northwest Territories
Canada X1A 2L9
(403) 873–7200

Calculating Costs

Canada continues to be a great travel/vacation value because U.S. citizens don't have to spend as much to get and stay there as you do for other international destinations. U.S. citizens also have the incentive of a highly favorable currency exchange rate, which, at this writing, ranges from 30 to 35 percent in your favor.

Because of fluctuating prices, this guide uses a scale of relative prices to indicate costs for accommodations and restaurant meals: *expensive*, *moderate*, and *inexpensive*.

Accommodations

An *expensive* double room in Vancouver, Victoria, Calgary, or Edmonton is likely to cost $100 and up a night in Canadian dollars.

But when you discount this figure by 30 percent and convert into U.S. dollars, your actual cost, minus taxes, is approximately $70, which is a pretty good deal. Even when booking a room at a deluxe hotel, ask about special discounts, such as weekend packages. Some hotels may have discounted rates for children, seniors, and salespeople. Special rates are usually not available during peak vacation periods, but if you don't ask, you won't save.

Accommodations rated *moderate* cost $50 to $100 a night Canadian. It is important to know that a moderately priced accommodation in a smaller Western Canada city or town may be equal to if not better in quality than some *expensive* places in the large metropolitan areas. An *inexpensive* accommodation is less than $50 a night Canadian.

Restaurants

Prices for restaurant meals are about the same throughout much of Western Canada, with the exception of remote areas and communities in the Yukon and Northwest Territories, where expensive transportation drives up the price of all goods. This means that a Big Mac costs about the same in Winnipeg as it does in Vancouver, but a similar hamburger costs more in Yellowknife and Whitehorse. The cost of a restaurant meal in Western Canada is also comparable to what you would pay for it in the United States, even taking into account the higher value of the U.S. dollar in Canada. There are few if any food bargains in Canada. Where you come out ahead is in buying regional specialties that may not be available back home.

An *expensive* meal for two at a top big-city restaurant can cost $75 and up. Add to this drinks, a bottle of decent wine, taxes, and tips and you've a large bill to settle. A *moderate* dinner for two can span from $30 to $75. An *inexpensive* meal costs less than $25 Canadian.

Although the restaurants designated *expensive* in this guide generally offer excellent ingredients and preparation, ambience, and service, those marked *moderate* and *inexpensive* have been selected also with regard to their high quality and value to customers. This guide's emphasis is on diversity—presenting a wide choice of dining opportunities. Not every meal has to be a memorable culinary experience. Many times it's more satisfying to have honest home cooking when you're far away from home, and some of those restaurants are in these pages as well.

Most resorts in Western Canada offer meal plans: Modified American Plan (MAP), breakfast and dinner daily; Full American

Plan (FAP), three meals daily. The menus under these plans also contain food items with an additional charge—for instance, shrimp cocktail might add $2.00 to your bill. Regardless of your food plan, you are expected to leave a tip, signed on your chit and charged to your account. Cocktails and wines are also extra charges.

If you want to save money when staying at a big-city hotel, avoid frequent use of room service. Take breakfast at a nearby coffee shop or diner, where the food is usually better, served faster, and considerably lower in cost. Also consider bringing to your room a deli sandwich, pizza, or carton of chicken wings.

Attractions

Admission to many of the attractions described in this book is *free*. Others are designated *admission charged* or *donation accepted*. Major attractions usually have several price categories—adults, children, seniors, groups, and so forth. During the peak summer vacation season, from the end of June to Canada's Labour Day (beginning of September), most attractions are open from 10:00 A.M. to 5:30 P.M. Some major attractions (amusement parks, historical villages, fairs, expositions) extend their hours into the evening during the peak season. Each attraction has its own method of operation. Sometimes, when a historic home or local museum, for example, is closed on a Sunday or Monday, the curator might open it up for you. Don't be too shy to inquire if your curiosity is aroused about a place. Local communities are very proud of their heritage, and they want to share it with interested visitors from distant places.

Gasoline

Gasoline is plentiful throughout Western Canada. The Canadian imperial gallon is about 1 liter more than the U.S. gallon, and the price per gallon is more than you would pay at home.

Food and Lodging in Western Canada

Accommodations

Accommodations in Western Canada—hotels, motels, resorts, bed and breakfast places, hunting or fishing camps, farm and country houses, inns, tourist homes, and so on—are comparable in quality

The dream of most skiers is to take on the magnificent downhill slopes of ▶ the Canadian Rockies.

and diversity to those in the United States and in any other highly developed, industrialized country. Accommodation standards—housekeeping, safety, amenities—are quite high in Canada. The level of personal service in luxury hotels is generally good to excellent, although not yet on a par with those of the best European hotels.

Both the federal and provincial governments have done a fine job in providing roadside and park camping areas. Many of these include power hookups, safe water, toilet and bathing facilities, fireplaces, picnic tables, and recreational offerings.

Canada has come a long way in developing country home/farm vacations (including bed and breakfast places). Here you enjoy the best in Canadian rural life, including superb home-cooked meals, for a reasonable cost. The hosts even invite you to take part in the chores. For more information, contact: Canadian Country Vacations Association, P.O. Box 2580, Winnipeg, Manitoba, Canada R3B 4C3; (204) 477–6591. This association has inspected and approved all homes on its lists.

Hostels are found in most Canadian cities and in rural areas. For details and locations, contact: Canadian Hostelling Association, National Office, 333 River Road, Tower A, Vanier City, Ottawa, Ontario, Canada K1L 8H9; (613) 748–5638.

From May to August, most Canadian universities and other schools welcome overnight guests. For a nominal charge, you have a room on campus. Some also offer a private bath, cafeteria services, and recreational facilities. It's a great deal that makes travel budgets stretch further. Contact your nearest Canadian consulate for more information or the housing office of individual universities (a directory of Canadian schools of higher learning should be in your local library).

Major Hotel Chains

The following major hotel chains offer fine accommodations in many Western Canada locations (all 800 numbers good from the United States and Canada):

Four Seasons Hotels: (800) 268–6282
Best Western International: (800) 528–1234
CN (Canadian National) Hotels: (800) 268–9143
CP (Canadian Pacific) Hotels: (800) 828–7447
Delta Hotels: (800) 268–1133

Holiday Inns: (800) 465–4329
Howard Johnson Hotels: (800) 654–2000
Hyatt Hotels: (800) 268–9000
Sheraton Hotels: (800) 325–3535
(800) 268–9330 (in Western Canada)
Travelodge: (800) 255–3050
Westin Hotels: (800) 228–3000

Dining

In Western Canada you can eat every kind of food from mass-produced hamburgers to the finest in gourmet cuisine, with prices to match. I recommend that you try the many regional foods, such as fresh salmon in British Columbia and beef in Alberta; both are incomparable. Most familiar fruits and vegetables are grown in abundance in Western Canada. Decent wines are being developed in British Columbia, and they are worth a try. Bread making is a high art; after all, the grain-producing provinces of Alberta, Saskatchewan, and Manitoba are the breadbasket of Canada, and they export considerable amounts of wheat to countries throughout the world. Ethnic restaurants abound. Here's your chance to sample the best of Ukrainian, Chinese, Greek, and Italian foods, to name just a few of the many possibilities. Prices for meals in Western Canada restaurants are about the same as in the United States.

Tipping

A service charge is not automatically added to bills in Canada. It is customary, however, to tip people who serve you 15 percent of the total amount on a bill, excluding sales tax. Excellent service in a restaurant, for example, warrants an additional 5 percent or more. Taxi drivers receive a 10 percent tip of the meter's total. People who handle your bags receive $1.00 per piece of luggage. Don't forget the person who tidies up your room, makes your bed, and cleans the bath; $1.00 to $2.00 a night shows appreciation for his or her efforts. Also as part of the tipping bottom line, indifferent or poor service warrants the usual—an empty plate.

Alcohol and Drug Laws

The legal drinking age in British Columbia, Saskatchewan, Northwest Territories, and Yukon is nineteen; in Alberta and Manitoba it is eighteen.

Bottled liquor is sold through provincial-government stores. Selling hours vary from province to province. Liquor can also be purchased in licensed restaurants and bars. Hours for sale at these establishments also vary.

Canada has very strict drug laws, sharp enforcement, and tough penalties, and it would be prudent to abstain while in this country.

Provincial Sales Taxes

All Canadian provinces, except for Alberta, Northwest Territories, and Yukon, have a sales tax, ranging from 4 to 12 percent, applied to purchases of most goods, food in restaurants, and for accommodations. In some provinces a sales tax refund is available when the goods you buy are taken out of the country. You should inquire about sales tax rebates when you make purchases.

Weather

The best time for most vacation travel in Western Canada is during the warm-weather months—from mid-May to the end of September. July and August are the peak summer months. Spring and fall, in terms of seasonal transitions, are relatively short periods, except for coastal British Columbia, where the weather is mild throughout much of the year. The mountain regions, of course, get snow early, and some peaks are white year-round. June can be a tricky month in the high mountains—at Banff, for instance, when one day it can be shirt-sleeves warm and the next a surprise snowstorm can drop a few inches. In winter the mountains offer some of the best skiing in the world. The plains region of Alberta, Saskatchewan, and Manitoba is like a bowling alley down from the Arctic whence high winds and cruel temperatures flow. On the other hand, during the summer, it can get hot enough to fry eggs on the Trans-Canada Highway. Along British Columbia's coast, during the late fall and winter, a great deal of rain falls, and people wonder if they'll ever see the sun again; it's much like the weather in Seattle. But the heavy rains help to grow the lush forests and profusion of lovely flowers, some blossoming through winter. Very little snow falls along the southern coast, and what does quickly melts. Overall, during the primary vacation-travel months, the weather throughout Western Canada is near perfect.

As to how you should dress for the weather, tailor your wardrobe to the season and the kind of outdoor activities you'll want to do. A stout windbreaker, warm sweater, and basic rain gear should be standard, even in summer. In case you forget, all of these can be purchased virtually anywhere in Canada. There are some terrific values in English and Scottish woolens, in just about every form of clothing (weaving, pattern, colors) you want. Unless you are going up to the Arctic reaches of the Northwest Territories, the clothing you bring should not be different from that which you would take if you were going to northern California, Oregon, Washington, or the coast of Maine.

Time Zones

Western Canada is divided into three time zones: Central Standard Time (Manitoba, Saskatchewan); Mountain Standard Time (northwest Saskatchewan, Alberta, eastern British Columbia); Pacific Standard Time (British Columbia and Yukon); the Northwest Territories span all these time zones, plus Eastern Standard Time and Atlantic Standard Time. There is a one-hour difference between time zones (e.g., 12:00 P.M. Mountain Standard Time in Calgary is 11:00 A.M. Pacific Standard Time in Vancouver).

Telephone Area Codes

Telephone area codes for Western Canada are as follows:

Alberta	403
British Columbia	604
Manitoba	204
Northwest Territories (Yellowknife)	403
Saskatchewan	306
Yukon (Whitehorse)	403

Toll-free "800" numbers are in common use throughout Canada, and you should use them if possible before making a toll call. Many establishments don't offer toll-free numbers, but enough do to make your effort worthwhile. This book features toll-free numbers wherever possible.

Pay phones in Canada charge 25 cents Canadian for local calls. You can use your phone company credit cards in Canada.

How to Get to Western Canada

Your Travel Agent

Travel anywhere these days has become so complicated and costly that even the sophisticated traveler needs help to get through the maze of details and figures with satisfaction. You need go no further than your local travel agent for help. He or she can book your accommodations, meal plans, transportation, tours, rental cars, and many other aspects of your trip. Everything will be arranged to fit the budget you specify. In addition, your travel agent will give advice based on his or her own familiarity with popular places and special programs in Western Canada.

Your local travel agent delivers a tremendous amount of service at no extra cost to you, though you may be charged for special services. Travel agents receive a commission from the hotels and transportation companies, but you pay the same rates as when you book yourself. Some of the best travel agents belong to the American Society of Travel Agents (ASTA); look for the ASTA symbol when you select your agent. Not all travel agents are as we would like them to be—top-notch professionals who place the well-being and satisfaction of their clients first. Ask your friends and business associates for recommendations. Don't be timid to shop around until you get the best for your needs. After all, it's your hard-earned money and your hard-earned vacation.

Discount Fares

Travelers over sixty-five years of age are eligible to receive discounts on air, rail, and bus fares in some provinces. You must show proof of age when tickets are purchased. Those between the ages of thirteen and twenty-one can also travel by air at reduced rates by providing proof of age (birth certificate or driver's license). Discounts are offered for children under the age of twelve. Get full details on these money-saving discounts from your local travel agent or transportations company ticket clerk.

Package Tours, Cruises, and Vacations

Through your local travel agent, you can book many different kinds of package tours and vacations to Western Canada—for example, bus tours of every kind, fly-and-drive packages, ski and resort packages, big-city tours, hunting and fishing packages, railroad and cruise packages. Many escorted tours include accommodations, meals, sightseeing, transportation, tour managers and guides, entertainment, and special events.

For example, Maupintour, 1515 St. Andrews Drive, Lawrence, KS 66044, (913) 843–1211, is one of the "blue chip" companies in this business in terms of quality services and customer satisfaction. Maupintour offers packages to the Canadian Rockies, the resorts of Banff, Jasper, and Lake Louise, and the cities of Vancouver, Victoria, Calgary; train packages across Canada; cruises through the Inside Passage along the coasts of British Columbia and Alaska; and special Christmas and New Year's tours of the Canadian Rockies.

The following, recommended companies also offer a wide variety of touring, adventure and/or vacation packages to Western Canada; the "800" designation means a toll-free number:

Westcan Travel (403) 283–4500
Air Canada: check local listing or toll-free "800" number
American Automobile Association (AAA): contact local office
American Express: contact local travel agent
American River Touring Association: (415) 465–9355
Amtrak: check local listing
Cartan Tours: (800) 426–0364
Canadian Airlines: check local listing or toll-free "800" number
Cooke's Travel: (519) 733–2391
Thomas Cook Travel: check local listing
Cosmos: (800) 221–0090
Cunard Cruises: (212) 880–7500
Discovery Tours: (503) 241–2520
Exploration Holidays & Cruises: (206) 625–9600
Four Winds Travel: (800) 248–4444
Globus-Gateway: (800) 221–0090
Hanover Holiday Tours: (519) 364–4911
Holiday House: (416) 364–2433
Holland America Cruises: (206) 281–3535
Horizon Holidays: (800) 387–2977
Johansen Royal Tours: (800) 387–2977
Laughlintours: (213) 552–9393
Lindblad Travel: (203) 226–8531
Northwest Adventures: (800) 635–1379
Norwegian American Cruises: (800) 221–2400

Paquet French Cruises: (212) 757–9050
Pathway Tours: (800) 265–1224
Princess Cruises: (800) 421–0522 (United States); (800) 663–3591
    (Canada)
Princess Tours: (800) 426–0442
Royal Viking Line: (800) 346–8000
Salen Lindblad Cruising: (800) 243–5657
Sitmar Cruises: (213) 553–1666
Tauck Tours: (203) 226–6911
Thomson Vacations: (312) 467–4200
Touram: (514) 874–4405
UTL Holiday Tours: (312) 952–4000
Via Rail Canada: (800) 665–8630
Vista Tours: (800) 826–4642

Major Canadian Transportation Companies

Air Canada (check local listing or call "800" operator for toll-free number) is the national (government-controlled) airline of Canada. Air Canada's regularly scheduled flights provide service to most urban centers in the country and direct flights to Canadian destinations from a number of U.S. cities (New York, Boston, Washington, Los Angeles, Miami, and others). This carrier also works with a number of leading package-tour operators, providing travelers with a wide variety of package tours to Western Canada—touring, skiing, big-city holidays, and so on.

Canadian Airlines, a recent merger between Canadian Pacific and Pacific Western airlines (check local listing or contact your travel agent), provides regularly scheduled service to Western Canada destinations from many centers in Canada. This carrier also offers vacation packages to British Columbia.

Wardair (ask your travel agent for details) is an excellent charter airline that provides high quality group travel and vacation packages.

Via Rail—call (800) 561–3949—the national rail service of Canada, provides regularly scheduled passenger rail service throughout much of Canada, including one of the world's great rail trips—from Halifax, Nova Scotia, on the Atlantic to Vancouver, British Columbia, on the Pacific. Departures for Western Canada are from most major cities—Halifax, Québec, Montréal, Ottawa, Toronto, Winnipeg, Calgary, Vancouver. Sleeping accommodations and dining cars are on board. Western Canada package tours are also available.

Direct Flights to Western Canada Cities from U.S. Cities

Vancouver is served by direct flights from these U.S. cities: Chicago, Los Angeles, San Francisco, Dallas, Denver, New York, Washington, D.C., Honolulu, San Diego, Reno, Seattle.

Calgary has direct service from Boise, Chicago, Dallas, Denver, Houston, Las Vegas, Los Angeles, New York City, Palm Springs, Phoenix, San Diego, San Francisco.

Edmonton is directly served from Chicago, Dallas, Denver, Houston, Las Vegas, Miami, Minneapolis, Phoenix, San Francisco, Seattle.

Winnipeg can be reached directly from Chicago, Denver, Fort Lauderdale, Los Angeles, Miami, Minneapolis, New York, Phoenix, San Francisco, Seattle, Tampa.

Travelers from other U.S. locations can reach any Western Canada destination through connecting flights. For the convenience of many eastern seaboard U.S. travelers, Western Canada flight connections are made through airports in Toronto or Montréal. Ask your travel agent for details.

Airport Services

Major airports providing international services in Western Canada are in Vancouver, Victoria, Calgary, Edmonton, Regina, and Winnipeg. These airports provide foreign exchange, lockers, telephones, duty-free shops, bars, restaurants, newsstands, bookstores, drugstores, and various other shops and services. Hotels and motels are conveniently located near all international airports.

They also offer ground transportation to city center by bus, taxi, or limousine. The major car-rental companies have facilities at the airports.

These terminals have special facilities for the handicapped, including ramps, washrooms, and automatic doors.

Primary Gateways to Western Canada from the United States and Eastern Canada by Car

You can come into Western Canada through the following gateways:

From Eastern Canada, eastern United States (New York, Pennsylvania, New Jersey, New England, Washington, D.C.), Toronto, and other Ontario cities: via the Trans-Canada Highway, through the gateway of Winnipeg, Manitoba. The Trans-Canada Highway runs across the country, from sea to sea, essentially east/west, connecting most of the major cities.

From Detroit, Cleveland, and midwestern, mid-Atlantic, southern U.S. cities: via Interstate 75 to Sault Sainte Marie, to the Trans-Canada, thence to Winnipeg.

From Chicago, Saint Paul/Minneapolis, midwestern and southern U.S. cities: via Interstate 94 to Fargo, North Dakota, then Interstate 29 to Manitoba Highway 75, to Winnipeg.

From U.S. cities in the Rocky Mountain and southwestern states: to Interstate 15, which runs north/south through Montana, to Alberta Highway 4 leading to Lethbridge, and thence to Highway 2 to Calgary and Edmonton.

From U.S. cities in California and the Pacific Northwest: to Vancouver, via Interstate 5; to British Columbia, Highway 99; also from Port Angeles on Washington's Olympic peninsula to Victoria, British Columbia, via ferry.

There are a number of other access routes into Western Canada from the United States. Consult your atlas to find the routing and entry points most convenient to you.

Road Distances to Western Canada from Selected North American Cities

The following list gives driving distances from major North American cities to various destinations in Western Canada. For example, traveling from east to west, the distance from Winnipeg (the gateway to Western Canada for those coming into the region from the east) to Regina is 571 kilometers/343 miles; to Calgary, 1,336 kilometers/802 miles; to Edmonton, 1,357 kilometers/814 miles; to Vancouver, 2,232 kilometers/1,339 miles; or to Victoria, 2,337 kilometers/1,402 miles.

Canada

Toronto, Ontario, to Winnipeg = 2,099 km./1,303 mi.
Ottawa, Ontario, to Winnipeg = 2,218 km./1,377 mi.
Montréal, Québec, to Winnipeg = 2,408 km./1,495 mi.
Québec City, Québec, to Winnipeg = 2,678 km./1,663 mi.
Halifax, Nova Scotia, to Winnipeg = 3,656 km./2,270 mi.

United States

Fairbanks, Alaska, to Edmonton = 1,840 mi./2,962 km.
Fairbanks, Alaska, to Vancouver = 2,207 mi./3,553 km.
Los Angeles, California, to Vancouver = 1,437 mi./2,314 km.
San Francisco, California, to Vancouver = 1,013 mi./1,631 km.
Seattle, Washington, to Vancouver = 144 mi./232 km.
Washington, D.C., to Winnipeg = 1,641 mi./2,642 km.
Chicago, Illinois, to Winnipeg = 895 mi./1,441 km.
St. Paul/Minneapolis, Minnesota, to Winnipeg = 436 mi./702 km.
Detroit, Michigan, to Winnipeg = 1,182 mi./1,903 km.
Philadelphia, Pennsylvania, to Winnipeg = 1,630 mi./2,624 km.
New York, New York, to Winnipeg = 1,854 mi./2,985 km.
Boston, Massachusetts, to Winnipeg = 1,835 mi./2,954 km.

Services and Safety Tips

Rules of the Road for Safe Driving

Everyone in your vehicle should wear seat belts when driving in Canada. Strict seat belt laws are in effect throughout Canada, with the exception of Alberta, Yukon, and Northwest Territories.

U.S. drivers should remember that maximum speed limits are posted in kilometers per hour (km/h), as are distances (e.g., Vancouver 1,244 km.; 771 mi.) One hundred km./h. equals 60 mph, the maximum speed on major highways.

Studded tires are permitted without seasonal limitation in Saskatchewan, the Northwest Territories, and Yukon, but only during the winter in the other provinces.

Use of radar-detection devices is illegal in Alberta, Manitoba, Northwest Territories, Yukon, and in some of the eastern provinces. If you are driving across the country, pack yours away in a suitcase.

Emergencies

In an emergency, simply dial "O" on the telephone and ask the operator for the police, who have been specially trained to handle all types of emergencies.

If someone has an urgent need to get in touch with you but does not know where or how, he or she should contact the RCMP (Royal Canadian Mounted Police) in the area where you are traveling (leave your itinerary with a friend or relative back home). Several times each day many of the CBC (Canadian Broadcasting

Corporation) radio outlets broadcast the names of individuals traveling in their areas of Canada, requesting them to contact the nearest RCMP office for an emergency message. This excellent service should be used only for genuine emergencies.

Auto Clubs

The Canadian Automobile Association (CAA) extends full services to the American Automobile Association (AAA), Alliance Internationale de Tourisme (AIT), Federation Internationale de l'Automobile (FIA), Federation of Interamerican Touring and Automobile Clubs (FITAC), and Commonwealth Motoring Conference (CMC). These services, obtainable upon presentation of your membership card, include travel information, itineraries, maps, tour books, road and weather conditions, accommodation reservations, emergency road and travel agency services. For more information, contact: Canadian Automobile Association, 1775 Courtwood Crescent, Ottawa, Ontario, Canada K2C 3J2; (613) 226–7631.

Bear and Forest Fire Safety

The rugged mountain and wilderness areas of Western Canada, in British Columbia and Alberta, are home to North America's king of beasts—the bear. This is their natural and legitimate place. You are merely a guest in their territory. Grizzly and black bears are most common, and many have been spoiled by well-meaning humans with handouts of food. Forget about how cute your "teddy bear" is back home. Here you're dealing with dynamite that can kill. You can assume that these magnificent animals are always unpredictable and very dangerous, especially mothers with cubs. Most people never come close enough to a bear to fear an attack. However, when hiking, make enough noise on the trail so that bears will scoot off and avoid you. Never get between a mother and her cub. When you spot a bear, keep a safe distance between you and it. The bear is considerably faster than you and is about as powerful an animal as they come. Resist moving in closer for a better camera shot.

When camping, keep your area clean. This means wrapping all food items in airtight packages and placing the supply caches

◄The wilderness is endless in Western Canada, but a top bush pilot and his nimble plane make almost everywhere in this awesome land accessible to visitors.

33

away from your tent. Clean up all traces and scents of food that can attract bears. Avoid bringing any food, such as a sandwich or snack, into your tent before going to sleep. If you have problems with a bear, make a report to the nearest wildlife officer. When entering a national or provincial park, be sure to get the latest information on bear sightings and advice on what to do should you have a problem.

The forests of Western Canada are among the great riches of the continent. Enjoy them and protect them from destruction by fire. Be careful in the use of matches and lighting instruments. Make sure that anything that was burning (match, campfire) is out cold. Do not dispose of your smokes until you are certain that they are no longer burning. Build your campfires on hard, clear ground and away from vegetation, leaves, pine needles, and other materials that can accidentally catch fire and spread flames throughout the forest. When entering a national or provincial park, be sure to get current information on fire regulations, use of wood, and safe campfire locations.

Safe Driving on Gravel Roads

Throughout most of your travels in Western Canada, if you are driving, you will find the hard-surface roads are well engineered and constructed for various terrain and climatic conditions, with escape roads for runaways and plenty of scenic overlooks and rest areas. Roads are well maintained during periods of bad weather, such as snow and ice, and directional, warning, and destination signs are well placed and easy to read. Service stations, restaurants, and accommodations are along most routes. However, if you plan on doing some off-the-main-highway exploring or taking the famed Alaska Highway, which will usually place you on gravel roads, the following safe-driving tips will make your touring adventure more secure and enjoyable.

Gravel sections of the Alaska Highway (most of the Alaska Highway is now paved, but gravel sections remain) and major roads in northern British Columbia, Alberta, Yukon, and Northwest Territories are generally safe and well maintained. They are paved with loose gravel because of harsh climatic conditions during certain times of the year. For example, the rapid deterioration of asphalt or concrete surfaces during severe weather (freezing and thawing) causes road hazards and difficult maintenance. Gravel surfaces, on the other hand, provide better, safer traction in snow, ice, and mud. Also, be careful of slippery road conditions after heavy rains or thaws. A four-wheel-drive vehicle is ideal for north-country driving. Studded tires are recommended for ice and hard-packed snow.

Make sure that your vehicle is in top mechanical condition. Repair shops are scarce on long stretches of road and bills for work performed are high. Take some spare parts and tools with you—a spare tire in prime condition, fan belt, spark plugs, wrenches, and so on. Take a container of extra gas, a jug of coolant, some extra motor oil, and plenty of windshield washer fluid.

Protect your gas tank from being punctured by loose gravel by fastening a rubber mat to the surface that faces the road. Protect your headlights from rocks by attaching plastic shields and your radiator from swarms of bugs with an appropriate screen. Most of this auto equipment can be bought at your local supply store or at stores in Western Canada. Many garages located near major gravel roads can help equip your vehicle.

Take the following personal gear should you get stranded for a while: sleeping bags, warm coats, sweaters, hats and mittens, insect repellent, basic pots and pans, drinking water, enough food for a couple of days, fuel and fire-making tools, first aid materials, emergency flares, and, if possible, a CB radio. If you have to spend a night off the road, the best bet is to sleep in your vehicle. This saves your skin from insects and your hide from bears. Be alert to animals suddenly getting in your way on the road. Hitting an elk at 60 mph is not much different from smashing into a brick wall.

Keep a good distance between your vehicle and the one in front. This helps to keep rocks from being spun up and cracking your windshield. Anticipate that you may very well have bits and pieces of gravel hitting the glass and metal of your vehicle when trucks and cars, which travel at high speeds on these roads, pass you. Most travelers get through their journey without having any damage, but don't be surprised if it happens. It's part of the way of travel in these parts, and your insurance policy should help set things right again when you're back home. During dry periods, moving cars and trucks send up thick plumes of dust—another reason to keep a long distance between you and the next car. Keep your headlights on at all times—whether it's dusty or not—while traveling the gravel roads. Keep your windshield washer filled with fluid and use it frequently. When being overtaken by a truck, pull over to the shoulder and let him pass, but don't stop—keep moving.

Don't let your gas tank go below half full. Top it off at frequent intervals. Know how far it is to the next gas station, and don't let yourself come up short.

Don't drive tired. Take plenty of rest stops and enjoy the scenery. Share the wheel with your partner. Be alert at all times.

Do enjoy the country you're passing through. It's among the great adventures of a lifetime.

Free Culture on the Road

One of the great treats while touring Western Canada by auto is tuning into a CBC (Candian Broadcasting Company) radio station. A federal government–operated network, CBC provides some of the finest news, discussion, cultural, and entertainment programming in the English-speaking world. Its broadcasts of classical music are outstanding in variety and amount.

Marina Services

Full marina services are available for travelers sailing their private boats into British Columbia ports. During the peak summer season, however, available moorages are hard to get, particularly in or near the popular cities of Victoria and Vancouver. Yachting is a major recreational activity along the British Columbia coast, and many people can afford it. For information on reserving moorages in ports you want to visit, inquire through your local yacht club.

Hunting and Fishing Regulations

Hunting is regulated by federal, provincial, and territorial laws. You must obtain a license from that province or territory in which you plan to hunt. A federal migratory game bird hunting permit is required for such species; these are available at most Canadian post offices. Many of Canada's provincial parks and reserves and adjacent areas prohibit entry with any type of weapon. The Northwest Territories requires an export permit for all unprocessed wildlife that is taken out.

Fishing is also regulated by law. You must obtain a nonresident license for the province in which you wish to try your luck.

In British Columbia, you need a license for tidal-waters sport fishing. Contact: Department of Fisheries and Oceans, Communications Branch, 1090 West Pender Street, Vancouver, British Columbia, Canada V6E 2P1; (604) 666–2074.

Also, in British Columbia you cannot export salmon or other game fish beyond the possession limit without written authorization from a fishery officer. No more than 40 kg. gross weight of canned salmon, taken by sport fishing, can be exported from the province in any year.

A special fishing permit is needed in all national parks and can be obtained at any national park site for a nominal fee; they are valid throughout Canada.

Non-Canadian fishing guides cannot work in Canada without approval from the Canada Employment and Immigration Commission, and it must be obtained *before* you come to Canada (contact your nearest Canadian Consulate).

For more information on parks, reserves, hunting and fishing laws, licenses, and wildlife conditions, contact the following:

ALBERTA
Fish and Wildlife Division
8th Floor, South Tower
Petroleum Plaza
9915 108 Street
Edmonton, Alberta
Canada T5K 2C9

Alberta Provincial Parks
Suite 60, 16th Floor
10405 Jasper Avenue
Edmonton, Alberta
Canada T5J 3N4

BRITISH COLUMBIA
Fish and Wildlife Branch
780 Blanshard Street
Victoria, British Columbia
Canada V8V 1X5

MANITOBA
Travel Manitoba
Department 6020
155 Carlton Street, 7th Floor

Winnipeg, Manitoba
Canada R3C 3H8

NORTHWEST TERRITORIES
Wildlife Service
P.O. Box 2668
Yellowknife
Northwest Territories
Canada X1A 2P9

SASKATCHEWAN
Tourism Saskatchewan
2103 11th Avenue
Regina, Saskatchewan
Canada S4P 2V7

YUKON
Tourism Yukon
P.O. Box 2703
Whitehorse, Yukon
Canada Y1A 2C6

NATIONAL PARKS OF CANADA
Parks Canada
Ottawa, Ontario
Canada K1A 1G2

CHAPTER 3

Canada for
Non-Canadians

The Canadian Nation

Canadians are governed by a parliamentary form of democracy in contrast to the republican form in the United States. Elizabeth II, queen of the United Kingdom, is also queen of Canada. The governor-general, usually a noteworthy Canadian citizen appointed by the prime minister and approved by the queen, is her representative. When the queen is not present in the country, the governor-general acts as the symbolic chief of state. The prime minister, who is also a member of Parliament and the leader of the political party having a majority of members in Parliament, is the chief executive officer of Canada. Unlike the U.S. system, which separates the executive and legislative branches, the Canadian political system combines both, similar to the United Kingdom's. There are two major political parties in Canada—the Progressive Conservative party and the Liberal party. All members of a prime minister's cabinet must be elected members of Parliament—another difference from the United States where a president's cabinet members are appointed and cannot hold elective office. Ottawa, in the province of Ontario—between Toronto and Montréal—is Canada's federal capital.

Canada is a member of the United Nations, NATO, and the Commonwealth of Nations. Because of its generosity to people in need everywhere around the globe and its reasonable position on many key international issues, Canada is one of the most respected nations in the world.

The following are the provinces of Canada and their capital

cities (similar in concept to states, but possessing far more powers of self-government): Newfoundland/Labrador (St. John's), Prince Edward Island (Charlottetown), Nova Scotia (Halifax), New Brunswick (Fredericton), Québec (Québec City), Ontario (Toronto), Manitoba (Winnipeg), Saskatchewan (Regina), Alberta (Edmonton), and British Columbia (Victoria). Canada also has two vast land areas in the north that are awaiting designation as provinces, Yukon Territory (Whitehorse) and Northwest Territories (Yellowknife). On the provincial level, the queen of Canada is represented by lieutenant governor-generals, whose functions are chiefly ceremonial. Lieutenant governor-generals are usually outstanding citizens of their respective provinces. When the queen and members of the Royal Family visit the provinces of Canada, the lieutenant governor-generals are their chief hosts. Political power in the provinces lies with the legislative assemblies and the premiers who hold dominant power in the executive and legislative branches and within the majority political party. The operational form of government here is similar to what is on the federal level.

Canada has a population of more than 25 million. Close to two-thirds of Canadians reside in the provinces of Ontario and Québec, and about 75 percent of all Canadians live within one hundred miles of the U.S. border. (Most of the important urban centers of Canada are near the border.) About 30 percent of all Canadians are French; more than 40 percent are of British stock (English, Irish, Scot, Welsh); and the remainder are of various groups, such as Ukrainians, Poles, Germans, Italians, Chinese, West Indians, Greeks, and many others. Unlike the United States, which thinks of itself as the "melting pot" where all groups are assimilated into the dominant Anglo-Saxon culture, Canada considers itself a "cultural mosaic" whose citizens can be equally proud of their ethnic and Canadian heritage. This "cultural mosaic" concept has become institutionalized in most aspects of Canadian life, and it is the official cultural policy of every level of government throughout the country. A majority of Canadians are Christians of various denominations. There are also large concentrations of Jews, Muslims, and many other religious groups.

Canadians enjoy one of the highest standards of living in the world. For example, through government subsidies, low-cost medical care is available to all citizens. Also through government subsidization, the cost of higher education is considerably lower than in the United States.

In April 1982, Canadians witnessed a historic event when Elizabeth II, queen of Canada, sat before a crowded assembly of the House of Commons and Senate of the Parliament of Canada in Ottawa and presided over the proclamation of the Constitution Act of 1982. This great moment in history marked a number of important changes in Canada's constitution and is a milestone in this country's political evolution. With the proclamation of the Constitution Act, Canada repatriated from the British Parliament its constitution and shed a outmoded vestige of its colonial past. Canada now progresses into the future as a fully independent nation.

Entry into Canada

Canada Customs clears foreign visitors for entry into Canada. Its checkpoints are located on all highways that cross the border between the United States and Canada and at international airports and seaports. The French word for Customs is *Douane*, and it is part of the official bilingual signature of this vital federal department. You will find the people of Canada Customs to be courteous and professional. They try hard to make your entry into Canada a most pleasant start to your trip. They are, however, masters of their craft—among the best of their kind in the world—and it is highly inadvisable to attempt to slip illegal drugs and undeclared goods past their keen senses. Many have tried, much to their regret.

Citizens or permanent residents of the United States do not require passports or visas and can usually cross the U.S.–Canadian border without difficulty or delay. However, it is strongly recommended that you carry some sort of valid personal identification, such as proof of residence and citizenship (birth certificate or other document that provides legal evidence). Naturalized U.S. citizens should carry their naturalization certificate or other evidence of citizenship. Permanent residents who are not citizens should carry their alien registration receipt card (U.S. Form I–151 or Form I–551). Persons under eighteen years old who travel to Canada without an adult must have a letter of permission from a parent or guardian. U.S. citizens can enter Canada from any other country without a passport or visa.

All other persons, except U.S. citizens or legal residents, citizens of France residing on the islands of Saint Pierre and Miquelon, and residents of Greenland, require a valid passport, visa, or other acceptable travel document to gain entry into Canada. If you are entering Canada from the United States, make sure that your travel documents are acceptable to the U.S. Immigration Service before you leave the United States so that you won't have trouble reentering.

Employment and Study

If you want to study in Canada—and thousands of non-Canadians do so every year—you must obtain a student authorization before coming to Canada. Your own school or Canadian Studies Program should be able to help you with this kind of red tape. You will also need an authorization for working in Canada. Employment authorizations are usually not issued if there are qualified Canadians or permanent residents available for the kind of work you are seeking. Those who are being transferred by their companies to positions in Canadian offices and operations should seek the assistance of their human resources (personnel) departments. Another good source of information about employment or study in Canada is your nearest Canadian Consulate. See page 16 for addresses and telephone numbers in the United States.

Clearing Canada Customs

By Car

The entry of vehicles and trailers into Canada for touring purposes, for periods of up to twelve months, is generally a quick, routine matter that does not require the payment of duty. Motor vehicle registration forms should be carried, as well as a copy of the contract if you are driving a rented vehicle. If you are driving a vehicle registered to someone else, you must carry that person's authorization to use the vehicle. All national driver's licenses are valid in Canada, including the International Driver's Permit.

By Private Aircraft

Visiting aviators should plan to land at an airport that provides Customs clearance. You must report to Canada Customs immediately and complete all documentation. In emergencies, you can land at other fields, but then you must, as soon as possible, report your arrival to the nearest regional Customs office (see above telephone

numbers) or the nearest detachment of the RCMP (Royal Canadian Mounted Police). For more details on flying your own plane to Canada, contact your nearest Canadian Consulate General (see page 16). The publication *Air Tourist Information—Canada* is available from Transport Canada, AISP/A, Ottawa, Ontario K1A 0N8; (613) 995–0197.

By Private Boat

If you're planning to come to Canada on your own boat, contact the regional Canadian Customs office nearest to where you intend entering Canadian waters (see above telephone numbers) for a list of ports of entry that provide Customs facilities and their hours of operation. When you arrive, you should immediately report to Customs and complete all documentation. If you have an emergency, report your arrival, as soon as possible, to the nearest regional Customs office or to the local detachment of the Royal Canadian Mounted Police.

Personal Exemptions

Everything you bring into Canada must be declared and is subject to being inspected by Canada Customs on your arrival in the country. The following are commonsense rules and should present no real burden to the average traveler.

Tobacco. If sixteen years of age or older, you can bring in duty-free 50 cigars, 200 cigarettes, and 2 pounds of processed tobacco.

Alcoholic beverages. You can bring into Canada duty-free 40 ounces of liquor or wine or 288 ounces of beer or ale. You must be at least nineteen years of age in British Columbia, Northwest Territories, Saskatchewan, and Yukon; eighteen in Alberta and Manitoba.

Gifts. You can bring in duty-free gifts for friends and relatives provided that the value of each gift does not exceed $40 (Canadian funds) and that the item is not tobacco, liquor, advertising material, or any good that is not intended as a gift according to Customs definitions. Contact your nearest Canadian Consulate (see page 16) if you have any questions.

◀The pioneers traversed Western Canada in covered wagons. You can do the same with a lot more fun and without the hardship.

Business equipment and materials. Printed materials, commercial samples, blueprints, charts, audiovisual materials, convention and exhibit displays, and the like brought into Canada may be subject to the full rate of duty and tax or a portion thereof, or may be duty- and tax-free. Canada wants business travel to be as easy and convenient as possible. Contact the Commercial and Trade Division at your nearest Canadian Consulate (see page 16) for answers and information. This is what Canadian Customs says about its system regarding business and convention visitors: "We have taken steps to simplify customs and excise requirements and to reduce border-crossing formalities."

Pets. Canada is a pet-loving nation. You can bring your dogs and cats into Canada provided each animal has a certificate from a licensed veterinarian that confirms vaccination against rabies within the preceding thirty-six months. Puppies and kittens under three months and Seeing Eye dogs accompanied by their owners can enter Canada without certification or restriction.

Pet birds, songbirds, and birds of the parrot family, up to two per family, can be brought into Canada provided that the owner accompanies the birds and declares on arrival that the birds have been in the owner's possession during the preceding ninety days and have not been in contact with other birds during that period.

Pet monkeys, other small pet mammals, fish, and most reptiles can come into Canada without restriction. Pet foxes, skunks, raccoons, and ferrets, however, can come into Canada without health certification or a Canadian import permit only when they are accompanied by the owner. Turtles and tortoises require an import permit before admission.

Livestock, horses, wild or domestic fowl, and commercial shipments of animals, including all species of birds, are subject to veterinary health inspection on arrival in Canada. Contact the Chief of Imports, Animal Health Division, Food Production and Inspection Branch, Agriculture Canada, Ottawa, Ontario K1A 0Y9; (613) 995–5433.

Endangered species. The importation of endangered species of animals and plants, and their products, is restricted and may require the prior issuance of an import permit. This restriction also applies to certain animal skins and mounted animals and trophies. For more information, contact Administrator, Convention on International Trade in Endangered Species, Environment Canada, Canadian Wildlife Service, Ottawa, Ontario K1A 0E7; (613) 997–1840.

Plants, fruits, and vegetables. House plants can be brought into Canada without phytosanitary (plant health) certification when carried as personal items. All other plants require phytosanitary certification, which is issued by your nearest offices of the U.S. Department of Agriculture. Visitors from other countries should contact their national agricultural agency.

You can bring most fruits and vegetables into Canada; however, there are restrictions regarding certain types, and these change from time to time. Contact your nearest Canadian Consulate (see page 16) for current information.

Food. Food for two days' personal use can be brought into Canada.

Recreational boats and vehicles. You can bring in your boats, motors, trailers, snowmobiles, and other types of recreational vehicles duty- and tax-free under a temporary entry permit, which is issued by Canadian Customs when you arrive, on condition that such vehicles are for personal use only and are to be brought out of the company at the end of your visit.

Recreational equipment. You can bring in the following items duty- and tax-free provided they are only for your personal use: fishing tackle; camping, golf, tennis, scuba, and skiing equipment; radios, television sets, typewriters; camera equipment with a reasonable amount of film; and other recreational or hobby items.

Radio communication equipment. Radio equipment that has a power output of 100 milliwatts or less, operating in the 26.97/27.7 MHz band or on the carrier frequencies of 49.830, 49.845, 49.860, 49.875, or 49.890 MHz, may be operated in Canada without licensing.

Visitors to Canada are permitted to operate aircraft, ship, amateur, and citizens band radio stations provided that such stations are properly licensed by the government of the United States or by the government of your national origin.

The following stations, which must have a U.S. license, require a Canadian permit for operation in Canada: citizens band (CB) radio-telephone stations and radio-telephone stations in vehicles that move back and forth across the international border, or that are operated through a common carrier to connect with the telephone system. Permits may be obtained by writing the Director General, Radio Regulatory Branch, Department of Communications, Ottawa, Ontario K1A 0C8. Visitors must carry their Canadian permit and national license at all times.

Nonresident household goods. A nonresident of Canada who purchases, constructs, owns, or leases for at least three years a seasonal residence (not a mobile home or other movable residence) may qualify for the duty- and tax-free entry of furniture and household goods.

Firearms. Firearms having no legitimate sporting or recreational use (e.g., handguns) are not permitted entry into Canada. Canada has strong handgun laws, and they are enforced to the hilt. Don't even try it. If you are traveling through Canada to get to Alaska, you must ship your prohibited or restricted weapons by commercial carrier. Don't bring them in with you! If you fail to report your weapons to Customs, they can be legally taken away from you.

If you bring in a handgun for shooting competition, you must obtain a permit in advance from a local Canadian registrar of firearms.

Long guns, those used for hunting and competition shooting, can be brought into Canada and used without a permit by visitors sixteen years of age and older. Nonresident hunters may bring in 200 rounds of ammunition (per person) duty-free. Nonresident marksmen competing in meets recognized by the Amateur Trap Shooting Association, the Shooting Federation of Canada, the Dominion of Canada Rifle Association, or the National Skeet Shooting Association may bring in 1,000 rounds of ammunition (per person) as personal baggage. For more information contact your nearest Canadian Consulate (see page 16) and your hunting/ shooting organization, such as the National Rifle Association in the United States, or Revenue Canada, Customs and Excise Commercial Verification and Enforcement, Connaught Building, Mackenzie Avenue, Ottawa, Ontario K1A 0L5; (613) 954–6831.

Firearms in British Columbia. A nonresident carrying a firearm in British Columbia, while not on an arterial (main) or secondary highway, must have either a British Columbia firearms license or a hunting license.

Explosives, ammunition, fireworks, and pyrotechnics. Blasting explosives and detonators, propellant explosives and ammunition, and all types of fireworks and pyrotechnic devices may not be brought into Canada without an official permit. For more information, contact the Chief Inspector of Explosives, Explosives Branch, Energy, Mines and Resources Canada, Sir William Logan Building, 580 Booth Street, Ottawa, Ontario K1A 0E4.

Reentry into the United States

U.S. citizens and residents must satisfy U.S. Immigration authorities of their right to return to the United States. You can do this by presenting some form of identification or proof of citizenship (copy of birth certificate or passport; driver's licenses are generally not good forms of identification at border crossings).

Make a list of all your purchases in Canada that you're taking across the border, keeping sales slips ready for inspection. Pack these purchases separately for easy inspection. Don't hide anything. They'll find it.

You can take out of the United States and bring into it up to $5,000 in U.S. currency. You must report amounts above this limit to U.S. Customs.

Items of cultural, historical, or scientific value to the heritage of Canada that are more than fifty years old (e.g., antique furniture and paintings) cannot be taken out of the country without official permission. For information, contact the Secretary, Canadian Cultural Property Export Review Board, Department of Communications, Ottawa, Ontario, K1A 0C8; (613) 990–4900.

You can bring plants of Canadian origin into the United States provided that you have obtained a phytosanitary certificate from the Plant Products and Quarantine Division, Agriculture Canada. Offices are located in major urban centers throughout Canada.

Exemptions

By staying in Canada for at least forty-eight hours, you can bring into the United States up to $400 (U.S. dollars) of purchases duty-free.

Every member of your family is entitled to this exemption regardless of age. Members of the same family can pool their exemptions into a larger duty-free total. For example, if five of you are traveling together and Mother falls in love with a $2,000 designer gown in Vancouver, she can bring it back home duty-free, because your family has five $400 exemptions that total a $2,000 one. All duty-free purchases must accompany you back across the border.

You can also bring home duty-free 100 cigars, as long as they have not been made in Cuba; 200 duty-free cigarettes; and 1 liter of liquor (minimum age to bring in alcohol is twenty-one).

Duty-free gifts can be sent to friends and relatives from

47

Canada to the United States if the value of each gift does not exceed $50. The package should be marked "Unsolicited Gift."

Your Health while Traveling

Some unexpected health problems may happen on a trip. You may need the services of a doctor and even stay in a hospital. The best way financially to protect yourself and members of your family is to make sure that your health insurance plan provides the coverage you might need while traveling—adequate to pay for the costs of treatment. Canadians are protected by the health care system administered by their province, but the benefits therein are not available to nonresidents. Daily rates for hospital care vary from hospital to hospital and from province to province. Charges for adult in-patient care can start at $800 per day; charges for children in specialized hospitals can be even higher. Some provinces impose a surcharge of up to 30 percent on care for nonresidents. Before you come to Canada, seek advice on your present health care benefits and what additional coverage you may need from your organization's human resources department (personnel), your insurance agent, auto club, or travel agent. Also be sure to bring copies of your prescriptions in the event that they have to be renewed by a Canadian doctor.

Special Auto Insurance Identification

All provinces in Canada require motorists to produce evidence of financial responsibility in case of an accident. U.S. motorists are advised to obtain from their insurance agents a Canadian Nonresident Interprovincial Liability Insurance Card, which is issued free of charge. If you have an accident in Canada and don't have this card, your vehicle can be impounded, and other serious legal action can be taken against you. *Don't leave home without it.*

Canadian Holidays

Many services—banks, government offices, factories, business offices, and so on—are closed during the national and provincial holidays listed here. However, places of accommodation, many restaurants, and some services are open for the convenience of travelers.

National Holidays
New Year's Day
Good Friday
Easter Monday
Victoria Day (3rd Monday in May)
Canada Day (formerly Dominion Day), July 1
Labour Day (1st Monday in September)
Thanksgiving Day (mid-October)
Remembrance Day (memorial for Canadian men and women who served in the military), November 1
Christmas Day, December 25
Boxing Day, December 26

Provincial Holidays
Alberta
Heritage Day, 1st Monday in August

British Columbia
British Columbia Day, 1st Monday in August

Manitoba, Saskatchewan, Northwest Territories
Civic Holiday, 1st Monday in August

Yukon
Discovery Day, 1st Monday in August

The Metric System
All measurements in Canada follow the metric system, which is commonplace in most countries except the United States.

Temperature is given in degrees Celsius; gas is sold by the liter, groceries by grams and kilograms; and road speeds are posted in kilometers per hour.

If you are not already familiar with the metric system, the following measurements will be helpful during your travels in Canada:

Speed
15 miles per hour = approximately 25 kilometers (km.) per hour
30 miles per hour = approximately 50 kilometers (km.) per hour

50 miles per hour = approximately 80 kilometers (km.) per hour
60 miles per hour = approximately 100 kilometers (km.) per hour

Length
1 inch = 2.54 centimeters (cm.)
1 foot = 0.3 meters (m.) or 30 centimeters
1 yard = 0.9 meters or 90 centimeters
1 mile = 1.6 kilometers or 1600 meters

Mass
1 ounce = 28 grams (g.)
1 pound = 0.45 kilograms (kg.) or 450 grams

Volume
1 fluid ounce = 28 milliliters (ml.)
1 Imperial pint = 0.57 liters (l.) or 570 milliliters
1 Imperial quart = 1.14 liters or 1140 milliliters
1 Imperial gallon = 4.5 liters or 4500 milliliters

When buying gasoline in Canada, remember that the Imperial gallon is close to a liter larger than the U.S. gallon. The Imperial gallon will at first seem to cost more but the price tends to equal out in the total of how much gas goes into your car and what you pay for it.

Temperature
86°F = approximately 30°C (a hot summer day)
68°F = approximately 20°C (room temperature)
32°F = approximately 0°C (water freezes)
−6°F = approximately −20°C

The following is a formula for temperature conversion, which may be useful only to mathematicians:

To convert Celsius to Fahrenheit $(°C × \frac{9}{5}) + 32 = °F$

To convert Fahrenheit to Celsius $(°F − 32) × \frac{5}{9} = °C$

Money Matters

The Canadian System

The monetary system of Canada, like that of the United States, is based on dollars and cents. The denominations of coins

Put on stout hiking boots and what you need on your back and experience ▶
the wonder of the Canadian Rockies by being close to the boundless land
and the sky.

and paper bills is the same, except that the $2.00 bill is more commonly used than in the United States. In addition, each denomination of Canadian paper money is of a different color, which makes it easier to tell a $1.00 bill from a $10.00 bill.

More Value for Your Travel Dollars

The value of the Canadian dollar averages about $.30 *below* the U.S. dollar. While the West German mark, the British pound, and the Japanese yen have risen in value against the U.S. dollar (at this writing), the value of the Canadian dollar has remained more stable against the United States. For every U.S. dollar that is converted to Canadian, a 30 percent exchange rate is realized (sometimes more and sometimes less, depending on fluctuations in world currency markets). For example, a traveler converting $100 United States with a 30 percent exchange rate should receive $130 Canadian. Although some goods and services cost more in Canada, you should be able to stretch your U.S. travel/vacation money further in Canada than in many other popular destinations around the world, perhaps even to splurge on a few pleasures (e.g., a new fur coat, Canadian crafts) that otherwise might not be possible.

Where to Convert to Canadian Money

U.S. currency, including major traveler's checks and credit cards, is widely accepted throughout Canada for the purchase of goods and services. Some places will even give you a better exchange rate just to get your business. The canny traveler will keep a sharp eye out for these.

It's a good idea to convert some of your money into Canadian currency at your hometown bank (about $100 for initial expenses, such as cabs, tips, fast food, and so on). The larger U.S. banks usually handle Canadian currency. You can also buy traveler's checks in Canadian denominations before you leave on your trip. Both your local banks and traveler's check–issuing companies must give you the benefit of the prevailing exchange rate.

Canadian banks are usually the best places in which to convert your money to Canadian currency (that is, if you want to get the best rate of exchange). Places of accommodation are not, unless they use a more favorable exchange rate as a promotion to attract your business. The only advantage of converting your money at a hotel is that their cash departments keep longer hours than banks and are open on weekends and holidays. Canadian banking hours are usually from 10:00 A.M. to 3:00 P.M. Monday through Friday. Almost all banks have extended hours of operation (set by individual banks) on certain days of the week, such as Saturday.

Automatic Teller Machines (ATM)

Need cash? The CIRRUS network has Automatic Teller Machines (ATM) located in major cities in British Columbia, Alberta, Saskatchewan, and Manitoba. These cash-dispensing machines are in service under the following names: Instabank, Select Service, Money Machine, Money Mark, and Magicbanc. To use the CIRRUS network just insert your bank card in any machine displaying the CIRRUS symbol, enter your Personal Identification Number (PIN), and follow the machine's instructions. When in doubt, call toll-free (800) 4–CIRRUS for information on locating your nearest CIRRUS machine. There are also several other major ATM systems and networks operating in Canada. Check with your bank card company to find out which one in the Western Canada provinces will provide the instant-cash services you might need.

Many ATMs will make cash advances on major credit cards as well; be sure to inquire about the availability of this option in Canada at your credit card company before you leave home.

Credit Cards

All major national and international credit cards (such as American Express, Visa, and MasterCard) are widely accepted throughout Canada. Major credit cards are necessary for renting automobiles and are used as a form of identification when checking into places of accommodation. In hotels, restaurants, shops, and other places of business be sure to check beforehand that your card is accepted.

United States Consulates in Western Canada

The following U.S. consulates are located in Western Canada to assist you in emergencies (lost passports, personal documents, and so on) and to provide information regarding your commercial and tourism involvements in Canada:

Calgary, Alberta
Room 105
615 MacLeod Trail S.E.
Calgary, Alberta T2G 4T8
(403) 266–8962

Vancouver, British Columbia
21st Floor
1075 W. Georgia Street
Vancouver, British Columbia V6E 4E9
(604) 685–4311

Winnipeg, Manitoba
6 Donald Street
Winnipeg, Manitoba R3L 0A7
(204) 475–3344

Postal and Telecommunications Services

Canadian postage stamps must be used on all mail sent from Canadian locations. As of this writing, first-class letters sent from Canada to a U.S. address must have a 39-cent Canadian stamp. First-class letters sent from the United States to a Canadian address carry a 22-cent U.S. stamp. You can have mail sent to you in Canada by using the General Delivery system in the location where you are staying. Your mail should be addressed in this manner:

Your name
c/o General Office
Main Post Office
City and province
Postal code

General Delivery mail must be picked up within fifteen days, or it will be returned to the sender.

For next-day or sooner delivery, use Telepost, which combines telecommunications with letter-carrier service. Just telephone your message to the nearest CN/CP Public Message Center (call directory assistance for the number) for delivery anywhere in Canada or the United States. Telepost is available twenty-four hours a day.

Through Intelpost you can transmit documents or photographs via satellite to destinations in Canada, the United States, and Europe. This service is available at main post offices in Canada.

Electricity and Water

Travelers from the United States can use their electric appliances—shavers, hair dryers and curlers, irons, and so on—as they would at home. Special adapters are not needed.

Drinking water throughout Western Canada is safe to use from the tap.

Business Hours

Business hours in Canada are similar to those in the United States. Most offices are in full operation by 9:00 A.M., and work for most people usually ends by 5:00 P.M. Executive lunches are as long as needed. Most stores are open from 10:00 A.M. to 6:00 P.M. Many have extended hours on busy shopping days. Some are open on Sundays. Late-hour drugstores and newsstands can be found in most large cities. The hourly routine of everyday life is not very different in Canada from what it is in the United States.

CHAPTER 4

Touring British Columbia

British Columbia in Brief

British Columbia is Canada's third-largest province, after Québec and Ontario. It is also the third most populous, with more than 3 million inhabitants. More than 90 percent of its people speak English as their first language. Most British Columbians are of British stock—English, Scottish, Welsh, Irish—and this is Canada's most British province, not just in name but in attitudes and lifestyle. There are also large groups whose ethnic roots are Germanic, Scandinavian, Slavic, and Oriental. Almost all of the world's ethnic, racial, and religious groups are represented in British Columbian society. The vast majority of British Columbians reside in the southern part of the province, close to the U.S.–Canadian border along the 49th parallel.

The capital city of British Columbia (the province is known most typically in Canada as "B.C.") is Victoria, named in honor of the "Great Queen" and empress of what was once a significant empire. Victoria is located on the southern tip of Vancouver Island, well below the 49th parallel. The largest city in British Columbia is Vancouver, third in importance after Toronto and Montréal. Other large B.C. cities are Prince George, Kamloops, Kelowna, Nanaimo, and Penticton.

B.C. entered the Canadian Confederation in 1871, about four years after Upper Canada, Lower Canada, Nova Scotia, and New Brunswick came together in a united country. British Columbia has always felt itself far removed from the centers of economic and political power represented by Toronto, Ottawa, and Montréal. The linking of B.C. with the rest of Canada through the transcontinental railroad in the nineteenth century ended some of this isolation, as did the Trans-Canada Highway and the advent of transcontinental air travel.

In recent years, B.C. has turned its attention toward the thriving nations of the Pacific Rim, and its future growth and prosperity will depend increasingly on the Far East. The province also has a close affinity with the nearby states of Alaska, Washington, Oregon, and California, and the majority of American tourists who visit B.C. come from these states. The actual borders of British Columbia are the Yukon to the north, Alberta to the east, the states of Montana, Idaho, and Washington to the south, and the Pacific Ocean to the west.

The climate along the Pacific coast throughout the year is mild: dry and sunny during the summer, rainy and foggy during the winter. Coastal areas receive little if any snow during the winter, except in the high mountains. It is not unusual to see delicate, colorful flowers blooming in Victoria throughout the winter. On Vancouver Island one can see many trees that are hundreds of years old and that have grown to incredible heights. The heavy rainfall here has created lush vegetation, such as giant ferns and thick moss. From the Coastal Mountains to the Rockies on its far eastern border, British Columbia is rippled with mountain range after mountain range. All of these ranges and valleys are thickly forested, except for the southern part of the Okanagan region where the terrain is desertlike, similar in many respects to Arizona's or New Mexico's. The north central interior flattens out into a rolling plateau. Throughout the interior are countless lakes, rivers, streams, waterfalls, and glaciers. Some of the great national parks of Canada, such as Yoho, Glacier, and Kootenay, are in eastern British Columbia. Near the Alberta border is Mount Robson, the highest point in the Canadian Rockies (however, Mount Fairweather at 4,663 m./15,300 ft. is the highest in the province). In contrast to the coast, which is either sunny or rainy, the climate of the interior is more typical of North America, with four distinct seasons.

A major part of British Columbia's economy is based on developing and processing natural resources—lumber, minerals, food (cattle, fruits, and vegetables), and the fisheries. Travelers to British Columbia dine on such treats as Pacific salmon and province-grown fruits and vegetables of almost every kind. In the 1800s the province was a center for the fur-trading operations of the Hudson's

Bay Company and for the discovery of gold in the northwest. The city of Vancouver today is an important North American business center, with banking, investment ventures, and insurance leading the way. It will soon become a banking free zone, which will stimulate increased foreign investments through its financial institutions.

British Columbians enjoy an exceptionally high standard of living. There is a great deal of affluence and a high level of culture. The educational system is superb, particularly the major universities, and the same can be said for the quality of health care, which is heavily subsidized by the government and available to all. British Columbians are extremely law-abiding, civilized people, and the amount of crime and violence is very low in comparison with that in the United States.

Tourism is the second most important economic sector, and its infrastructure—accommodations, restaurants, shops, parks, transportation, attractions, entertainment—is generally excellent in all parts of the province, especially in the prime vacation areas—Vancouver, Victoria, the Okanagan, and the Rockies.

No other province in Canada has such a diverse range of magnificent scenery that is largely accessible to most visitors. In the final analysis, it is this glorious spectacle of nature that one remembers the most about British Columbia. B.C.'s motto, concerning its beauty and quest for excellence, is, therefore, most apt: *Spendor Sine Occasu* (splendor without diminishment).

Tourism British Columbia

In Canada the main source of information (including maps and brochures) about this province is:

Ministry of Tourism, Recreation and Culture
Parliament Buildings
Victoria, British Columbia V8V 1X4
(604) 387-1642

Outside of Canada, Tourism British Columbia offices are located in the following cities:

London, England: 1 Regent Street; 01-930-6857
Los Angeles, California: Suite 34, Ambassador Hotel, 3400 Wilshire
    Boulevard; (213) 380-9171

San Francisco, California: 100 Bush Street, Suite 400; (415) 981-4780

Seattle, Washington: March & McLennan Building, 720 Olive Way; (206) 623-5937

Regional Tourist Agencies

The following regional tourist agencies will be happy to provide you with information on all-seasons sports, attractions, culture, dining, and accommodations in their areas:

Vancouver Island: (604) 382–3551
Southwestern B.C. (Vancouver metro area): (604) 688–3677
Okanagan-Similkameen: (604) 861–8494
Kootenay Country: (604) 365–8486
Canadian Rockies (B.C. section): (604) 427–4838
High Country: (604) 372–7770
Cariboo-Chilcotin: (604) 392–2226
North by Northwest: (604) 847–5227
Peace River/Alaska Highway: (604) 785–2544

Touring British Columbia

Note: See Chapter 5 for information on the city of Vancouver and environs, Whistler resort area, and Gulf Islands; see Chapter 6 for information on the city of Victoria, Vancouver Island, the Inside Passage, and Prince Rupert to Prince George.

The Sunshine Coast

Exploring British Columbia's Sunshine Coast brings you into a magnificent area of islands, mountains, and sea, all within close proximity to the city of Vancouver. You can take a one-day trip here or make it into a major touring adventure. Because of its great beauty and relative closeness to Vancouver, the Sunshine Coast is home to writers, craftspersons, and those who wish to live a more independent life a bit removed from the hassles of civilization. In addition to touring, this region offers sport fishing, camping, hiking, canoeing, wild bird and animal photography, beach walking, heritage museums, Canadian cultural displays, fishing and sightseeing charters, horseback riding, golf, tennis, and local festivals.

It's easy to get to the Sunshine Coast. Take Highway 99 north to the ferry terminal at Horseshoe Bay. From here you take a B.C. ferry (in Vancouver call (604) 685–1021 for information or (604) 669–1211 for recorded information 24 hours a day; in Victoria call (604) 386–3431 or (604) 656–0757)—across Horseshoe Bay, passing between Bowen and Gamier islands, to Langdale, the beginning of the Sunshine Coast tour. From Langdale follow Highway 101 up the coast to Gibsons, Sechelt, Secret Cove, Madeira Park, Pender Harbour, Irvines Landing, Garden Bay, and Earls Court. At Earls Court take another ferry across Jervis Inlet to Saltery Bay, Lang Bay, and Powell River. The ferries running from Powell River can take you across the Strait of Georgia to Comox on Vancouver Island. From Comox head north to Port Hardy and the Inside Passage trip on the B.C. ferry M.V. *Queen of the North;* head south to Qualicum Beach, which will take you to Highway 4 and thence to the west coast of the island, facing the open Pacific, and the Pacific Rim National Park; or go farther south to the city of Victoria (see Chapter 6). At Powell River take the ferry to Texada Island or stay on the mainland and keep driving north on Highway 101 to the end of the road at Lund (the communities north of Lund to Prince Rupert are served by ferries and airplanes).

Accommodations and attractions on the Sunshine Coast are varied. At **Gibsons** visit the Elphinstone Pioneer Museum, the Captain Vancouver Cairn, or stroll along the sea walk. Sea Cavalcade and jazz festivals are in July.

Sunshine Lodge is 4 km. (2.4 mi.) west of ferry terminal, (604) 886–3321. Moderate.

In **Davis Bay,** the **Bella Beach Motel,** on Highway 101, (604) 885–7191, has a restaurant and rooms with an ocean view. Moderate.

While in **Sechelt** visit the Sunshine Coast Arts Centre, featuring paintings, graphics, sculpture, and crafts by local area artists; open Wednesday to Sunday; (604) 885–5412. There is a Sunshine Coast Golf Course in this town.

Driftwood Inn, on Highway 101, (604) 885–5811, has a restaurant and a swimming beach. Moderate.

In **Halfmoon Bay, Lord Jim's Resort** has a dining room, scuba diving, and a heated pool, (604) 885–7038. Moderate.

Sundowner Inn is bed and breakfast at a historic site in **Garden Bay,** (604) 883–9676. Moderate.

In **Powell River** visit Willington Beach, Valentine Mountain lookout, the archaeological display, and the salmon hatchery. There are canoe circle routes from here and a ferry to Texada Island. Try the Powell River Golf Course.

Beach Gardens Resort Hotel, on Highway 101, (604) 485–6267, has a restaurant and landscaped grounds; the rooms have views of water and mountains. Moderate.

Lund Breakwater Inn, on Highway 101 in **Lund,** (604) 483–3187, has a dining room. Inexpensive.

Metro Vancouver to Lake Louise, Alberta, via the Trans-Canada Highway 1

The Trans-Canada Highway 1 goes across lower British Columbia and over some of the most varied topography in North America. Beginning your trip in Vancouver, travel through the sprawling eastern suburbs of the city: Burnaby, Port Coquitlam, New Westminster, and Surrey. From the Langley area to the town of Hope, you'll be paralleling the Fraser River as you move through the Fraser Valley. The Fraser Valley is broad, flat, rich agricultural land, with many fruit, vegetable, grain, and livestock farms and pretty communities that serve them. The Fraser River along this stretch meanders toward its delta in a leisurely fashion and empties into the Strait of Georgia just below city center Vancouver.

As you travel east, the valley narrows, with the walls of mountains pulling closer to the road. The road begins climbing in elevation, and the Fraser River flows through rock gorges in angry torrents. At Hope there is a junction of the Trans-Canada and the Crowsnest Highway 3. The Crowsnest dips south and then moves east, hugging the U.S.–Canadian border (see page 79 for a description of this route to Banff, Alberta). From Hope the Trans-Canada goes north until it reaches Cache Creek. Here you move away from the eastern slopes of the Coast Mountains, on the western side of which are thick forests and much rain in the winter months, and enter a more arid, almost desertlike, region to the south. The Trans-Canada and Highway 97 meet at Cache Creek. Highway 97 takes you north through the Cariboo-Chilcotin region and eventually to the Alaska Highway, which leads to the Yukon, the Northwest Territories, and the state of Alaska.

At the city of Kamloops, the Trans-Canada heads in an easterly

Mountain range follows mountain range in British Columbia, each one ▶ ahead seemingly more splendid than the one most recently passed.

direction toward the Canadian Rockies, Lake Louise, and Banff. Along the way you will cross several mountain ranges, such as the Monashee, the Selkirks, the Purcells, and the Great Divide at the Canadian Rockies themselves. Kamloops is the gateway to the Okanagan region, one of the province's prime four-season vacation areas. The Okanagan is also famous for its many fruit orchards, vineyards, and wineries. Once you pass the Okanagan Valley and begin moving toward Revelstoke, the topography becomes alpine, with high snow-capped mountains, lush forests, long lakes, and such attractions as Rogers Pass and Glacier National Park.

The distance between Vancouver and Banff, Alberta, is 858 km. (515 mi.). The drive along the Trans-Canada is not only the most direct road route between these two points, but also one of the most scenic and interesting drives in Canada. There are plenty of accommodations, restaurants, parks, recreational opportunities, and gas/repair stations along the way.

As you head east out of Vancouver, via Highway 1A, you may want to take a side trip to **New Westminster** to see these interesting attractions.

Canadian Lacrosse Hall of Fame, 65 East Sixth Ave; call (604) 521–7656 for hours and visiting information. Lacrosse is one of Canada's national sports, and here you can see photographs and memorabilia of its history in the country.

Museum of the Royal Westminster Regiment, The Armoury, 530 Queen's Avenue; call (604) 526–5116 for hours and visiting information. Displays of the regiment's history from 1863.

Samson V Maritime Museum, on the waterfront between 8th and 10th streets; call (604) 521–7656 for hours and visiting information.

Fort Langley National Historic Park, via Highway 10, off the Trans-Canada, about 75 km. (45 mi.) from Vancouver city center; (604) 888–4424. Open daily except Christmas, Boxing Day, and New Year's. Admission charged. A restored Hudson's Bay Company post, with one building dating back to 1840. All buildings are furnished in the mid-nineteenth-century period, and costumed inhabitants are engaged in the crafts and chores of the fur-trading pioneers and those who worked provisioning the company's Columbia District.

Abbotsford is famous for its **International Air Show,** held annually in early August at the airport on Highway 401; call (604) 533–3713 for information. For accommodations, try the following, which have dining rooms and other amenities:

Country Inn Motor Hotel, 2073 Clearbrook Road, (604) 859–6211. Moderate.

Best Western Bakerview Motor Inn, 3467 Delair Road, (604) 859–1341. Moderate.

In the **Mission/Hatzic** area, via Highways 11 north to 7 east, Westminster Abbey, a community of Benedictine monks, provides a place of natural beauty for rest and prayer; call (604) 826–3975 for visiting hours.

Harrison Hot Springs Resort Area can be reached via the Trans-Canada to Bridal Falls, then north across the Fraser to Highway 7 (the Sasquatch Highway); turn left on 7 and then right on 9 north. Harrison Hot Springs is on Lake Harrison. It is in the deep woods of this area that the man/ape creature known as Sasquatch (Big Foot) is supposed to roam. So far no one has been able to get near it, although some have taken photos of a strange being purported to be Sasquatch. Perhaps it is better for it and for us that Sasquatch remains a mystery. Within this popular vacation area are hot springs for bathing, golf courses, and the Sasquatch Provincial Park, with hiking trails and camping. Accommodations include the following:

The Harrison, (604) 521–8888. Lake/mountain setting, golf, pools, boating, tennis, fine dining room, dancing, and entertainment. Expensive.

Harrison Village Motel, (604) 796–2616. Overlooking lake, some rooms with patios, heated pool. Moderate.

South Shores Resort Motel, (604) 796–2185. Housekeeping units, rooms with mountain or lake view; opposite sandy beach. Moderate.

Campgrounds; call the Chamber of Commerce, (604) 796–3425, for information.

Originally a Hudson's Bay Company post, **Hope** was laid out by royal engineers in 1858. Later, gold seekers came here to find fortunes in the sandbars of the Fraser River. The Dewdney Trail, the first pack trail, was opened here in 1860. In 1965 the side of a mountain (a 100 million ton slide of mud, rock, and snow) broke away and crashed down on many homes in an area near town; the people, homes, and autos remain buried in a common grave under the rubble from the mountain. Also near Hope is the Hell's Canyon Airtram (see below); a doll museum and mini-golf are in the area. The Crowsnest Highway 3 joins the Trans-Canada at Hope.

All accommodations have dining rooms and other amenities:

Imperial Motel, 350 Hope/Princeton Highway, (604) 869–9951. Moderate.

Maple Leaf Motor Inn, 377 Hope/Princeton Highway, (604) 869–7107. Moderate.

Skagit Motel, 655 3rd Avenue, (604) 869–5220. Moderate.

Yale was once known as Fort Yale, in its Hudson's Bay Company days. St. John the Divine, located here, is B.C.'s oldest Anglican church. Visit the Pioneer Cemetery, Spirit Cave Hiking Trail, the National Monument to Chinese Pioneers (those who helped build the transcontinental railroad), and the Cariboo Wagon Road National Monument. During August the Fraser River Barrel Race takes place.

Hell's Canyon Airtram, on the Trans-Canada, is just northeast of Yale, (604) 867–9277. Open May to October. Admission charged. A twenty-eight passenger airtram takes you high above the Fraser Canyon, through which the mighty Fraser River surges in a torrent. This facility also has floral gardens, landscaped grounds, a gift shop featuring British Columbian jade items, and a restaurant serving grilled salmon and salmon chowder.

Cache Creek, at the junction of the Trans-Canada and Highway 97, is the gateway to the Cariboo-Chilcotin region and on the route to Alaska Highway (see page 87 for accommodations).

Kamloops, with a population of 140,000, is one of British Columbia's largest cities. It serves as the transportation, retail, and service center for much of the southern interior of British Columbia. Kamloops is also the northern gateway to the Okanagan vacation region (take the Trans-Canada east to Highway 97 south). Also at Kamloops, a section of the Yellowhead Highway 5 north provides direct access to Jasper National Park in Alberta, via the main section of the Yellowhead Highway 16. This route takes you past Mount Terry Fox, named for the courageous, young Canadian who, suffering from cancer, jogged across the country on one healthy leg and one artificial one. His example inspired Canadians as no one has done for many decades. You also pass Mount Robson, the highest point in the Canadian Rockies (3,954 m./12,972 ft.) and go through Yellowhead Pass (1,146 m./3,717 ft.), after which this scenic highway is named.

Attractions in Kamloops include the following:

Kamloops Museum and Archives, 207 Seymour Street, (604) 828–3576. Closed Mondays and holidays. Free. Displays of local history, Amerindian cultures, fur trade, ranching, and railroading.

Kamloops Waterslide and R.V. Park, east of city center on the Trans-Canada, (604) 573–3789. Admission charged. Six water slides, mini-golf, hot tubs, children's playground, RV facilities.

Kamloops Wildlife Park, east of city center on the Trans-Canada, (604) 573–3242. Admission charged. Displays of live wild animals, mini-train rides, nature trail.

All accommodations have restaurants and other amenities:

The Place Inn, on the Trans-Canada, (604) 374–5911. Moderate.

The Dome Motor Inn, 555 West Columbia Street, (604) 374–0358. Moderate.

Panorama Inn, 610 West Columbia Street, (604) 374–1515. Moderate.

Hospitality Inn, 500 West Columbia Street, (604) 374–4164. Moderate.

Sandman Inn, 550 Columbia Street, (604) 374–1218. Moderate.

Coast Canadian Inn, 339 St. Paul Street and 3rd Avenue, (604) 372–5201. Moderate.

David Thompson Motor Inn, 650 Victoria Street, (604) 372–5282. Moderate.

Rider's Motor Inn, 1759 Trans-Canada, east of the city, (604) 374–2144. Moderate.

Courtesy Inn Motel, 1773 Trans-Canada, east of the city, (604) 372–8533. Moderate.

David Crocket Motel, 1893 Trans-Canada, east of the city, (604) 372–2122. Moderate.

Highway 97 south joins the Trans-Canada at Kamloops. It leads to one of British Columbia's major vacation areas—the **Okanagan/Similkameen** vacation region—frequented by travelers from the West Coast of the province, Americans from south of the border, and those from Alberta who want to relax and have fun in a different environment from their own.

Whether you are traveling east or west along the Trans-Canada (or on the Crowsnest Highway 3 to the south), you will probably want to take a side trip through the Okanagan/Similkameen region, even for a day or two. Okanagan Lake, a long stretch of warm water, is perfect for swimming, windsurfing, boating, fishing, and waterskiing. It even has its own resident monster—affectionately called "Ogopogo"—who is supposed to be a cousin of the one in Scotland's Loch Ness.

This is a major fruit-producing area, and you'll find stands selling freshly picked crops throughout the region. Accommodations, from bed and breakfasts to deluxe resorts, are plentiful, and the golf is excellent, as are tennis, trail riding, skiing, and just about any other sports activity you enjoy. Be sure to visit the vineyards and their wineries. Many wineries offer free samples at the end of tours.

The key vacation cities in the Okanagan are Vernon, Kelwona, and Penticton. Smaller communities, such as Enderby, Armstrong, Westbank, Peachland, Summerland, Keremeos, and Osoyoos (see page 79), though a bit quieter, also offer most of the vacation features and attractions of the three main cities.

Okanagan Festivals

Blossom Festival, Penticton, early May
Arabian Encampment Horse Show, Kelowna, end of June
Hobie Cat Regatta, Kelowna, end of June
Big Cheese Country Music Festival, Armstrong, mid-July
Highland Games, Penticton, mid-July
Peach Festival, Penticton, end of July to end of August
Square Dancers Jamboree, Penticton, early August to mid-August
Canadian International Ultra Triathlon, Penticton, end of August to September
International Festival of the Arts, Kelowna, September
Labatt's Open Racquetball Tournament, Kelowna, Labour Day weekend
Okanagan Wine Festival, throughout the region, end of September into early October

Wineries in the Okanagan

In addition to being one of British Columbia's top vacation regions, the Okanagan is the province's wine-producing country. Botanist G. W. Henry was the first to plant grapevines in B.C. in 1899. In 1926 J. W. Hughes, a Kelowna rose grower, planted the first vineyard in the Okanagan on the same site that Father Charles Pandosy planted the region's first apple orchard in 1862. Both men knew that the soil and climate were suitable for fruit growing and that the growing season was long (five and a half months), considering the region's northern location. Dr. Eugene Rittich, a Hungarian with extensive experience in wine making in France, Germany, and Austria, came into the Okanagan in the early 1930s, and the region's involvement in this most enjoyable industry began because of his know-how and efforts.

Today the Okanagan has several wineries producing a wide variety of wines. Some are excellent, though others have a way to go in terms of their acceptance by connoisseurs. What is impressive is that through scientific research and advanced agriculture, Okanagan wines are improving and might one day challenge some of the best from France and California. If you are in the region from late September to mid-October, be sure to attend the Okanagan Wine Festival, featuring various events and the tasting of the region's best wines; call (604) 861–8494 for more information. The wineries listed below welcome visitors.

Calona Wines, 1125 Richter Street in Kelowna. Tours from the end of May to the end of October; (604) 762–9144.

Casabello Wines, 2210 Main Street in Penticton. Tours daily during the summer; call for hours, (604) 492–0621.

Claremont Estate Winery and Vineyards, off Highway 97 in Peachland. Tours end of May to Labour Day; (604) 767–2992.

Divino Estate Winery, Road 8 in Oliver. Open end of May to Labour Day; (604) 498–2784.

Gray Monk Estate Cellars, Camp Road in Okanagan Centre. Tours May to end of October; (604) 766–3168.

Okanagan Vineyards, R.R. 1, Road 11 in West Oliver. Tours April to September; (604) 498–4041.

Sumac Ridge Estate Winery, Highway 97 north. Tours end of May to Canadian Thanksgiving; (604) 494–0451.

Uniacke Estate Winery, off Highway 97, south of Kelowna. Tours from May to end of October; (604) 764–8866.

A major vacation center in northern Okanagan, **Vernon** offers every kind of water sport, plus fine entertainment, culture, accommodations, dining, and shopping. Three lakes and five mountains are close by—and so are gold, skiing at Star Mountain, hot springs bathing, hunting, and trail riding. This is a friendly and relaxing place to stop during your travels across the province. Attractions in Vernon include the following:

Vernon Museum, 3009 32nd Avenue at the Civic Centre, (604) 542–3142. Open Monday through Saturday. Free. Exhibits on the paddle-wheel boats that sailed on the lake and on the lifestyle of the early settlers.

O'Keefe Ranch, on Highway 97, (604) 542–7868. Open mid-May to Canadian Thanksgiving. Admission charged. Established in

1867, this ranch, consisting of about 20,000 acres, was once the biggest cattle empire in the Okanagan. You can visit the ranch buildings and see the mansion and furnishings of the O'Keefe family as well as St. Ann's Church.

Topham Brown Art Gallery, 3009 32nd Avenue in the Civic Centre; call (604) 545–3173 for hours. Exhibitions by local artists and traveling shows.

Accommodations are varied. Below are some possibilities for you to consider:

Village Green Inn, junction of Highway 97 and Silver Star Road, (604) 542–3321. Awarded four diamonds for excellence by the Canadian Automobile Association and the American Automobile Association in 1986. Excellent accommodations and dining, indoor and outdoor pools, championship tennis courts, near lake, beaches, golf courses, and skiing. Moderate.

Lake Side Motor Inn, Okanagan Landing Road, (604) 542–2377. Sandy beach, indoor pool, dining room. Moderate.

Vernon Lodge Motel, 3914 32nd Street, (604) 545–3385. Indoor pool, dining room, nightclub. Moderate.

Best Western Villager Motor Inn, 5121 26th Street, (604) 549–2224. Moderate.

Vernon Sandman Inn, 4201 32nd Street, (604) 542–4325. Indoor pool, dining room. Moderate.

Willy's Motor Inn, 3309 39th Avenue, (604) 545–3351. Rooms with balconies, outdoor pool, dining room. Moderate.

Swiss Hotel Silver Lode Inn, at Silver Star Mountain Ski Area, (604) 549–5105. At base of lifts; Swiss-style dining room, sauna, and swimming pool. Moderate.

Vance Creek Hotel, at Silver Star Mountain Ski Area, (604) 549–5191. At base of lifts; dining room, lounge, rooftop hot tubs. Moderate.

Kelowna is in the middle of the Okanagan vacation region. It boasts thirty-one parks, with nine of them on Okanagan Lake. Hot Sands Beach, for example, perfect for sunbathing and swimming, is right in city center. Kelowna's cultural life includes the Okanagan Symphony and the Sunshine Theatre for live drama and comedy. Knox Mountain offers hiking and terrific views of the city and surrounding landscape. There are excellent accommodations, restaurants, and shops in Kelowna. It prides itself on treating vacationers very well, and it succeeds.

Listed below are some of the main attractions in Kelowna:

Father Pandosy Mission, Benvoulin Road, (604) 762–4907. Admission charged. Founded in 1859, this mission was the first permanent white settlement in the Okanagan Valley. There are several restored log buildings and displays of equipment.

Kelowna Centennial Museum and National Exhibit Centre, 470 Queensway, (604) 763–2417. Free. Exhibits by local artists and traveling shows.

Gold City Auto Museum, on Highway 97. Call (604) 763–1000 for hours. Admission charged. A display of forty-five antique and show vehicles.

Centennial Museum, 470 Queensway Avenue. Open daily during the summer. Free. Displays about local history, including Chinese house and store, and McDougal's Trading Post. Also a 1910 street scene, the first Kelowna radio station, and the interior of a Salish Amerindian home.

Wild Waters, on Highway 97. Call for hours and fees, (604) 765–5194. Four giant water-slide flumes, mini-golf, and hot tubs.

Accommodations abound. Here are several suggestions:

Lake Okanagan Resort, a Canadian Pacific hotel on the lake near Kelowna, (604) 769–3511, toll-free (800) 268–9411. This is one of the finest resort hotels in central British Columbia. It has been awarded the AAA four-diamond award for excellence. The resort is located on more than 300 acres and includes one mile of shoreline on the lake. Excellent rooms and dining facilities, seven championship tennis courts, par-3 golf, swimming, horseback riding, and hiking. Moderate to expensive.

Capri Hotel, 1171 Harvey Avenue, (604) 860–6060. Modern hotel, nicely appointed rooms; suites available. Swimming pool, restaurants, grills, and lounges. Convenient to all recreational attractions in the area. Moderate.

Seclusion Bay Resort, 19 km. (11.4 mi.) south of Kelowna, (604) 768–3885. Moderate to expensive.

Lakeshore Villa Resort, R.R. 3, Gellatly Road, (604) 768–5634. Moderate to expensive.

The Park Lane Motor Inn, 1675 Abbott Street, (604) 860–7900. Moderate.

Gyro Beach Resort, 3409 Lakeshore Road, (604) 762–3227. Moderate.

Lodge Motor Inn, 2170 Harvey Avenue, (604) 860–9711. Moderate.

Best Western Country Motor Inn, 2402 Harvey Avenue, (604) 860–1212. Moderate.

Safari Motor Inn, 1651 Powick Road, (604) 860–6204. Moderate.

Big White Mountain Ski Area Central Reservations, (604) 861–1511, for booking hotel rooms and condo units at this popular ski area.

Das Hofbrauhaus, in the Big White Mountain Ski Area, (604) 736–0411. Condos, fireplaces, dining room, deli, entertainment, indoor pool. Moderate.

Between Kelowna and Penticton, on Highway 97, is the community of **Peachland.** When passing through, stop and visit the **Peachland Museum** at 5890 Beach Avenue, (604) 767–3441; open June through August. The museum is housed in the former Peachland Baptist Church, built in 1910, a unique eight-sided wood structure. Its collection tells about some of the first orchards in the Okanagan, which were planted in this area.

Penticton, on Lake Okanagan, is encircled by mountains, and located nearby are many beaches, orchards, and vineyards. You might call it "Eden," and for those who stay a while it is. What could be better than attending the Peach Festival or staying at a deluxe resort or sailing on the lake or dining on schnitzel at Karl's restaurant or playing golf on lush fairways or watching parading beauties on the beach? All vacation amenities are here. Some of Penticton's attractions are listed below:

The Okanagan Summer School of the Arts offers classes in music, the visual arts, drama, dance, creative writing, and voice; call (604) 493–0390 for information.

Casabella Princess, cruises from the Delta resort, (604) 493–5551. A vintage stern-wheel paddler takes you on pleasant lake cruises.

Art Gallery of the South Okanagan, 11 Ellis Street and Front Street, next to the Delta resort; call (604) 493–2928 for hours. Changing exhibitions of painting, photography, pottery, and drawings. World's first art gallery operating on passive solar energy.

Dominion Radio Astrophysical Observatory, Whitelake Road off Highway 97, (604) 497–5321. Open daily. Free. A visitor center has displays on the scientific work being conducted at this facility. There are both radio and optical telescopes, and astronomers are on hand to explain their science.

Okanagan Indian Project, 110-304 Martin Street, (604)

493–6651. Open May through August, Monday through Friday. Free. Information on the history and culture of the Okanagan Amerindians.

Reg Atkinson Museum, 785 Main Street, (604) 492–6025. Open Monday through Friday. Free. Collection of Salish and local archaeological artifacts, natural history specimens, the Braun collection of mounted animals, military memorabilia, and pioneer tools.

Okanagan Game Farm, on Highway 97. Open daily; no telephone number. Admission charged. A wide variety of North American and African animals (zebra, cougar, grizzly, timber wolf) roaming 560 acres overlooking Skaha Lake.

For accommodations and dining in the Penticton area, try the following:

The Delta Lakeside, 21 Lakeshore Drive, (604) 493–8221. One of the premier resorts in the Okanagan, the Delta Lakeside fronts on Okanagan Lake and has its own sandy beach for sunbathing and swimming. The spacious rooms have balconies; there are fine restaurants, saunas, a health club, an indoor pool, and tennis courts. Arrangements for skiing, snowmobiling, skating, ice sailing, and trail riding can be made through the hotel. Expensive.

Best Western Telstar Motor Inn, 3180 Skaha Lake Road, (604) 493–0311. Near beach, indoor and outdoor pools, restaurant. Moderate.

Sandman Inn, 939 Burnaby Avenue, (604) 493–7151. Moderate.

Penticton Travelodge, 950 Westminster Avenue, (604) 492–0225. Moderate.

The Rochester Motel, 970 Lakeshore Drive, (604) 493–1128. Moderate.

Spanish Villa, 890 Lakeshore Drive, (604) 492–2922. Moderate.

Bowmont Motel, 80 Riverside Drive, (604) 492–0112. Moderate.

Three Gables Hotel, 353 Main Street, (604) 492–3933. Fireside dining room, pub, entertainment. Moderate.

Waterfront Inn, 3688 Parkview Street, (604) 492–8228. Moderate.

El Rancho Motel, 877 Westminster Street, (604) 492–5736. Moderate.

Black Forest Motel, 707 Westminster Street, (604) 492–0028. Moderate.

After a time in the Okanagan, if you wish to continue east on the Trans-Canada, follow Highway 97 to 97A north, which connects with the Trans-Canada at **Revelstoke.** (If you are traveling west, take 97 north to the Trans-Canada and Kamloops, or if you want to take the Crowsnest Highway 3 east [see page 79], follow 97 south.)

Situated on the source waters of the Columbia River and between the Selkirk and Monashee mountains, Revelstoke was named in honor of Lord Revelstoke, head of a British bank that helped to finance the transcontinental railroad at a critical time in its development. In the late 1800s the town became the mountain divisional center for the CPR (Canadian Pacific Railroad), and it continues to function as an important transportation and supply center for its mountain region. While in Revelstoke, visit the following:

Revelstoke Art Gallery, 315 West 1st Street, (604) 837–3067. Open June to September; call for hours. Free. Works by local and regional artists and traveling shows.

Revelstoke Museum, same address and phone number as above. Displays of the history and development of the town, focusing on the railroad, mining, lumbering, and riverboats.

All of the following accommodations have restaurants and other amenities.

Three Valley Gap Motor Inn, 19 km. (11.4 mi.) west of town, (604) 837–2109. Moderate.

Sandman Inn, off the Trans-Canada, (604) 837–5271. Moderate.

Best Western Wayside Inn, 1901 Laforme Blvd., (604) 837–6161. Moderate.

Swiss Chalet Motel, 1101 Victoria Road, (604) 837–4650. Inexpensive to moderate.

The MacGregor Motor Inn, 2nd Street, (604) 837–2121. Moderate.

Other attractions in the area include **Nakusp Hot Springs** on Highway 23 south from the Trans-Canada at Revelstoke, (604) 265–4234, which offers natural hot springs bathing (44°C/105° to 112°F); waterskiing; helicopter skiing; golf.

Access to **Mount Revelstoke National Park** is off the Trans-Canada in the Revelstoke area. The 263-square-mile park is located on the western slope of the Selkirk Mountains. There are wonderful views of mountain peaks, glaciers, alpine meadows, and lakes. Hiking trails (65 km./40 mi. of them), such as Skunk Cabbage, Giant

Cedars, and Mountain Meadows, take you into the interior of the park. A road off the Trans-Canada goes to Mount Revelstoke and its alpine meadows. Also in this area is Balsam Lake. From Mount Revelstoke a hiking trail, along which the natural beauty of the wilderness is both poetic and awesome, goes farther into the park to Eva Lake. Campgrounds are located at Mountain Creek, Loop Brook, and Illecillewaet. The interpretive or information center is at Rogers Pass. For more information, contact Superintendent, Mount Revelstoke and Glacier National Parks, Box 350, Revelstoke, British Columbia V0E 2S0; (604) 837–5155.

Glacier National Park (same address and telephone as Mount Revelstoke National Park described above) can be reached from the Trans-Canada. The community of Rogers Pass is at the center of the park. There are over one hundred glaciers in this national park, and dense stands of hemlock and cedar. During the winter and thawing seasons, this is avalanche country, and the frequent plunge of millions of tons of ice and snow down the slopes made the Rogers Pass area one of the most difficult obstacles to overcome in the building of the transcontinental railroad and the Trans-Canada Highway. Today howitzers are used to break up the snow and prevent avalanches from becoming a danger to travelers. Guided hikes begin at the Illecillewaet Campground and move through diverse ecological zones. If you are interested in hiking on the glaciers themselves, check for full details with your local mountaineering club or with the Sierra Club branch in your area. Among the trails in Glacier National Park (140 km./93 mi. of them) are Trestle, Loop, Meeting of the Waters, and Abandoned Rails. There are campgrounds in the park.

In 1881 A. B. Rogers, an employee of the CPR, found a pass through the Selkirk Range (later named in his honor), so that one of the final links in the transcontinental railroad could be built. The railroad was put through **Rogers Pass** (elevation 1,323 m./4,302 ft.) at great effort and expense in 1885 and 1886. As the area was subject to frequent avalanches, the 8-km. (4.8 mi.) Connaught Tunnel was built in 1916 to protect lives and the passage of trains. The Trans-Canada Highway came through here in 1962. Avalanches are still a problem, but an excellent safety program protects travelers moving through this area.

Rogers Pass Information Centre is on the Trans-Canada, (604) 837–6274. Open mid-June to Labour Day; call for times during rest of year. Free. The Information Centre, operated by Parks Canada, is located at the top of Rogers Pass. It provides information on the building and operation of the transcontinental railroad through this rugged part of the country and the natural history of the area—glaciers, avalanches, caves, alpine meadows, and wildlife—and it shows a movie on the secrets of the Nakimu Cave System. Well worth the stop to understand the magnificent landscape you are passing through.

For accommodation try the **Best Western Glacier Park Lodge,** off the Trans-Canada, (604) 837–2126. Great location; dining room and lounge. Moderate.

The town of **Golden,** on the Trans-Canada between the Selkirk Mountains and Glacier National Park and the Rockies and Yoho National Park, was once known as Kicking Horse Flats. You'll find golf, hunting, fishing, wild river rafting, hiking, and access to some of the top national parks in Canada here. Call (604) 344–7125 for complete information on touring and vacation opportunities in the Golden area. The **Golden Rim Motor Inn,** off the Trans-Canada, (604) 344–2216, has saunas, an indoor pool, and a dining room. Moderate.

The main access to **Yoho National Park** is off the Trans-Canada Highway, and the park's office is in the community of Field. Yoho and Kootenay are "Siamese twin" parks in that they join each other at the B.C.–Alberta border. Yoho, the northern park, runs along the spine of the Canadian Rockies, and Kootenay is the southern park. There's no mistaking that you are in high mountain country here, with a landscape of deep forests, icy glaciers, wild rivers, pure lakes, and an abundance of wildlife. Within its shale area—particularly Burgess, now a World Heritage site—are fossils from prehistory. They're protected and not for collecting, but you can see the remains of ancient creatures by hiking into the shale zone.

Among the many features of the park are the Spiral Tunnels Viewpoint, Kicking Horse Pass, Kicking Horse River, Lake O'Hara (the Alpine Club of Canada has a shelter here), Emerald Lake, Takakkaw Falls, Yoho River, Twin Falls, Laughing Falls, Point Lace Falls, Angel's Staircase Falls, Yoho Glacier, Hamilton Falls and Lake, and Natural Bridge. There are numerous hiking trails (360 km./225 mi. of them), such as the Deer Lodge Trail and the Avalanche Trail, and the following campgrounds—Kicking Horse,

British Columbia's Pacific Rim National Park is an ever-changing natural ▶ **environment of sea, sky, and shore. The moods of nature here evoke poetry and soul searching of positive force.**

Hoodo Creek, Chancellor Peak, Takakkaw Falls, and Lake O'Hara. Trout fishing is allowed in Yoho, but you have to get a permit from park authorities; canoeing is possible on Lake O'Hara and Emerald Lake; and you can go horseback trail riding from a stable at Emerald Lake. For more information, contact Superintendent, Yoho National Park, Box 99, Field, British Columbia V0A 1G0; (604) 343–6324.

In addition to its impressively high mountains, **Kootenay National Park** is famous for its wild rivers, glaciers, canyons, and hot springs. Access is from many points along the Banff-Windermere Highway 93 and from the Trans-Canada and Highway 95. The southern end of the park, Radium Hot Springs, is a bit more arid than the northern part at Vermilion Pass (Lake Louise and Banff can be reached from here). These dual climate zones make for diverse vegetation and animal and bird life. Kootenay is a naturalist's paradise, and when he or she gets through trekking and observing, there are natural hot springs to soak away fatigue and reestablish a more complete tranquility. The many hiking trails (200 km./125 mi. of them), such as Marble Canyon, Paint Pots, Fireweed, Valley View, and Juniper, lead throughout the park. Paint Pots is a bed of ochre that was used in long-gone days by the local native peoples. A suspension bridge, reached via the Paint Pots Trail, crosses the powerful Vermilion River.

The hot springs at Radium (noted on page 86) are world famous, and people come from all over North America and many foreign countries to seek a cure for what ails them. A soak in these hot mineral waters is the perfect ending to a long day's drive or hours on nearby ski slopes.

Camping with facilities for recreational vehicles is at Redstreak, off Highway 95 near the Trans-Canada; McLeod Meadows to the north of Radium Hot Springs; and Marble Canyon. Kootenay also offers fishing (permit required) and canoeing on the Kootenay and Vermilion rivers.

For more information, contact Superintendent, Kootenay National Park, Box 220, Radium Hot Springs, British Columbia V0A 1M0; (604) 347–9615; (604) 347–9331.

Highly recommended for accommodations in this area is **Emerald Lake Lodge,** near Field, off the Trans-Canada, about 30 minutes from Lake Louise, Alberta; (403) 343–6321; in Canada, (800) 661–1367. This is a historic, chalet-type lodge in Yoho National Park. It has been popular with sophisticated travelers seeking tranquility for more than eighty-five years, and it has been recently restored and renovated to contemporary standards. The outstanding setting takes advantage of the essential beauty of the Canadian Rockies. Within the Emerald Lake area you can canoe, fish, trail ride, hunt for fossils, cross-country ski, and go dog sledding. Nearby are Lake O'Hara, Takakkaw Falls, and Yoho Glacier. The main lodge has a dining room and an 1890s Yukon saloon. Entertainers (singers, musicians, dancers, comics) are brought in from Banff. Expensive.

The Canadian Rockies: The B.C.–Alberta Border. The Trans-Canada Highway crosses the **Continental Divide** and enters the province of Alberta through **Kicking Horse Pass** (1,647 m./5,402 ft.). Just a few miles past the border, near the Trans-Canada, is Lake Louise. If you head north on Highway 93, you'll reach Jasper (connecting with the Yellowhead Highway 16 east to Edmonton). Highway 93 south leads to Banff and Calgary.

Metro Vancouver to Banff, Alberta, via the Crowsnest Highway 3

The Crowsnest Highway 3 (and Rocky Mountain Trench Highway 93/95 east in the Kootenay region) takes you through or near towns with familiar and odd-sounding names: Princeton, Osoyoos, Greenwood, Trail, Castlegar, Creston, Yahk, Kitchener, Cranbrook, Wasa, Skookumchuck, Fairmont Hot Springs, Invermere, and Radium Hot Springs. You travel over several mountain ranges, through thickly forested valleys, arid ones, and those lush with fruit orchards, until you come to the Kootenays and the Canadian Rockies. View after view of gorgeous alpine scenery and fields of wild mountain flowers is breathtaking. All along the way are museums, historical sites, and places for swimming, fishing, camping, boating, skiing, tennis, hiking, horseback trail riding, wild river rafting, and golf. The accommodations in the towns are fine; some of the resorts are as outstanding as those you'll find anywhere in the world. Although there are few gourmet restaurants as such, most places serve good, honest cooking—both North American and ethnic cuisines—that will satisfy the appetites of travelers. If you've traveled across B.C. before along the Trans-Canada, you'll find this southern route a nice change and see new aspects of this beautiful province. U.S. travelers coming from eastern Washington, Idaho, and western Montana will also find this an enjoyable route to Vancouver.

Osoyoos is the southern gateway to the Okanagan vacation region. In architecture and style, Osoyoos reminds one of a town in Arizona or New Mexico—in fact, it's called the Spanish Capital of

Canada. Although the hills around the town are almost desertlike, the land in the valley is irrigated to support extensive orchards and vegetable crops. In July the folks here hold a **Cherry Festival** to honor the fruit they grow in such abundance. Just to the south of town is **Osoyoos Lake,** which is a perfect place for swimming, sunbathing, boating, fishing, and windsurfing. The **Osoyoos Museum,** (604) 495–6723, welcomes visitors who want to learn about the history of this pleasant community. Osoyoos is just a "stone's throw" away from the B.C.–Washington border, and U.S. travelers can enter the province via U.S. Highway 97.

The following accommodations have restaurants and other amenities:

Desert Motor Inn, on Highway 3, (604) 495–6525. Moderate.

The Sahara Hotel, in town, (604) 495–7211. Moderate.

Grand Forks is right on the B.C.–Washington border, and U.S. Highways 21 and 395 give access to the province at this point. Within the town there are a local history museum and a Doukhobor museum as well as an art gallery. **Grand Forks Motor Inn,** in town, (604) 442–2127, has a restaurant and a pool. Moderate.

Both gold and copper were discovered in the **Trail** area in the late 1800s. Today its primary economic activity is smelting minerals (zinc, lead, and silver) from the region's mines. U.S. travelers coming from Washington take Washington Highway 25 to B.C. Highway 22. In the city are the Birchbank eighteen-hole golf course, Beaver Creek Provincial Park, Wright Public Pool, Gyro Park, and Seven Mile Dam. Other attractions include:

City of Trail Museum, in City Hall. Open weekdays from June through September. Free. Exhibits of local history.

Italian Community Archives, 584 Rossland Avenue in the Colombo Lodge. Open July through August; call (604) 368–9556. Records, photos, and artifacts of Italian immigrants.

Rossland Historical Museum, in Rossland. Open from mid-May to mid-October, (604) 362–7722. Admission charged. Displays on the geological history of the area. Le Roi Gold Mine underground tour here. Home of B.C. Ski Hall of Fame.

Also in the Rossland area are the **King George VI Provincial Park** and **Red Mountain Ski Area.**

The following accommodations have restaurants and other amenities:

Victoria Place, 898 Victoria Place, (604) 368–5577. Inexpensive.

Glenwood Motel, 2769 Glenwood Drive, (604) 368–5522. Moderate.

Castlegar is well worth the side trip on Highway 22 north from Trail. The Doukhobors, a unique community of people who live here, came from the steppes of czarist Russia, where they were persecuted for their strong religious beliefs. They were pacifists and refused to serve in the military; they lived in a highly structured communal society; they were vegetarians; their religious practices were simple and basic in comparison with those of the Byzantine Russian Orthodox.

The writer Tolstoy and the North American Society of Friends (the Quakers, whom the Doukhobors resemble in attitudes and religious practices) helped the Doukhobors leave Russia and settle in Canada. They originally settled in Alberta and Saskatchewan, carving out farms on the prairies. Because of disputes with the provincial governments, they had to move on again and, at last, found refuge in south central British Columbia. The Doukhobors are famous for their choirs, which have performed to enthusiastic audiences throughout Canada, the United States, and other countries. Visit the Zuckerberg Island Heritage Park, the Kootenay Indian Pit House, the Russian Chapel House, the Doukhobor Bridge, and Verigin's Tomb. Peter "Lordly" Verigin was the Doukhobor spiritual leader who brought them to Canada. Castlegar is also the gateway to the Arrow Lakes, via Highway 6, for great fishing, swimming, camping, hiking, and sunbathing. While in Castlegar, be sure to see the following:

Doukhobor Historical Museum, across from Castlegar Airport. Open daily; (604) 365–6622. Admission charged. Buildings show the communal character and lifestyle of the Doukhobors and tell of their history in Russia and Canada. Sample Russian culinary specialties, such as borscht and pirogi, at the Doukhobor Restaurant, where all dishes are vegetarian.

West Kootenay National Exhibition Centre, next to Doukhobor Museum. Open daily; (604) 365–2411; Free. One of twenty-three National Exhibition Centres in Canada. Exhibits from local and international cultures.

The following inns have restaurants and other amenities:

Sandman Inn, 1944 Columbia Avenue, (604) 365–8444. Inexpensive to moderate.

Fireside Motor Inn, 1810 8th Avenue, (604) 365–2128. Moderate.

Creston, on the Kootenay River on Highway 3, is famous for its fruit orchards and fields (strawberries, raspberries, cherries, apricots, peaches, plums, pears, and most kinds of apples). A visit here in the spring when the blossoms are out, or in the summer when apples are ripening, is a memorable experience in human-cultivated beauty set against a backdrop of magnificent nature. There's a golf course in town.

If you have extra time for exploring, take Highway 3A north to the **Kootenay Lake** area, where there are several golf and fishing resorts. At Kootenay Bay you can take a ferry to Balfour and then Highway 3A to the hot springs at **Ainsworth.** This area can also be visited by taking Highway 3A north from Castlegar to Nelson or Highway 6 to Nelson and then Highway 3A. U.S. citizens coming to Creston from Idaho should take U.S. Highway 95, to Idaho Highway 1 to the border, and then B.C. Highway 21 to Creston.

The annual **Blossom Festival** is held in May. Other attractions in Creston include:

Creston Valley Museum, off Highway 3, (604) 428–9262. Call for hours. Admission charged. Housed in the old Stone House; depicts the town's agricultural heritage.

Creston Valley Wildlife Management Area, outside of downtown. Open throughout the year. Free. Seventeen thousand acres of lakes, streams, and marshes supporting a wide variety of wildlife; guided walks, canoe trips, films, talks, gift shop, and snack bar. For campground, call (604) 428–3260.

Wayside Garden and Aboretum, on Highway 3. Open May to October, (604) 428–2062. Admission charged. Beautiful floral displays: rose garden, rhododendron dell, water lily and fish ponds, perennial borders, rock garden and lily beds, tea house, and gift shop.

Recommended accommodations follow:

Ponderosa Motel, on Highway 3, (604) 428–4009. Moderate.

The Hacienda Inn, in town, (604) 428–2224, has a dining room. Inexpensive to moderate.

City Centre Motel, in town, (604) 428–2257. Moderate.

Budget Host Motel, on Highway 3, (604) 428–2229. Moderate.

U.S. travelers entering British Columbia in the **Cranbrook** region can take Montana Highway 93 or Idaho Highway 95. Both these highways come into the city of Cranbrook, and they continue north through the eastern part of the province to Banff, Alberta; the Trans-Canada; and Lake Louise. If you are headed for Banff and then Calgary, leave the Crowsnest Highway at Cranbrook and continue on Highway 93/95 north.

Cranbrook was developed in the late 1800s when the railroad serving this region selected it over Fort Steele as terminal point. Today Cranbrook serves as one of the major commercial and transportation centers for the lower Kootenay region. There are fine accommodations, restaurants, shops, and services in this city.

Don't miss **Sam Steele Days** in June, and if you're interested in the railroads, visit **Cranbrook Railway Museum** in downtown Cranbrook, (604) 489–3918. It's open daily throughout the summer and limited hours in the winter. Admission is free. There are restored luxury railway cars—1920s vintage—and a caboose for children to explore.

All of the following accommodations have restaurants and other amenities:

Sandman Inn, 405 Cranbrook Street, (604) 426–4236. Moderate.

Heritage Estate Motel, 362 South Van Horne Street, (604) 426–3862. Inexpensive.

Mount Baker Hotel, 1017 Baker Street, (604) 426–5277. Moderate.

Town and Country Motor Hotel, 600 Cranbrook Street, (604) 426–6683. Moderate.

Inn of the South, 803 Cranbrook Street, (604) 489–4301. Moderate.

Best Western Coach House Motor Inn, 1417 Cranbrook Street, (604) 426–7236. Moderate.

From Cranbrook the Crowsnest Highway 3 continues east to the Alberta border where, at Pincher Creek, Alberta, it forms a junction with Highway 6. By heading south on 6 you come to Waterton Lakes National Park (see pages 227–28). Just below Waterton, actually adjoining it, is Glacier National Park in Montana. Between Cranbrook and the Alberta border is the Fernie Ski Area, and just past the town of Sparwood, you go through Crowsnest Pass (elevation 1,382 m./4,533 ft.) at the border of the two provinces.

This region of British Columbia (between Cranbrook and the Alberta border) has numerous resort areas offering everything from skiing and white-water rafting to horseback riding and golf. While you're in the area, be sure to visit the following:

Fort Steele Historic Park, 13 km. (7 mi.) north of Cranbrook on Rocky Mountain Trench Highway 93/95; (604) 489–3351. Open daily. Free. Fort Steele is the main historical attraction in the Kootenay region and should not be missed. A canny fellow by the name of John Galbraith, no relation to the famous economist, saw the potential of this site as settlers, miners, and merchants began moving in, and started a ferry line. Then there came disputes between the whites and local natives. In 1887 Superintendent Samuel B. Steele and seventy-five North West Mounted Police ("D" Division) came in Galbraith's Ferry to establish law and order, and here they built the first NWMP post in British Columbia. Fort Steele, on the bank of the Kootenay River, became a transportation, commercial, and social center for this area. However, in 1898, after the B.C. Southern Railway chose Cranbrook as its divisional point, Fort Steele declined into oblivion. It was brought back to life as a historic park, and today you can stroll Fort Steele's streets and visit its buildings as they were in the 1800s. You can step into the millinery shop; the blacksmith shop; Bleasdell's drugstore; Dr. Watt's office; the Kershaw family store; Coventry's opera house; the Presbyterian, Anglican, and Roman Catholic churches; the Windsor Hotel; and numerous private residences from the Victorian period. Vaudeville shows are performed at the Wild Horse Theatre. There's also a Tea Room for snacks and an interesting museum of local lore.

The city of **Kimberley,** a highly recommended side trip via Highway 95A, tucked away in the Purcell Mountains, is Bavaria in Canada. Its architecture is a mix of southern German, Austrian, Swiss, and English Tudor. The Platzl (town center) in downtown draws people to shops, restaurants serving schnitzel, outdoor cafés, and the sight of Happy Hans jumping out from what the people here say is the world's largest cuckoo clock. There are outdoor band concerts and strolling musicians. Residents wearing lederhosen and dirndls are a common sight during the summer.

One of Kimberley's main attractions is an eighteen-hole, par-71 CPGA golf course set in the midst of magnificent scenery. The **Alpine Slide,** a 2,700-foot thrilling run down the side of a mountain, is in operation from July to Labour Day. Kimberley's annual festivals include **The International Old-Time Accordion Festival** in July. The **Bavaria City Mining Railway** gives rides from the end of June until Labour Day. Be sure to visit the **Kimberley Heritage Museum,** located above the public library in the Platzl, and the **Comico Gardens** with its flowers and plantings.

The following accommodations are highly recommended:

Top of the World Ranch, off Highway 93/95, between Fort

Steele and Fairmont Hot Springs; (604) 426–6306. Top of the World is a family-owned ranch high in the Canadian Rockies (Kootenay region). It takes guests year-round and offers the authentic western ranch experience: trail rides, camp fires, hearty home-cooked food, comfortable accommodations, the panorama of changing seasons, and the sight of wild animals and birds, the glory of the mountains, barbecues, fishing, and the knowledge that you have escaped civilization and are enjoying it. Moderate.

Fairmont Hot Springs Resort, in Fairmont Hot Springs on Highway 93/95; (604) 345–6311. The largest natural mineral hot pools in Canada are at Fairmont Hot Springs Resort, which has been a favorite with families since 1922. In addition to swimming and hot springs bathing, it features a championship eighteen-hole golf course, deluxe villas and hotel, and excellent facilities for camping at its RV park. Its natural hot spring pools have a clear, odorless water with temperatures of 35° to 45°C (90° to 106°F).

The resort also offers tennis, racquetball, squash, trail rides on horseback, hiking, helicopter sightseeing, and canoeing, fishing, and windsurfing on nearby Columbia Lake as well as a game room for children. In the winter, it operates its own ski center with 10 mi. runs (see page 92). The resort is located at the base of the Kootenay section of the Canadian Rockies, and the alpine and lake scenery is fantastic. Fairmont, considered one of Canada's top family resorts, is worth a visit or a prolonged stay. Reservations are essential during peak summer and winter seasons. Moderate to expensive.

Invermere, a small resort community, is at the northern end of Windermere Lake, which flows into Columbia Lake, the source of the mighty Columbia River. The lakes in this area are good for swimming, canoeing, fishing, and windsurfing. There are a number of places of accommodations (such as the Fairmont and Panorama resorts), restaurants, and stores in this scenic area. Be sure to visit the following:

Invermere Museum, in town, (604) 342–9769. Open June through August. Admission charged. Museum in old railroad station; pioneer log cabins, old school house; copy of David Thompson's journal (early explorer, fur trader, surveyor, map maker who helped to establish the border between Canada and the United States); pleasant park setting.

Food and lodging are available at the following:

Invermere Inn, in downtown, (604) 342–9246. Dining room, lounge, pub, sauna, large pool and water slide, hot tubs. Moderate.

Panorama Resort, in the Invermere area; (604) 342–6941. Panorama is one of Canada's finest alpine resorts. It's actually a self-contained village of deluxe hotel and inn rooms and condos. Grocery, liquor, sports equipment, and gift shops are within the Panorama complex. It offers horseback trail rides, wild river rafting trips, guided treks through the rugged wilderness, tennis, and winter sports (see page 92). Golf is nearby, and so is swimming in Columbia Lake. In late August the resort is the host site for the **Annual Scottish Gathering.** Moderate to expensive.

Radium Hot Springs, at the junction of Highways 93 and 95, bordering Kootenay National Park; (604) 347–9331, is one of the world's famous hot springs. Before the coming of the whites, Amerindians sought to cure their ills in these baths (40°C/102°F). So did Winston Churchill during one of his trips to Canada. Thousands of people believe that these odorless, clear waters heal, and many have indeed experienced relief. The Aquacourt accommodates both bathers and swimmers. It is open to all every day of the year, with summer hours from 8:30 A.M. to 11:00 P.M. At the Radium Hot Springs Resort an eighteen-hole golf course and facilities for squash, racquetball, and tennis are available. Within the area there are also water slides, wild river rafting trips, hiking trails, helicopter hiking trips, and horseback trail rides. Other places to visit are the nearby Bugaboo Ski Area and Our Lady of Peace Shrine.

White Water Trips, Glacier Raft Company, (604) 347–9218, provides thrilling wild river raft trips on the Vermilion and Kootenay rivers: horseback trips through Yoho National Park, the Continental Divide, and Top of the World Provincial Park; other trips on the Alberta side of the Rockies.

Accommodations in the area are listed below:

Radium Hot Springs Resort (mentioned above); (604) 347–9311. Moderate.

Motel Bavaria, (604) 347–9915. Moderate.

Alpen Motel, (604) 347–9823. Moderate.

Radium Hot Springs Lodge, (604) 347–9622. Moderate.

Mount Assiniboine Lodge, in Mount Assiniboine Provincial Park, bordering Kootenay and Banff National Parks; (403) 678–2883. Access by hiking trail, helicopter, or cross-country skiing. Log lodge overlooks Magog Lake. Reservations essential. Expensive.

The Canadian Rockies: The B.C.–Alberta border. If you are heading for the Canadian Rockies in Alberta, take Highway 93 east through Kootenay National Park, which crosses the Great Divide at

Vermilion Pass (1,637 m./5,367 ft.) and enters Banff National Park. It joins the Trans-Canada in Alberta just south of Lake Louise. Highway 95 splits off from 93 and continues north until it joins the Trans-Canada at Golden, B.C. From here you can head east, entering Alberta through Kicking Horse Pass, just a few miles north of Lake Louise or south of Jasper National Park.

Metro Vancouver to the Yukon and Alaska via Highway 97: The Cowboy and Gold Fever Country of the Cariboo

Cache Creek, at the junction of the Trans-Canada and Highway 97 north, might be a good place to stop for the night if you have come up from Vancouver without stopping and intend to go north on Highway 97. The following accommodations have restaurants and other amenities:

Sandman Inn, (604) 457–6284. Moderate.

Cache Creek Travelodge, (604) 457–6224. Moderate.

This part of British Columbia—near **100 Mile House**—attracted persons in quest of furs and gold in the 1860s. 100 Mile House is one hundred miles from the town of Lillooet, which is at "mile 0" on the Cariboo Wagon Road. In the 1930s Lord Martin Cecil came into the area to manage his father's ranch. This is prime western ranchland for the raising of cattle, and lumbering, mining, and tourism are also major industries.

For fun and adventure, try the following:

Cariboo Cowboy Adventures, (604) 395–2345. Trail rides and overnight excursions in the countryside.

The Great Cariboo Ride Society, (604) 395–4096. A nine-day horseback trek across the Fraser Plateau to Gang Ranch; great meals; fishing and dips in waterfalls.

Annual Festivals

Western Days—May

South Cariboo Square Dance Jamboree—June

All-Breed Horse Show—July

Great Cariboo Ride—August

Accommodations include the following:

Red Coach Inn, in the village, (604) 395–2266. Moderate.

Imperial Motel, in the village, (604) 395–2471. Moderate.

Williams Lake is named after Chief William of the Sugar Cane

Reserve. Its Indian name is "Colunetza," which means "gathering place of the lordly ones." Williams Lake serves the many cattle ranches in the area. Lumbering and mining are also important economic activities. While in town visit the Bullion Gold Mine, see the downtown murals, and tour the Gibralter mines.

The Williams Golf and Tennis Club, (604) 392–6026, has an eighteen-hole golf course, three tennis courts, and a restaurant.

Annual Events
Stampede—late June to early July
Quarter Horse Show—August
Kinsmen Inner Tube Race—August

All of the following accommodations have restaurants and other amenities:

Sandman Inn, 664 Oliver Street, (604) 392–6557. Moderate.

Fraser Inn, 285 Donald Road, (604) 398–7055. Moderate.

Williams Golf and Tennis Club, (604) 392–6026. 18 holes, 3 tennis courts, restaurant.

From Williams Lake take Highway 20 to **Bella Coola** on the coast, a long journey of 465 km. (279 miles). The first fourth of the way, up to **Hanceville,** is paved road, and the rest of the way is gravel. If your vehicle is in good condition and prepared for some rough spots, this trip could be a nice adventure from the interior of the province to the coast. The scenery along the way is beautiful. You pass through several small towns and **Tweedsmuir Park.** You can camp and enjoy the wilderness along the way. If you are bringing along a canoe, all the better. Be careful not to stir up a grizzly en route. The paved road picks up again at the western end of Tweedsmuir Park and takes you to Bella Coola, which is at the Labouchere, Dean, and Burke channels, just east of the Inside Passage (see page 189). There are accommodations, supplies, gas, and food in the villages and in Bella Coola. Midsummer is a good time to do this trip, and it is best not to travel under a tight schedule.

In the old days, **Quesnel,** on Highway 97, was a supply center and steamboat landing for the gold-mining town of Bakersville, which is now a historic park. Today it continues as a transportation center for the local mining and lumbering industries. Both natural gas and oil potential have been found here, and Quesnel may be important to our future as a source for energy.

Barkerville Historic Park, at end of Highway 26 east, is 82 km. (49 mi.) from Quesnel. Open daily, (604) 994–3316. Free. A restored village from the Gold Rush period in the late 1800s. During the summer, there are stage shows and demonstrations of how people lived and worked in those days. The buildings include a blacksmith shop, saloon, miner's cabin, churches, Chinese herbal shop, general store, and many more. Barkerville does a good job of telling its story. It takes some extra time to get there, but it's well worth it.

The Alexander Mackenzie Heritage Trail, between Quesnel in Cariboo's interior and Bella Coola on the coast, is a demanding but immensely satisfying hiking trek through beautiful and historic country; for more information, call Heritage Service in Victoria— (604) 387–1011—or write Alexander Mackenzie Trail Association, P.O. Box 425, Kelowna, B.C. V1Y 7P1.

Western Cariboo Outfitters, 566 Edkins Street, Quesnel, (604) 992–2287, sponsor pack trips, trail rides, scenic and photography trips into the wilderness heart of Cariboo high country, and a fifteen-day adventure trip from Nazko to Tweedsmuir Park over the Rainbow Mountains to the coast at Bella Coola.

Annual events in Quesnel include the **Oldtime Fiddlers Contest** in June and the **Billy Barker Rodeo** in July. For accommodations, try the following:

Cascade Inn, 383 St. Laurent Avenue, (604) 992–5575. Moderate.

Talisman Inn, 753 Front Street, (604) 922–7247. Moderate.

As you travel north from Quesnel, you'll pass through Prince George (described on page 195), the next major city along Highway 97. There are a few routes you can take from here. If you are still headed for the Alaska Highway, continue on Highway 97 north until you come to Chetwynd. At the junction, take Highway 29 north, which reconnects with Highway 97 just above the town of Fort St. John. This loop will save you a great deal of time and mileage. Once you commit yourself to the Alaska Highway going north, your only other option (should you decide to turn south) is to take Highway 37 (above Watson Lake in the Yukon) to Prince Rupert; otherwise, you have to backtrack until you reach Prince George.

The Yellowhead Highway 16 bisects Highway 97 in Prince George, and at this point, if you wish to turn east, take the Yellowhead to Jasper and then to Edmonton. From Jasper you can go south on Highway 93 through Jasper National Park and to the

Trans-Canada to Lake Louise, Banff, and Calgary. Near the British Columbian border the Yellowhead passes through Mount Robson Provincial Park, where Mount Robson, the highest point in the Canadian Rockies, and Mount Terry Fox, named in honor of the brave Canadian cross-country runner, are located.

On the banks of the Peace River, once a link in a chain of fur-trading posts, **Fort St. John** became in recent times a center for oil and natural gas exploration and development in this part of the province. Attractions here include a monument to Alexander Mackenzie, the North Peace Museum of local history, and the North Peace Art Gallery. The World Gold Panning Championship is held in July, and in August, the Black Powder Shoot.

The following accommodations have restaurants and other amenities:

The Coachman Inn, 8540 Alaska Road, (604) 787–0651. Moderate.

Pioneer Inn, 9830 100th Avenue, (604) 787–0521. Moderate.

In 1800 the North West Company established a trading post in **Fort Nelson** (410 km./246 mi. north of Fort St. John), and the Hudson's Bay Company took over in 1865. Exploration for oil and natural gas has improved the economy here. Lumbering is a major activity.

Accommodations are available at the **Coachhouse Inn,** 4711 50th Avenue, (604) 774–3911. Dining room and lounge. Moderate.

To the B.C.–Yukon border: The distance between Fort St. John and the Yukon border is 940 km. (564 miles). The only community of any size en route is Fort Nelson, which is about halfway, although there are some small villages. Your best bet is to make sure your vehicle is okay for the trip in Fort St. John. It's a good place for getting supplies, gas, and whatever else you need. The Alaska Highway going through B.C. is paved, except for a stretch just before the Yukon border. As mentioned above, there are accommodations and hot meals in Fort Nelson. It's a good stopping point if you're there in the afternoon; night driving can be hazardous because of the wild animals that cross the road. Of course, you can camp almost anywhere. Two provincial parks with facilities—Muncho Lake and Stone Mountain—are located on the highway north of Fort Nelson. After you enter the Yukon, the first town of any size is Watson Lake, where there are accommodations, food, and auto and other services.

Winter Sports in British Columbia

British Columbia has more opportunities for enjoying winter sports than any other of the Western Canadian provinces (Alberta comes in a close second with its Rocky Mountain area). Within B.C. you can ski downhill, cross-country; be dropped off on virgin powder from helicopters or Snow-Cats; ice-skate, snowshoe, ice climb, and fish. The province's infrastructure of resorts, hotels, restaurants, transportation system, après-ski activities, shops, and ski schools is among the very best on the continent. If you haven't yet enjoyed winter in B.C., you've got a cornucopia of treats and thrills waiting for you.

Downhill Skiing

For twenty-four-hour information on conditions at recreational ski areas, call:

Vancouver: (604) 688–8011
Calgary: (403) 262–7575
Edmonton: (403) 451–6686
Seattle: (206) 621–8889
Spokane: (509) 483–1150

Mount Washington, in the Courtney area of Vancouver Island; (604) 338–1386. Twenty downhill runs; lodges and condos; ski school; après-ski dining and entertainment; week packages; equipment rentals.

Grouse, in North Vancouver, a few minutes from city center (see page 123); (604) 984–0661. All runs are lit until 11:00 P.M.; Bavarian beer garden; snow-making; CSIA ski school; 1,110 m. (3,641 ft.) summit; close to city accommodations and restaurants.

Whistler/Blackcomb, one of the top world-class ski resort areas in Western Canada; over sixty marked runs for every level of expertise; (see page 116 for more details); call (604) 932–4222 for information on packages and hotel reservations.

Hemlock Resort, two hours from Vancouver city center in Hemlock Valley, via Highway 7; 500 acres of skiing terrain; Winter Carnival; helicopter skiing; Hemlock Inn; ski school; night skiing; (604) 797–4411.

Gibson Pass, in the Cascades; 157 km. (94.2 mi.) of marked trails; cross-country skiing; equipment rentals; lodges and après-ski actvities; horse-drawn sleigh rides; snowmobiling trails; (604) 840–8822.

Apex Alpine, in the Okanagan region (Kamloops area); thirty-six runs—2,000-foot vertical drop; ski school; ice rink; hot tubs; condos; (604) 292–8221.

Big White Ski Village, in the Okanagan region (Kamloops area); forty-one runs—1,900-foot vertical drop; ski packages; ski school day-care facility; (604) 765–4111.

Silver Star, in the Okanagan region (Kamloops area); thirty-two runs; new accommodations; equipment rentals; ski school; (604) 542–0166.

Tod Mountain, in the Okanagan region (Kamloops area); 3,100-foot vertical drop; expert FIS runs; slalom runs; ski school; 1,700 rooms available in the area; (604) 578–7151.

White Water, in the southeastern corner of the province, the Selkirk Range of the Canadian Rockies; eighteen runs; helicopter skiing on virgin powder; accommodations in Nelson; (604) 354–4944.

Red Mountain, in Castlegar area; 2,800-foot vertical drop; powdery alpine meadows; hot racing slopes; ski school; equipment rentals; helicopter skiing; (604) 362–7384.

Panorama, located south of the Bugaboos; 3,800-foot vertical drop; cross-country trails; helicopter skiing; luxury accommodations; outdoor hot tubs; (604) 342–6941.

Fairmont Hot Springs, in the heart of the Canadian Rockies; runs for all levels of expertise; cross-country trails; excellent accommodations; ski packages; (604) 345–6311.

Kimberley Resort, called "Little Bavaria" in the Rockies because of German-style architecture in town and restaurants; 2,300-foot vertical drop; longest night skiing run in North America; ski school; plenty of accomodations, entertainment, and restaurants; (604) 427–4881.

Fernie Snow Valley, in the Canadian Rockies near Cranbrook; 2,400-foot vertical drop; excellent accommodations, restaurants, and entertainment in area; ski school; (604) 423–6041.

Helicopter Skiing

Helicopters take you to mountaintops where there are unlimited runs of virgin powder. Top professional guides show you the way down, and the safety standards in equipment and on the runs are among the best in the world. Helicopter skiing in the Canadian Rockies is one of the thrilling wonders of this world. The following organizations offer the thrill of helicopter skiing in the mountain ranges of British Columbia:

Canadian Mountain Holidays, the Bugaboos, Cariboos, Bobbie Burns, and Monashees; (604) 342–6941.

Mike Wiegele Helicopter Skiing, the Cariboos and Monashees; (403) 762–5548.

Kootenay Heli-Skiing, the Selkirks and Monashees; (604) 265–3121.

B.C. Powder Guides, the Spearhead and Chilcotin ranges; (604) 932–5331.

Panorama Resort Heli-Skiing, the Purcells; (604) 342–6941.

Selkirk Tanglers Heli-Skiing, the Selkirks and Monashees; (604) 344–5016.

Valkyrie Heli-Ski, the Valkyrie Range; (604) 362–9662.

Mountain Canada, the Purcells and Selkirks; (604) 344–5410.

Northwest Mountain Holiday, the Babine and Bulkley ranges; (604) 846–5336.

Snow-Cat Skiing

A twelve-passenger Snow-Cat vehicle takes to the top of a virgin powder run—no lifts, no crowds, you have the mountain mostly to yourself—up to 18,000 feet of glorious skiing per day. This type of skiing offers all the advantages of helicopter skiing without the helicopter.

Selkirk Wilderness Skiing, five-day, all-inclusive packages; (604) 366–4424.

Great Northern, two- to six-day, all-inclusive packages; (604) 832–9500.

Nordic and Cross-Country Skiing

British Columbia has some of the most spectacular ski-touring areas in North America. Within or near the national and provincial parks are bed and breakfast places, ranches, motels, and resorts. A number of resorts have their own cross-country skiing trails.

National Parks: Yoho, Kootenay, and Glacier.

Provincial Parks: Assiniboine, Garibaldi, Manning, Alice Lake, Brandywine Falls, Champion Lakes, Kokanee Creek, Maclure Lake, Nancy Greene, Strathcona, Top of the World, Wells Gray, Whiteswan, Beaton, Bugaboo Glacier, Cypress, Kitsumkalum Mountain, Kokanee Glacier, Mount Seymour, Stageleap, Ten Mile Lake, Wasa, West Lake, and Mount Robson.

Call Ministry of Lands, Parks, and Housing at (604) 387–1067 for information on these provincial parks.

CHAPTER 5

Vancouver: Camelot by the Pacific

Metro Vancouver • Whistler The Gulf Islands

What Makes Vancouver Special

A few years ago Bob Hope played Vancouver and paid the city a most generous compliment: "People say that they've left their hearts in San Francisco. But they haven't seen Vancouver!" For those who have seen Vancouver, however, these words are well understood. It would perhaps be a bit too much to say that Vancouver is better than San Francisco, but describing them as similar in many respects is fairly accurate—both enjoy laid-back lifestyles and excellence in creative and commercial effort.

Vancouver has a mild climate most of the year, although it gets bountiful doses of rain from time to time, just as nearby Seattle. The hazards of snow and ice rarely plague drivers here, but when the slush does hit, there is mayhem on the roads because people have forgotten or never learned how to drive in the mush. It offers skiing and sailing, both within an hour of each other. Its backyard sprawls over millions of acres of thick forests, tall mountains, wild rivers, and pure lakes. Some, such as native medicine men and scientists, say the legendary but shy "Big Foot" lives nearby in the deep woods.

Vancouver lacks the violent crime of California cities, and visitors from the States appreciate the generally law-abiding ways of Vancouverites. Vancouver also tends at times to be a starchy, smug city of the strait-laced and the self-satisfied. In Vancouver, as elsewhere, the puritanical and the licentious are in constant struggle. Every kind of alternative lifestyle and cult is here. Stiff, upper-lip British traditions are very strong—more so in Victoria—but they've been slotted into a wider spectrum of cultures of the Poles, Greeks, Ukrainians, Chinese, Italians, Pakistanis, Indians, and Portuguese, to name but a few from the city's mosaic of peoples. Both the proper and the strange coexist without too many noses put out of joint. Perhaps this is the way people were meant to live, not as clones of one another but in diversity and in harmony.

To Canadians living in the East, Vancouver is often thought of as their country's Lotus Land, the place to pull yourself together again after a divorce or any kind of bad luck. Once you feel psychically on top again, you can return to Ottawa, Montréal, Toronto, or Halifax. But few, it seems, end up going back East permanently. Life is that good in Vancouver, except for the havoc the winter rain can cause with one's sinuses.

Among the noteworthy persons who have lived in the Vancouver area are the artist/writer Emily Carr; Malcolm Lowry, author of *Under the Volcano;* and Ayn Rand, the famous writer and promoter of rugged individualism. The best of contemporary Canadian architecture has its roots here through talented designers such as Arthur Erickson. Its University of British Columbia surely must be considered among the "Ivy League" of Canadian higher education. So-called beautiful people abound in Vancouver. The religions of health, fitness, and narcissism are pursued with the fervor of Ponce de León seeking the Fountain of Youth. But this is, after all, the west coast. The mind-set and ways are similar to those in California. Exceptional affluence is expressed everywhere in order to be seen, in fashions, cars, homes, and all sorts of other fancies. Poverty is hardly a virtue here, and the theological concept of predestination based on wealth beats mightily in the breasts of many well-heeled Vancouverites.

Vancouver is a city of opera, symphony, rock and roll, live theater, motion-picture production, gourmet restaurants, diverse museums, and folk arts and crafts. Great music has yet to be created in Vancouver, but time is on this city's side. Maybe a new Beethoven or Mozart won't be hatched here, but neither has New

York City or Toronto produced one. The possibility of some talent a few notches lower merits hopeful expectation.

Vancouverites love sports—hockey, soccer, lawn bowling, sailing, cricket. They are prime candidates for a major league baseball team. They are fanatical about sports oddities also, and in a nearby suburb, during the summer, there is an annual belly-flopping contest, in which men weighing in the 350-pound-and-up range jump into a pool to determine who can make the biggest splash.

If Vancouverites have any hang-up about where they live it's their sense of isolation from the Eastern power centers of Canada. In the past they felt this apartness politically, economically, socially, and culturally. Now their loneliness is mainly political. No one would bet that a politician from Vancouver would ever become prime minister of Canada, although John Turner, leader of the Liberal party and representing the riding of Vancouver Quadra, was prime minister for a short time after the resignation of Pierre Trudeau—but even then he was more of an Ontario figure. The way federal politics are moving in Canada, there's a good chance that Turner will become prime minister again. At any rate, Vancouver has wisely turned its face firmly to Asia—China, Japan, and the other thriving countries of the Pacific. Its prosperous destiny lies more in this direction than toward the Old Boys' Networks back East. Here in the Pacific Rim area a "brave new world" is opening like the petals of the lotus flower at dawn, and Vancouver is very much a part of it all. What makes Vancouver special? Not any tangible thing. It is something far more valuable: a continuing freshness combined with ongoing potential.

A Brief Look at Vancouver's History

The first inhabitants of the area that is now the city of Vancouver were the Coast Salish people, noted for their high culture. Their descendants continue to live near the city, keeping alive an honored heritage through their arts and crafts. Captain James Cook was the first European to sail along here, and a few years later, Captain George Vancouver mapped this part of the Northwest Coast and claimed what he saw for George III, king of England—hence the name Strait of Georgia, the strait on which the city bearing the explorer's name lies.

It was not until the early 1860s, however, that any significant number of white people moved in to settle permanently. They were attracted by the prospect of making money in the lumber industry. In those early days, Vancouver was a raw, rough, grimy, but booming logging town, inhabited by tough timber and sawmill workers, shrewd entrepreneurs, and those who made big money on the periphery, such as "Gassy Jack" Deighton, a colorful saloon keeper who has been immortalized in local folklore. Another economic boost came with the completion of the transcontinental railroad, which linked this burgeoning port with the great cities of Eastern Canada, such as Toronto and Montréal. Sir William Cornelius Van Horne, chairman of the Canadian Pacific Railroad, helped to accelerate the city's growth as a major port by using it to ship grain from Alberta, Saskatchewan, and Manitoba to foreign buyers. Also from this port, in the nineteenth century, men crazed with "gold fever" sailed for fortune or misery up to the Yukon and the Klondike "mother lodes." The opening of the Panama Canal in the early part of this century increased Vancouver's importance as a seaport. Although the early population was mostly of British and American origin, a sizeable Chinese community began to develop from among those who had helped to build the transcontinental. During succeeding years, the city rapidly expanded as an influential business and population center, attracting new money and ever-increasing numbers of new people.

Unlike Montréal, Toronto, Halifax, and other east coast Canadian cities, Vancouver has had a relatively bland history. It has never experienced destruction from war and the anguish of rebellion and foreign occupation, as have places in Eastern Canada. Conflicts with coastal Indian tribes and later with Chinese "tong" societies do, however, give the Vancouver story some drama. The dismal years of the Great Depression of the 1930s, the sequestering in concentration camps of its native Japanese population in the World War II years, and the mistreatment of Pakistani immigrants during the 1960s and early 1970s are black marks on the proud heritage of an otherwise tolerant, highly civilized society.

Actually, the most exciting part of Vancouver's history is happening right now. The extraordinary success of Expo 86 was solid evidence of the city's present and future achievement. Because of its dynamism, location, climate, population, and financial strength, Vancouver is very much Canada's city of the future. Today it ranks third in importance, after Toronto and Montréal. Although Toronto will remain Canada's dominant city for some time to come,

Vancouver will likely soon surpass Montréal and take second place. In little more than one hundred years, the progress of Vancouver from a rude logging camp to the bright light on the Pacific has been phenomenal. The use of such superlatives in Vancouver's case is not excessive.

The following are key dates and events in Vancouver's history:

1778 Captain James Cook, British explorer, sails into the area, but he keeps on going.

1792 Another Briton, Captain George Vancouver, takes possession of the area for the "Empire." Vancouver had been a junior officer when Cook first sailed into this part of the world.

1793 Another intrepid explorer, Alexander Mackenzie, treks to the Pacific Coast, becoming the first white man on record to journey across Canada.

1867 What is now downtown Vancouver—the West End—is sold for just about peanuts: 114 pounds, 11 shillings, and 8 pence. Today it is one of the most expensive real estate areas in North America. Also this year, "Gassy Jack" Deighton opens his saloon to satisfy thirsty lumber workers and gold seekers. Today a glitzy section of boutiques and cafés occupies this section, but it continues to be known as "Gastown" in Jack's honor.

1886 The town of Granville becomes a city and officially takes the name of Vancouver. In twenty minutes, this year, Vancouver is destroyed by fire. The city's first fire engine arrives over a month later.

1887 The first passenger train arrives from Montréal.

1897 The first Vancouver ship departs for the great "gold rush" in the Klondike.

1907 Vancouver's stock exchange is incorporated. (Today it's the third most important exchange in Canada.)

1909 The city gets its first skyscraper. (Today's city center is a forest of gleaming skyscrapers.)

1915 The Vancouver Millionaires hockey team wins the coveted Stanley Cup.

1944 Vancouver and Odessa, U.S.S.R., become sister cities.

1957 Queen Elizabeth, queen of Canada, and Prince Philip make their first of several visits to Vancouver.

1976 University of British Columbia's outstanding Museum of Anthropology opens.

1986 Expo opens and logs 22 million visits, making it one of the most successful world's fairs in history. The Dr. Sun Yat-Sen

Gardens open in Chinatown. Vancouver celebrates its one hundredth birthday as a city.

1987 The British Columbia World Trade and Convention Centre, one of the largest and best-equipped on the North American continent, opens.

Vancouver Today: Some Basic Facts

Vancouver is located in the Southwest corner of British Columbia, about thirty miles from the U.S. border.

Vancouver itself is only 44 square miles, but its metropolitan area, consisting of several municipalities, is 1,076 square miles.

Vancouver is Canada's third-largest city in terms of population. The city itself has close to 420,000 inhabitants; the metro area has nearly 1.3 million people.

Vancouver is one of North America's busiest seaports, especially for shipping raw materials produced in Canada (coal, metals, petroleum, potash, grain, timber, and so on) to the industrial countries of Asia. It has companies involved in the lumber industries and in fisheries, which are mainstays of the region's economy. It is one of Canada's major service and financial centers, in sectors such as banking and brokerage companies. Both federal and provincial governments have sizeable operations in the metro area. Tourism is another major industry, with attractions and amenities among the finest anywhere.

University and medical facilities are known throughout the world for their excellence. They attract outstanding talent from throughout Canada, the United States, and other countries.

How to Get to Vancouver

An important North American city and Canada's door to the Pacific Rim region, Vancouver is served by major transportation companies—domestic and international airlines, transcontinental passenger rail service, buses, and cruise ship lines from Los Angeles and Seattle (ship itinerary usually includes the Yukon and Alaska also). U.S. interstate and Canadian interprovincial highways, such

Vancouver is a city of valid adjectives—dynamic, big, frenetic, vibrant, ▶ beautiful, progressive, tolerant, sophisticated, cultured, naughty. It has everything and gets better all the time.

as the Trans-Canada Highway 1, give direct, quick access to the city.

By Plane

The following air transportation companies provide service to Vancouver: Air Canada (from major Canadian, U.S., and international departure points); Air B.C. (from British Columbian towns and cities, Seattle, and Calgary); Canadian Airlines (a merger of Canadian Pacific Air and Pacific Western Airlines); also United, Japan, Western, Quantas, British Airways, Lufthansa, Wardair, Cathay Pacific, KLM, Air California, Air New Zealand. Call the toll-free operator at (800) 555–1212 for the information numbers of these companies, or contact your local travel agent for schedules and fares.

Vancouver International Airport is located on Sea Island near Richmond, a short ride on Granville Street from city center Vancouver (about twelve miles; twenty-five minutes). It is one of Canada's busiest and most modern air travel facilities. Shuttle buses and cabs make frequent runs between the airport and city center, and a number of hotels in city center provide airport transportation services or are regular stops for the shuttles. All the major car rental companies have booths in the main terminal. The main terminal itself has an array of dining places, lounges, money-changing offices, duty-free and gift shops, and bookstores. Adjacent to the airport are many fine hotels and restaurants. When you arrive at the airport you must clear Canadian Customs. If you're returning to the States you can also clear U.S. Customs at the airport.

By Car

The main road to Vancouver from Eastern Canada is the Trans-Canada Highway 1. The distance on the Trans-Canada, for example, from Calgary, Alberta, to Vancouver is 652 miles. Highway 3 is another route from the Alberta border that takes you through some beautiful country in southern British Columbia, along the border with Montana, Idaho, and Washington. From the Trans-Canada you can pick up Highway 95 a few miles north of Banff, which goes by Kootenay National Park and connects with Highway 3 at either Cranbrook or Fort Steele.

If you are traveling north from U.S. West Coast cities, Interstate 5 is your best route. The distance from Seattle to Vancouver is 144 miles, or a three-hour drive at 55 mph and a stop at Canadian Customs. Interstate highways from the East make a direct connection with I–5 (check your map for routing). I–5 connects at the U.S.–Canadian border with British Columbia Highway 99. Canada Customs is in the B.C. town of White Rock, and U.S. Customs is in Blaine, Washington.

A more interesting way of traveling to Vancouver from the south is first to tour the magnificent Olympic National Park area of Washington (the Olympic peninsula), then take the car ferry from Port Angeles on the Strait of Juan de Fuca to the charming capital city of Victoria, British Columbia, on Vancouver Island. From Sidney take another car ferry through the Gulf Islands to the city of Vancouver (the ferry docks at Tsawwassen just south of the city center, a forty-five- to sixty-minute drive). You might also want to tour Vancouver Island, which is on the open Pacific (see page 178 for more details), and return to Vancouver via car ferries from Nanaimo.

By Train

Both VIA Rail, the Canadian passenger rail system, and Amtrak, passenger trains serving U.S. destinations, provide service to Vancouver. In the case of VIA Rail, you can count on regularly scheduled daily service from most points east of Vancouver. You can come into Vancouver either through the Rocky Mountain portals of Calgary and Banff National Park or through Edmonton and Jasper National Park. On the return trip east, you have the option of visiting the national park you missed on your way west. VIA Rail will also help you book hotels, rental cars, and package tours in Canada. Call this operator for VIA Rail's toll-free number serving your area: (800) 555–1212.

Amtrak will take you via Chicago to Seattle, where you take a Greyhound bus for Vancouver. Amtrak trains provide service to Seattle from U.S. West Coast cities also. Amtrak will help you make reservations for hotels, rental cars, and tours as well. Call this toll-free number for full details: (800) 872–7245.

Vancouver's rail station is located at 1150 Station Street, in the False Creek section of the city, at Main and Terminal.

By Bus

Bus transportation from U.S. and Canadian destinations arrives at and departs from the Greyhound Bus Depot, located at 150

103

Dunsmuir Street. Call (604) 662–3222 for information and schedules.

By Boat

A number of cruise ship lines, such as the "Love Boats" of Princess, include Vancouver as a major port stop on their Northwest Coast sailings through the Inside Passage and up to Alaska. Contact major package tour operators listed on pages 27–28 or your local travel agent for details and prices.

As a major port and sailing center, Vancouver has marina facilities for visiting yachtsmen, but docking space is especially tight during busy seasons.

How to Get Around Vancouver

City center Vancouver, where most tourist and business activity is focused, is but a tiny part of this large metropolis. It is actually a huge peninsula. Along its north coast is a fjord known as the Burrard Inlet, which splits off into Indian Arm. To its south, the mighty Fraser River forms a delta and flows into the Strait of Georgia. Between Vancouver's Point Grey and the separate municipality of West Vancouver is English Bay, the city's broad front yard of water. Vancouver is surrounded by several municipalities that together compose Metro Vancouver—West Vancouver, North Vancouver, Burnaby, Coquitlam, New Westminster, and Richmond.

Except for side trips to certain attractions, you will probably spend most of your time in the central core of Vancouver, and so it shouldn't be too difficult to get around. Pender, Dunsmuir, Georgia, and Robson streets, running northwest/southeast, are parallel with one another. Burrard, Hornby, Howe, Granville, Richards, Homer, Hamilton, and Cambie bisect the others at right angles. These are the main streets of city center Vancouver, where you'll find some of the major hotels, shops, office buildings, art museums, and restaurants. The best way to orient yourself is to use the Hotel Vancouver, with its green copper, mansard roof, as your center point (Robson Square here will also do). Other landmarks in the area are the Birk's Clock and the Vancouver Art Gallery, both on Georgia Street. The hotel faces Georgia Street, which runs northwest toward Stanley Park. A few blocks beyond the back of the hotel is English Bay, and beyond that Vancouver Island. A few blocks past the front of the hotel is the waterfront on Burrard Inlet, the location of the new

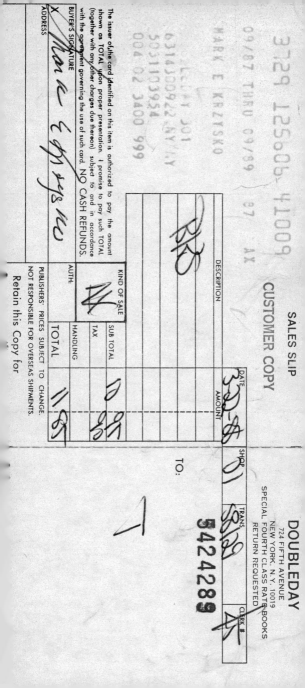

SALES SLIP

CUSTOMER COPY

DOUBLEDAY
724 FIFTH AVENUE
NEW YORK, N.Y. 10019
SPECIAL FOURTH CLASS RATE-BOOKS
RETURN REQUESTED

3729 125006 41009

09/87 THRU 09/89   87   AX

MARK E KRZYSKO

631430922 NY/.Y
503110395 4
004 02 3400 999

DESCRIPTION	KIND OF SALE	SUB TOTAL	AMOUNT	DATE	SHOP	TRANS	CLERK #
		TAX			01	342428	
	AUTH.	HANDLING					
		TOTAL	11.85				

The issuer of the card identified on this item is authorized to pay the amount shown as TOTAL upon proper presentation. I promise to pay such TOTAL (together with any other charges due hereon) subject to and in accordance with the agreement governing the use of such card. NO CASH REFUNDS.

BUYER'S SIGNATURE
X

ADDRESS

PUBLISHERS' PRICES SUBJECT TO CHANGE.
NOT RESPONSIBLE FOR OVERSEAS SHIPMENTS.
Retain this Copy for

TO:

convention center and the cruise ship docks. The nearby snow-capped mountains (Coast Mountains) that you see are north of the city. Most of the streets are nicely laid out in an easy-to-comprehend grid pattern.

Most city center attractions, including Stanley Park, can be seen the best and least expensive way, on foot. Free maps are available at your hotel or at the **Vancouver Travel Info Centre,** 562 Burrard Street, (604) 683–2000. The Centre will also provide a stack of free literature and answer any question you have about the city. It is an excellent place to start your tour of Vancouver.

Vancouver has superb public transporation to most sections of the city. **B.C. Transit** operates the city's bus system, with frequent service from 4:00 A.M. to midnight. Call (604) 261–5100 for fare and schedule information. A Seabus, actually two 400-passenger catamarans, connects city center with North Vancouver. The sailing across the Burrard Inlet takes less than fifteen minutes. You can take aboard a bike on weekends and holidays for an additional, minor cost. It departs from the old CPR station near Granville Square in city center Vancouver and from Lonsdale Quay in North Vancouver. For more information, call (604) 324–3211. The Seabus, part of B.C. Transit, is a great tourist attraction, but avoid weekday rush hours.

One of the main themes of Expo 86 was public transportation. The fair was a good excuse to build a new transit system: ALRT (Advanced Light Rapid Transit) system is run by computers, although a security officer rides along. In city center ALRT is called Skytrain, part of B.C. Transit, because it moves on elevated rails. The ALRT system takes commuters and visitors all the way from New Westminster to the waterfront at the new trade and convention center. The return trip takes about an hour. Call (604) 324–3211 for schedules and fares.

Taxi cabs are everywhere, but nowhere when you need one the most. Have your hotel get a cab for you, or call Yellow Cab, (604) 681–3311, yourself; also Black Top, (604) 681–2181, and Maclure's, (604) 731–9211. Yellow Cab, by the way, will give you a tour of the city at the meter rate.

Business and Convention Services

Business hours: 9:00 A.M. to 5:00 P.M. weekdays; many retail stores open to 9:00 or 9:30 P.M. Thursdays and Fridays, and from noon to 5:00 P.M. on Sundays.

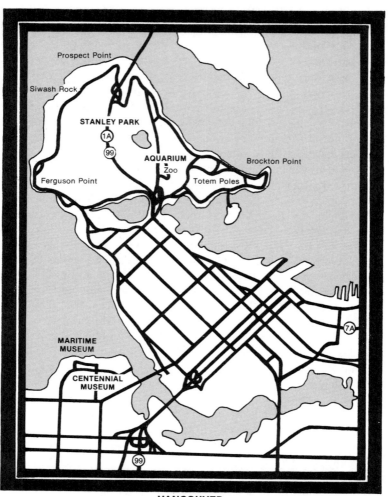

VANCOUVER

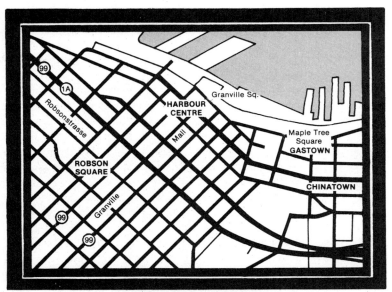

DOWNTOWN VANCOUVER

Bank hours: 10:00 A.M. to 3:00 P.M. weekdays; 10:00 A.M. to 5:00 P.M. on Fridays; some banks are open to 8:30 P.M. and on Saturdays.

World Trade Centre and Vancouver Board of Trade: Suite 400, 999 Canada Place; (604) 681–2111.

Convention Facilities: Vancouver is a world-class convention city, as proved by the success of Expo 86. The city has the meeting facilities, ancillary services and equipment, hotel space, restaurants, entertainment, and attractions necessary to successfully cater to any size convention. The city's new British Columbia Convention Centre, a stunning modern building with a roof of five sails (a metaphor to Vancouver's maritime heritage and as much a landmark for the city as the Opera House in Sydney, Australia), is the top place in Western Canada for large and small conventions. Actually, it looks like a sleek ocean liner ready to move to distant lands. Cruise ships headed up the Inside Passage to Alaska dock beside it and the lower levels of this facility serve as the city's main terminal for these ships.

Located on the waterfront, the Convention Centre offers associations up to 117,000 square feet of column-free convention space. It can seat up to 5,000 persons for meetings or for dining. There are twenty-one breakout meeting rooms suitable for groups of 50 to 700 persons. Also part of this unique convention complex is the Pan Pacific Hotel, Vancouver's newest deluxe accommodation. Its gleaming tower appears like the bridge of a sleek cruise ship. The Convention Centre is within walking distance or a short cab ride of all downtown attractions, restaurants, entertainment, and shopping. For more information on this excellent facility, contact Director of Marketing, British Columbia Convention Centre, Suite 200, 999 Canada Place, Vancouver, British Columbia, (604) 641–1987, telex 04–507702.

Your next best source of information regarding meeting facilities in the city is the Greater Vancouver Convention & Tourism and Marketing Association, located at 1055 West Georgia Street (mailing address: Box 11142 Royal Centre, Vancouver, British Columbia V6E 4C8); (604) 682–2222.

Business networks: B.C. Ministry of Industry and Small Business Development, 800 Robson Street, (604) 660–3900; Economic Development Office, City of Vancouver, 601 West Broadway, (604) 873–7212; Canadian Business Centre, Department of Regional Industrial Expansion, 1101-1055 Dunsmuir Street, (604)

666–0434; International Trade and Commerce Department, Vancouver Board of Trade, (604) 681–2111.

Vancouver Stock Exchange: 609 Granville Street, (604) 689–3334.

Limousine service: Classic Limousine, (604) 669–5466.

Translating service: Berlitz Language Centres of Canada, 830 West Pender Street, (604) 685–9331; Community Translation Service, (604) 254–2321.

Secretarial service: Kelly Services, 865 Hornby Street, (604) 669–1236.

Messenger service: Western Carrier, 3525 East 11th Avenue, (604) 438–6361.

Useful Information

Emergencies:
Police, Fire, Ambulance—dial 911 or 0 for operator.
Doctor—(604) 736–5551 (College of Family Physicians of Canada will provide referrals to foreign language–speaking doctors); after 5:00 P.M., (604) 683–2474.
Dentist (College of Dental Surgeons of B.C.)—(604) 736–3621.
Poison—(604) 682–5050 or 682–2344.
Rape—(604) 872–8212.
Crisis—(604) 733–4111.
Veterinarian—(604) 733–9312.
Canadian Coast Guard (marine and aircraft distress)—(604) 666–7888.
Vancouver General Hospital—855 West 12th Avenue, (604) 875–4111.
Road Service—twenty-four-hour service (must be a member of an auto club), (604) 736–5971.

Time zone: Pacific (three-hour difference from New York, Toronto, and Montréal)

Telephone area code: 604

Climate: Sunny but not very hot summers; usually dry, invigorating weather. Rainy in autumn and winter, but very little snow at or near sea level. For the latest report on road conditions, call (604) 660–9775 for southern B.C. or (604) 660–9781 for northern B.C.

109

Special clothing: Bring a light raincoat, hat, and an umbrella, also a warm jacket and sweater for evenings.

Local holiday: B.C. Day, celebrated first Monday in August.

Mass Media: *Vancouver Province* (morning newspaper), *Vancouver Sun* (afternon newspaper); all other major national and international newspapers and magazines are available at newsstands. Both Canadian and American television, including cable programming, and radio are available at the flick of the dial.

Free tourist information: Vancouver Travel Info Centre, 562 Burrard Street, (604) 683–2000.

Liquor: All bottled liquor is sold in government owned and operated stores located throughout the city. Their usual hours are from 10:00 A.M. to 6:00 P.M.; some stay open to 9:00 or 11:00 P.M. Check with your hotel's concierge for the one nearest you. Liquor is, of course, served in restaurants and lounges until 1:00 or 2:00 A.M. Vancouver police are very strict on drunk drivers and keep a keen eye out for them.

Sales tax: There's a 7 percent sales tax on goods, except for food, prescription medicines, children's clothes, and books without advertisements. There's also a 7 percent sales tax on meals over $7.00.

Churches, temples, and fraternal organizations: Most hotels list the addresses of places of worship and their schedule of services. If you want to attend a local meeting of your international fraternity— Freemasons, Knights of Columbus, Eastern Star, Shrine, Lions, Rotary, and so on—get details for admission before leaving home. During Expo 86, many lodges and organizations warmly welcomed their kin from afar, and there is every reason to expect that this good fellowship will continue.

Special Events

Although Expo is no longer, Vancouver has special events happening throughout the year to keep its citizens and visitors entertained. The two biggest special events are the **Sea Festival** in July and the **Pacific National Exhibition** in August and early

September. Below is a listing of some of the top ones and telephone numbers for information about attending or participating:

January/February
Chinese New Year Celebrations in Chinatown; (604) 687–0729.

April
Vancouver Wine Festival; (604) 280–4411.

May
Pacific Rim Kite Festival; (604) 261–5425.
Vancouver International Marathon; (604) 669–3626.
Cloverdale Rodeo; (604) 576–9461.
Vancouver Children's Festival; (604) 687–7697.

May/June
Vancouver International Film Festival; (604) 685–0260.

June
Asia Pacific Festival, week-long celebration of song, theater, dance, crafts, and food from the city's Asian cultures (604) 873–7487.
Greek Day; (604) 266–7148.

July
British Columbia Highland Games; (604) 936–0315.
Canada Day, various entertainments, including fireworks, celebrating Canada's premier national day.
Italian Day; (604) 430–3337.
Vancouver Sea Festival, fireworks, salmon barbecues, parades, and the great Nanaimo to Vancouver bathtub race; (604) 669–4091.
Vancouver Folk Music Festival; (604) 879–2931.
World Invitational Hang-Gliding Championship, flights from Grouse Mountain; (604) 984–0661.

August
Taste of Vancouver, Richards Street Festival, international food booths, wine tasting, and the annual, spectacular waiters' race; (604) 689–3448.
World Championship Logging Competition at Squamish; (604) 892–9244.
International Airshow at Abbotsford; (604) 895–9211.

August/September
Pacific National Exhibition, one of the great agricultural and industrial fairs of the Pacific Northwest (fifth largest in North

America), held since 1910. There are countless exhibits and demonstrations, top star entertainment, a demolition derby, a beauty contest, a midway, and lumberjack competitions. The PNE is held in Exhibition Park and operates from 10:30 A.M. to 10:30 P.M., mid-August to Labour Day. Call (604) 253–2311 for schedule and events information.

October
Octoberfest; (604) 661–7373.

November
Christmas Fair.

December
Christmas Craft Fairs in various parts of the city.

Christmas carol music from boats, young carolers on board the *Carol Ship*, which sails throughout the harbor to different locations on each of the three evenings of this beautiful event. They go as far as Point Grey, Deep Cove, and Port Moody; (604) 687–9558.

Special Tours Outside of Vancouver

Royal Hudson Steam Train, board at B.C. Rail Station, 1311 West 1st Street in North Vancouver; call (604) 687–9558 for schedule and fares (advance reservations are advised).

The Royal Hudson, the last steam train carrying passengers in Canada, takes you along the beautiful coast north of Vancouver. This is a two-hour, forty-mile trip to the lumber community of Squamish. You pass by Horseshoe Bay with its many islands (Gambier and Bowen islands), near tall Douglas firs and the Coast Mountains. The views are spectacular; don't forget to bring your camera. If you let your imagination take wing, you could very well be in the fjord country of Norway. Squamish, the final destination, has restaurants and gift shops. You can return on the Royal Hudson, or take a bus to a dock where you board the M.V. *Britannia*, a comfortable boat with such amenities as a snack bar offering sandwiches, soft drinks, and beer. The M.V. *Britannia* sails along the coast back to Vancouver, but the perspectives of the landscapes

Vancouver's position between sea and mountains allows you to ski on fresh ► **snow at a nearby peak one hour and windsurf or sail in the harbor the next hour.**

and seascapes from its decks are entirely different from the views out the windows of the Royal Hudson. Keep a sharp eye out for bald eagles. The round trip consumes the better part of a day, but it's a memorable experience for all ages.

Marine Drives. There are two Marine Drives: one that goes along the same basic route as the Royal Hudson, and another one that goes around Point Grey on the opposite side of English Bay. When you take the **Northern Marine Drive,** you can visit Lighthouse Park, explore many of the small communities along the coast, stop a while and cast a line for fish, take a ferry over to Nanaimo on Vancouver Island, hike trails in thick, primeval woods, and see awesome waterfalls on the way to Squamish via Highway 99. While on this northern route you can also drive, along with a couple of extra ferry rides, as far as Powell River on the mainland. The road stops a few miles above Powell River. After that is nothing but wilderness and a few coastal Indian reserves until Prince Rupert, B.C., and Alaska. If you wish to see more of this exceptionally beautiful northern coast, take a cruise ship voyage or a B.C. ferry from the northern tip of Vancouver Island through the Inside Passage to Prince Rupert, the Yukon, and Alaska. It's one of the great adventures of North America. The town of Squamish, north of Horseshoe Bay, is about as far as most people go in their brief forays from Vancouver. But if you continued inland on Highway 99, you would come to one of British Columbia's prize summer and ski resort areas, Whistler.

The second Marine Drive is less adventuresome but not without its rewards. This route is officially called **North West Marine Drive** and melds into **South West Marine Drive**. It goes around Point Grey, offering wonderful views of English Bay, the skyline of city center Vancouver, the Strait of Georgia, Vancouver Island, and the Gulf Islands. Along the way you pass a number of beaches for swimming, sunbathing (including nude), windsurfing, and picnicking. You also circle the campus of the University of British Columbia, with its many museums, including the fabulous Museum of Anthropology; the exquisite Nitobe Memorial Garden (Japanese); and the extensive University Endowment Lands, where you can hike in botanical splendor. You reach North West Marine Drive via Burrard and Cornwall. The private homes along the way are extraordinary and so are their gardens and landscaping. They evoke envy in even the most innocent. There are several golf courses along the South West Marine Drive section; McCleery is open to the public.

Victoria. No visit to Vancouver would be complete without a side trip to Victoria, the tranquil, blossom-festooned capital of British Columbia. Regularly scheduled ferries connect the two cities at Tsawwassen, from city center Vancouver via Highways 99 and 17. (See Chapter 6 for a complete description of Victoria.)

Gulf Islands, reached via ferries from Tsawwassen terminal; call (604) 669–1211 for schedules and fares (reservations required).

In this part of the Strait of Georgia, the Canadian–U.S. international border zigzags to the extent that it's often difficult for a sailor to figure out just which country he's in on any given tack. Also here are a large number of small islands, some belonging to British Columbia and others to the state of Washington. The Gulf Islands are Canadian, and the San Juan Islands are American, because they are nearest the Strait of Juan de Fuca, which separates the tip of Vancouver Island from the north shore of the Olympic Peninsula. If it all sounds confusing, it is, until you look at a map.

In addition to local fishing families, many professionals and people with artistic bents live on the Gulf Islands. They are small, rural islands, tucked away from the frenetic pace of the city, but also close enough to it so that one can easily go into Vancouver for a gourmet meal, a concert, or a stage show. You can visit these lovely islands with a car, but a bike or good walking shoes are the best ways for exploring them. Generally, the people who live on the islands are friendly, and the institution of the general store on some of them continues to be the center of gossip and simple fun. The many beaches, cliffs, and forest parks are good areas to see bald eagles and sea otters. Visit the studios of artisans and buy their elegant wares. The primary islands and their ferry ports are **Galiano Island** (Montague Harbour and Sturdies Bay); **Mayne Island** (Village Bay); **Saturna Island** (Saturna); **North Pender Island** (Otter Bay); **Saltspring Island** (Long Harbour, Vesuvius Bay, and Fulford Harbour).

There are good accommodations on the Gulf Islands. For example, the **Bodega Resort,** on Galiano Island, (604) 539–2677, offers log chalets with fireplaces and stained glass windows, kitchen facilities, two trout ponds, on twenty-five acres of meadows and trees, overlooking mountains and sea. Some have dining and lounge facilities, and recreational offerings, such as horseback riding, scuba diving, tennis, swimming pools, golf, and trout fishing. For more information on accommodations here, pick up the "Accommodation Guide" from a B.C. Travel Infocentre.

Whistler Resort Area, located seventy-five miles north of Vancouver via Highway 99, about two hours (use caution driving as road can be hazardous at times, especially under slippery conditions).

The Whistler Resort Area has the best skiing closest to Metro Vancouver. It features the highest vertical drop of any mountain in North America—5,208 feet (1,609 meters) at Blackcomb Mountain. It has chair lifts, T-bars, and a gondola to take you to the top. There are more than sixty runs, with the longest being seven miles, and 50 percent of them are in the intermediate skill range. There are trails for cross-country skiing and snowshoeing also. Equipment rentals are available at Whistler Village Sports, (604) 932–3327, and other outlets. The Whistler area gets about 450 inches of snow a year, making for a long, satisfying season. Helicopter skiing is also offered here during the winter, and helicopter hiking in the summer. These nimble whirlybirds take you high up on the Coast Mountains, and you come back down on your own over virgin snow or on foot through magnificent forests, picking a bouquet of wildflowers on the way. For more information and rates, call Whistler Heli-Skiing/Hiking, Ltd., (604) 932–4105.

In the warm-weather months the Whistler area is a great getaway for fishing, horseback riding, tennis, golf—an eighteen-hole Arnold Palmer–designed course, (604) 932–4544—and boating. The Whistler Mountain gondola gives a splendid high-rise ride, where the view from the top is outstanding. Dine at the restaurant on the summit or bring your own picnic. In its setup and ambience, Whistler is similar in concept to Vail and Aspen in Colorado, attracting the well-heeled, the young and beautiful, and just plain folks.

Recommended places of accommodation in the Whistler area include Crystal Lodge, (604) 932–4700; Fitzsimmons Creek Lodge, (604) 932–3338; The Vale Inn or Highland Lodge, (604) 932–5525; Whistler Creek Lodge, (604) 932–4111; Whistler Resort & Club, (604) 932–5756; Whistler Springs, (604) 932–2340. Most of these places have restaurants and many recreational and entertainment amenities. For example, the **Delta Mountain Inn,** (604) 932–1982, toll-free (800) 268–1133, is close to ski lifts, shops, and other attractions. It offers golf, boating, windsurfing, fishing, swimming pool, and tennis courts, as well as a gourmet restaurant and a nightclub. The rates at Whistler accommodations are in the moderate to expensive range.

Recommended nonhotel restaurants include **Keg at the Mountain,** (604) 932–5151, for steaks and salads (moderate), and **Isabelle's,** (604) 932–6611, popular dining place for continental cuisine in a friendly environment, moderate to expensive. For some swinging night life, try **Club 10,** (604) 932–1010, showplace for top international talent, and **The Longhorn Pub,** (604) 932–5999, which has live bands every night. Both **Carlberg's,** (604) 932–3554, and **Inge's,** (604) 932–3353, are the places to shop for fine gifts and handicrafts. For both kids and grownups, there's a super water-slide complex in Whistler Village.

During the warm, dry-weather months, if you want to keep touring this beautiful, mountain- and lake-strewn part of the province, continue heading north on Highway 99, until you reach the town of Lillooet. From here go south on Highway 12 to the community of Lytton, where you pick up the Trans-Canada Highway 1. Once you are on the Trans-Canada, you can easily come back to Vancouver or move east toward the great national parks of the Rockies (Banff and Jasper) and the cities of Calgary and Edmonton. Because of dangerous road conditions, this ordinarily pleasant tour beyond Whistler is not recommended in the winter or during any prolonged rainy period. The distance from Whistler to Lytton is about 105 miles.

Touring Services

Most of your best touring in Vancouver will be done on your own. There are, however, times when you want to let someone else make the effort while you just go along to learn and enjoy. The following companies offer sightseeing tours of Vancouver and nearby attractions:

Johnathan's Luxury Cruises, (604) 688–8081, Granville Island; motor yacht cruises on Vancouver waters.

Sailing on English Bay, (604) 733–6660, Beach Avenue Marina; sailboat cruises on English Bay; summer cruises only.

Gray Line Tours, (604) 681–8687, from Hotel Vancouver or free pickup at your hotel; trips to Capilano and Grouse Mountain areas; Stanley Park and Vancouver Aquarium; Royal Hudson/M.V. *Britannia* trip; Victoria and Butchart Gardens.

Jo's Studio Tours, (604) 266–6949; visits to the studios of leading British Columbia artists and craftspersons; groups of fifteen persons only.

BC Rail, (604) 984–5246; rail trips to Whistler and Lillooet.

Harbour Air, (604) 688–1277; float plane takes off from harbor near Westin Bayshore Hotel; aerial tour of Vancouver area.

S.S. *Beaver* Cruises, (604) 682–7284, located at Coal Harbour. Replica of B.C.'s first steamship (1835), built in 1966, provides day and evening cruises daily during the summer; also available for charters.

Vancouver Vintage, (604) 683–6464, will pick you up. Rolls-Royce with chauffeur shows you the city in high style to which you are accustomed; also nightclub tours.

Maverick Coach Lines, (604) 255–1171; makes pickups at leading hotels; tours of Metro Vancouver and Victoria.

Westwind Balloon Tours, (604) 888–1919; departs from Langley Airport, weather permitting. Balloon trips over Vancouver area; champagne toast at end of trip; in operation from May to November.

Malibu Princess, (604) 685–8468; tours of Vancouver waters and up to Howe Sound; landings at various points en route for sightseeing on shore.

City and Nature Sightseeing, (604) 254–5015; tours of the city and natural areas in and near Vancouver.

Neighborhoods

Four special neighborhoods are among Vancouver's most popular attractions: Chinatown, Granville Island, Gastown, and Robson Square/Robsonstrasse. These are walking places where discoveries are made and pleasures taken at a leisurely pace. To miss visiting them is to dismiss an important part of the Vancouver experience.

Chinatown

Vancouver has the second-largest Chinatown in North America, although the Chinatowns of Los Angeles and Toronto will soon rival Vancouver's in population size (San Francisco's is still the first). Vancouver's Chinatown is located just east of city center, or a few minutes' walk from the Hotel Vancouver/Vancouver Art Gallery area. Pender, Keefer, Main, Gore, and Carrall are the principal streets in this section. The architecture of many of the buildings is reminiscent of that of the Orient. Both the Chinese Cultural Centre and Dr. Sun Yat-Sen Classical Chinese Garden, much of which was donated by the People's Republic of China, are worthwhile places to visit. Chinatown has many restaurants serving the varied cuisine of "this most ancient culture"—Cantonese, Mandarin, Szechuan, and Vietnamese. There are also plenty of dim sum places. The best part of Chinatown is exploring it on foot, poking in and out of Chinese grocery stores, curio shops, and herbal medicine stores. If you take a car, expect difficulty in finding a place to park, particularly on Sundays. Exploring Vancouver's Chinatown is a wonderful experience, and most of the people who live and work here welcome your presence.

Granville Island

Granville Island is in fact a peninsula in the False Creek area of Vancouver. Only a few minutes from city center, it can be reached under the Granville Street Bridge. It's best to take a car, taxi, or a tour to this unusual part of city center Vancouver, or False Creek Ferry, (604) 684–7781, and bus service on #50 from city center. Bus #51 also goes to the island. Until the early 1970s, Granville Island was a grubby industrial area, but it has since been spruced up. The industrial companies have gone elsewhere, and a new "people oriented" community has come into being. The Granville Island Public Market is one of its major attractions; here you can buy almost every kind of food you like, from fresh basil to freshly caught or smoked salmon. You can rent a boat here; visit the galleries of the Emily Carr College of Art and Design; play tennis; fish in Alder Bay; see plays at three different theaters; and watch potters, printmakers, glassblowers, and goldsmiths create beautiful things that you can purchase. Granville Island has a hotel (see page 133) and several seafood restaurants, cocktail lounges, and many views of the harbor and city. It's a pleasant place within the city but removed from it by a more low-key attitude.

Gastown

"Gassy Jack" Deighton, the local saloon proprietor mentioned earlier, bequeathed Gastown its unusual name. Once a rough-and-tumble area frequented by lumberjacks and seafarers, today's Gastown is one of the most interesting areas in city center. Water, Cordova, Columbia, Richards, and Cambie are the main streets that run through Gastown. A statue of "Gassy Jack" in Maple Tree Square depicts him standing on a barrel of booze near the spot where his saloon was located. At Water and Cambie streets is a steam clock, said to be the world's first. It blows its whistle on the quarter hour, delighting anyone passing near enough. Here you can browse in boutiques and unusual shops, take a bite at small restaurants and comfortable cafés, and wander in what was once "skid row."

Robson Square and Robsonstrasse

Robson Square is the heart of city center Vancouver. Facing Georgia Street is the Vancouver Art Gallery (see page 126). Behind it and sandwiched between Hornby and Howe streets is the two-block-long Arthur Erickson–designed complex that houses law courts, government offices, restaurants, a food fair, shops, an ice-skating rink, and a theater. Because this complex lies so close to the ground and is so long, it is difficult for one to admire it. It's similar in nature to the Les Halles complex in Paris, which has received mixed reviews. The Erickson complex is confusing to the first-time visitor and its first impression is to keep people out rather than welcome them in. The logic of the place seems inside out.

Robsonstrasse or Robson Street (it crosses the middle of Robson Square) received its Teutonic name from German-speaking people who frequented the many shops that catered to their special tastes for food, fashions, and publications. The new name stuck, and it makes a nice tourist gimmick in a province that is mostly Anglo-Saxon. Along Robsonstrasse you can buy all kinds of sausages and dark breads and the latest magazines published east of the Rhine River. This is also a street of fashionable and expensive boutiques. Strolling down the Robsonstrasse, chomping on wurst-in-rye, and eyeing Paris gowns priced in the thousands is chic and fun to do when bored with all else in an attraction/entertainment-rich Vancouver.

Parks, Gardens, and Beaches

Because of its long growing season (as compared with those of other parts of Canada), relatively mild climate, high amount of rainfall, and the botanical knack of its citizens, Vancouver has some of the most beautiful parks and gardens in North America. This penchant to grow plants and flowers and to manipulate their arrangement stems partly from the British and Japanese gardening influences that are so strongly expressed here. Gardening mania is everywhere, both in public and private places. Lawns surrounding homes appear so uniformly perfect that one would think there surely must be an inspector going around measuring the length of grass and comparing its lush tone of color against some official chart. At any rate, whatever way the landscaping is accomplished, one of the great joys of visiting Vancouver is smelling its lovely flowers (even roses in December) and walking among its giant trees.

Stanley Park: You haven't been to Vancouver if you haven't been through Stanley Park (named in honor of Governor-General Lord Stanley). This magnificent park, all 1,000 acres of it, lies right next to city center Vancouver and a few minutes' walk from most of the top hotels. Established for the public's enjoyment in 1888, Stanley Park is one of the largest and most beautiful city parks in North America. You can walk or jog over its forested trails without worrying about cutting through squads of muggers as in many other city parks. Stanley Park lies to the north of city center, between Burrard Inlet on the east and English Bay to the west. It's a peninsula that points to West and North Vancouver on the other shore. The city's famous Lion's Gate Bridge connects these communities with city center at Stanley Park.

The attractions within the park are many and varied. Regardless of your age, there's something pleasant for you here. The children's zoo and the sensational aquarium are described on page 125. In addition, there are trails through tall Douglas firs and western red cedars. A seawall walk that goes around the periphery of the park has a seaside part for walkers and a forestside part for bikers. It gives access to beaches for swimming and sunbathing and other areas for splendid views. This 5.5-mile-long seawall was built under the supervision of Master Stonemason James Cunningham. Cunningham worked on the wall for forty years, from the 1920s to the late 1960s—even after his formal retirement—as an expression of his desire to bring this unique project closer to completion. The seawall was finally finished in this decade. Also within Stanley Park is a lawn bowling club that welcomes visitors, a display of B.C. coastal Indian totem poles (carved by Haida Kwakiutl artisans), and a small zoo of mammals. The charming Teahouse Restaurant, Victorian garden house, is a favorite with Vancouverites and visitors alike. Take your favorite person here; sunset is a perfectly romantic time. Call (604) 669–3281 for reservations. You can take a car tour of the park and stop for a picnic. More vigorous souls can rent bikes, including tandems, or roller skates for enjoying the park; Stanley

Park Bike Rentals, at 676 Chilco Street, opposite Lost Lagoon, (604) 681–5581.

Perhaps the best part of Stanley Park is going on a solitary walk among the giant trees and long ferns of the Northwest. You feel as if you are in the Garden of Eden and light years from a bustling civilization. Every once in a while, you stop and remember that that civilization is just beyond the treetops, and then, reluctant to leave, you find your pace slowing.

Queen Elizabeth Park, off Cambie Street, a few miles south of city center; best to take a taxi. From the highest hill at Queen Elizabeth Park you have the second-best view of the skyline of Vancouver (the first being from the top of Grouse Mountain, mentioned below). Queen Elizabeth Park, named after the present monarch, contains superior botanical displays, with sunken gardens and creatively designed floral and shrubbery displays everywhere you walk. The floral exhibits within Q.E. Park are so beautiful that it is hard to imagine that this site was once a dismal rock quarry. For the convenience of visitors, the park has a restaurant, picnic areas, tennis courts, and the Bloedel Conservatory.

Bloedel Conservatory, in Queen Elizabeth Park; (604) 872–5513. Open daily, except for Christmas. Admission charged. The Bloedel Conservatory sits on the highest hill within the jurisdictional limits of Vancouver. It is from here that you get the dramatic view of the city skyline with its background of snow-capped mountains. On the plaza surrounding the Conservatory is a huge Henry Moore sculpture. In the morning, on a nice day, it is not unusual to see a number of elderly Chinese men and women performing solitary Tai Chi exercises that are close to ballet movement in their grace and elegance. The Bloedel building itself is a Buckminster Fuller–style geodesic dome, inside of which are tropical and desert environments. Each one has its indigenous plants and flowers. A wide variety of tropical birds fly around the space at will. Bloedel is the park's extraordinary *pièce de résistance*.

Nitobe Memorial Garden, on University of British Columbia campus, near Museum of Anthropology. Open daily during the summer and weekdays the rest of the year. Admission charged. Nitobe, a perfect example of Japanese skill and artistry in botany and landscape architecture, is my favorite garden in Western Canada. Exceptional balance and harmony are achieved through the arrangement of plantings (Japanese flowering shrubs and trees) within a limited area. There are also classical Japanese accents, such as a tea house (for display only), a curved bridge, a gazebo overlooking a tranquil pond alive with prize carp, and a stone pagoda memorial in honor of Inazo Nitobe, the garden's benefactor. Inazo Nitobe was one of Japan's representatives to the League of Nations and a major force for linking the best interests of the nations of Asia with those of North America. His remains are interred in Victoria, British Columbia.

VanDusen Botanical Gardens, located at 37th Avenue and Oak Street. Open daily. Admission charged. The VanDusen Gardens are famous for walks thickly flanked by pink, purple, red and white rhododendrons. There is a wide assortment of trees, shrubs, flowers, and other plants, all well labeled. Band concerts are held within the park during the summer. There is a restaurant, and **MacMillan Bloedel Place,** (604) 266–7194, houses exhibits telling the fascinating story of the Northwest Pacific Coast lumber and paper industries.

Lighthouse Park, via Marine Drive in West Vancouver. Free. Lighthouse Park, a few minutes drive from city center, offers wonderful woodland and sea-cliff walks. Site of picturesque Point Atkinson Lighthouse, this is a virgin forest of 200-foot fir trees, which are some two-and-a-half millennia in age (2,500 years). While hiking over its thirteen kilometers of trails, keep a sharp eye out for bald eagles swooping to their nests in the trees. There are great views of the ships in English Bay, distant Vancouver Island, city center Vancouver, and Point Grey, where the campus of the University of British Columbia is located. You can climb or sunbathe on the rocks and enjoy a picnic in this exquisite wilderness setting.

Grouse Mountain Recreational Area, in North Vancouver, via Highways 1A and 99, over Lion's Gate Bridge, and then to Capilano Road; (604) 984–0661. Admission charged for the aerial tramway ride to the top.

From the top of 4,000-foot (1,200 meters) high Grouse Mountain you have the best view in this region of the lower mainland and greater Vancouver. You can see all of Metro Vancouver, a good swath of Vancouver Island, surrounding waterways—Strait of Georgia, Burrard Inlet, English Bay, and even south to Mount Baker in the state of Washington. A thrilling aerial tramway ride takes you up and down the mountain, and all ages enjoy the experience. It is not unusual to spot a black bear or a deer on the slopes below. At the summit there is a restaurant with superb views, café, and a gift shop. You can hike around Blue Grouse Lake or attend concerts and theatrical productions that are held from time to time. Brief but spectacular helicopter rides high above the Grouse Mountain area give you views of the surrounding lakes and forest wilderness and make you realize that sophisticated Vancouver is right on the edge of a vast, virtually uninhabited landscape extending to the North Pole.

During the winter, Grouse Mountain is the closest skiing area to city center. An adage in Vancouver says, "In the morning we go skiing on Grouse Mountain. In the afternoon we come down to go sailing in English Bay." There are easy runs for beginners, and instruction is available.

North Vancouver Parks, on the way to Grouse Mountain, via Lion's Gate Bridge. The main attraction here is **Capilano Suspension Bridge,** reputed to be the longest of its kind in the world. The great fun of walking across the narrow bridge is that it swings from side to side 450 feet above a raging river. It's an unforgettable experience, to say the least. A restaurant and gift shop are located here; (604) 985–7474. Admission charged. Also in the area is the **Capilano Regional Park and Salmon Hatchery,** offering tours showing British Columbia's top money-making fish in different stages of growth; (604) 987–1411. Free. The park has hiking trails and places for picnics. On the road to Grouse Mountain is **Cleveland Dam,** forming Vancouver's reservoir. There are picnic places and hiking trails in adjacent Capilano Park. This is a fine viewing point of the twin mountain peaks known as "The Lions." North Vancouver has another swaying suspension bridge and an interesting ecology center with woodland walks at **Lynn Canyon Park,** best access from Second Narrows Bridge and via Lynn Valley Road, (604) 987–5922. Free.

Beaches: The following public beaches for swimming, sunbathing, windsurfing, and picnicking are located in Vancouver:

Point Grey—Kitsilano Beach, Jericho Beach, Locarno Beach, Spanish Banks Beach, Wreck Beach (nude).

Stanley Park—English Bay Beach, Second Beach (saltwater pool in this area), Third Beach. Most have facilities for picnics (tables, fireplaces) and can be reached by public transportation. Some have food concessions.

Attractions

Museum of Anthropology, on the campus of the University of British Columbia, (604) 228–3825. Closed on Mondays, Christmas, and Boxing Day. Admission charged. The Museum of Anthropology is one of Vancouver's top three attractions (the other two being Stanley Park and the view from Grouse Mountain). If you have but a brief time to spend in the city, this museum should be at the head of your list. If you are staying in city center, you best bet is to take a cab to the museum.

There are two impressive aspects to the museum: the architecture and the collection. Arthur Erickson's design is based on the Amerindian long houses once so typical along the Northwest Coast. High windows, framed by a sequence of stark concrete post and lintel portals, look out on a set of fascinating, authentic totem poles. Beyond them are Point Grey Cliffs, English Bay, the towers of the city, and the Coast Mountains. The building is a photographer's delight because it offers so many striking angles. I consider the Museum of Anthropology to be Erickson's finest building.

The museum's collection, the best of its kind in the world, concentrates on artifacts from the Northwest Coast tribes. Many anthropological scientists consider the Northwest tribes to have developed the most sophisticated and most beautiful visual arts and crafts in North America (the only exception being the advanced cultures of Mexico). Artifacts from the cultures of the Pacific region, Asia, and Latin America are exhibited as well. Featured items are dramatically displayed and accessible to viewers; you can actually open the drawers of display cases and see the rare and precious. The museum offers both conducted and self-guided (audio) tours and a full schedule of special presentations.

Vancouver Aquarium, in Stanley Park, (604) 682–1118. Open every day. Admission charged. In beautiful Stanley Park is Canada's largest aquarium. The stars here are the killer whales (*Orcinus orca*), who put on daily shows for visitors. A common sight along the British Columbian coast, these highly intelligent mammals are killers only in the sense that in the wild one of their food sources is live seals. If you have ever visited Sea World or Sea Land, you know how smart and gentle they are. The thousands of other live sea species displayed at Vancouver Aquarium include beluga whales, sharks, and tropical fish. An Amazon River display is inhabited by tropical birds, boas, and piranhas. The whale pools have underwater windows through which you can see them look at you. The aquarium complex itself is one of the best on the continent.

Children's Zoo, in Stanley Park. Open every day. Free. Here is a perfect place for young children to see and pet gentle farm animals. Also in the area are pony rides and a miniature steam train ride; there is a charge for the rides.

Vancouver Museum, in Vanier Park complex near Burrard Street Bridge, (604) 736–7736. Open every day. Admission charged. The most distinctive architectural feature of the Vanier complex of museums is a circular, funnel-shaped roof symbolizing the ceremonial hats worn by Northwest Coast Indians. Within this striking complex is the Vancouver Museum, which has a number of interesting exhibits portraying the city's colorful history. Among the exhibits are Indian artifacts, a car from the first transcontinental passenger train to come into the city, furnishings from the Edwardian age, and a re-creation of an early trading post.

Gordon Southam Observatory, in Vanier Park complex near Burrard Street Bridge, (604) 736–4431. Call ahead for schedule; open during summer evenings in clear weather. Free. This is hands-on astronomy, where you learn about the heavens from a scientist and see them for yourself through a telescope.

Maritime Museum, in Vanier Park complex near Burrard Street Bridge, (604) 736–4431. Open every day. Admission charged. Vancouver's past, present, and future are inexorably linked to the sea. The city is Canada's door to the Pacific, with all its immense trading possibilities. The Maritime Museum chronicles this rich heritage. Among its exhibits is the *St. Roch,* a two-mast schooner, the first ship to sail through the fabled Northwest Passage.

City of Vancouver Archives, in Vanier Park complex near Burrard Street Bridge, (604) 736–8561. Closed Saturday and Sunday. Free. The archives contain books, maps, papers, newspapers, and photographs of historical value. Both scholars and casual visitors are warmly welcomed.

H. R. MacMillan Planetarium, in Vanier Park complex near Burrard Street Bridge, (604) 736–3656. Closed Mondays. Admission charged. A trip through the galaxy is presented in the afternoon and in the evening. For those already well versed on constellations, planets, and interstellar happenings, there are more theatrical shows. A cafeteria in this part of the complex offers views of the harbor.

Vancouver Art Gallery, 750 Hornby Street in Robson Square; (604) 682–5621. Closed Monday. Admission charged. Housed in what was the city's old courthouse, of stolid neoclassical design with a brilliantly modern interior, Vancouver Art Gallery has four floors of well-lighted exhibition space. There is a special children's gallery on the ground floor. This art museum is best known for its extensive collection of paintings by Emily Carr, British Columbia's most famous artist. An impressionist of sorts, often considered within the "Group of Seven" (immortal Canadian artists), Carr painted scenes of the Northwest Coast and forests, totem poles, and remote native villages. There is a mystical quality to her works that sticks in one's imagination. The Vancouver Art Gallery is in the heart of city center and should be visited for the Carr collection alone.

University of British Columbia Museums, Point Grey section of Vancouver, a short drive southwest of city center. UBC, as it is called by local folks, is Western Canada's top institution of higher learning. Located on the end of Point Grey, UBC is worth visiting just to stroll its pleasant, attractive campus; there's very much of an "established, elite" feel to it. There are also low-cost dormitory accommodations here; see "Accommodations" section in this chapter. Adjacent to the main campus are the **University Endowment Lands,** an area of 2,500 forested acres where you can hike or jog in lovely natural surroundings. Endowment Lands are inhabited by small mammals, including deer, and it is not unusual to spot bald eagles, which are ubiquitous along British Columbia's coast. Marine Drive, which goes around Point Grey, offers some beautiful views, and Wreck (nude bathing here) and Spanish Banks beaches are in this area. Among other reasons for visiting the UBC campus are its excellent museums:

Anthropology Museum; see above description.

M. Y. Williams Geology Museum; extensive mineral and fossil collection; (604) 228–5586. Closed weekends. Free.

Nitobe Memorial Gardens; see above description.

Fine Arts Gallery; (604) 228–2759; located in Main Library. Free.

TRIUMF; (604) 222–1047. One of the world's largest cyclotrons for subatomic research.

Fantasy Garden World, in Richmond, just off Highway 99, between turn-off roads for Vancouver International Airport and the ferry for Victoria; (604) 271–9325. Open daily. Admission charged. If you are traveling to Vancouver from the state of Washington on B.C. Highway 99 or going south on this same road, visit Fantasy Garden World. This floral theme park features millions of flowers and beautiful landscaping, a farm with many small animals for the kids to pet, miniature-train ride, stocked trout lake, a biblical

127

garden with a giant Noah's Ark, a European village where you can sample the foods from several nations, greenhouses, a pretty little chapel where many Vancouverites tie the knot, and a pavilion that serves English tea in the afternoon. This fine theme park, created by Vander Zalm, a premier of British Columbia, reflects his Dutch and Canadian heritages at their best.

Simon Fraser University Campus, located on Burnaby Mountain in Burnaby, approximately forty minutes' drive east of city center. Simon Fraser, designed by architects Arthur Erickson and Geoffrey Massey, has one of the most stunning university campuses in the world, both in terms of its contemporary architecture and its setting on Burnaby Mountain with the backdrop of distant snow-capped mountains and great views of the city and sea inlets. Visit SFU's **Art Gallery,** (604) 291–4266, and its **Museum of Archaeology and Ethnology,** a fine display of artifacts from Northwest Coast Indian tribes; (604) 291–3325. Open every day, noon to 3:00 P.M. on weekends. Free. For information on SFU theatrical events, classical and experimental, call (604) 291–3514. Free tours of the university; call (604) 291–3210.

EXPO (was located along the banks of False Creek, a few blocks south of city center). Alas, the glory of EXPO, which received such intensive worldwide publicity and 22 million visitors, is no more. It is considered one of the most successful world fairs ever held, coming soon after a big loser in New Orleans that almost killed this entertainment concept. EXPO 86 featured more than eighty pavilions, plazas, and theaters. There were some 260 live performances every day. Visitors enjoyed almost every type of entertainment, from high-tech exhibits expressing the fair's main theme of transportation and communication to shows by world-class entertainers. Most of the pavilions have been dismantled and planners are now at work finding new, profitable uses for this large site. No doubt it will be developed into housing and office buildings. It's probably just as well. When Montréal's EXPO 67 ended its highly successful first season, Mayor Jean Drapeau kept the facility going for close to twenty additional years. Each year the attractions grew more decrepit and less interesting, and the park itself came to resemble abandoned steel mill complexes. Finally, Montréal's powers-that-be said "enough is enough," and they mercifully closed the gates for good. The wheelers and dealers of Vancouver, however, have been smarter. They created a fantastic show with EXPO 86, providing a terrific time for millions, and they knew to pull down the final curtain before it became a money-losing bore. However, all is not lost. Some structures remain and are worth seeing if you missed EXPO's glory or want to relive it again. The monumental Beijing Summer Palace Gate is still there, as is a nine-meter-high Balinese one from Indonesia. In addition, a six-meter granite Inukshuk sculpture from the Northwest Territories has become a permanent Vancouver fixture.

The 224-acre land site known as B.C. Place, once a shabby waterfront area, has been enhanced by close to $100 million of landscaping and other improvements. Eventually 30,000 people will work in its offices and other facilities, and 20,000 will live in its apartments, condos, and townhouses. On the other side of the city, Canada Place, with its marvelous roof of five white sails, has become Vancouver's stunning convention center, spacious enough to hold thousands of delegates. If you have some extra time, it is worthwhile to take a nostalgic visit to the place where EXPO once played to and thrilled millions. Vancouver's EXPO will long continue in memory as a supreme example of intelligent, creative civic achievement on a global scale.

Arts and Sciences Technology Center, 600 Granville Street; (604) 687–8414. Open every day. Admission charged. Similar in nature to science museums in most major cities, offering hands-on exhibits that are enjoyed by children and adults.

Burnaby Village Museum, 4900 Deer Lake Avenue in Burnaby; (604) 294–1233. Open daily during the summer months; closed January and February. Admission charged. Heritage Village takes visitors back to a simpler time. Here you can visit with a small-town blacksmith, see a sawmill in operation, taste the treats at an ice cream parlor, and poke into an early log cabin, general store, and schoolhouse.

Accommodations

Vancouver, as the third most-important city in Canada and Western Canada's "Number One" destination, has a large number of hotels, motels, and guest houses. Most are priced in the moderate to expensive range, although some decent inexpensive accommodations are available generally outside city center. During the busy tourist season—from late May to mid-September—rooms at the more desirable hotels are difficult if not impossible to book on short notice. In addition, during other peak periods delegates to

129

large conventions make booking a room frustrating for the casual traveler. It's smart to make advance reservations any time; during busy times, they are essential. You can book rooms through the toll-free 800 numbers of the major hotel/motel chains; see pages 22–23 for numbers.

Consult with your local travel agent and auto club for their accommodation reservation services, which are usually available at no extra cost. Many places require a cash deposit prior to arrival and/or evidence of credit; both can be accomplished through a major credit card.

Some places of accommodation in this listing are described as "good value accommodations with many amenities," which means that they are recommended and offer such features as swimming pools, pleasant settings, and/or other conveniences to make your stay comfortable. This designation has been used to increase the number of recommended places to stay during peak seasons.

In British Columbia a 7 percent hotel and motel tax is added to the room accommodation portion of your bill. Those places of accommodation displaying a blue "Approved Accommodation" sign or decal have been inspected by the provincial government and conform to high standards of courtesy, comfort, and cleanliness.

Complaints regarding accommodations should be sent to Manager of Accommodation Services, Tourism British Columbia, 1117 Wharf Street, Victoria, British Columbia V8W 2Z2.

If you would like to stay at a Vancouver area bed and breakfast, contact this agency for more information and rates: West Coast Bed & Breakfast Association, Box 593, 810 Broadway, Vancouver, British Columbia V5Z 4E2, (604) 276–8616.

City Center Accommodations

The following hotels are located in city center, with convenient access to major attractions (parks, museums, and so on), business and government offices, shopping areas, entertainment and sporting venues, and restaurants.

Vancouver's Finest

The hotels in this first category are considered by travelers to be the best in Vancouver in terms of customer satisfaction, guest services, facilities, and management. They are also among the most expensive, averaging well over $100 a night.

Four Seasons Hotel, 791 West Georgia Street, (604) 689–9333;

toll-free (800) 268–6282. Certainly one of the premier hotels in the city, with excellent amenities and service. Its main restaurants are Chartwell's (named after Winston Churchill's estate in Kent, England) and Harvester; lunch is served in the Garden Lounge and, in the summer, beside the outdoor pool. There's an indoor/outdoor pool. Free indoor parking is available. The Four Seasons is connected to Pacific Centre Mall and its more than 150 shops. The Four Seasons is my top choice in Vancouver. Expensive.

Vancouver Mandarin, 645 Howe Street, (604) 687–1122. The Mandarin is adjacent to the Pacific Centre. The rooms and suites are luxurious, and the service is first-rate. It features a health club, squash and racquetball courts, a billiard room, swimming pool, and sauna. Cristal, one of the city's best dining places, and Le Café are its restaurants, and Clipper and Captains are Mandarin's lounges. Expensive.

Westin Bayshore, 1601 West Georgia Street, (604) 682–3377; toll-free (800) 228–3000. This excellent hotel in the Westin chain is located near beautiful Stanley Park. There are both an indoor and an outdoor pool, as well as a marina with services for your yacht. The Westin offers a family plan and free parking. Its restaurants and lounges include Trader Vic's, Marine Lounge, Garden Lounge, and Garden Restaurant. Expensive.

Hotel Vancouver, a Canadian National hotel, 900 West Georgia Street, (604) 684–3131; toll-free (800) 268–9143. The first Hotel Vancouver was opened in 1887. The present and third Hotel Vancouver, completed in 1939, is the city's landmark place of accommodation, much in the same manner as the Chateau Frontenac in Québec City. It would be difficult to imagine city center Vancouver without this venerable hotel. The service here is high class, and the rooms are spacious and pleasant. Dining and dancing in the Panorama Roof restaurant is a city tradition. There are also the Timber Club and the Spanish Grill. Expensive.

Hotel Meridien Vancouver, 845 Burrard Street, (604) 682–5511; toll-free (800) 543–4300. The Meridien provides luxury in the European manner, both with regard to the rooms and service. Its restaurants include Gerard and Café Fleuri. The Rivoli Bar is the place to relax after a busy day or before a busy night in Vancouver. Expensive.

Pan Pacific Vancouver Hotel, 999 Canada Place, (604) 662–8111; toll-free (800) 663–1515. A new deluxe hotel, the Pan Pacific is part of the dramatic Canada Place complex, located on the waterfront. Its main function is to provide top accommodation to convention delegates, but other travelers are also welcomed. It features a pool, health club, racquetball courts, and twenty-four-hour room service. For dining there are a Japanese restaurant, Five Sails for continental cuisine, and Café Pacifica. Expensive.

Hyatt Regency Vancouver, 655 Burrad Street (in Royal Centre), (604) 687–6543; toll-free (800) 228–9000. This Hyatt—more than thirty sparkling floors—offers luxury and all the amenities you need, including a charming lounge and a gourmet restaurant. The Hyatt's situation couldn't be better. It's in the heart of downtown Vancouver and connected to the Royal Centre, an attractive indoor shopping mall. Expensive.

Other Fine Accommodations

Hotel Georgia, 801 West Georgia Street, (604) 682–5566; in Canada, toll-free (800) 663–1111. A fine, centrally located hotel with friendly personal service. An English pub called George V, restaurants, and lounges. A favorite with frequent visitors to the city. Moderate.

Abbotsford Hotel, 921 West Pender Street, (604) 681–4335. Located in the financial center. An older hotel with newly refurbished rooms. Restaurants and lounges. A good value in downtown. Moderate.

Best Western Chateau Granville, 1100 Granville Street, (604) 669–7070; toll-free (800) 528–1234. Offers discounts to seniors. Rooms have balconies or patios, with views of the city, waterfront, or mountains. There are a dining room and place for cocktails and live entertainment. Expensive.

Coast Georgian Court, 773 Beatty Street, (604) 682–5555; in Canada, toll-free (800) 663–1144. Intimate, high-class hotel in European manner. Its William Tell restaurant is one of the best in the city. Near B.C. Place Stadium. Expensive.

Ramada Renaissance at Denman Place, 1733 Comox Street, (604) 688–7711; in Canada, toll-free (800) 663–9494. Nice location near Stanley Park and English Bay. Rooms have balconies and refrigerators. Some have kitchens. There are an indoor pool, rooftop restaurant, and a bar. Expensive.

Ming Court Hotel, 1160 Davie Street, (604) 685–1311. Rooms have balconies with excellent views of English Bay. Pool and free parking; dining room and lounge. Close to beaches and city center. Expensive.

Best Western Sands, 1755 Davie Street, (604) 682–1831; toll-free (800) 528–1234. A block up from English Bay. Some rooms have balconies. The Sands has restaurant and lounge facilities. Moderate.

Century Plaza Hotel, 1015 Burrard Street, (604) 687–0575. An apartment-type accommodation with large rooms; some have balconies and kitchen facilities. Indoor pool, sauna. Dining room, coffee shop, and nightclub. Live entertainment in the Rum Runners Lounge. Moderate to expensive.

Holiday Inn City Centre Harbourside, 1133 West Hastings Street, (604) 689–9211; toll-free (800) 465–4329. Downtown location. Rooms with views of the city or the harbor. Revolving Top of the Inn restaurant, indoor pool; lounge offers live entertainment. Family plan. Airport limo service. Expensive.

Sandman Hotel, 1110 Howe Street, (604) 684–2151; in Canada, toll-free (800) 663–6900. Indoor pool, free parking, takes pets, family plan. Lounge has entertainment; dining in Heartland Restaurant. Moderate to expensive.

Shato Inn Apartment Hotel, 1825 Comox Street, (604) 681–8920. All rooms have kitchen facilities. Pleasant garden. Nice section of the city and near Stanley Park and beaches. Moderate.

Pacific Palisades Hotel, 1277 Robson Street, (604) 688–0461. Offer full kitchen facilities; Puffin's dining room; health club and indoor pool; free parking; executive suites. Expensive.

Sheraton Landmark Hotel, 1400 Robson Street, (604) 687–0511; toll-free (800) 325–3535. Rooms with balconies. A revolving restaurant on top, called Cloud Nine, gives super views of the city, ocean, and mountains. Family plan. Jazz bar with live entertainment. Moderate to expensive.

Best Western O'Doul's Hotel, 1300 Robson Street, (604) 684–8461; toll-free (800) 528–1234. Has smoking and nonsmoking floors, twenty-four-hour room service, indoor pool, Jacuzzi, exercise room. O'Doul's Restaurant, lounge, and sidewalk café. Expensive.

Granville Island Hotel, 1253 Johnston Street, (604) 683–7373. Located in an interesting part of the city noted for food, the arts, and marine activities. Most rooms have water views. Dining in the Pelican Bay restaurant. Jacuzzi, sauna, outdoor garden, and marina. Expensive.

Wedgwood Hotel, 845 Hornby Street, (604) 689–7777. City center location, balconies, fireplaces; Wedgwood Room, one of the best restaurants in the city. Expensive.

Sheraton Plaza 500 Hotel, 500 West 12th Avenue, (604) 873–1811; toll-free (800) 325–3535. Offers kitchen facilities, balconies, free parking, dining facilities, and family plan. Moderate.

Holiday Inn Broadway, 711 West Broadway, (604) 879–0511; toll-free (800) 465–4329. Features Le Bistro Restaurant and Cherry Tree Lounge. Live entertainment, indoor pool, sauna, and free parking. Moderate to expensive.

Vancouver Vicinity

The following places of accommodation are within a thirty- to forty-five-minute drive of downtown Vancouver and should be considered when hotels in city center are filled. Accommodations in suburban Richmond, located south of city center, are close to the Vancouver International Airport and may be preferable to businesspeople.

Airport Inn Resort, 10251 St. Edwards Drive in Richmond, south of city center Vancouver and near airport, (604) 278–9611. Next to the airport and twenty-minute drive from downtown. A resort on twelve acres offering three swimming pools, tennis and squash courts, exercise and game rooms. They even have a special fun place for children. This resort offers Japanese ambience in its Suehiro Steakhouse and Samurai Lounge. The best accommodation in the airport area. Moderate to expensive.

Best Western Coquitlam Motor Inn, 319 North Road in Coquitlam, east of city center Vancouver; (604) 931–9011; toll-free (800) 528–1234. Located about ten miles from city center. Pool, sauna, tropical courtyard, Beef n' Barrel restaurant, and lounge with live entertaiment. Moderate.

Best Western Kings Motor Inn, 5411 Kingsway Street in Burnaby, east of city center Vancouver; (604) 438–1383; toll-free (800) 528–1234. Good value accommodations with many amenities. Restaurant. Moderate.

Delta River Inn, 3500 Cessna Drive in Richmond, south of city center Vancouver and near airport; (604) 278–1241; toll-free (800) 268–1133. Located on the bank of the Fraser River, within minutes of downtown and the airport. Swimming pool and private marina for sailing, cruising, or fishing charters. Seafood served at Place at the Pier and a more varied menu at the Deckhouse Grill. Moderate to expensive.

Richmond Inn, in downtown Richmond, 7551 Westminster Highway, south of city center Vancouver and near airport; (604)

273–7878. Nice rooms, heated pool, saunas, health club. Restaurants and lounge with entertainment. Moderate.

Sheraton Villa Inn, 4331 Dominion Street in Burnaby, east of city center Vancouver; (604) 430–2828; toll-free (800) 325–3535. Indoor/outdoor pools, dining facilities, live entertainment, family rates. Moderate to expensive.

Abercorn Inn, 9260 Bridgeport Road in Richmond, south of city center Vancouver and near airport; (604) 270–7576. A wee bit of rural Scotland in British Columbia in architecture and ambience. Restaurant and whirlpool. Moderate.

Best Western Poco Motor Inn, on Highway 7, east of Vancouver city center, in Port Coquitlam; (604) 941–6216; toll-free (800) 528–1234. Good value accommodations with many amenities. Dining room. Moderate.

Best Western Tsawwassen Inn, in Tsawwassen, about three miles from the Victoria ferry terminal and about a fifteen-minute drive south of Vancouver; via Highways 99 and 17; (604) 943–8221; toll-free (800) 528–1234. Good value accommodations with many amenities. Dining room. Moderate.

Delta Town and Country Inn, near the Victoria ferry terminal in Tsawwassen, junction of Highways 99 and 17; (604) 946–4404. Good value accommodations with many amenities. Dining room. Moderate.

International Plaza Hotel, 1999 Marine Drive in North Vancouver, within a few minutes of city center Vancouver; (604) 984–0611. Near Lion's Gate Bridge, which leads to Stanley Park. Close to such attractions as Grouse Mountain and magnificent coastal drives. Dining and lounge facilities, pool, tennis courts, and entertainment. Moderate.

Lake City Motor Inn, on Highway 7 in Burnaby, east of city center Vancouver; (604) 294–5331. Good value accommodations with many amenities. Some rooms have kitchens. Coffee shop. Moderate.

Park Royal Hotel, in West Vancouver, north via the Lion's Gate Bridge, on the Capilano River; (604) 926–5511. A Tudor-style country inn set in beautiful surroundings. Minutes from city center Vancouver. Dining room. Moderate to expensive.

Lonsdale Quay Hotel, waterfront hotel at Lonsdale Quay, northern terminus for the Seabus connecting North Vancouver with city center Vancouver; (604) 986–6111. Health facility, restaurant, lounge, and pub. Moderate to expensive.

Inexpensive but Good Places to Stay

University of British Columbia, Walter Gage Residence, Boulevard at Westbrook Mall, southwest of city center Vancouver, (604) 228–5441. Low-cost accommodations for singles, doubles, and families on this attractive campus, a major area attraction in itself, are available from early May until late August. Meals are available at the Student Union. Downtown is about twenty minutes away. University of British Columbia offers one of the best accommodation values in this popular travel destination; highly recommended. Inexpensive.

Vancouver Hostel, 1515 Discovery Street, (604) 224–3208. About a half hour out from downtown, Vancouver Hostel is next to an excellent beach, tennis courts, and Jericho Park. You can cook your own meals or eat at the hostel's cafeteria. No children under five years of age and no pets. Inexpensive.

YWCA Hotel, 580 Burrard Street, (604) 662–8185. This is a fine, co-ed accommodation (welcomes couples and families), located in downtown Vancouver. Bathrooms are on a share basis, and there are kitchen facilities. Only female residents have use of the swimming pool and gym. Inexpensive.

Camping Areas near Vancouver

Contact your camping association and auto club for a complete listing of privately operated campgrounds. The following two government-operated camping facilities offer the best of two worlds: easy access to a great, sophisticated city and proximity to the natural beauty of the province.

Mount Seymour Provincial Park, North Vancouver, (604) 929–1291. In a beautiful setting. Close to mountains, sea, and city. There are no power hookups for trailers, but park has food, water, wood, and toilets. Inexpensive.

Parks Canada Recreational Vehicle Inn, Highway 17; via 52nd Street exit; northeast of ferry terminal to Victoria; (604) 943–5811. In operation from April to October. Facilities include washrooms, toilets, heated pool, recreation lounge; near water-slide park, grocery and gift shops, and golf.

Dining

There are more than 2,300 restaurants in Vancouver, representing the cuisines of about twenty ethnic groups. The deluxe hotels in Vancouver pride themselves on having at least one superb restaurant each, and you probably won't be disappointed in dining at least one evening at yours. Throughout the city there are also the familiar fast-food franchises when you need something fast and cheap. Regardless of your budget, kids seem to prefer fast-food burgers, French fries, and pizza to châteaubriand and flaming pepper steak. Vancouver's best foods are those which come from nearby areas, such as fresh seafood, especially salmon, fresh vegetables, and fruit. Wines are being produced in British Columbia, and you should sample some of them. They're okay, but it would be unfair to compare them with what comes out of Bordeaux or California. Having the second-largest Chinese population in North America, Vancouver has an abundance of Chinese restaurants. Although several excellent Chinese restaurants are recommended below, it's a bit of an adventure going into Chinatown and discovering the one that may become your favorite. Other ethnic groups have their eateries as well. Those serving continental cuisine—meaning French—are among the best of all restaurants. There are also fine Italian, Greek, and Portuguese places. As long as you have money to spend, you won't go hungry for great food to eat in Vancouver. The following recommended places are a small sampling of what's available in Vancouver:

The Teahouse Restaurant, in the Ferguson Point area of Stanley Park, (604) 669–3281. The Teahouse in Stanley Park is Vancouver's sentimental favorite place for a light snack or a full-course meal. It is a traditional British greenhouse with a most uplifting decor and splendid views from its windows. The atmosphere is relaxed and civilized in the English manner. Toasting an achievement or a loved one seems to take on special meaning at the Teahouse. Moderate to expensive.

Yang's, 4186 Main Street, (604) 873–2116. If you want to have some of the finest Chinese food in Vancouver, come to Yang's. It doesn't have the glitz of tourist-type Chinese restaurants, but Yang's has the secret ingredient of excellent cooking—chefs who create art as well as substance for the palate. Inexpensive.

Cheshire Cheese Inn, 4585 Dunbar Street, (604) 224–2521. Similar in name to one of Dr. Samuel Johnson's favorite London pubs, the Cheshire Cheese serves typical English fare—steak and kidney pie, bangers and mash, and good ale on draft. Inexpensive.

Binky's Oyster Bar, 784 Thurlow Street, (604) 681–7073. Fresh oysters and fish dishes are the specialties. Moderate.

La Bodega, 1277 Howe Street, (604) 684–8815. A popular Spanish bistro. Tapas dishes—small succulent servings of meats, seafood, cheese, vegetables—and Spanish wines and sherries are served here. **Chateau Madrid,** (604) 684–8814, serving more substantial Spanish fare, is in the same building. Moderate.

Chartwell's, at the Four Seasons Hotel, 791 West Georgia Street, (604) 689–9333. One of Vancouver's elegant restaurants. Menu selections, wines, ambience, decor, and service are excellent. Continental and nouvelle cuisine prepared with artistry, with strict emphasis on fresh ingredients available in season. Expensive.

Kibune Restaurant, 1508 Yew Street, (604) 734–5216. Excellent Japanese cooking served in traditional Nippon decor. Moderate.

Hy's Mansion, 1523 Davie Street, (604) 689–1111. A fine restaurant set inside a "Sugar Baron's" home. It's a nice change-of-pace treat. Moderate to expensive.

Pink Pearl Chinese Seafood Restaurant, in Chinatown, 1132 East Hastings Street, (604) 253–4316. A favorite restaurant with both Chinese and Caucasian patrons. A vast menu of Cantonese specialties will whet your appetite. Peking Duck and Rainbow Lettuce Wrap are just two of innumerable delicious dishes. Moderate to expensive.

Umberto's, 1380 Hornby Street, (604) 687–6316. Here you can feast on some of the best northern Italian cooking in British Columbia. Moderate.

Cristal, at the Mandarin Hotel, 645 Howe Street, (604) 687–1122. Elegance in decor and ambience and excellence in continental cuisine and service characterize this fine restaurant. It's a special place for special occasions. Expensive.

Salmon House on the Hill, 2229 Folkestone Way, West Vancouver, (604) 926–3212. One of the best places in the Vancouver area for Pacific salmon grilled over alderwood, Amerindian style. Get it served with wild rice and fiddleheads. This is also the place for romantic views of the harbor and distant Vancouver Island. Moderate to expensive.

William Tell, Georgian Court, 773 Beatty Street, (604) 682–5555. Seafood and steak dishes are well prepared. Both service and dining comfort get high marks. Expensive.

Quilicum Westcoast Indian Restaurant, 1742 Davie Street,

◀ Vancouver's skyline gleams with purpose during the day. Its towers sparkle like jewels at night.

(604) 681–7044. Try not to leave Vancouver without dining at this Northwest Coast Amerindian restaurant. The chefs use ingredients, such as salmon, duck, and oysters, which the native people in this region thrived on for millennia. Dishes are prepared using ancient traditions brought up to date for modern tastes. Moderate.

The Cannery, 2205 Commissioner Street, (604) 254–9606. Get a table with a view of the harbor and order your choice of seafood. Decor is that of an early, Northwest Coast fish cannery. Moderate.

Café de Paris, 751 Denman Street, (604) 687–1418. A top gourmet restaurant, with superb service and an extensive wine list. Highly recommended. Expensive.

Robson Schnitzel House, 1156 Robson Street, (604) 682–4850. Excellent German restaurant in the heart of city center. Offers a selection of beers from several countries. Moderate.

Bridges, 1696 Duranleau Street, (604) 687–4400. Meals served al fresco on a spacious deck in the quaint ambience of Granville Island and the marina world of boats, flapping sails, and screeching gulls. Bridges has a formal enclosed dining room and a wine bar also. Moderate to expensive.

A Kettle of Fish, 900 Pacific Street, (604) 687–6661. A fine seafood place with a menu that changes according to the availability of fresh fin fish and shellfish. Congenial environment in a greenhouse packed with plants, making for an uplifting meal on an overcast day. Moderate.

The Triangle, 302 West Cordova Street, (604) 684–2712. One of the best "greasy spoons" in Vancouver. Here you can satisfy your hunger for good, honest home cooking. Inexpensive.

Wedgwood Room, 845 Hornby Street, in Wedgwood Hotel, (604) 689–7777. North American, Westcoast, and French cuisines. Moderate to expensive.

Timber Club, in the Hotel Vancouver, (604) 684–3131. This is the Hotel Vancouver's top restaurant, which serves continental cuisine. It honors the city's long history with decor recalling the folklore of the province's vast forests and the economy made possible by the lumber industry. Expensive.

Trader Vic's, in the Westin Bayshore Hotel, (604) 682–3377. Seasoned travelers have found Trader Vic's restaurants in many cities and made them a popular part of their dining and entertaining. This one is excellent, concentrating on a wide variety of seafood and oriental dishes. Expensive.

The Noodle Maker, 122 Powell Street, (604) 683–9196. Here you can dine on gourmet Chinese cooking without having to worry about having an allergic reaction to the additive MSG used in most oriental restaurants. There's a huge live fish pond right in the center of the main dining room. A very popular place. Inexpensive to moderate.

Chardonnay's, 808 West Hastings Street, (604) 684–1511. Exceptional continental cuisine prepared by master chefs and served within sophisticated surroundings. Moderate to expensive.

Harbour House Revolving Restaurant, in the Harbour Centre complex at Hastings and Granville streets, (604) 669–2220. Revolving restaurant. Dine on a steak or salmon while the beauty of Vancouver's natural surroundings moves into view. Other excellent revolving restaurants are at the Sheraton Landmark Hotel (considered by many to have a better view) and at the Holiday Inn Harbourside. Moderate to expensive.

Entertainment

Vancouver, as is typical of large, important cities, has all forms of entertainment, from the highbrow to the seamy. If you are staying at a major hotel or motel, in addition to dining and lounge facilities, there's a good chance it offers some form of live entertainment—a dance band, pop singers, comedians, dancers, stage revues. There are movie houses throughout the city. Nightclubs and theaters are listed below. You can buy tickets to concerts, plays, sport games, and special events through Vancouver Ticket Centre, (604) 280–4411; charge tickets by phone using major credit cards.

Nightclubs

The following are chic drinking and dancing places, where you can bring your own date or come yourself and see the possibilities:

Bombay Bicycle Club, 921 West Pender Street, (604) 681–4335.

Richard's on Richards, top bar for young singles, 1036 Richards Street, (604) 687–6794.

Pelican Bay, in Granville Island Hotel, (604) 683–7373.

Amnesia, 99 Powell Street, (604) 682–2211.

Club Soda, 1055 Homer Street, (604) 681–8202.

Daddy Long Legs at the International Plaza Hotel, 1999 Marine Drive, North Vancouver, (604) 984–0611.

Heaven, 1251 Howe Street, (604) 689–5256; going strong from 11:00 P.M. to 5:00 A.M.

The Cotton Club, 364 Water Street, (604) 681–0541.

Landmark Jazz Bar, at the Sheraton Landmark Hotel, (604) 687–9312.

Punchlines Comedy Theatre, 21 Water Street, (604) 684–3015.

Rose and Thorne Pub, 757 Richards Street, (604) 683–2921.

Metro, rock and roll, 1136 West Georgia Street, (604) 687–5566.

Systems, disco, 350 Richards Street, (604) 687–5007.

Club Mardi Gras, in the Century Plaza Hotel, 1015 Burrard Street, (604) 687–0575.

Music and Theater

The music and theater scene in Vancouver is very active, with enough offerings to satisfy the interests of most visitors. Local talent and performers from other parts of Canada put on splendid shows and some go on to be stars. Both Michael J. Fox and Arthur Hill, leading actors in films and television, originally came from the area. Vancouver is a main stop on the tours of top international performers. There's a good chance you can see some of your favorites when you visit. In addition to the theaters listed below, both **B.C. Place Stadium** and **Pacific Coliseum** at Exhibition Park are major venues for important concerts and performances.

Orpheum Theatre, on Seymour Street, (604) 683–2311. Built in 1927 and recently renovated, this highly ornate theater is now the home concert hall for the **Vancouver Symphony Orchestra,** (604) 875–1661, the **Vancouver Chamber Choir,** (604) 738–6822, the **Vancouver Bach Choir,** (604) 921–8012, and other music groups.

Queen Elizabeth Theatre and Playhouse, on Georgia Street, (604) 683–2311. The Q.E. Theatre seats 2,800 and is home for four major performances a year by the **Vancouver Opera Association,** (604) 682–2871. The 650-seat Playhouse has its own resident company, which puts on experimental and popular productions from autumn to spring. The **Fesitval Concert Society,** (604) 736–3737, has concerts at the Playhouse.

Firehall Theatre, 280 East Cordova Street, (604) 689–0926; various dramatic productions and concerts.

City Stage, 751 Thurlow Street, (604) 688–1436; a small theater for live performances.

Theatre in the Park, outdoors in Stanley Park from July through August, (604) 687–0174; popular Broadway musicals.

Waterfront Theatre, on Granville Island, (604) 685–6217; performs works by British Columbia writers.

Kitsilano Showboat, 2305 Cornwall Street, (604) 734–7332; free shows—bands, tap dancers, comedians—outdoors; summer only.

Arts Club Theatre, 1181 Seymour Street; a small theater with three stages, operating throughout the year. Also, two stages at Granville Island, where full-scale dramas and musicals are performed, including cabaret-style productions with table service. Call (604) 687–1644 for information on performances and tickets for the Arts Club theatres.

Shopping

Vancouver is Western Canada's largest shopping center. It has everything you need. There are a number of bargains for visitors from the United States—considering the favorable exchange rate. Fashions for women and men are of as high style and quality as those you would find in New York and Toronto. On the other hand, you can purchase some special products here that would be hard to get elsewhere, such as sun-dried Pacific salmon (also fresh salmon airmailed to your home) and Northwest Coast Amerindian arts and crafts. Large national chain department stores—Eaton's, The Bay—are here, as well as Woodward's, a home-grown one of distinction.

Some of Vancouver's most interesting shopping sections include Robson Street (Robsonstrasse); Robson Fashion Centre for Canadian and international designs; Gastown; Chinatown; Granville Island; and the South Granville Street area.

The major multistore malls in city center are listed below:

Pacific Centre, Georgia at Granville—130 shops and three department stores; **Eaton's** and eight floors of departments in this mall. In the area are also **The Bay** and **Holt Renfrew.**

The Landing, Water Street, near Convention Centre—two levels of exclusive shops and boutiques.

Royal Centre, on Burrard and Georgia.

Harbour Centre, on Hastings Street, between Seymour and Richards.

In West Vancouver, **Park Royal Centre** sprawls for acres on both sides of Marine Drive. As can be expected, it has a large number of shops, several department stores, and supermarkets.

The following is a listing of shops that may be of special interest to visitors:

Laura Ashley, 1171 Robson, (604) 688–8729, pretty Victorian English look in fashions and home furnishings.

Marks & Spencer, in Pacific Centre, (604) 685–5741, a well-known British department store, selling a wide range of British-made goods—from underwear to shortbread.

Bacci Design, 2788 Granville Street, (604) 732–7317, a super-fashionable, super-expensive boutique, catering to women who are and can afford to be.

Jaeger Fashions, at Holt Renfrew, (604) 687–4242, top quality fashions for women.

Pappas Furs, 449 Hamilton Street, (604) 681–6391, a well-known furrier, offering classic and contemporary styles; one of North America's largest collections.

Edward Chapman, 833 West Pender Street, (604) 685–6207, quality, conservative clothing for men, with an English bent.

Tiffany Glass Centre, 2210 Cambie Street, (604) 874–4422, beautiful reproductions of Tiffany lamp shades.

Millar & Coe, 419 West Hastings Street, (604) 685–3322, English bone china and Waterford crystal at reasonable prices.

Jade World, 1696 West 1st Avenue, (604) 733–7212, offers all manner of objects made of jade mined in British Columbia, and you can visit the studios where the raw material is formed into objects of great beauty.

Inuit Gallery, 345 Water Street, (604) 688–7323, an impressive collection of Inuit (Eskimo) carvings, prints, and tapestries.

Brinkhaus Jewellers, in the Hotel Vancouver, (604) 689–7055, designer and dealer in exquisite objects of precious metals and gems.

Les Must de Cartier, upper level of the Pacific Centre, (604) 689–9411, internationally known for fine jewelry.

Professional Sports

Except for the **Canucks,** a National Hockey League team, the professional sports teams of Vancouver are not widely known throughout North America. They, nevertheless, offer top-notch sports excitement and entertainment. There is reason to expect that in the not-too-distant future Vancouver will be awarded a major league baseball franchise. When that happens, Vancouver will join the Toronto Bluejays and Montréal Expos.

B.C. Place Stadium, 1 Robson Street at Beatty, (604) 661–3664, ten-acre stadium with air supported roof.

Exhibition Park, at Hastings and Renfrew Streets, (604) 253–2311.

NHL Hockey, the Vancouver Canucks, at the Coliseum in Exhibition Park; call (604) 254–5141.

Canadian Football League, the British Columbia Lions, at B.C. Place Stadium; call (604) 588–5466.

Harness Racing, Cloverdale Raceway; (604) 576–9141; season is from late October to mid-April; horse racing is at Exhibition Park, (604) 254–1631.

Recreation

Sports play a big role in this health-conscious city. Most sports activities are organized on an ad hoc basis or just enjoyed individually. **Sport British Columbia** is a central source for information regarding most sports activities taking place in the province. The people in this agency will be happy to answer your questions and suggest how you can participate in a sport of interest to you; (604) 687–3333.

Public Golf Courses (Contact your own club about playing the private courses in the Vancouver area.)
Fraserview—(604) 327–3717
University Endowment Lands—(604) 224–1818
McCleery—(604) 261–4522

Tennis
Stanley Park—(604) 688–8786
Queen Elizabeth Park—see page 122

Public Indoor Pools (Most of the major hotels and motels listed in this guide have swimming pools.)
University of British Columbia Aquatic Centre—(604) 228–4521
Vancouver Aquatic Centre, 1050 Beach Avenue, (604) 689–7156

Outdoor Saltwater Pools
Kitsilano Beach—(604) 731–0011
Second Beach at Stanley Park

Skiing

Whistler Resort Area—see page 116

Grouse Mountain—see page 123

Mount Seymour Provincial Park—ten miles from city center in North Vancouver; three runs, chair lifts, and rope lifts.

Excellent downhill skiing is also available at Mount Baker in the state of Washington.

Ice-Skating

Lower level of Robson Square in city center.

Sailing

Sea Wind Sailing School—(604) 669–0840, 1818 Maritime Mews, Granville Island; rentals of vessels can be bareboat or with captain.

Scuba Diving

For such a northerly area in the Pacific, the sea life here is fabulous—close to 200 varieties of animals, including whales and octopus, and over 325 kinds of fishes—making for many fascinating dives. For suggestions on where to dive and equipment to rent, contact Diver's World, (604) 732–1344; The Diving Locker, (604) 736–2681; or Adrenalin Sports, (604) 682–2881.

Windsurfing

Windsurfing is a big sport on the waters off Vancouver. Many of the beaches (see page 124) have people giving instruction. For more information on the popular spots and equipment rentals, contact Windsure Windsurfing, Ltd., (604) 734–0212, or Wind Tech, (604) 681–8324.

Running/Jogging

The best place for running in the city is Stanley Park. Also try the Endowment Lands at the University of British Columbia.

Salmon Fishing Charters

The following companies offer salmon-fishing trips from Vancouver:

Barbery Coast Yacht Basin—(604) 669–0088

Westin Bayshore Yacht Charters—(604) 682–3377

Coho Fishing and Guides—(604) 324–8214

Paradise Racquet Yacht Charters—(604) 688–5231

They supply everything you'll need—food for the fish and you, gear, and even the fishing license.

Small Boating

You can rent kayaks at Granville Island Marina, (604) 681–3474, and Cove Canoe and Kayak Rentals, in North Vancouver, (604) 929–2268.

Bicycling

For information on routes and laws regarding biking, call (604) 687–3333. The scenic routes in the city for biking are in Stanley Park (see page 121) and the University of British Columbia Endowment Lands. Rentals are available at Bayshore Bicycle Rentals, (604) 689–5071, and Stanley Park Rentals, (604) 681–5581.

CHAPTER 6

Victoria: England by the Pacific

Victoria • Vancouver Island • The Inside Passage • Prince Rupert to Prince George

What Makes Victoria Special

No city in Canada is more British in mood and trappings than Victoria, British Columbia. Just as Québec City expresses the essence of *ancien régime* of France in North America, Victoria does the same for Canada's other founding nation/culture, Great Britain. And just as Halifax, Nova Scotia, was a major seaport for the Royal Navy on the North Atlantic, so was Victoria on the Pacific. Through several decades, British naval officers found the climate and lifestyle of Victoria to their liking, and many retired here, thus permeating many of the city's institutions with their Mother Country's styles, manners, and attitudes: Afternoon high tea with crumpets, scones, and delicate sandwiches served on English bone china with bright sterling settings is as common as the red double-deck London buses plying Government Street. Downtown stores sell Scottish woolens, Waterford crystal, Doulton china, tweed jackets, Stilton cheeses, and exquisitely wrapped bon bons. You can order a made-to-measure suit from a London tailor and buy the same styles that Princess Diana is currently wearing. Union Jack flags in all sizes and souvenirs with pictures of members of the Royal Family are available just about everywhere. The genuine and pseudo–Brits of

Victoria tend to be a bit more prim and proper, stodgy and stiff-upper-lipped than the citizens of the Mother Country, but it all contributes to the special atmosphere that many tourists, especially Anglophiles, seem to enjoy and expect. While the British influence is undeniably strong, residents from many other ethnic backgrounds contribute to the high quality of life here—Dutch, Germans, and Chinese, to name but a few. While the British demeanor is often a temporary façade, the people are more often warm, smiling, and helpful than not.

Although metropolitan Victoria is large in area and population, the downtown section, where most visitors tend to stay, gives the impression of being smaller and more intimate than it really is. You can visit most of the attractions, shops, restaurants, and places of entertainment on foot. Victoria is an immaculately clean city. Most of the older buildings have been declared heritage places and have been refurbished into boutiques, dining spots, and professional offices. Visually, the city is most attractive—particularly around the Inner Harbour area, which is used primarily for pleasure boats—with its parks and shore walks and flower baskets hanging from lampposts. It has a slower pace, as compared with that of Vancouver.

Victoria has the mildest weather in British Columbia. Although there is a great deal of rain in the winter, as is the case all along the coast, many colorful flowers bloom in February, and during this otherwise harsh season, duffers in tweed knickers are out shooting a round of eighteen holes at the local golf clubs. Spring, summer, and early autumn are truly magnificent, with mostly bright skies and dry air. The grass is lush and flowers grow everywhere. Almost everywhere are views of the sea and distant mountains—those on Vancouver Island and in the state of Washington. Washington's snow-capped volcano, Mount Baker, is a familiar sight, and so are the peaks of the Cascades and those in Olympic National Park.

Victoria is a city of walkers, joggers, bikers, sailors, golfers, and tennis players. All ages participate in exercise and recreation that they like. It's not a dynamic business center, as are Vancouver and Toronto, but the people exude their own kind of dynamism. This is a beautiful place and far from sleepy. There's a feel of being in utopia here. The Christmas season is a special time in Victoria. Both the hotels and the city attempt to create a Dickensian holiday feel, and people come here just to enjoy a Victorian Noël. It takes a little extra effort to get to Victoria, but few visitors have come away disappointed. Most, in fact, plan to return in the near future.

A Brief Look at Victoria's History

The human history of the Victoria area is many millennia old. Northwest Coast Amerindian tribes developed an advanced civilization based on fishing and hunting and created art that many connoisseurs consider the finest produced by the indigenous peoples of North America. Their culture went into decline with the coming of the Europeans. In 1843 James Douglas, who was the chief factor for the Hudson's Bay Company at Fort Vancouver (on the Columbia River in what is now the state of Washington), chose the tip of this peninsula jutting into the Strait of Juan de Fuca as the site of Fort Victoria. The political reason a trading fort was established here is that the United States and Great Britain were in the process of establishing the 49th parallel as the international boundary between much of British North America (Canada) and the United States. The tip of Vancouver Island at Fort Victoria extended a considerable distance below the 49th. By maintaining sovereignty over all of Vancouver Island and its valuable resources in this manner, further U.S. territorial claims were blunted. If you look at a map, you'll see that the U.S./Canada border follows the 49th parallel for thousands of miles until it hits the West Coast where it loops around the southern end of Vancouver Island.

As fur trading faded away in Victoria, the city became a major port for the processing and shipment of the island's rich lumber and mineral resources. Gold was also discovered in the Fraser River region in 1858, and Victoria became a boom town for men en route to seek wealth there. During the mid-1800s, the city was a contrast of bawdy houses and saloons, beautiful mansions and churches, the rough and crude, the gentle and cultivated. It became a city in 1862. At nearby Esquimalt Harbour, in 1865, the British Admiralty established a naval base. Victoria became the capital of Vancouver Island, and later a part of the province of British Columbia in 1871. It remained the major city of British Columbia until the transcontinental railroad linked the vast territory between the Atlantic and Pacific coasts to Vancouver. From then on the economic importance

This re-creation of Anne Hathaway's cottage in Victoria is a charming ▶ symbol of the strong English influence in coastal British Columbia.

of Victoria diminished while Vancouver's rose. The provincial capital was originally in New Westminster, former name of the city of Vancouver, but protests forced the seat of government to be moved to Victoria in 1868 where it has remained since.

Victoria Today: Some Basic Facts

Although there is some light manufacturing (furniture, machinery, food, rubber and plastic products, and so on) in the city, Victoria's main occupation and preoccupation is government, both provincial and federal. Thousands of people are employed in the government bureaucracy. The second most important economic activity is tourism, followed by education, retail sales, and various kinds of personal and professional services. Fishing, ship repair, agriculture, and the shipment, through its seaport, of the island's natural resources (lumber, fish, minerals, and farm products) are other important ways the people of Victoria make their living.

The population of greater Victoria is about 263,000. The people live in Victoria proper and in the surrounding communities of Esquimalt, Oak Bay, and those on the Saanich Peninsula.

Victoria is a popular retirement community, attracting hundreds of new inhabitants because of its mild climate, high quality of life, and excellent services for the elderly. There is, however, a good mix of all ages here.

The central city has no excessively tall buildings, except for a few multistory hotels. Almost every structure is on a human scale. There are plenty of nice parks and walking areas, gardens and floral displays, magnificent views of mountains and sea, and top-quality goods in stores. The cultural life—music, stage, and the visual arts—is quite rich and diverse. When discussing Victoria, one finds few defects to complain about.

How to Get to Victoria

Although on an island, Victoria is easy to reach by private or rented car, by bus, and by air. On Vancouver Island the Trans-Canada Highway itself extends from Nanaimo and ends at mile "0" in Victoria. The B.C. ferries are modern, large-capacity vessels that link the island with the mainland at several points and also provide trips through the famous Inside Passage (see page 189).

By Car

From Vancouver: The quickest way to get here is by Highway 99 south to 17, which leads to the ferry terminal at Tsawwassen. (This is also the best way for those coming up from Washington, Oregon, and California. Highway 99 north, connecting with U.S. Interstate 5, is your best route in B.C.) Another way, which allows you to tour more of Vancouver Island, is to take the Lion's Gate Bridge to North Vancouver, then the Trans-Canada Highway to the ferry terminal at Horseshoe Bay.

From Seattle, Washington: The ferry terminal is located off Elliott Avenue at Elliott Bay.

From Anacortes, Washington: Take U.S. Interstate 5 north to Highway 20 west to the ferry terminal in Anacortes.

From Olympia, Washington, via the Olympic peninsula to Port Angeles: Take Highway 101, which circles the peninsula. If you have extra time, tour the west side of the peninsula, which borders on the open Pacific and Olympic National Park, one of the most splendid natural areas in the United States.

By Ferry

The most pleasant way to get to Victoria/Vancouver Island is on one of the B.C. ferries. It's amazing how many cars and campers these modern vessels can carry. Tractor-trailer trucks go into the bottom hold, while cars are carried on the second level. The enclosed passenger decks have comfortable nonsmoking and smoking sections, coffee bar, cafeteria, and a newsstand. The open decks have chairs for relaxation and plenty of space for strolling about. En route the scenery is gorgeous with lovely islands and plenty of birds—including bald eagles.

From Vancouver to Victoria, using the terminals of Tsawwassen on the mainland and Swartz Bay on the island: During the summer (late June to early September) there are sailings every hour from 7:00 A.M. to 10:00 P.M.; the same schedule applies for return trips. The sailing time is approximately one hour and thirty-five minutes.

From Vancouver to Nanaimo, using the terminals at Horseshoe Bay on the mainland and Departure Bay on the island: same schedule and sailing time as above. From Nanaimo you can go farther "up island" to Port Hardy, across the island to Port Alberni and the Pacific Rim National Park, or "down island" to Victoria, which is 112 km. (67.2 mi.) south via the Trans-Canada.

You should be at the ferry terminal at least an hour to forty-five minutes prior to sailing. Travel is on a first-come–first-served basis; no reservations (except for the Inside Passage trip). Check on length of waiting time during peak months of July and August. For more information, call B.C. Ferries' twenty-four-hour recorded messages—Vancouver, (604) 685–1021; Victoria, (604) 656–0757; Nanaimo (604) 753–6626; for other clerk-answered information—Vancouver, (604) 669–1211; Victoria, (604) 386–3431; Seattle, Washington, (206) 682–6865.

Ferry service is also available on Washington State ferries— (206) 464–6400 in Washington; (604) 656–1531 in B.C.—via Anacortes, Washington; three sailings daily in the summer and one during the winter. Sailing time is three hours and twenty minutes. Blackball Transport—(206) 457–4491 in Port Angeles; (604) 386–2202 in Victoria—has four sailings daily between Port Angeles, Washington, on the Olympic Peninsula, and downtown Victoria. Sailing time is one hour and thirty-five minutes. The most romantic, vintage ship that carries passengers and a few cars (fifty of them) from Seattle to Victoria is the *Princess Marguerite*, an old, but safe, seaworthy steamship with the Union Jack emblazoned on its twin smokestacks. It has a pub and a dining room. The *Princess Marguerite* sails daily from May to October. Call (604) 386–6731. Reservations are required for all but B.C. ferries.

By Plane

The following airlines provide regularly scheduled service between the mainland at Vancouver International Airport and Victoria: Air Canada (with connections to major North American and international cities), Air B.C. (this airline provides service throughout the province, even to remote coastal areas), Burrard Air, Canadian Airlines, San Juan Airlines (has several trips daily to and from Seattle), and Skyline Airlines. The Victoria International Airport itself is located in Sidney, off Highway 17, 30 km. (18 mi.) north of Victoria, and a few miles south of the Vancouver ferry terminal at Swartz Bay, Rental cars are available at the airport.

By Bus

Frequent, comfortable bus/ferry service is available between Vancouver and Victoria on Pacific Coach Lines. In Victoria, call (604) 385–4411; the terminal is at 710 Douglas Street near the

Empress Hotel; in Vancouver, (604) 662–3222; the terminal is in city center at 150 Dunsmuir Street.

By Rail

Via Rail—(800) 665–8630—provides Vancouver Island rail service between Victoria and Courtenay with stops at Nanaimo. From the Victoria area you can get ferries to the United States and to Vancouver via Swartz Bay. From Nanaimo you can take the ferry to the mainland—Horseshoe Bay to the city of Vancouver.

How to Get Around Victoria

The best way to get around downtown Victoria is on foot. Most of the major attractions are here—the Provincial Museum, the stores, the wax museum, Inner Harbour, high tea served at the Empress Hotel, and so forth. You can orient yourself on the front steps of the Empress Hotel. Directly across from you is Inner Harbour with its promenade and yacht moorings. The street in front is Government Street. If you go north on Government, you pass by most of the fine shops selling woolens, china, books, and so on. Government will take you to Fisgard Street, which, in this section of the city, is Chinatown. From the Empress going north, Government bisects Humbolt, Courtney, Broughton, Fort, View, Yates, Johnson, and Pandora. It runs parallel with Gordon, Broad, Douglas, and Blanshard. Within this general area are shops, department stores, boutiques, cafés, restaurants, malls, and theaters. Going south on Government, you cross Belleville Street, on which are located the Parliament buildings (at a right angle to the Empress on Inner Harbour), Royal London Wax Museum, Undersea Gardens, hotels, the Archives, the Provincial Museum, Thunderbird Park, the bus station, and Crystal Garden. Douglas Street, which runs parallel to Government, heading south, goes by Beacon Hill Park and ends at Dallas Road, part of the Marine Drive. Other areas and their attractions can be easily reached by car, taxi, or bus—for example, the campus of the University of Victoria is off Highway 17, via McKenzie Ave. Butchard Gardens is off Highway 17 north; follow signs. As a matter of fact, signs leading to attractions are very good in the Victoria area, and you should not get lost.

Public Bus Service

B.C. Transit provides bus service on downtown routes from 6:00 A.M. to midnight every day of the week. The company sells day

VICTORIA

passes for unlimited rides. Call (604) 382–6161 for information and rates.

Taxis, Rental Cars, Bikes

Ask the concierge or desk clerk at your hotel or motel for assistance in securing a cab, or call Bluebird (604) 384–1155/382–4235. Budget Rental Car—(604) 388–5525. Island Sun Rentals, (604) 383–4424, 434 Kingston Street, rents cars, scooters, jeeps, tandems, mopeds, and motorcycles.

Visitors Information Centre

At the junction of Wharf and Government (812 Wharf Street), on the Inner Harbour, across from the Empress Hotel, the Information Centre is a good source for maps, brochures, directions, and accommodation information on Victoria. Call (604) 382–2127 for tourism information at any time of the year.

Parking

A number of public parking garages are scattered throughout downtown. The "P" sign will lead you to one in the area you want to visit. There is metered street parking, but pay attention to the time limits and keep the meter honest. Victoria has a terrible reputation for having its tow trucks waiting in the wings to scoop up the vehicles of visitors and residents alike. This situation is one of the few blemishes on an otherwise superb city.

Business and Convention Services

Victoria is a perfect place for business meetings and small conventions. Spouses love touring the attractions, especially the gardens, museums, and historic homes, while their mates deliberate. And after the meetings are over, both can enjoy the romantic charm of the city together. Construction is now underway for the Victoria Conference Centre. It has a prime location on Douglas Street next to the Empress Hotel and overlooking Inner Harbour. It will accommodate conventions of up to 1,500 persons, and have about a dozen function rooms. For more information about the new convention center and existing convention/meeting facilities (hotels and universities) in the city, contact the Tourism Association of Vancouver Island, The Penthouse, 612 View Street, Victoria, B.C. V8W 1J5, (604) 382–3551/382–1665.

Useful Information

Police—(604) 383–1313
Doctor—(604) 383–1193
Inhalator or Fire—(604) 384–1122
Ambulance—(604) 595–9911
Poison Control—(604) 595–9211
Royal Jubilee Hospital—(604) 595–9200
Victoria General Hospital—(604) 727–4212
Emergency Road Services—(604) 383–1155 (twenty-four hour); (604) 386–6311 (CAA and AAA members)
Prescription Chemists (drugstore)—(604) 384–1195 (provides delivery to hotels and motels)

Special Events

January
New Year's Day Levess, a fun and entertainment celebration
Polar Bear Swim
Victoria Symphony

February
Various musical, theatrical, and visual art events
Bloomin' Flower Count

March
Various musical, theatrical, and visual art events

April
Hobby Show
Dixieland Jazz Party

May
Jazz Festival
Victoria Day holiday
Annual Exhibition and Fair
Harbour Festival
Crystal Garden Spring Craft Fair
Swiftsure, yacht race

June
Oak Bay Tea Party
Folkfest International Village

July
Canada Day holiday

August
Chinatown Street Festival of the Arts
Classic Boat Festival
Victoria to Skooe Open Ocean Kayak Race

September
Classic Boat Festival

October
Royal Victoria Marathon
Chinatown Lantern Festival
Goldstream Salmon Run

November
Christmas Craft Fair, Crystal Gardens
Christmas at Craigdarroch

December
Christmas at Craigflower Manor
Christmas Craft Fair, Empress Hotel
Santa Claus Parade
Nutcracker, Royal Theatre

Touring Services

The following touring services provide sight-seeing in Victoria and attractions on the island:

Harbor Tours, (604) 381–1511, from May to October. Departs from Inner Harbour dock across from Empress Hotel, hour tours of coastal area from Inner Harbour to Esquimalt Harbour; also sunset cruises.

Mesouda Yacht Tours, departs from dock at the Oak Bay Beach Hotel, (604) 598–4556. Operates throughout the year (departs from Inner Harbour in the winter). Provides tours of the local coast and harbors and fishing charters.

Grayline Tours, free pickup at major hotels, (604) 388–5248. Sightseeing of local area attractions; trips to Butchart Gardens.

Tally-Ho Sightseeing, (604) 479–1113. Located beside Parliament buildings and opposite Royal London Wax Museum. Provides one-hour horse-drawn tours of Victoria.

Walk-A-Bout Victoria, (604) 382–2127, Visitors and Information Centre, 812 Wharf Street. A guided walking tour through some of the city's most interesting and colorful sections; operates during the summer only.

Vancouver Island Helicopters, (604) 656–3987. Tours from Victoria and Nanaimo of beautiful, secluded places on the island.

Attractions

Butchart Gardens, located fourteen miles north of Victoria, via Highway 17. Call (604) 652–5256 (recorded information), (604) 652–4422 (questions). Open throughout the year; because of heavy traffic during the peak July and August season, admittance into the gardens may be limited. Admission charged.

If there is a North American "Paradise" for horticulturists and simple lovers of flowers and landscaping, it is Butchart Gardens. Here you will be dazzled by splendid displays of innumerable kinds of flowers, plants, shrubs, and trees, all arranged along a walking tour that takes you through the very heart of Eden itself. Butchart features Italian, English Rose, Japanese, and Sunken Gardens. There are ponds, waterfalls, a dancing fountain, two restaurants, and a coffee bar. Books, seeds, plants, and gardening tools can be purchased at the Seed and Gift Shop. Entertainment—fireworks, stage shows, and music—is provided every day, except Sunday, from mid-May through September. Write or phone for a copy of the *Butchart Gardens Entertainment Guide*. When you're on site, they'll loan you umbrellas, cameras, wheelchairs, and pushcarts for babies. Moorages are also available for visitors in the area on their own yachts. Buses provide frequent transportation to Butchart Gardens from Victoria and from the city of Vancouver. When you walk through the sumptuous gardens, it is hard to image this place was once a drab limestone quarry. The late Jennie Butchart was the main force in transforming gouged-out land into one of the premier horticultural attractions in the world (the work began in 1904). To visit British Columbia and miss experiencing Butchart Gardens is to turn one's back on the beauty the hand of God and that of humans have wrought together.

The Marine Drive follows the coastline along Dallas Road and offers spectacular views of the distant Olympic Mountains across the Strait of Juan de Fuca. It passes through parts of the swank Rockland residential area and continues past the lovely Victoria Golf Course, which is in full operation during the winter, and through the prestigious Oak Bay community. The drive continues through the high-priced area of Uplands to the Saanich Peninsula and on to Cordova Bay. There are many stopping places along the way where you can enjoy the views and stroll or jog the promenades. Sealand of the Pacific is along this scenic route in the Oak Bay section.

Thunderbird Park, located at the corner of Belleville and Douglas, next to the Provincial Museum, is a small grass area decorated with tall totem poles and a Kwakiutl dance house. Here's a perfect spot to take pictures of your friends in front of the fantastic carvings of the region's Amerindians.

Beacon Hill Park, between Douglas and Cook streets and bordering Marine Drive (a five-minute walk from the Empress Hotel), is a 154-acre enclave of flower beds, ponds, oaks, and cedars. There are communities of royal swans and many different birds, including the giant black raven. At the Marine Drive end of the park is one of the world's tallest totem poles. Also within Beacon Hill Park is a Children's Farm replete with chickens, pheasants, peacocks, goats, and lambs. Children have a place where they can pet the young animals.

Parliament Buildings, Belleville Street, facing Victoria Harbour and at right angle to Empress Hotel. Call (604) 387–3046 for tour information. Tours given in French and German also; tours are conducted during the summer months, but building is open throughout the year. Free. The Parliament (provincial legislative) buildings are impressive enough to grace the capital of a good-size country. It could certainly accommodate Canada's federal Parliament, should it ever decide to move out of Ottawa. Completed in 1898, this complex for enacting legislation and governing the province is a massive building of domes, towers, and arches. The interior is rich with marble. If the legislature is in session while you're passing through, you may observe the proceedings of the lawmakers. During the evening, the outline of the complex is illuminated with thousands of bulbs, giving it a Christmasy feel even in mid-summer. A large expanse of lawn flows from the center building down toward Victoria's Inner Harbour. Set back a few feet from Belleville Street and in a straight line to the main portal of the complex is a majestic statue of Queen Victoria (one of the best sculptures of her in Canada), from whose patronage this city takes its name.

B.C. Provincial Museum, 675 Belleville Street, near Parliament buildings, (604) 387–3701. Open daily, except Christmas and New Year's Day. Free. This extensive museum is Victoria's best attraction, and it's free. The B.C. museum concentrates on the peoples, industries, and ecology of the province. The displays of Amerindian art are superb. There are mounted animals (the Wooly Mammoth is awesome), fish, and birds common to B.C. One display recreates a frontier town, allowing you to walk through as one who has zoomed backward several decades in time. A tea room and gift shop are on the main floor.

Helmcken House, 638 Elliot Street, (604) 387–3440. Open Wednesday to Sunday. Free. This historic 1852 residence belonged to Dr. J. S. Helmcken, a man who brought medical science to a needful community in its pioneering days. You can see the original furnishings and medical instruments of that bygone era.

Sealand of the Pacific, 1327 Beach Drive in the Oak Bay section via Marine Drive, (604) 598–3373. Open daily from March to mid-October; Wednesday to Sunday from mid-October to February. Admission charged. Sealand bills itself as "Canada's largest oceanarium," which is true. Its main attractions are shows put on by orca whales, sea lions, and seals. It also has an underwater viewing area where you can see live displays of octopus, salmon, and many other species.

Point Ellice House, 2616 Pleasant Street, (604) 385–3837. Open Tuesday to Friday. Free. A magistrate by the name of Peter O'Reilly built this fine house in 1861. The house itself, its original furnishings, and displays will give you a fair idea of how well the "establishment" lived at a rugged and wooly time in the city's early history.

Pacific Undersea Gardens, 490 Belleville Street, (604) 382–5717. Open daily. Admission charged. This museum of marine life is well worth a visit. In an undersea gallery, you see living specimens of thousands of marine animals. The Northwest Coast is an exceptionally rich environment for a wide diversity of marine life, including the world's largest octopi. A scuba diver puts on a show working with a huge Pacific octopus.

Victoria Heritage Village, 321 Belleville Street, (604) 384–3232. Open daily. Admission charged to some attractions. Heritage Village is a complex of shops and tourist attractions: Explore Victoria Bicycle Rentals, 381–BIKE; Christmas Shop, decorations from around the world, 388–XMAS: Haunted Mansion, built by a gold crazy Scotsman, has resident ghosts and goblins; the

Cricket Grill, light meals and snacks, 382–3344; Tickles Gift Shoppe, 384–3232; Victoria's Enchanted Garden, a beautiful world in miniature, 384–3232; the Victoria Foreign Exchange buys and sells all currencies and cashes checks; Snakes & Ladders & Dazy Maze Miniature Golf.

Royal London Wax Museum, 470 Belleville Street, (604) 388–4461. Open every day with extended hours during the summer. Admission charged. Figures of British royalty, Canadian greats, and famous and infamous figures from throughout history—more than 180 of them, made in Longdon—are here authentically costumed and set in displays portraying their times. The kids love the horror and fantasy displays, and Anglophiles adore the renditions of the queen and members of her family.

Crystal Garden, 713 Douglas Street, (604) 381–1213. Open daily. Admission charged. The setting is that of a tropical garden containing 150 species of plants and 50 species of exotic birds, monkeys, and reptiles. It has several souvenir boutiques and restaurants also.

Classic Car Museum, 813 Douglas Street, (604) 382–7118. Open daily. Admission charged. This is the place for auto buffs— rotating displays of antique cars that you'd like to take out on the road for a spin. The museum also has replicas of the Crown Jewels of England and a gift shop selling china and crystal.

Miniature World, 635 Humboldt Street (at the Empress Hotel), (604) 385–9731. Open daily. Admission charged. Things miniature have always been popular with people. At this attraction you'll see what is purported to be the "world's largest doll house" (which sounds like a contradiction), a neighborhood in "ye olde London," as well as "one of the world's largest rail scenes and the world's smallest operational sawmill."

Mile "0," where Douglas Street meets Dallas Road. Although Mile "0" doesn't sound like much of anything, it is the western starting point of the Trans-Canada Highway, *the world's longest national highway—7,820 km./4,860 mi.* For those of us who have traveled long stretches of the Trans-Canada in all kinds of weather, this is a major attraction!

The Emily Carr Gallery of the Provincial Archives, 1107 Wharf Street, (604) 387–3080. Closed Sundays during the summer; in the winter open Tuesday through Saturday. Free. The Gallery shows paintings by Emily Carr, B.C.'s most famous artist, and documents relating to her life and work. Exhibitions of the works of other artists are also held. Films about Emily Carr are shown, and special tours give visitors a fuller appreciation of the contributions of one of Canada's cultural immortals. Reproductions of her paintings are for sale here.

Bastion Square, entrance off Government Street, between Yates and Fort streets at the foot of View Street. Here was the original site of Fort Victoria, established by James Douglas of the Hudson's Bay Company in 1843. There are several buildings of historic importance in Bastion Square: Board of Trade Building (1893); the Court Building (1889), Victoria's first concrete building, now houses a maritime museum; Law Chambers (turn-of-the-century) now has several shops; Burns House (1882) once was a brothel; Strousse Warehouse (1885) supplied gold miners.

Maritime Museum of British Columbia, 28 Bastion Square, (604) 385–4222. Open daily. Admission charged. The Maritime Museum has a wide assortment of marine artifacts, ship models, exhibits focusing on Captain Cook who sailed hereabouts in the eighteenth century, and displays portraying the history of Britain's Royal Navy and the Canadian Navy as they relate to British Columbia. The museum houses the *Tilkum* and the *Trekka*, two famous B.C. sailing vessels that circumnavigated the globe.

Art Gallery of Greater Victoria, 1040 Moss Street, (604) 384–4101. Closed Mondays. Admission charged. The Art Gallery collection includes European prints and drawings, English decorative art, and Canadian art, both historical and contemporary. Its excellent collection of Japanese art is one of the finest on the continent. A café and shop are within the Spencer mansion complex.

Government House, 1401 Rockland Avenue, is the official residence of the lieutenant governor of British Columbia and where Elizabeth II, queen of Canada, and other members of the monarchy stay when visiting this part of the province. The beautiful grounds, however, are open to the public, except of course when royalty is in residence or during special events. There are a sunken rose garden, formal lawns and other gardens, a lily pond, and many exquisite botanical features, both indigenous and specially planted.

Craigdarroch Castle, 1050 Joan Crescent, (604) 592–5323. Open daily. Donations accepted. Scots have a penchant for building grand castles for themselves. This was so with Robert Dunsmuir, who in 1851 left the heather-covered hills of Scotland to settle in Victoria. Dunsmuir, known as the "coal king of British Columbia," made a great deal of money and spent $650,000 (a king's ransom in those days) building Craigdarroch Castle. Completed in 1889, Craigdarroch is not a castle in the classic medieval sense. But as an immense, impressive mansion, there are few other similar places in Canada that can top Craigdarroch. There are guides to answer questions to make a visit here memorable.

Craigflower Manor, 110 Island Highway, (604) 387–3067. Open Wednesday through Saturday. Free. The farmhouse and schoolhouse on this site were part of a Hudson's Bay Company farm established in 1853. The farmhouse contains furniture from this mid–nineteenth-century period (most of the pieces originally from Scotland).

Craigflower School, 2765 Admirals Road, (604) 387–3067; call for hours and tours. For those interested in Canada's pioneering heritage, Craigflower School is the oldest standing schoolhouse in Western Canada, built around 1855.

Dominion Astrophysical Observatory, 5071 West Saanich Road (best taken in when going to or from Butchart Gardens), (604) 388–3157. Open from Monday through Friday, May through August. Free. There is a giant telescope here and interesting exhibits dealing with astronomical phenomena. The public can view the heavens through the telescope on Saturday evenings. A fine panoramic view of the countryside can be had from this facility.

Chinatown, on Fisgard Street, is a compact section of small restaurants and stores selling Oriental goods. The food is quite good here. The Chinese community has a number of festivals throughout the year. The entrance to Chinatown is marked by an ornate gate where Fisgard bisects Government Street.

Centennial Square, off Douglas Street, is the location for City Hall and the McPherson Theatre, where many entertainments are performed. Shops and restaurants surround a landscaped courtyard.

Fable Cottage Estate, 5187 Cordova Bay Road, (604) 658–5741. Open from the end of March to third week in October. Admission charged. Fable Cottage is a lovely estate on the waterfront, featuring a handcrafted mansion (à la Disney), an outdoor animation display, beautiful gardens, great views of the sea, gift shops, and a tea pavilion.

Fort Rodd Hill and Fisgard Lighthouse, 501 Belmont Road, (604) 380–4662. Open daily, except end of year holidays. Free. The Fort Rodd/Fisgard Lighthouse area (designated a national park) offer many acres of lovely tranquil parkland overlooking Esquimalt Harbour. Explore the nineteenth-century artillery installations. Fisgard is the oldest lighthouse in B.C., built in 1859.

Royal Roads Military College, via Highway 1A to Colwood, on Sooke Road, next to Fort Rodd Hill, (604) 380–4660. Open daily. Free. Although much of this military educational facility is off-limits to visitors, it is worth making the trip to see the beautiful grounds and gardens and catch some of the martial ambience. Hatley Castle, built in 1908 by a coal baron, is on this site. Royal Roads is one of three military and staff colleges in Canada (formerly called Canadian services colleges). They both train cadets and commission officers for careers in the armed forces. When I visited this attraction, no "Visitors Welcome" sign was seen, but military buffs should persist and wade onto the grounds nevertheless.

Fort Victoria, 340 Old Island Highway, four miles west of the city, (604) 479–8112. Open June through September. Admission charged. Fort Victoria was originally built in 1843 by Sir James Douglas as a Hudson's Bay Company trading post. Visitors can see replicas of the bastions and officers' quarters; a museum with displays of early days in Victoria, tools, charts, cannons; and a cozy jail cut out of solid rock.

Gonzales Weather Station, 302 Denison Road, (604) 388–3350. Open Monday through Friday. Free. Not only can you see antique meteorological instruments here, but you also get the best high-level view of the city of Victoria from the rooftop observation deck.

Maltwood Art Museum and Gallery, at the University of Victoria, (604) 721–8298. Open daily. Free. By visiting this art museum you will also have a chance to stroll the pleasant campus of the University of Victoria. The main gallery, located at University Centre building, features art exhibits and the Katharine Maltwood collection of decorative arts, paintings, sculptures, graphics, archaeological artifacts, glass, textiles, ceramics, and furniture. Exhibitions by contemporary artists are held at the McPherson Library Gallery.

The Carillon, at the corner of Belleville and Government streets in Heritage Court. Recitals given every Sunday at 3:00 P.M. and on all holidays at noon. Concerts are given during the Advent/ Christmas season also. With sixty-two bells, this is the largest carillon in Canada and the seventh largest in the world. You can climb eighty-five steps to the carillonneur's playing cabin and see him or her in performance. The Carillon is a gift to the province from Canadians of Dutch ancestry.

Swan Lake–Christmas Hill Nature Sanctuary, 3873 Swan Lake Road, 6½ km. (4 mi.) north of downtown on the Pat Bay Highway, (604) 479–0211. Closed December and January. One hundred acres of lake, marsh, fields, and thickets. Arrange tours and natural history programs by calling the above number.

All Fun Waterslide Park, north on the Trans-Canada Highway 1, 13 km. (8 mi.) from Victoria, (604) 474–3184. Open June weekends and every day from July to Labour Day. Park has ten water slides, white-water river ride, car museum, mini-golf.

Accommodations

Victoria is one of Canada's most popular tourist cities, and advance reservations during the summer season and over the Christmas holidays are essential. Call ahead or have your travel agent do it for you.

The Empress (a Canadian Pacific Hotel), 721 Government Street, (604) 384–8111; toll-free (800) 268–9411. The Empress is to Western Canada what the Château Frontenac is to Eastern Canada. A "landmark" hotel known to sophisticated travelers throughout the world, the Empress reflects the essence of bygone elegance in its neogothic architecture, ambience, service, and civility. Central to all attractions and within steps of the Parliament buildings, the hotel overlooks Victoria Harbour and the moorings of expensive yachts. The Empress features fine restaurants (the Empress Dining Room, Garden Cafe, Bengal Lounge, Library Bar), shops, and many amenities. It has become a popular place to stay during the Christmas season, when Victoria takes on a Dickensian feel, and a number of tour companies offer special Christmas holiday trips to Victoria with stays at the Empress; contact your travel agent for details. The most popular tradition at the Empress is afternoon tea, in the English manner. The best of the house is served on bone china with sterling: English honey crumpets, fruit salad, homemade scones with jersey cream and strawberry jam, assorted tea sandwiches, Empress cakes, and Empress blend tea. There are four sittings during the summer months and three during the winter. Because of its popularity, having afternoon tea at the Empress requires a reservation (call 384–8111). Expensive.

Executive House, 777 Douglas Street, (604) 388–5111. Excellent accommodations, including luxury penthouse suits. Indoor pool, sauna, free parking, and "Raven's," a fine restaurant. This hotel is central to everything—attractions and government and commercial offices. Moderate to expensive.

Huntington Manor Inn, 330 Quebec Street; (604) 381–3456. A top-of-the-line hotel with most amenities. Excellent location. Moderate to expensive.

Captain's Place, 309 Belleville Street; (604) 388–9191. A venerable hotel (1897) with antique furnishings and painted fresco ceilings. Full breakfast is included in the room rate. Dining room overlooks Inner Harbour. Moderate to expensive.

Laurel Point Inn, 680 Montreal Street; (604) 386–8721. One of Victoria's best hotels—super location, all rooms with balconies and water view, swimming pools, tennis, dining room, and lounges. Free parking. Expensive.

The Beaconsfield Inn, 998 Humboldt Street; (604) 384–4044. Elegant rooms in an English-style mansion located near Inner Harbour. Some rooms have canopy beds. There are fireplaces and down comforters, a guest library, and a sunroom. Moderate to expensive.

Crest Harbourview Inn, 455 Belleville Street, (604) 386–2421; toll-free (800) 663–7474. Excellent downtown location, fine accommodations, car and bike rentals, indoor pool, lounge, pleasant lawns and patio, and parking. Moderate.

Oak Bay Beach Hotel, 1175 Beach Drive, via Marine Drive, (604) 598–4556. A lovely Tudor-style hotel right on water's edge with views of snow-capped mountains in the distance. In addition to the usual hotel amenities, Oak Bay has an English-style pub, a fine dining room overlooking the water and mountains, and a forty-one-foot custom yacht that's available for fishing, sightseeing, or private dinner cruises. This is a very friendly place whose staff members are eager to please. Expensive.

Olde England Inn, 429 Lampson Street, (604) 388–4353. A very well-known accommodation that transports you back to Elizabethan times. You can sleep in a canopy bed previously used by royalty and feast on roast beef and Yorkshire pudding—along with several pints of good stout ale, of course. Part of this complex is

◀ **The Empress Hotel on the yacht harbor in Victoria is one of the world's famous hotels. Here the tradition of English-style afternoon tea is sacred, ample, and punctual.**

Anne Hathaway's Cottage, an authentically furnished sixteenth-century dwelling that seems as if it had been plucked from a street in Stratford-on-Avon. It's filled with furnishings from that period, and the guides are costumed as Tudor wenches. Highly recommended. Moderate to expensive.

Harbour Towers, 345 Quebec Street; (604) 385–2405, toll-free (800) 663–7555. A full-service hotel near the Inner Harbour, shopping areas, and downtown attractions. Moderate.

Château Victoria, 740 Burdett Avenue, (604) 382–4221; toll-free (800) 663–7000 (U.S. and B.C.), (800) 663–7565 (Canada). One of Victoria's top hotels, offering indoor pool, sauna, satellite TV, free parking, central location, and the city's only rooftop restaurant. Moderate.

James Bay Inn, 270 Government Street, (604) 384–7151. Comfortable accommodations, convenient location, reasonable rates, family restaurant. Inexpensive.

Embassy Motor Inn, 520 Menzies Street, (604) 382–8161. Located next to the Parliament buildings and within a few steps of the promenades circling the Inner Harbour, the Embassy has kitchenettes, a sauna, a pool, parking, and a restaurant. Moderate.

Royal Scot Motor Inn, 425 Quebec Street, (604) 388–5463; toll-free (800) 663–7515. The Royal Scot gives you good value by providing a suite for the price of a room. Free local calls, indoor pool, saunas, Jacuzzi, masseur, tea room, exercise facilities. Moderate.

Inn on the Harbour, 427 Belleville Street, (604) 386–3451. Close to Seattle ferry and downtown attractions. Some rooms have kitchenettes. Restaurant, lounge, outdoor pool. Moderate.

Crystal Court Motel, 701 Belleville Street, (604) 384–0551. Downtown location, some housekeeping units, free parking. Inexpensive.

Ingraham Rodeway Inn, 2915 Douglas Street, (604) 385–6731; toll-free (800) 228–2000. Decent accommodations at fair prices. Dining room, a cabaret, and coffee shop. Moderate.

Sussex Apartment Hotel, 1001 Douglas Street, (604) 386–3441. Comfortable, good location, reasonable rates. Accommodations available with kitchenettes. Free parking and coffee shop. Moderate.

University of Victoria Housing Services, P.O. Box 1700, Victoria V8W 2Y2; (604) 721–8395. From May 1 to August 30, comfortable rooms are available at the University of Victoria, located a few minutes' drive north of downtown, also on the bus route. Price includes breakfast and free parking. An excellent value for the thrifty. Inexpensive.

Bed and Breakfast Reservation Services

The following agencies provide information and make reservations at bed and breakfasts for Victoria, other parts of Vancouver Island, and the Gulf Islands:

Garden City Bed & Breakfast Reservation Service, P.O. Box 6398, Station C, Victoria, B.C. V8P 5N7, (604) 479–9999.

V.I.P. Bed & Breakfast Reservation Service, 1786 Teakwood Road, Victoria, B.C. V8N 1E2, (604) 477–5604.

Travellers Bed & Breakfast Reservation Service, 1840 Midgard Avenue, Victoria, B.C. V8P 2Y9, (604) 477–3069.

Pacific Rim Host Homes, P.O. Box 6647, Station C, Victoria, B.C. V8P 5N7, (604) 592–5256.

Heritage Homes Bed & Breakfast Registry, 809 Fort Street, Victoria, B.C. V8W 1H6, (604) 384–4014.

Dining

Victoria offers a wide choice of restaurants. Seafood and traditional British dishes are featured. Ethnic fare, such as Chinese, Japanese, Greek, Italian, is also widely available. French cuisine is excellent. The Bombay Room at the Empress serves Indian dishes with chutney and other condiments. Its seafood with chutney on Fridays is a must.

The Blethering Place, 206-2250 Oak Bay Avenue, (604) 598–1413. Cornish pastries, Welsh rarebit, New Zealand Canterbury lamb chops, steak and kidney pie. Moderate to expensive.

Café Francais, 1635 Fort Street, (604) 595–3441. This dining room is decorated with eighteenth-century French antiques. Bouillabaisse is a specialty. Desserts, such as cheesecake, are concocted in the kitchen. Moderate to expensive.

Chez Daniel, 2524 Estevan Avenue, (604) 592–7424. Chef Daniel Rigollet, a member of "Confrerie de la Chaine des Rotisseurs," selects fresh ingredients for his menu offerings. Also has a good list of fine imported and North American wines. Expensive.

Chez Ernest, 4496 West Saanich Road, (604) 479–2123. One of Victoria's best French restaurants, in operation since 1947. Rack of lamb, roast pheasant, breast of duck, and Châteaubriand Forestière are specialties of the house. Expensive.

The Cricket Grill, 660 Oswego Street, (604) 382–3344. Offers eighty-five beers from twenty-five countries, plus gourmet hamburgers and smoked salmon. Moderate.

The Dingle House, 137 Gorge Road East, (604) 381–4412. An 1870s house decorated with paintings and stained glass windows. European cuisine served on Royal Albert china and with English silver. Moderate to expensive.

India Curry House, 2561 Government Street, (604) 384–6522. Fresh dishes daily. No MSG, preservatives, or additives; homemade condiments. Serves tandoori dishes—chicken, prawns, lamb—also vegetarian dishes. Inexpensive to moderate.

Rattenbury's, 703 Douglas Street, (604) 381–1333. Summer salmon barbecue, prime rib, steaks; al fresco dining in good weather. Moderate.

Villa Roma, 2900 Douglas Street, (604) 386–1113. Pizza, steaks, ribs, seafood, and salads. Will make free deliveries to your hotel. Inexpensive to moderate.

Periklis, 531 Yates Street, (604) 386–3313. Delicious Greek food—lamb dishes, seafood, and steaks. Guests are treated to Greek dancers and belly dancers. Moderate.

The Parrot House, in the Château Victoria Hotel, (604) 382–9258. Victoria's only rooftop restaurant. Spendid views of the Inner Harbour and distant mountains. The food here is good. Moderate to expensive.

Gazebo Tea House and Gallery, 5460 West Saanich Road, between Victoria and Butchart Gardens, (604) 479–7787. Lunch, afternoon tea and early dinner served in the English manner in a lovely country garden. Inexpensive and moderate.

Portt's Restaurant, 910 Government Street, (604) 388–7333. One of Victoria's most popular seafood restaurants; also serves steaks. It's right on the harbor with nice views all around. A good dining value. Moderate.

Murchies Tearoom Restaurant, 1111 Government Street, (604) 381–4181. Great afternoon teas and more substantial meals in an elegant setting with rich appointments. Popular with visitors and residents. Moderate.

Raven's, in the Harbour Towers Hotel, 345 Quebec Street, (604) 386–7444. Continental and West Coast cuisines. A splendid interior decorated with Amerindian art. Expensive.

Yokohama, 980 Blanshard Street, (604) 384–5433. If you lust for sushi, this is the place to get your fill. Moderate.

Jack Lee's Chinese Village, 755 Finlayson Street, (604) 384–8151. An extensive menu of Cantonese, Szechuan, and Mandarin dishes. Moderate.

The Keg, 500 Fort Street, (604) 386–7789. Serves what it considers the ultimate sharing snack—strips of steak or chicken sauteed with green peppers and onions served hot with relish, cheeses, and soft tortilla. Also has seven-layer dip, two-way salmon, and cajun popcorn shrimp. An unpretentious, fun place where the British stiff lip is out of place. Inexpensive.

Harbour House, 607 Oswego Street, (604) 386–1244. A top seafood place in a convenient location on the Inner Harbour and near the Empress Hotel and where the *Princess Marguerite*, the Victoria–Seattle ferry, docks. Moderate.

Holyrood House, 2315 Blanshard Street, (604) 382–8833. Scottish motifs—Clan Room, Scotia Dining Lounge—and Scottish offerings such as steak pie; also North American–style steaks, grilled salmon; a smorgasbord on weekends. Moderate.

Maiko Gardens, 940 Fort Street, (604) 383–3421. A full range of Japanese dishes served by kimono-clad waitresses in a Far East setting. Moderate to expensive.

The Captain's Palace, 309 Belleville Street, (604) 388–9191. Breakfast, luncheon, afternoon tea, and dinner elegantly served in a historic Victoria mansion. Good location on the Inner Harbour. Bed and breakfast accommodation also available here. Moderate.

Princess Mary, 344 Harbour Road, (604) 386–3456. A fine restaurant in an old ship. Seafood and beef dishes; special children's menu. Moderate.

Four Mile House, 199 Old Island Highway (ten minutes from downtown), (604) 479–2514. English country cooking in the fourth oldest building in Victoria (built in 1858). Ten minutes from downtown. Moderate.

Norman's R, 1280 Fairfield Road, (604) 383–1615. In the residential area of Fairfield. You create your own dinner out of thirty-five items: soups, salads, appetizers, and entrées. You can have a flambé made at your table or dig into delicious cheesecake. Moderate.

Chantecler, 4509 West Saanich Road (between Victoria and Butchart Gardens), (604) 727–3344. A lovely Tudor-style country house serving excellent continental fare. A good choice on the way to or from Butchart Gardens. Moderate to expensive.

Entertainment

Most of the major hotels have live entertainment (singers, comedians, dance bands, and so on) in their lounges and some in their dining rooms. For current entertainment events ask your concierge or call the organizations listed below. The following groups and theaters feature plays, dance, and musical events throughout the year or in their formal seasons:

Victoria Symphony Society, 631 Superior, (604) 385–6515
Pacific Opera Association, 1316 Government, (604) 385–0222
The Royal Theatre, 805 Broughton Street, (604) 383–9711
Phoenix Theatre, at the University of Victoria, (604) 721–8000
McPherson Playhouse, 3 Centennial Square, (604) 386–6121
Bastion Theatre, 1002 Wharf Street, (604) 386–8301
Belfry Theatre, 1291 Gladstone, (604) 385–6815
Kaleidoscope Theatre Productions, 255-560 Johnson, (604) 383–8124

Nightclubs
Yuk Yuks, 514 Fort Street, (604) 386–1792; comedy dinner theater
Merlins, 1208 Wharf Street, (604) 381–2331; club and bistro

Sports and Recreation

For the visitor, most sports and recreation will involve touring Victoria on foot. It is also a wonderful city for jogging. Almost everywhere you'll see people of all ages briskly walking, jogging, or cycling. The following additional options are offered:

Public Golf Courses
Douglas Golf Lands, 5273 Cordova Bay, (604) 658–5522; long par 3
Cedar Hill Municipal Golf Course, 1400 Derby off Cedar Hill Road, (604) 595–3103; eighteen holes, par 67
Henderson Park Golf Course, 2291 Cedar Hill Road (Oak Bay recreational area), (604) 595–7946; nine holes, par 3

Public Swimming Pools
Crystal Pool, 2275 Quadra, (604) 383–2522
Recreation Oak Bay, 1975 Bee, (604) 595–7946

Public Tennis Courts
Beacon Hill Park Courts, off Cook Street
Recreation Oak Bay, 1975 Bee, (604) 595–7946

Public Skating Rinks
Memorial Arena, 1925 Blanshard, (604) 384–0444
Recreation Oak Bay, 1975 Bee, (604) 595–7946

Racquet Sports
Quadra Court House, 3950 Quadra, (604) 727–2277
YM/YWCA, 880 Courtney Street, (604) 386–7511

Fishing Charters
Magna Charters, 902 Deal Street, (604) 598–4213
Brentwood Inn Boat Charters, 7212 Penden Lane, Brentwood Bay,
    near Butchart Gardens, (604) 652–1014

Sailing Charters
Victoria Sailing School, 1010 Wharf Street, (604) 384–7245

Harness Racing
Sandown Thoroughbred Autumn Race, thirty minutes north of
    downtown via Highway 17; 1810 Glamorgan, Sidney; call (604)
    656–7206 for information

Shopping

Your best buys are imported goods from Great Britain, locally
made candies, Amerindian-made sweaters, jewelry (B.C. jade and
silver) and carvings, books on Canada, and arts and crafts by the
province's other artists (weavings, pottery, fashions, paintings, and
so on).

Admiral Stamp & Coin, 827A Fort Street, (604) 384–1315.
Stamps, coins, bullion, war medals, and postcards.

Ivy's Book Shop, 1507 Wilmot Place, (604) 598–2713, has been
in business for close to a quarter of a century and is widely known
as one of Canada's top book shops. It has a broad selection of British
and Canadian books.

Gallery of the Arctic, 611 Fort Street, (604) 382–9012. Inuit
(Eskimo) sculpture in stone and old whalebone, stone-cut prints
from Cape Dorset and Pangnirtung.

The Quest Gallery, 1023 Government Street, (604) 382–1934.
Excellent objets d'art from the best of Canadian craftspersons.

Market Square, 201-560 Johnson Street, in the heart of "Old
Town," (604) 386–2441. More than thirty stores and restaurants are
set in refurbished heritage buildings, surrounding an old-style
covered market. This is an enjoyable place for all ages, whether you

buy or just poke around. Special entertainment and recitals are held here throughout the year.

Harbour Square Shopping Mall, 910 Government at Broughton Street, (604) 388–4632. This is an indoor mall with many shops and eateries.

Hudson's Bay Company, 1701 Douglas at Fisgard, (604) 385–1311. Canada's well-known department store featuring furs, more than 300 patterns of top brands of English china, a Canadiana Shop offering works by local artists and artisans (10 percent off on purchases made in the shop), woolens from England and Scotland, and famous Hudson's Bay point blankets.

Mayfair Shopping Center, 221 Mayfair, one mile from downtown at Douglas and Finlayson, (604) 383–0541. More than one hundred fashion boutiques. Mayfair is one of the most elegant shopping malls on Vancouver Island. Bus service is available from downtown.

Rogers' Chocolates, 913 Government Street, (604) 384–7021. This is the place for connoisseurs of fine chocolate goodies. Rogers' has been in business for more than one hundred years, and their Victoria Creams make taste buds sing heavenly tunes. Dieters beware.

Rosemary and Wendy Antiques, 620 Broughton Street, (604) 385–9816. Estate and antique jewelry is sold here, as well as art from the Orient.

Alcheringa, 665 Fort Street, (604) 383–8224. Museum-quality art from New Guinea, selected from remote villages on the Sepik River.

Bolen Books, Hillside Centre, 1644 Hillside Avenue, (604) 595–4232. A wide selection of books and tour guides.

Celtic Casuals, Harbour Square Mall, 910 Government Street, (604) 388–6122. Fine quality woolens from Scotland, Wales, and Ireland.

Montague Bridgman, Ltd., 650 Fort Street, (604) 383–0821. The city's oldest store selling fine china and crystal. They stock over 300 dinnerware patterns.

The Victoria Hand Loom, Ltd., 641 Fort Street, (604) 384–1011. The focus here is on beautiful, original Canadian handi-

◀ **The city of Victoria exudes elegance, style, and class. Its location on the Pacific coast allows flowers to grow throughout the year, even in the dim days of late January.**

crafts: Haida argillite carvings, B.C. jade, pottery, handwoven tweeds, and so on.

The Beehive, 619 Fort Street, (604) 383–9821. An excellent selection of imported and domestic knitting woolens; also skirt and sweater kits from Scotland.

The Orient, 1411 Government Street, (604) 383–6223. A vast array of imports from the Far East: silks, brass, carvings, wicker, teak, embroidery.

Munro's Books, 1108 Government Street, (604) 382–2464. One of the finest bookshops in Western Canada; browsing through their extensive collection is an unhurried pleasure. Housed in one of Victoria's heritage buildings, with high ceilings and colorful wall hangings by Carole Sabiston.

Victoria Limited Editions, 919 Fort Street, (604) 386–5155, has Victoria's largest selection of stemware. Offers low prices on Waterford crystal.

The Blue Window, 1607 Douglas Street, (604) 383–5815. A top quality gift shop featuring Bosson Heads, Pen Delfin rabbits, Hummel figurines, and hand-painted military figurines.

The English Sweet Shop, 738 Yates Street, (604) 382–3325. British candy, toffee, teas, biscuits, and chocolates. If you forgot to stock up on such goodies at Fortnum & Mason's in London, here's your next best chance to do so.

Baden-Baden Boutique, 667 Fort Street, (604) 386–5252. European fashions with German quality and style.

Nootka Court, on the corner of Douglas and Humbolt streets. An unusual shopping center with a variety of shops, restaurants, a liquor store, and a theater.

Trounce Alley, off Government Street. A quaint little passage with stores and dining places.

Vancouver Island

Touring "Up Island"

Most visitors to the coast of British Columbia concentrate on the cities of Victoria and Vancouver. Both certainly have enough attractions to keep you busy for an extended period of time— fishing, golf, touring, whale watching, crafts shopping, hiking, camping, mountain climbing. However, while in this area, it would be a shame to miss out on experiencing the natural magnificence of

Vancouver Island. Here are long stretches of unspoiled beaches, impressive mountains, and forests containing some of the tallest trees in the world. If you've never seen whales or bald eagles, you can do so here; this is their natural habitat. All you need is a sharp eye, binoculars, and a camera. You can fish for salmon and trout and not be disappointed. There are beaches for swimming and slopes for skiing. While it rains a lot in winter, Vancouver Island is Canada's mildest zone during this otherwise harsh season. Unless you go to a high elevation, there's generally no snow. It's not unusual to see flowers growing outdoors during the cold-weather months, whereas most of Canada and the United States have to wait until April to realize the first blossoms.

Vancouver Island is 510 kilometers/320 miles long and 40 to 80 miles wide, making it the largest Pacific island off the coast of North America (for comparison's sake: the province of Prince Edward Island is 2,184 square miles; Vancouver Island, which is part of a province, is 13,024 square miles). The island extends from just below the 50th parallel to about the 48th. About one-fifth of the island, the southwestern tip containing the city of Victoria, extends close to 1 degree below the 49th parallel, along which almost the entire U.S.–Canadian boundary line runs. In fact, the city of Victoria is far closer to Washington's Olympic National Park than either Bellingham or Seattle, major cities in that state.

The center spine of the island is a range of high mountains; on the East Coast, facing the Strait of Georgia, are most of the communities and broad expanses of agricultural land; and the West Coast, facing the open Pacific, is very rugged, wind- and rain-swept through much of the year, and relatively uninhabited. As you tour Vancouver Island, search out West Coast Indian sites and villages that reveal an ancient way of life. There's a mystical aspect to the native people, a depth of understanding about life and nature, that seems more profound than our own.

Highway 14 goes around the southern tip of Vancouver Island, from Victoria to Sooke, Jordan River, and Port Renfrew. At **Sooke** visit **Region Museum,** (604) 642–3121, with a collection of weavings and carvings by the Salish and Nootka people and exhibits on early pioneer life; open through the year. Free. Be sure to see **Leechtown Gold Rush Site**—call Sooke Museum above for details—where gold was discovered in 1864. **Botanical Beach,** between Sooke and **Port Renfrew** at Botany Bay, has natural aquariums, tidal pools, and a great deal of intertidal marine life to see. Be careful of rough seas and winds when exploring in this area. At Port Renfrew you can get over to the West Coast hiking trail with some effort, but you would be better off to start the trail at Bamfield, which can be reached from Port Alberni, about a third of the way "up island."

Camping at Provincial Parks

Provincial parks that offer camping facilities are listed below. Call (604) 929–1291. Camping is on a first-come–first-served basis. There is a small fee for use of camping facilities. Most campgrounds have showers, firewood, and toilets, but the actual range of facilities may vary from park to park.

Bamberton, on the Saanich Peninsula, north of Victoria
Elk Falls, on the Quinsam River, near Campbell River
Englishman River Falls, in the Parksville/Qualicum area
Goldstream, just north of Victoria on the Trans-Canada
Gordon Bay, on Cowichan Lake, north of Victoria
Little Qualicum Falls, off Highway 4 between Parksville and Port Alberni
McDonald, close to Swartz Bay, near the Vancouver ferry terminal
Rathtrevor Beach, south of Parksville
Sproat Lake, near Port Alberni
Buttle Lake Campground and Ralph River Campground, both in Strathcona Park

The following tour starts in Victoria and moves in a northwest direction "up island":

As you drive from the outskirts of Victoria on the Trans-Canada Highway 1, you go over Malahat Drive, which offers superb views of deep forests and distant islands. **Goldstream Provincial Park** is here and a good place to stop and grab a bite to eat and walk among the tall trees.

In **Duncan** you can purchase thick, exceedingly warm Cowichan sweaters knitted by native women who live in or around this community. Be sure to visit the following:

British Columbia Forest Museum, off Trans-Canada Highway 1, (604) 748–9389. Open from May to September. Admission charged. Indoor/outdoor exhibits on the forest industry in B.C., woodland walking trails, and steam train rides.

Cowichan Valley Museum, 200 Craig Street, (604) 748–1143. Open throughout the year. Free. Small, local historical museum.

The Glass Castle, off the Trans-Canada, (604) 746–6518. Open evenings during July and August. Admission charged. An eccentric house made from 180,000 glass bottles.

Whippletree Junction, off the Trans-Canada, (604) 748–1100. Open daily. Admission charged. Re-creation of turn-of-the-century pioneer village; includes an early Chinatown.

Sixteen giant murals decorate the buildings of **Chemainus.** These beautifully rendered murals depict this tiny town's heritage from the time of the native people to pioneering days and great moments in its history. A charming, unique place that's well worth the side trip on Highway 18.

In **Ladysmith** stop at the **Black Nugget,** 12 Gatacre Street, (604) 245–4846 (call for hours and admission fee), a local historical museum in an 1881-vintage hotel.

Crown Forest Industries Arboretum and Museum, off the Trans-Canada, (604) 754–3206, is open throughout the year. Free. Tree specimens from all over the world; early logging and railroad equipment displays.

Accommodations in Ladysmith are available at **Inn of the Sea,** Yellowpoint Road, (604) 245–2211. Full-facility waterfront resort, fireside dining, pool, tennis, Jacuzzi.

Nanaimo is the second-largest community on Vancouver Island. There are plenty of accommodations, restaurants, and shopping malls. The terminal for ferries to the mainland and the city of Vancouver is here; sailing time is one hour and thirty-five minutes. Call (604) 753–6626 for information. The oldest remaining Hudson's Bay Company bastion still guards the harbor. Attractions here include the following:

Harmac Arboretum, 65 Front Street, (604) 753–1112. Open throughout the year. Free. Displays of exotic trees.

Madrona Exposition Centre 900, 5th Street; (604) 753–3245; call for hours. Donation. Changing exhibits on various aspects of B.C. life.

Nanaimo Centennial Museum, 100 Cameron Street, (604) 753–1821. Open throughout the year. Donations. Historical and art exhibitions, Chinese art, coal-mine re-creation, local archives.

Annual Events
Highland Games—mid-May
Shakespeare Plus Festival—July–August

Great International Bathtub Race—mid-July
Vancouver Island Exhibition—August

For dining, try the following restaurants:

The Lighthouse, 50 Anchor Way, (604) 754–3212. Unusual lighthouse restaurant on the water, serving seafood. Moderate.

Chez Michel, 10 Front Street, (604) 754–1218. French cuisine; tables with water view. Moderate to expensive.

Accommodations can be found at **Coast Bastion Inn,** 11 Bastion Street, (604) 753–6601. The best in town; rooms have water views, gourmet restaurant, health facility, nightclub and lounge. Moderate to expensive.

The following have dining rooms, lounges, and other amenities:

Best Western Harbourview Motor Inn, on Trans-Canada south, (604) 754–8171. Moderate.

Tally-Ho Island Inns, 1 Terminal Avenue, (604) 753–2241. Moderate.

Highlander Motor Inn, 96 North Terminal Avenue, (604) 754–6355. Moderate.

Nanaimo has several large shopping malls where you can find just about any kind of item. It's about equal to Victoria in having such retail complexes.

Woodgrove Centre, on the North Island Highway, (604) 390–2721, is one of the largest on the island.

Harbour Park Mall is in downtown, (604) 754–3234.

Rutherford Mall is on the north Island Highway, (604) 758–8111.

The main route heading north out of Nanaimo becomes Highway 19.

The **Parksville-Qualicum Beach** area is best known for its long sandy beaches, and during the summer season, it is a major vacation spot for both B.C. residents and visitors. It's also popular with fishers, hikers, and spelunkers. Visit **Craig Heritage Park** in Parksville, (604) 248–6433. Open on Sundays. Collection features Amerindian and pioneer artifacts. Qualicum Beach is perfect for swimming and sunbathing. Golf, lawn bowling, live theater, and nature hikes are also offered. **Qualicum Falls Provincial Park** has hiking trails and provides areas for overnight camping. The Old Time Fiddle Contest and the Sand Castle Competition are held in July.

Recommended restaurants:

The Judges Manor, 193 Memorial Avenue, (604) 248–2544. Continental cuisine in a hertiage house. Moderate to expensive.

Ma Maison, next to the Bayside Inn, (604) 248–5859. Excellent French dishes, nice dining room by the sea. Moderate to expensive.

All accommodations have dining rooms and other amenities:

Tigh-Na-Mara Lodge, off the Trans-Canada, (604) 248–2072. Moderate to expensive.

The Bayside Inn, 240 Dogwood Street, (604) 248–8333. Best in town. Moderate to expensive.

Best Western College Inn, Qualicum Beach, (604) 752–9262. Moderate.

Sand Pebbles Inn, Qualicum Beach, (604) 752–6974. Moderate.

From Parksville you can travel to the western side of the island and the Pacific Rim National Park by taking Highway 4.

Cathedral Grove, on Highway 4 going west to Port Alberni, has splendid stands of tall, 800-year-old Douglas firs and West Coast cedar. Cathedral Grove is within **MacMillan Provincial Park,** which also includes Cameron Lake. A small bathing beach is off the road.

Cameron Lake Resort, via Highway 4, (604) 752–6707, has housekeeping cottages, store, boat rentals. Moderate.

Port Alberni, the largest community in the center of the island, has several motels and restaurants. Port Alberni is famous for salmon fishing and has an annual derby offering a $10,000 first prize for a record catch. From here you can take a passenger ferry—M.V. *Lady Rose*—to Bamfield where the West Coast Trail begins or to Ucluelet at the southern end of Long Beach, a section of the Pacific Rim National Park.

Here are some of the attractions in Port Alberni:

Alberni Valley Museum, 4255 Wallace Street, (604) 723–2181. Open Tuesdays to Sundays. Free. Forestry and Amerindian displays.

Rollin Art Centre, 8th Avenue and Argyle Street, (604) 724–3412. Open Monday through Saturday. Shows local arts and crafts and traveling shows; garden setting.

Martin Mars Water Bombers, via Highway 3, Lakeshore Road, (604) 723–6225; call ahead for visiting information. World's largest fleet of flying water bombers used to fight forest fires. A "must visit" for aviation buffs.

All of the following accommodations have dining rooms, lounges and other amenities:

Timber Lodge Motor Inn, on Highway 2, (604) 723–9415. Moderate.

Hospitality Motor Inn, 3835 Redford Street, (604) 723–8111. Moderate.

Barclay Pacific Hotel, 4277 Stamp Avenue, (604) 724–6556. Moderate.

Ucluelet is a favorite jumping-off point for divers; they can explore shipwrecks around the Broken Group Islands and shake hands with giant octopi, king crabs, and other inhabitants below the surface.

Street addresses for the following accommodations are not necessary, since once you get into town you can't miss them; all have dining rooms unless otherwise noted:

***Canadian Princess* Resort,** (604) 726–7771. Historic steamship permanently moored in harbor, providing cabin accommodations, dining room, and lounge. Moderate.

West Coast Motel, (604) 726–7732. Moderate.

Thorton Motel, (604) 726–7725. Moderate.

Pacific Rim Motel, (604) 726–7728. Housekeeping units. Restaurants nearby. Moderate.

The West Coast Trail, part of the Pacific Rim National Park, runs from **Bamfield** to **Port Renfrew** (72 km./44 mi.). This challenging trek requires a great deal of preparation and physical stamina and takes several days to traverse. There are dangers from wind, rain, and rough seas, as well as on the rugged trail itself. Its rewards are many—opportunities to see surprises in nature, such as the marine, bird, and mammal life of the area, the quickly changing moods of the weather, and the joy of being solitary in a magnificent and dramatic natural environment. In the early part of the century this trail provided a route for shipwreck victims to find their way to the safety of human civilization. When the winds are right, you can almost hear the voices of those lost at sea off this beautiful but hazardous and mystical coast. To reach Bamfield, take the ferry from Port Alberni.

Bamfield accommodations include the following:

Bamfield Trails Motel, (604) 728–3231. Restaurant nearby. Moderate.

Aguilar House, (604) 728–3323. Cottages and family-style, home-cooked meals. Moderate.

Pacific Rim National Park, contact Superintendent, Pacific Rim National Park, Box 280, Ucluelet, B.C. V0R 3A0; (604) 726–7721/726–4212.

Pacific Rim National Park faces the open Pacific and consists of three sections: the West Coast Trail, the Broken Group Islands, and Long Beach. When you stand facing the Pacific here, the entire, immense nation of Canada is to your back. For most visitors to the park, the Long Beach area is the most accessible. You can get to Long Beach by car and easily tour its 34 km./20 mi.) length. By strolling its hard-packed sand surface, you can catch sight of sea lions, seals, schools of porpoises, and pods of orca whales. Within the woodland areas are blacktail deer, bald eagles, and many different species of birds. A great deal of rain falls along this coast, so take along "dirty weather" gear—slickers, warm sweaters, and water shedding hats. The road that goes the length of Long Beach doesn't always hug the shoreline. You'll have to look for access roads to get to the beach. A side road goes down to Quistis Point, and Sea Lion Rocks can be seen not far from the main road. To visit the Broken Group Islands, inhabited by many bald eagles, make arrangements for a boat-for-hire in Ucluelet. Pacific grey whales pass close to shore starting in late February, as they journey from the Bering Sea to the warm waters of Baja California. Be sure to bring binoculars and/or cameras with telephoto lenses regardless of what season you visit.

The main beach areas from Ucluelet to Tofino are Wya Point, Florencia Bay, Quistis Point, Wickaninnish Bay, Sandhill Creek, Long Beach, Cove Box Island, and Schooner Cove. The Willowbrae Trail goes along the entire stretch of this part of the park, giving you access to the intertidal zone. There are dramatic cliffs at Florencia Bay and Green Point. The Rain Forest Trail will take you into thick stands of cedar and hemlock.

Wickaninnish Centre, (604) 726–7333, in the Ucluelet area, is open daily from Easter to Canadian Thanksgiving. Free. Exhibits on the ecology of the park: the sea, land, birds, marine life, mammals, winds, tides, rain. You'll see the Seabird Mural, the Offshore Zone Mural, Explorer 10 Submersible, the *Great Ocean* film, and exhibits on the local Nuu-Chah-Nulth people. There are excellent interpretive programs where guides take you on walks through the different ecological zones and explain what you see. There's an interpretive theater at Green Point.

The two campgrounds in the park are at Green Point for those

185

with vehicles and Schooner Walk-In, which has limited facilities (water, wood, toilets, and so on) for tenters. More basic (frills-free) camping is on the Broken Group Islands at Benson, Hand, Clark, Gibraltor, Gilbert, Willis, and Turret islands. Accommodations and restaurants are available in Tofino and Ucluelet.

Boats can be rented in Tofino and Ucluelet. You must get a license to fish; they are available in Tofino and Ucluelet. Taking shellfish from the beach or waters for eating is usually not advised because of "red tide," dinoflagellates consumed by shellfish which can kill you. Check with local authorities if red tide warnings are up. The water around here is too cold for swimming, except for polar-bear types. There's a supervised swimming area at North Long Beach. This is the right place for other water sports—surfing (great waves here), kayaking, SCUBA diving (lots of unusual marine life to see). Although the powerful rollers coming off the ocean make canoeing dangerous, there are plenty of inlets, coves, bays, lakes, and streams for you to explore.

If you want to get away from civilization but still have a roof over your head, **Tofino** is the place. In addition to exploring the beaches and woodlands of Pacific Rim National Park, you can go deep-sea fishing and bathe in natural hot springs. You might also want to curl up beside a log fire and finally read *War and Peace* while a turbulent surf and fierce winds rage outside. Golf, whale watching trips, and restaurants are here. Visit the **West Coast Maritime Museum** in the center of town, Third and Campbell streets, (604) 725–3327; open June through August. Exhibits on the history of boats and fishing in this area, Nootka artifacts and those from sunken ships.

For accommodations, choose among the following:

Pacific Sands Beach Resort, (604) 725–3322. Moderate.

Crystal Cove Resort, (604) 725–4213. Moderate.

Silver Cloud, (604) 725–3998. Close to beach, courtesy boat, dining room and lounge. Moderate to expensive.

Duffin Cove Motel, (604) 725–3448. Moderate.

From Tofino you can return on Highway 4 to Highway 19, which runs north and south along the eastern side of the island.

Courtenay and **Comox** are sister communities located along Highway 19. In Courtenay see the exhibits at the **District Museum** on 360 Cliffe Avenue, (604) 334–2271, which include Coast Salish big house, logging equipment, and Chinese and Japanese artifacts. Wonderful fishing and birdwatching are in the area, as well as cruises to nearby islands. Swimming and hiking can be enjoyed at Comox Lake. In Comox visit the **Filberg Lodge,** housing the art of H. M. Laing, painter/ornithologist, (604) 339–2715. If you come here in the winter, there's skiiing at Mount Washington and Forbidden Plateau. At Little River you can take the ferry to Powell River, which is on the mainland's "Sunshine Coast," just above the city of Vancouver; sailing time is one hour and fifteen minutes. Call (604) 669–1211 for information.

All of the following hotels have dining rooms and other amenities:

The Westerly, 1590 Cliffe Avenue, (604) 338–7741. Moderate.

The Washington Inn, 1001 Ryan Road, (604) 338–5441. Moderate.

Mt. Washington Condominium Rentals, Mt. Washington Ski Area, (604) 338–1386. A wide variety of housekeeping units. Moderate (weekly rates).

The Alders Beach Resort, in Comox, (604) 337–5322. Housekeeping cottages with fireplaces; on the beach; salmon fishing. Moderate.

If there is a mecca for salmon fishing in B.C., it is **Campbell River.** In August and September Campbell River is "tooth and jowl" with fishers going after the giant "king" and "tye" salmon. There's great fishing throughout the year here—especially for trout in the local lakes—with accommodations ranging from rustic fishing camps to comfortable resorts. Visit the **Campbell River Museum,** depicting native cultures—open May to September, (604) 287–3103—and take the ferry to Quadra Island to see excellent Amerindian arts and crafts at the **Indian (Kwakiutl) Museum** at Quathiaski Cove.

Campbell River also gives access, via Highway 28, to **Elk Falls Provincial Park** and **Strathcona Park,** the largest on Vancouver Island. Strathcona offers superb camping, mountain climbing, and canoeing. Highway 28 continues to **Gold River** on the Muchalat Inlet—Canada's "caving capital," with North America's deepest vertical cave. The *Uchuck III* will take you for a sail down the inlet to the site of an ancient Indian village where Captain Cook visited in 1778. It is said that his first contact with the native peoples of the coast was made here.

You can take a ferry from Campbell River across a narrow part of the Strait of Georgia to **Whale Town,** which is on an island adjacent to the B.C. mainland and its Sunshine Coast (see page 60).

From Whale Town via ferries and Highway 101 to 99, you can get back to the city of Vancouver. This trip is convoluted and time-consuming, but very worthwhile in experiencing the great scenery and seeing the interesting ways people live so far from civilization and yet so close to it.

Accommodations in the area include the following:

Coast Discovery Inn, 975 Tyee Plaza, (604) 287–7155. Rooms with water view, dining room, lounge, and marina. Moderate.

The Island Inn, 1430 South Island Highway, (604) 923–7255. Moderate.

Rod and Reel Resort, (604) 923–5250. Inexpensive.

Bachmairs Bavarian Apartment Hotel, 492 South Island Highway, (604) 923–2848. Moderate.

April Point Lodge and Fishing Resort, on Quadra Island, (604) 285–2222. One of the best fishing resorts in the region. Expensive.

The Austrian Chalet Village, 462 South Island Highway, (604) 923–4231. Moderate.

Coast Gold River Chalet, in Gold River, (604) 283–2244. Moderate.

Peppercorn Trail Motel and R.V. Park, in Gold River, (604) 283–2443. Moderate.

Valley of a Thousand Faces is forty-five miles north of Campbell River, via Highway 19. Open May to September. Admission charged. One thousand faces and 500 birds and wildflowers painted on cedar slabs hanging on trees in a woodland area.

A ferry from Port McNeil will take you to **Alert Bay** on Cormorant Island where you will find the tallest totem pole in the world. Visit the Alert Bay **Library and Museum** on Front Street, (604) 974–5721 (open July and August with exhibits of Kwakiutl and local history) and **St. George's Anglican Chapel.** Also visit **U'Mista Cultural Centre** on Front Street (604) 974–5403; open May to September. This cedar building looks like a Kwakiutl big house and has a potlatch collection.

Accommodations are available at **Haida-Way Motor Inn,** in Port McNeil, (604) 956–3373, and **Oceanview Camping and Trailer Park,** in Alert Bay, (604) 974–5213. Inexpensive.

Port Hardy is the departure point for the famous Inside Passage journey on the B.C. ferry M.V. *Queen of the North* (see page 189).

Port Hardy was named after Vice Admiral Sir Thomas Masterman Hardy of the British Royal Navy. During the Battle of Trafalgar, as captain of H.M.S. *Victory*, Hardy is depicted as holding the dying Lord Nelson in his arms. Once a Hudson's Bay Company post, this is the last major town of any size or importance on the northern tip of Vancouver Island. Kwakiutl arts and crafts are available for sale in this area. You can take a ferry from here through the Inside Passage to Prince Rupert on the B.C. mainland, and then to southern Alaska. While in Port Hardy, visit the following:

Port Hardy Museum and Archives, 7110 Market Street, (604) 949–8143. Open daily during the summer. History of white settlers in the area.

Fort Rupert, Beaver Harbour. Open in the summer. Hudson's Bay Company fort and trading post built in 1849.

Whaling Station, Coal Harbour. Open in the summer. A place where whales were processed for various markets. There's a twelve-foot-high whale-jawbone arch here.

All of the following hotels have restaurants:

Best Western Port Hardy Inn, 9040 Granville Street, (604) 949–8525. Moderate.

Glen Lyon Inn, 6435 Hardy Bay Road, (604) 949–7115. Moderate.

Seagate Hotel, (604) 949–6348. Moderate.

The Inside Passage

A voyage through the magnificent Inside Passage is one of the great trips of the world. It's an adventure that takes you through thickly forested mountains that rise up from the sea and whose walls are almost perpendicular to the surface of the water. The scenery is truly spectacular. As you sail through the Passage, you'll see bald eagles, orca and humpback whales, sea lions, loons, porpoises, and many other kinds of wildlife. The traditional way to travel is on a luxury cruise ship, beginning the voyage in Los Angeles, San Francisco, Seattle, or the city of Vancouver, then sailing between the magnificent islands along the British Columbia coast to destinations in Alaska. This voyage takes several days and can be quite expensive. However, there is another way to experience the Inside Passage that's quicker and less expensive. It also allows you to go ashore to explore remote communities en route and to take your vehicle along: B.C. Ferries operates the M.V. *Queen of the North,* which sails from Port Hardy on the northern tip of Vancouver Island to Prince Rupert, the province's largest city on the upper coast of its mainland. Prince Rupert is just a few miles south of the B.C.–Alaska border. If you are exploring the mainland of B.C., you can sail down the Inside Passage on the M.V. *Queen of the North* from Prince Rupert to Port Hardy. Port Hardy itself is about an eight-hour drive from the city of Victoria. You can also get on Vancouver Island and thence to Port Hardy from the mainland by taking a B.C. ferry from Horseshoe Bay (Metro Vancouver) or Powell River on the Sunshine Coast (north of Metro Vancouver). There are both bus and air service to Port Hardy from Victoria and Vancouver: Air B.C. (800) 663–0522 (toll free in B.C.); bus information, (604) 385–4411 in Victoria, (604) 662–3222 in Vancouver.

Northbound sailings on the M.V. *Queen of the North* begin in the first week of May. The last sailing is in mid-October. Southbound sailings are also on this schedule. For day-cruise reservations, write B.C. Ferries, 1045 Howe Street, Vancouver, B.C., V6Z 2A9, Canada. For information, call (604) 669–1211 (Vancouver); (604) 386–3431 (Victoria); (206) 682–6865 (Seattle, Washington).

The summer day cruise between Port Hardy and Prince Rupert takes fifteen hours one way, most of it during daylight; the length of the voyage is 274 nautical miles. The M.V. *Queen of the North* carries 750 passengers and 157 vehicles. Long-term parking is available at both the Port Hardy and Prince Rupert terminals. The vessel itself offers overnight cabins, buffet dining room with a dance floor, cafeteria, children's playroom, video arcade, bar, parents' room, observation lounge, promenade decks, newsstand, gift shop, and other amenities.

Sailing north en route to Prince Rupert, you will pass Scarlett Point, site of many shipwrecks in the past; Pine Island with its lighthouse that marks the entrance to the Inside Passage; Queen Charlotte Sound, countervailing currents make this area dangerous for inexperienced mariners; Egg Island Lighthouse, marks approaches to Fitz Hugh Sound and Smith and Rivers inlets; Addenbroke Island, site of an unsolved murder (Namu whirlwinds blow in the area with great strength and mountains tower over 1,000 m./3,279 ft.), Pointers Island, the Goldville family manned the lighthouse here for forty-two years. At Dean Channel, the great Canadian explorer Alexander Mackenzie ventured into this area. Ocean Falls is a lumber-producing community, Bella Bella is a prosperous fishing and logging town. Dryad Point marks Lama Passage for ships. Ivory Island is the site of an 1898 lighthouse. Milbanke Sound is an active salmon-fishing area. Many marine tragedies took place in the waters of McInnes Island. Boat Bluff is where the lighthouse keeper wanted a transfer because of the many wolves on the island. Swanson Bay is where paper and shingle mills once operated. In Butedale fishing, lumbering, and mining once thrived. Grenville Channel is considered the most spectacular channel in the Inside Passage, surrounded by mountains that rise 1,500 to 3,000 feet, densely wooded with pine and cedar. Ridley Island is a modern bulk-shipping terminal with goods going to all points around the world.

Prince Rupert to Prince George

The end (or beginning) of the Inside Passage voyage is **Prince Rupert,** named after the cousin of King Charles II of England and Grand Factor of the Hudson's Bay Company. Before the coming of the whites, this area was a gathering place for Tshimshian and Haida peoples. Prince Rupert, with a population of approximately 17,000, is called the "City of Rainbows" and the "Halibut Capital of the World"; its main economic activity is serving as terminal for natural resources (coal, lumber, and wheat) and finished goods being shipped to all parts of the world. The city also has fish canneries and pulp and paper processing factories. During World War II many American military persons departed from here for service in Alaska and in the Pacific.

Located at the mouth of the Skeena River and set in the midst of fjords, islands, and mountains, Prince Rupert is often referred to as the "gateway to the North." Fishing, hunting, sailing, diving, and exploring the interior mainland are some of the activities of this area. The city has a mild climate, with very little snow, mostly rain; gardens thrive here. A few miles north of Prince Rupert are Wales and Pearse islands, which form part of the border between British Columbia and mainland Alaska.

While in Prince Rupert visit the **Museum of Northern British Columbia,** First Avenue and McBride Street, (604) 624–3207. Open mid-May to mid-August. Local history of the settlement and exhibits on Northwest Coast Amerindian cultures.

Prince Rupert Accommodations listed below have dining rooms and other amenities:

Crest Motor Hotel, 222 1st Avenue West, (604) 624–6771. Moderate.

Highliner Inn, 815 1st Avenue West, (604) 624–9060. Moderate.

Prince Rupert Hotel, 2nd Avenue at 6th Street, (604) 624–6711. Moderate.

Rupert Motor Inn, 1st Avenue and 6th Street, (604) 624–9107. Moderate.

Slumber Lodge, 909 3rd Avenue West, (604) 627–1711. Inexpensive to moderate.

From Prince Rupert you can take a B.C. ferry to visit Skidegate and Masset on the **Queen Charlotte Islands**. At Second Beach, Skidegate, Queen Charlotte City, visit the **Queen Charlotte Islands Museum,** (604) 559–4643. Open throughout the year. Exhibits are of Haida totem poles, maritime history, pioneer settlement. The Queen Charlottes are wonderful for camping, exploring, and fishing. If you're up in the province to fish, stay at **Langara Fishing Lodge,** (604) 873–4228 (call collect), on Langara Island off Graham in the Charlottes. They offer a package that includes fine accommodations, meals, equipment, air transportation from the city of Vancouver, the advice of fishing experts, and catch care. Expensive, but a good value for the dedicated fisher.

You can also go from Prince Rupert to Alaska on the Alaska State ferry system. Between May 1 and September 30, Alaska ferries sail four times a week from Prince Rupert to Skagway (Highway 98 connects Skagway with Whitehorse in the Yukon and the Alaska Highway). Service between Ketchikan, Alaska, and Stewart, B.C., gives you access to the magnificent alpine scenery on Highway 37—the Stewart-Cassiar Highway (37 heading north links up with the Alaska Highway; communities are far apart on this highway so have supplies and extra gas). For information on the Yukon, see page 331; for information on Alaska, contact the Alaska Division of Tourism, P.O. Box E-86, Juneau, Alaska 99811, (907) 465–2010.

For more information on ferry service between B.C. and Alaska, contact Alaska Marine Highway System, Pouch R, Juneau, Alaska, 99811; (800) 544–2251.

If you and your vehicle arrive at Prince Rupert by ferry, you have several touring options on the mainland: You can take the Yellowhead Highway 16 (also see page 195) to Prince George (721 km./433 mi.) and, on the same route, continue east to the great national parks of the Canadian Rockies and the cities of Edmonton and Calgary in Alberta. From Prince George you can also head north to Dawson Creek and Fort St. John, which are on the Alaska Highway, and then northwest to the Yukon, the Northwest Territories, and Alaska. Going south from Prince George via Highway 97 to the Trans-Canada takes you to Vancouver.

When you are traveling between Prince Rupert and Prince George it seems as if you are at the northern part of the province. However, you are only in the middle of the province—north of you stretches a vast wilderness with few communities. The hardy people who live in this region farm, harvest timber, fish, trap fur-bearing animals, work in mining, provide services to the local people and to tourists, or work in government agencies. Pioneering is very much alive in these parts. This is also Amerindian country, and you'll have opportunity to experience something of a culture that predates the arrival of Europeans on this continent. This is a region of high mountains, thick forests, wild rivers, and sparkling lakes—home to eagles, moose, coyotes, grizzly and black bears (they are dangerous, so don't feed them and don't get out of the car when they are near). The many recreational opportunities along the way include camping, fishing, trail riding, and wild river rafting. Bring your camera and capture the beauty. Use common sense when traveling on remote stretches, plan your stops, and don't be the cause of a forest fire. Otherwise, it's all there for you to enjoy.

Terrace is a sizeable community about 140 km. (84 mi.) from Prince Rupert. Here you can find accommodations, gas, restaurants, tennis, swimming pools, theaters, and museums. **Terrace Heritage Park,** Kalum Street, (604) 635–2508, open from mid-May to end of August, has several old log buildings—a dance hall, barn, gold miner's cabin, and others—that represent pioneering life. Snow-capped Sleeping Beauty Mountain is a beautiful local landmark. On Copper River Road is a large bed of marine shell fossils. Highway 37 south from town takes you to **Lakelse Provincial Park** and the community of **Kitimat,** site of one of the largest aluminum-processing plants in the world (which you can tour). There's terrific salmon fishing in the Kitimat area. Visit the **Kitimat Centennial Museum,** 293 City Centre, (604) 632–7022, open June through September, which depicts the history of Kitimat's growth from a missionary village to an industrial town.

River Rafting Trips, Wilderland Explorations, Williams Creek Road in Terrace, (604) 635–9642, offer one-day and several-day adventure river trips on the Middle Bulkley, Lower Bulkley, Kitsumkalum, Skeena, Kitselas Canyon, Babine, and other rivers.

These wild river trips offer some of the best, unforgettable thrills in the province.

All of the accommodations listed below have restaurants and other amenities:

Desiderata Inn, 4034 Substation Avenue, (604) 638–0444. Moderate.

Inn of the West, 4620 Lakeside Avenue, (604) 638–8141. Moderate.

Sandman Inn, 4828 Highway 16, West Terrace, (604) 635–9151. Moderate.

At **Kitwanga** you can connect with Highway 37—the Stewart-Cassiar Highway—going north to the Alaska Highway. Kitwanga itself is famous for its number of one-hundred-year-old totem poles.

'Ksan Village, on the bank of the Skeena River, has one of the province's premier exhibitions of Northwest Coast Amerindian arts and crafts. It features seven decorated tribal houses: treasure, carving shed where native artisans create beautiful objects from their ancient heritage; the studio where silkscreen prints are produced by 'Ksan artists; the 'Ksan shop where you can purchase authentic arts and crafts; the firewood house where you can try your hand at craft making; the wolf or feast house where the potlatch feast is described; and the frog house, portraying the ways of a stone age culture. 'Ksan is a few miles north of Hazelton and well worth the diversion from the main route. There is a campground here. No admission charge to the village itself and to open buildings. Open from mid-May to mid-October, (604) 842–5544.

Smithers is a regional transportation center. Ranching, mining, lumbering, and services are the main economic activities here. Visit the **Smithers Art Gallery,** 1425 Main Street, (604) 847–3898, with exhibitions by local artists and traveling shows.

Trail Riding, Mountain View Ranch, Adams Road, (604) 847–5101, leads treks on horseback through the B.C. wilderness for a few hours or several days.

The following accommodations have dining rooms and other amenities:

Hudson Bay Lodge, on Highway 16, (604) 847–4581. Moderate.

Aspen Motor Inn, on Highway 16, (604) 847–2601. Moderate.

Fort Fraser is one of B.C.'s oldest communities. Simon Fraser established a post here for the North West Company, which was later merged with Hudson's Bay Company. In addition, the last spike of the Grand Trunk Pacific Railway, Canada's second transcontinental railroad, was driven in this area in 1914.

Fort St. James makes an interesting side trip via Highway 27 north off 16. Once capital of New Caledonia (the Scottish dream for a free homeland), it is the second-oldest community in B.C., founded by Simon Fraser and John Stuart in 1806. At Fort St. James National Historic Park the old fort has been reconstructed, with summer tours of the grounds, buildings, wharf and other facilities. Call (604) 996–7191 for information. In this area at Necoslie Reserve is the grave of the famous Chief Kwah. There are also memorials to Father Morice, a missionary who served the native people of the area. Our Lady of Good Hope, Father Morice's church, still stands and is open to visitors. Near the church is a propeller memorial to Russ Baker, a bush pilot who founded Canadian Pacific Airlines (CP Air was merged with Pacific Western in 1987 to create Canadian Airlines). A hike up Mount Pope (1,465 m./4,803 ft.) gives great views of the surrounding wild landscape. The annual 25 km. "Pope Peak Run" has a 650 m. (2,131 ft.) uphill section; call (604) 996–8233 for details.

Vanderhoof is a good place to stop for the night en route to Prince George. In June there's an old-style western rodeo; and in July there's the two-day **Vanderhoof International Airshow,** which is the top one of its kind in Canada; call (604) 567–9095 for details. Visit the **Nechako Bird Sanctuary** with its many different species and thousands of Canada geese. In early July, during the Canada Day celebrations, there's a River Days Festival, on the banks of the Nechako. The local museum—(604) 567–2991—displays a photograph of Herbert Vanderhoof, an odd-ball Chicago businessman who gave the town its name.

Accommodations are available at the **Vanderhoof Western Inn,** on 2351 Church Street, (604) 567–2115, which has dining room and lounge. Moderate.

Prince George, British Columbia's third-largest city, is at the junction of the Yellowhead 16 (east/west) and the Alaska 97 (north/south) highways. This city traces its history back more than 200 years ago, when the explorer Alexander Mackenzie came here and noted the location for his employer the North West Company. Simon Fraser came later, and Fort George was developed on the site. At that time, Fort St. James was the capital of this region, and Fort George had a secondary position. Today Prince George is one of the most important communities in B.C. This is a key place for finding accommodations, getting car repairs and extra supplies, and relaxing a bit before heading north on the Alaska Highway, east to the Rockies, or south to the city of Vancouver. **Vanier Hall** has performances by professional entertainers and the **Prince George Playhouse** presents live drama and comedy productions. There are a variety of shops and restaurants in the city.

Fraser-Fort George Regional Museum, 20th Avenue and Gorse Street, (604) 562–1612, is open May to September. Admission charged. Museum of local history; the Fort George Railway—coal-fired steam locomotive and vintage coaches—operates on weekends and holidays.

Prince George Art Gallery, 2820 15th Avenue, (604) 563–6447, is open Tuesday through Saturday. Free. Exhibitions by artists from the region and traveling shows.

All of the following accommodations have dining rooms and other amenities:

Holiday Inn, 444 George Street, (604) 563–0055. Moderate.

Connaught Motor Inn, 1550 Victoria Street, (604) 562–4441. Moderate.

Coast Inn of the North, 770 Brunswick Street, (604) 563–0121. Moderate.

Simon Fraser Inn, 600 Quebec Street, (604) 562–3181. Moderate.

Sandman Inn, 1650 Central Street, (604) 563–8131. Moderate.

Esther's Inn, 1151 Commercial Drive, (604) 562–4131. Moderate.

CHAPTER 7

Touring Alberta
Calgary • Banff • Icefields
Jasper • Edmonton • Lake Louise

Alberta in Brief

One might assume that Alberta was named after Prince Albert, the beloved consort of Queen Victoria. Queen Victoria played such an important role in Canadian history that her name has been liberally applied to cities, mountains, glaciers, and all sorts of things—she was that well loved, except perhaps in Québec. It would then make sense to name a province after Prince Albert, but, in fact, the Marquis of Lorne named the province in honor of Princess Louise Caroline Alberta, the fourth daughter of the "Great Queen." First, as governor-general of Canada he had the authority to do so. Second, the princess was his wife.

Until the coming of white explorers, trappers, mountain men, fur traders, settlers, ranchers, the Northwest Mounted Police, and the transcontinental railroad builders, the people residing on this magnificent landscape of prairies and mountains were Amerindians. These native people have lived here in what they call the "land of four directions" for thousands of years—some say 5,000 years, others close to 8,000; both may be gross underestimations. Today these people are known by the names of Cree, Blackfoot, Blood, Assiniboine, Piegan, Sarcee, Chipewyan.

The first whites—that is, those from Europe or of European ethnic origin—fur traders and missionaries, came into this region of Canada in the early eighteenth century. By and large, relations between the whites and the Amerindians were amicable. The whites wanted to trade and make money, but they were not

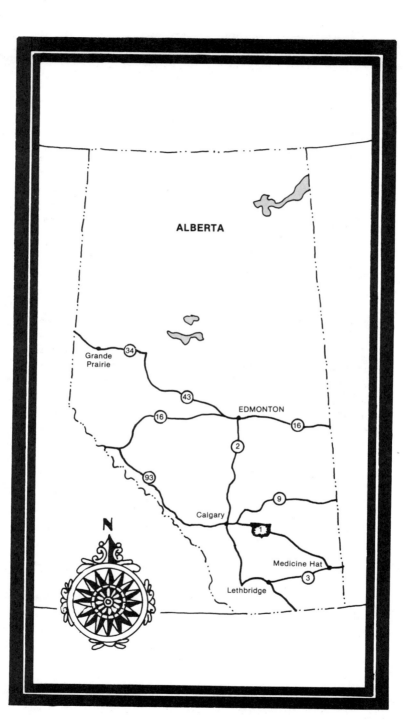

interested in developing the land. Appropriating ancestral lands was not a major issue here in the nineteenth century, as it was below the border, in the United States. However, trouble did come up north from the States in the form of rough-tough whiskey traders who built their own forts in the southern part of the province, exploited the native people, and created so much trouble that in 1873 the Canadian federal government established the Northwest Mounted Police (today's Royal Canadian Mounted Police), under command of such legendary strong men as Colonel Macleod, and sent them to this part of the prairies in 1874 to bring law and order by driving out the whiskey traders, protecting the native peoples, and opening up the area for development and settlement.

Settlement boomed after the tracks of the transcontinental railroad went through in the latter half of the nineteenth century. Villages, towns, and cities sprang up along the railroad as entrepreneurs seeking new ventures and immigrants from many foreign countries hungry for freedom and opportunity in this "promised land" flooded into the area. They turned Alberta into cattle ranches, wheat farms, and mining and forestry operations. Manufacturing, services, education, and culture blossomed, and by 1905 Alberta had grown enough to become a full-fledged province in the Canadian Confederation.

Vast reserves of oil and natural gas were discovered here in the early part of this century, and Alberta found it had more in common with Texas than Ontario or Québec—the oil and cowboy images were essentially the same in both places. The Great Depression of the 1930s hurt, but the post–World War II oil boom made Alberta exceedingly affluent, the envy of the rest of the country, and thousands of Canadians flocked here to get their piece of the pie. By the 1970s, cities such as Calgary and Edmonton were transformed into urban showplaces, and everyone seemed to be doing all right. But good times don't last forever, and Alberta's economy was dampened by the 1980s slide in oil prices. This is a "Can Do!" province, however, and optimism for the future is part of the essence of life here.

Geographically, Alberta is located between 60 degrees latitude north and 49 degrees at the Canadian–U.S. border. This is a large province of 661,000 square kilometers (255,200 square miles), with diverse topography, including many rivers, lakes, streams, and glaciers, and even sections of badlands (arid stretches of land with little or no vegetation), suitable more for trekking than development. In the southern region some of the most important paleontological finds in the world have been made. On its western border is British Columbia; on the east, the province of Saskatchewan. To the north are the Northwest Territories, and to the south is the state of Montana. Although the southern and central regions of the province are prairie farms and cattle ranches, the north is mostly forested wilderness and muskeg. Along the western border run the great Rocky Mountains, with their world-famous national parks and resorts—Banff, Lake Louise, Columbia Icefield, and Jasper.

Alberta winters are long and cold with low humidity and dry, crisp air; its summers are typically warm and pleasant. A great deal of snow falls in mountain areas—a boon for skiers and winter sports enthusiasts. During the winter, chinook winds, warm, dry winds that descend from the eastern slopes of the Rockies and across the prairies, lessen the severity of the cold and make it, at times, quite enjoyable. Because Alberta doesn't experience the amount of heavy rainfall that the Pacific coast does, travelers are assured of many sunny days to enjoy their vacations. On the other hand, when in the high mountains, don't be surprised to see brief periods of heavy snow falling in late June: but at that time of year, the snow quickly melts in the bright sun.

The population of Alberta is about 2.5 million, and the people represent many different ethnic and racial backgrounds—British (the majority), as well as German, Ukrainian, French, and Amerindian. There are more than 1,200 ethno-cultural groups throughout Alberta that are eligible to receive support from the province's cultural and linguistic programs!

Before the building of the transcontinental railroad, the only persons who traveled to this region were those in quest of fortune or the salvation of souls; once the railroad was built, however, close to two-thirds of the Canadian continent was opened up for exploration and/or enjoyment by more ordinary folk. With the development of such resort areas as Banff, Lake Louise, and Jasper, tourism here began in grand style. More and more people came to vacation in Western Canada, particularly the Rockies of Alberta, and they, in turn, told their friends of the natural glories and the highly civilized, plush resorts set in the middle of a wilderness. More and more people came to Alberta, and the tourism infrastructure grew and became more sophisticated to satisfy their demands. Today tourism is Alberta's third-largest economic activity. The diversity of tourism/vacation offerings is vast. You can be joyfully indolent in the midst of some of the most glorious scenery in the world or work your tail off climbing some of the highest mountains in the world. But the "bottom line" here is neither the scenery nor the attractions. It is the quality of the people of Alberta themselves, who welcome you with open arms and genuinely warm smiles, western-style.

Travel Alberta—Tourism Information

Travel Alberta, the provincial government's tourism agency, maintains a year-round toll-free telephone number, which can be used throughout the continental United States and throughout Canada. To request information, brochures, or maps, call (800) 661–8888.

If you are already traveling in the province and need information, dial toll-free (800) 222–6501.

Personal travel counseling is available by phone seven days a week, 8:15 A.M. to 8:00 P.M. mountain standard or mountain daylight time, from mid-May to mid-October. From mid-October to mid-May this service is available Monday to Friday, 8:15 A.M. to 4:30 P.M. mountain standard time. A recorded information tape is played in off-hours.

You will find Travel Alberta information centers at these locations (those open only from mid-May to September are marked with *):

*Walsh, on the Trans-Canada at the Alberta–Saskatchewan border
*Milk River, on Highway 4 near the Alberta–Montana border
*St. Mary, Montana, on U.S. Highway 99
*Fort Macleod, on the Crowsnest Highway 3 and Highway 2
*Sentinel, on the Crowsnest Highway 3 at the Alberta–British Columbia border
Gooseberry, Barrier Lake, and *Banff, on the Trans-Canada
*Golden, British Columbia, on the Trans-Canada
*Westaskiwin Rest Area, on Highway 2
*Oyen, Highway 9
Provost, Highway 13
*Wainwright, Highway 14
*Grand Centre, Highway 55, at the Alberta–Saskatchewan border
*Lloydminster, on the Yellowhead Highway 16, at the Alberta–Saskatchewan border
*Jasper, Highway 16

Specialized Vacation Information

Through Travel Alberta you can receive free of charge these brochures/maps for special vacations in the province (ask for them by name):

Canoe Alberta: Comprehensive information on all aspects of canoeing throughout the waterways of the province; includes an excellent topographical map showing the major canoeing routes and the level of expertise needed.

Alberta Forest Service Recreation Areas: Information and maps.

Alberta Provincial Parks: Details the offerings and facilities of provincial parks. A number of them, such as Writing-on-Stone, Dinosaur, and Dry Island Buffalo Jump, are immensely fascinating.

Alberta Country Vacations: This brochure tells you about farms and ranches that take guests. They are located throughout the province in scenic areas and offer home cooking and living with honest, down-to-earth people. Some places will even let you give a hand with the chores. This is a terrific vacation possibility for families with elementary school–age children.

Alberta Adventure Guide: This booklet lists outfits that offer trail riding on horseback, guest ranch vacations, fly-in fishing trips to the best places in the remotest areas, white-water rafting trips, touring and camping adventures in the subarctic, summer and winter mountaineering trips, and Rocky Mountain bicycle tours. (Hunting is not permitted in Alberta's provincial and national parks.)

Winter Activities Guide: Provides detailed information on downhill skiing and most other winter sports.

Accommodations

The government of Alberta inspects all accommodations in the province for cleanliness, comfort, construction, and maintenance. When traveling, look for the sign or decal "Alberta Approved Accommodation." Not all places of accommodation qualify for this endorsement. If you have any reason to complain, write to Travel Alberta, Industry Liaison, 10025 Jasper Avenue, Edmonton, Alberta T5J 3Z3.

If you need information about accommodations for persons who are disabled, contact Canadian Paraplegic Association by calling (403) 438–5046 or the Southern District Office at (403) 236–5060.

Sales Tax

None on shopping, accommodations, or restaurants—none at all on anything.

Alberta's Extra-Special Attractions

Southern Alberta

Cardston, via Macleod Trail Highway 2. C. O. Card Home and Museum, 337 Main Street. Open mid-June to end of August. Admission charged. Log cabin home that belonged to Charles Ora Card, the leader of forty Mormon families, who emigrated from Utah in 1887. A **Mormon Temple,** 348 3rd Street W., (403) 653–4142, offers tours of its visitor center. Also visit the **Remington Collection,** 339 Main Street, (403) 653–9879; coaches and carriages designed for Queen Victoria and King George IV. Open from June through August. Admission charged.

Crowsnest Pass, via the Crowsnest Highway 3 near British Columbia. Within this municipality are these points of interest: 100-million-year-old volcanic rocks; Sulphur Springs, cold waters used for their curative powers by the native peoples; Frank Slide (90 million tons of rock from Turtle Mountain crashed on the town of Frank in 1903 and killed seventy people); Hillcrest, site of one of Canada's worst coal-mining disasters in 1914; and Leitch Collieries, tours of old coal-mining complex; open mid-May to September. Free.

Cypress Hills Provincial Park, via the Trans-Canada to Highway 41 (at the Alberta–Saskatchewan border in the southeast corner of the province). Located on a plateau that was untouched by ancient glaciers, it supports fourteen species of orchids. Two hundred species of birds nest in the park, and deer, elk, moose, and beaver have habitats here. An archaeological dig found a 7,000-year-old native campground. Fishing, boating, camping, and hiking are all possible here. Rent boats at Cypress Hills.

Dinosaur Provincial Park, via the Trans-Canada and Highway 36 north (watch for signs for other access roads). A World Heritage

Site (designated as such by UNESCO), this important park (15,000 acres) protects one of the most extensive dinosaur fields in the world. Bus tours take you through the park for a small charge; camping facilities available.

Fort Macleod, at the Crowsnest Highway 3 and Macleod Trail Highway 2. A re-creation of the original Northwest Mounted Police fort built in 1874. A mounted police ride is held here daily during the months of July and August. The fort's official season is from mid-May to mid-October. Call (403) 553–4703. Admission charged. A guided walking tour of Fort Macleod takes you through the streets and buildings, describing the way the police, pioneers, and native people lived in this area. These free tours run from May to the end of August. Also within this area, via Highways 2 and 516, is **"Head Smashed In" Buffalo Jump,** a World Heritage Site (designated as such by UNESCO), where for more than 5,600 years the natives drove buffalo over the cliff and to their death. This was a primitive and cruel but nonetheless effective way of obtaining food and materials for clothing and shelter. Open from mid-May to the end of August. Free. Call (403) 553–2030 for more information.

High River, via Highways 2 and 2A. E. P. Ranch was owned by the Duke of Windsor for close to fifty years. It was bought by the Cartwright family in 1962. Visitors are welcome. You can enjoy lunch at the ranch or tea in the afternoon. Reservations are requested; call (403) 395–2418. Open weekdays from May to September.

Lethbridge, via the Crowsnest Highway 3 and Macleod Trail Highway 2, or Highway 4 from the Alberta–Montana border. Lethbridge is a thriving city just south of Calgary and north of the international border. In the 1800s it was a well-known coal-mining town, and American whiskey trading forts were strung out over the landscape in this region. Visit **Fort Whoop-up,** located in Indian Battle Park; call (403) 320–3997. A great battle took place here in 1870 between the Cree and the Blackfoot peoples. Near the park is the **Helen Schuler Coulee Centre,** which has several nature trails. Free. At 8th Avenue S., in Lethbridge, is **Nikka Yuko Japanese Gardens.** Open mid-May to mid-October; (403) 328–3511. Admission charged. The **Sir Alexander Galt Museum,** 1st Street and 5th Avenue, housed in a hospital built in 1891, has displays of local history; (403) 320–3898. Free. The city's crown jewel is the campus of the **University of Lethbridge,** a stunning complex designed by Arthur Erickson. Call (403) 329–2111 for free campus tours.

All of the following accommodations have dining rooms and other amenities:

Lethbridge Lodge Hotel, 320 Scenic Drive, (403) 328–1123. Moderate to expensive.

Sandman Inn, 421 Mayor Magrath Drive, (403) 328–1111. Moderate.

Lodge Motel, Mayor Magrath Drive and 7th Avenue, (403) 329–0100.

Medicine Hat, at the junction of the Trans-Canada and the Crowsnest Highway 3. If you are traveling west in the southern part of the province, Medicine Hat is the first large community you will come into after you pass the Saskatchewan border. From here you can go to Calgary on the Trans-Canada or straight to British Columbia through Lethbridge via the Crowsnest Highway.

In 1907 Rudyard Kipling said that Medicine Hat was a city "with all hell for a basement" in reference to its extensive natural gas field (discovered here in 1883). Today, Medicine Hat—a name that evokes images of the Old West—is a center for manufacturing and the distribution of agricultural products.

The Ataglass Plant, 613 16th Street S.W., is where artisans produce glass sculptures. Open weekdays; (403) 527–2339. Free.

The Medicine Hat Museum and Art Gallery, 1302 Bomford Crescent S.W.; museum, (403) 527–6266; art gallery, (403) 526–0486. The museum has interesting displays on the native peoples and pioneers of its region. Open throughout the year. Admission charged. The gallery presents exhibits of art, natural and ethnological history, and science. Open late May to September.

Most of the following accommodations have dining rooms and other amenities:

Best Western Flamingo Terrace Motel, 722 Redcliff Drive, (403) 527–2268. Moderate.

Circle T Lodge, 950 13th Street S.W., (403) 527–2275. Moderate.

Imperial Motor Inn, 3282 13th Avenue S.W., (403) 527–8811. Moderate.

Medicine Hat Lodge, on the Trans-Canada at Dunmore Road, (403) 529–2222. Moderate.

Travelodge Motor Inn, 1100 Redcliff Drive S.W., (403) 527–2275. Moderate.

Turner Valley, 54 km. (34 mi.) southwest of Calgary via Millarville and Highway 22. Turner Valley was one of Canada's richest oil-producing areas. Visit Dingman #1 and Royalite #4 wells, Christ Church (Anglican, circa 1910), the Fisher Ranch, John Ware cairn (John Ware was a famous black cowboy who had his own ranch in the area), and the Black Diamond Mine.

There are also a number of working ranches in the Turner Valley, and although they are private operations, as you tour the countryside, you may see cattle grazing and ranch hands riding or doing chores.

Writing on Stone Provincial Park, via Highway 2 to Milk River and then east on Highway 501. This park has many ancient petroglyphs (carvings and painting in sandstone cliffs by the native people who lived here). Naturalists conduct guided tours. There's a camping area among large cottonwood trees.

Central Alberta

Camrose, via Highway 21, south of Edmonton. Visit the **Centennial Museum,** 53rd Street and 46th Avenue, (403) 672–3298. Open June to September. Donations accepted. The museum has a pioneer church, an early schoolhouse, a log house, a mill, and a fire hall, all from settlement days.

Cochrane Ranch, on Highway 1A, west of the town of Cochrane. Open mid-May to September, (403) 932–3242. Free. Alberta's first large-scale cattle ranch was established here in 1881. The present site has 150 acres of parkland, lush with wildflowers and nature trails. On a hilltop is the large statue of a cowboy on his horse, who sits frozen in time as a perpetual symbol of Alberta's heritage.

Devon, west of Edmonton on the Yellowhead Highway 16 and then south on Highway 60. Here in Devon are the excellent University of Alberta **Devonian Botanic Gardens.** Open daily; (403) 987–3054. Donations accepted. There are an herb garden, native people's garden, alpine garden, and indoor floral and plant displays. A nature trail leads past a wide variety of plants, including those that grow in the desert.

In the **Drumheller** area, via the Trans-Canada to Highway 9 north, is the exceptional **Tyrrell Museum of Paleontology,** (403) 823–7707. Open from mid-May to September. Free. This new musem is well worth the side trip. The Tyrrell Museum, housed in a stunning modern building, tells the story of millions of years of the earth's history, through dinosaur, fossil, and geological exhibits, some of which interact with the viewer. Named in honor of the explorer and geologist Joseph Burr Tyrrell, who found the first dinosaur bones in this area in 1884, this is a wonderfully educating attraction for all ages.

Hoodoos, via Highway 10 southeast of Drumheller and toward East Coulee. The Hoodoos are huge geological mushroom-shaped rocks, formed by wind and water erosion. To walk among them is like walking on a planet in a science-fiction movie.

Gleichen, via the Trans-Canada east from Calgary to Highway 21. The **Blackfoot Museum** here features historical and cultural artifacts—from the signing of the treaty between Colonel Macleod and Chief Crowfoot, which occurred in the second half of the nineteenth century, to the present day. Open Monday to Friday, (403) 734–3862. Free.

Markerville, via Highway 54. The **Stephansson House** is located 4 km. (2.4 mi.) north of Markerville off Highways 592 or 781. In this pleasant house lived Stephan G. Stephansson (1853–1927), Iceland's national poet. Guided tours take you through this furnished, literary home, in which traditional Icelandic handicrafts are displayed. Open from mid-May to September, (403) 427–5708. Free.

Polar Park, via Highway 14, east of Edmonton. Open daily during the summer, (403) 922–3013. Admission charged. This is a special reserve for cold-climate mammals—more than one hundred species of them—from Canada, Northern China, Russia, and other countries.

West Central Alberta

Rocky Mountain House National Historic Park, via Highway 11. Open May to September, (403) 845–2412. Free. The interpretive center tells the story of fur trading and the forts serving the traders in this region between 1799 and 1875. There are nature trails and a ninety-acre buffalo paddock.

Siffleur, White Goat, and Ghost River wilderness areas, located along the eastern side of Banff and Jasper national parks, are preserved to protect their natural beauty and character. Visitors on foot are welcome. Development, impairment, hunting, fishing, trapping, motor vehicles, horses, and pack animals are prohibited. For more information, call Alberta Recreation and Parks at (403) 427–9429.

Grande Cache, via Highway 40, is the gateway to the

Willmore Wilderness and site of the second leg of the Smoky River's Great Canadian Riverboat Race.

Willmore Wilderness Park, located north of Jasper National Park, permits some activities, such as horseback riding, mountain bikes, hunting, and fishing. Write Willmore Wilderness Park, 11th Floor, Petroleum Plaza, South Tower, Edmonton, Alberta T5K 2C9.

Northern Alberta

Elk Island National Park, via Highway 16, just east of Edmonton. Call (403) 998–3999. A relatively small national park near the city, Elk Island is a tranquil place of meadows, lakes, and forests of aspen and spruce. It is also a preserve for elk and buffalo, which roam free in the southern portion of the park. There are hiking trails throughout the northern portion, an interpretive program, and canoe rentals.

Fort McMurray, via Highway 55 from Athabasca to Highway 63, is in the Athabasca Tar Sands region, a vast area of oil-bearing sand that will become a critical source of energy when other sources of petroleum dry up. The interpretive center explains the technology used to separate oil from sand. It is open from mid-May to September, (403) 743–7166. Free.

Saint Albert, via Highway 33, north of Edmonton, established in 1861, was one of the first independent communities in Western Canada. It was named after Father Albert Lacombe, a legendary missionary and friend of both the native, métis, and pioneering peoples of this region. His chapel, restored to look as it did in the 1860s, stands at St. Vital Avenue and welcomes visitors. Visit the museum here, the religious shrine, and Father Lacombe's crypt. The complex is open from mid-May to September, (403) 459–7663. Free.

Ukrainian Cultural Heritage Village, 50 km. (30 mi.) east of Edmonton on Highway 16. Open mid-May to September, (403) 662–3640. Free. This unique heritage village recreates an early Ukrainian settlement in Alberta. Within the park is Canada's famous Giant Ukrainian Easter Egg—7 m. long, 5.5 m. wide, and weighing 2,270 kg. The egg's decorations tell the story of settlement, religious faith, culture, good harvests, and protection received from the Royal Canadian Mounted Police. During the first weekend in July, the annual **Pysanka Festival** features Ukrainian food, song, dance, and crafts.

Wood Buffalo National Park, located in the extreme north of Alberta and overlapping into the Northwest Territories; access by air or by road from Fort Smith, N.W.T. (no road access from Alberta). Wood Buffalo is very much a wilderness area of great rivers, large lakes, extensive bogs, and thick forests that is home to moose, wolves, lynx, black bears, and eagles. It's a secure nesting ground for the endangered whooping crane as well. The park, which covers an area larger than Switzerland, has areas for camping, boating, and swimming. Park naturalists provide treks, and private outfitters will take you on tours by boat in the summer or dog team in winter. If you want to get away from it all, literally and figuratively, this is the right place. For more information, contact Superintendent, Wood Buffalo National Park, Box 750, Fort Smith, N.W.T., Canada X0E 0P0; (403) 872–2349.

Calgary: A World-Class Olympic Games City

What Makes Calgary Special

During a February 1987 broadcast of ABC's "Good Morning America," Olympic gold medal winner (decathlon in Montréal, 1976) Bruce Jenner gave a preview of Calgary, the host city for the fifteenth international Olympic Games, held in February 1988. Jenner said that he, as many others south of the border, had "misconceptions" about the city and that he had imagined it as a rough frontier town. A picture of an early pioneer settlement flashed across the screen, but then Jenner quickly continued with words and pictures extolling Calgary as a modern, sophisticated city, with skyscrapers rising up from the flatlands of the prairies, which end abruptly at the high walls of the Canadian Rockies. The image of the Old West persists in Calgary—it annually holds the largest rodeo in the world and authentic cattle ranches with real cowboys are but a short drive from city limits—yet Calgary can be best equated with such great cities of Texas as Dallas and Fort Worth. For Calgary is one of Canada's major petroleum centers. The oil companies are here, and this is where the deals are cut. The prosperity brought by the petroleum industry is reflected in the affluence of most of the people who live here, the modern city itself, and the recreational and cultural amenities it offers to residents and visitors alike. In addition to its many attractions, this host city for the 1988 Winter Olympic Games is the southern gateway to the great national parks of the Canadian Rockies: Banff and Jasper, with their awesome beauty, famous resorts, and many recreational opportunities. If you have never been to Calgary, you're in for a few surprises about a former Northwest Mounted Police post that in less than a hundred years has become a booming, gleaming modern city, very much in a class by itself.

A Brief Look at Calgary's History

The native peoples of the Calgary–southern Alberta prairie region can trace their history back 12,000 years. Their civilizations were based on hunting, particularly the buffalo, herds of which were in great abundance. Although explorers and fur traders for the North West Company and Hudson's Bay Company came through this area en route to what is now British Columbia, there were few white habitations as such. In the mid-1800s American buffalo hunters and whiskey traders, however, rode into this area, slaugh- tering these noble animals and exploiting the native people. The whiskey sellers in fact set up a string of their own forts to protect themselves and to discourage competition. Their presence became so objectionable that the Canadian federal government formed the Northwest Mounted Police to drive out these dangerous entrepre- neurs, protect the native tribes, and establish law and order throughout Western Canada. This outstanding military police force not only did their job exceedingly well, but prevented the lawless- ness and brutality that plagued several American states from happening in Canada. In addition, after the Battle of the Little Bighorn, chiefs such as Sitting Bull and their tribes fled to the prairies of Western Canada because they knew they would be protected by the Mounties. Not only did these people find safety, but they also received provisions and land for encampment from the government of Canada.

Calgary itself was founded in 1876 as a Mountie post called Fort Calgary (meaning "Bay Farm" in the Gaelic), located where the Bow and Elbow rivers come together, and in 1883 became an important center in the development of the transcontinental rail- road. Calgary was incorporated as a city in 1893 and continued to grow, serving as a center for processing cattle from local ranches into meat and for handling other agricultural products from area farms. For much of its history, until the boom times of petroleum, Calgary was primarily known as Canada's "cow town," much the same as Fort Worth, Texas. The first oil find was made nearby in Turner Valley in 1914, and the province's first refinery started operating in Calgary in 1923. The early promoters of Calgary as Canada's oil center were R. A. Brown, W. S. Herron, and A. W. Dingman. In 1947 a major reserve of oil was found at Leduc, and from that post–World War II time to just recently, Calgary has been an oil-boom town, and its skyline, affluence, and attractions reflect the money that was made here. During its boom years, thousands of Canadians, from slower-growth areas of the country, flooded into Calgary to seek their fortunes, and most of them prospered. However, when the price of oil sank to distressing lows, the glow faded, and thousands left Calgary for more promising opportunities in other areas, such as coastal British Columbia and southern Ontario. But the impressive characteristic about the more than 625,000 people of Calgary is their "Can Do!" spirit, which is not only seeing them through a time of slower growth but also giving them confidence that with pluck and imagination they'll continue to do well regardless of what happens to the price of oil. The pioneering spirit is not gone in Calgary—it's just been brought up to date.

How to Get to Calgary

By Plane

The following airlines serve Calgary International Airport: Air Canada, Canadian Airlines, Wardair, Continental, Western, Lufthansa, KLM, and United. The airport is approximately 18 km. (11.5 miles) or about thirty minutes from city center Calgary via Barlow Trail, McKnight Blvd, and Centre Street. The terminal itself is modern, with full facilities, including restaurants, duty-free shop, gift shops, lounges, magazine and book shops, and the booths of car rental agencies. There are taxis, limousines, and buses. The airport bus picks up on the half hour to and from the downtown Hotel Palliser.

By Car

From the east: Trans-Canada Highway 1.

From the west: Trans-Canada Highway 1, or the Crowsnest Highway 3 to Macleod Trail Highway 2 north.

From the south: U.S. Interstate Highway 15 to border at Sweetgrass, Montana, and Coutts, Alberta, which merges with Highway 4 north to Lethbridge and then via Macleod Trail Highway 2 north.

From the north (the city of Edmonton): Calgary Trail Highway 2.

By Bus

Greyhound provides service to and from Calgary. It operates from a terminal at 850 16 Street N.W. Call (403) 265–9111 for schedules and fares. The Red Arrow Express provides luxury bus service four times a day between Calgary and Edmonton. Its terminal is at the Westward Inn, 119 12 Avenue S.W., with pickups at Palliser Square; call (403) 269–2884.

By Rail

The VIA Rail station in Calgary is located in city center, 9th Avenue and Centre Street, at the Calgary Tower, with service west to Banff, Lake Louise, and Vancouver, and east to Regina, Winnipeg, Toronto, Ottawa, Montréal, and Québec City. For fare and schedule information, call (800) 555–1212 and ask opererator for VIA Rail toll-free number serving your area code. The toll-free number in Alberta is (800) 665–8630.

How to Get Around Calgary

The city, logically laid out in a grid pattern, is divided into four sections (quandrants), according to points on the compass—N.E., N.W., S.E., and S.W. City streets run north and south; avenues go east and west. Numbering of streets and avenues starts from city center, which is at Centre Street and 9th Avenue, near City Hall. City center's primary landmark is the Calgary Tower (190.9 m./ 626 ft.) at Palliser Square, 9th Avenue and Centre Street. Between 4th and 9th avenues in city center is where much of the city's daily hustle and bustle takes place.

The **Calgary Transit System** provides bus and LRT (Light Rail Transit) service throughout the city and to outlying shopping malls; call (403) 276–7801 for routes and schedules.

City Center Parking is available at metered street spaces and parking garages. Best bet is to park in a garage to avoid fines and towing.

CALGARY

Business and Convention Services

In addition to serving as a base for the petroleum and food processing industries, Calgary is a major financial and tourism center of Western Canada. Because of its many attractions, including the proximity of the great national parks of the Canadian Rockies, the city is also the place where many associations and organizations come to hold their meetings or conventions.

Business Hours: 9:00 A.M. to 5:30 P.M.

Bank Hours: 10:00 A.M. to 3:00 or 4:00 P.M. Some banks are open to 8:00 P.M. Fridays; most banks have extended hours.

Convention Facilities: Calgary Convention Centre, 120 9th Avenue S.E., (403) 261–8800, provides 227,000 square feet of exhibition/meeting space. Jubilee Auditorium, 1415 14th Avenue, (403) 289–5531, has theater seating for 2,700 and banquet space for 1,920. Roundup Centre, at Stampede Park, has 150,000 square feet of exhibition space. In addition, most of the major hotels have meeting facilities of their own.

Convention Information: Calgary Tourist and Convention Bureau, 1300 6th Avenue S.W., (403) 263–8510.

Calgary Stock Exchange: 300 5th Avenue S.W., (403) 262–7791.

Calgary Chamber of Commerce: 517 Centre Street S., (403) 263–7435.

Translating Services: Berlitz Translations, 550 6th Avenue S.W., (403) 265–3850.

Secretarial Services: Irene Clevering Agency, 707 7th Avenue S.W., (403) 269–3080. Most major hotels also provide secretarial assistance.

Newspapers: The *Sun* (morning) and the *Herald* (evening).

Tourist Information

The Calgary Tourist and Convention Bureau is your main source of information on how best to enjoy the city's accommodations, dining, attractions, sports, tours, and entertainment. The main office in city center is at 237 8th Avenue S.W., (403) 263–8510. It also has information booths at the Calgary Tower, Calgary International Airport, on the Trans-Canada Highway east; during the summer on the Trans-Canada west and the Macleod Trail Highway 2 south.

Useful Information

Local holiday: Calgary Day, first Monday in August

Time zone: Mountain

Area code: 403

Sales tax: none in Alberta

Emergencies of all kinds: dial 911

Hospital: Calgary General Hospital, 841 Centre Street E., (403) 268–9625

Ambulance: (403) 261–4000

Police: (403) 268–2311

Advice, information, direction: (403) 268–4656

Sexual Assault Centre: (403) 244–1253

Suicide crisis centre: (403) 252–3111

Distress/drug centre: (403) 266–1605

Post Office: at Eaton's and the Bay department stores in city center

Liquor: sold only at government stores; ask desk clerk or concierge at your hotel for closest location.

Foreign money exchange: The Royal Bank, 339 8th Avenue S.W., (403) 268–3910, and at other city banks.

Taxis: Prestige (403) 250–5911; Checker Cabs (403) 272–1111; Associated Cabs (403) 276–5312.

Entertainment and sports tickets: Bass outlets in the Bay department store, (403) 261–0300; Calgary Centre for the Performing Arts, (403) 266–8888.

Houses of worship:
Anglican Cathedral, 602 1st Street S.E.
United Church, 131 7th Avenue S.W.
Baptist Church, 1311 4th Street S.W.
Presbyterian Church, 1009 15th Avenue S.W.
Lutheran Church, 11,550 6th Avenue S.W.

Roman Catholic Church, 211 6th Avenue S.W.

Jewish Temple, 103 17th Avenue

Road emergency service: (403) 246–0606 (24 hours)

Road condition reporting service: (403) 246–5853 (24 hours)

Extra-Special Events

The Annual Calgary Exhibition and Stampede, ten days at the beginning of July. Call (403) 261–0101 or toll-free (800) 661–1260 for information. The Stampede takes place at Exhibition Grounds/ Stampede Park, just south of city center via Macleod Trail Highway 2. If you are a rodeo buff or have never been to one, the Calgary Stampede is the biggest and best in the world. But the rodeo is just part of this old-time western extravaganza:

Three-hour rodeo show every afternoon features saddle bronc, bareback, bull riding, steer wrestling, wild-horse riding, Indian buffalo riding. The Calgary Stampede made championship chuck-wagon racing the biggest thrill at rodeos. Next to Calgary-style chuck-wagon racing, the old Romans and their chariots seem feeble.

At night singers, dancers, comedians, and acrobats entertain you at the Grandstand Spectacular. A Vegas-style revue, top star performers, and a spectacular display of fireworks are among the highlights.

You can visit the agricultural displays and purebred livestock shows; take midway rides; eat everything from fast food to broiled Alberta steaks or ethnic dishes; compete in the annual $20,000 Blackjack Tournament; tour an Amerindian prairie village and see people demonstrating skills used in pioneering days; and watch the blows and hammers going at the World Championship Blacksmith Competition.

Calgary 1988 Winter Olympic Games, February 13 to 28. Call (403) 270–6088 for ticket information; tickets can be charged to VISA, which has been granted exclusive rights by the organizing committee to provide this service.

• Ice hockey and figure skating at the Olympic Saddledome, located in the city center (17,000 person capacity).

If you want to experience a wild west, rip-snorting rodeo on an extravagant ▶ scale, the Calgary Stampede is tops in North America.

- Second venue for ice hockey and figure skating at the Stampede Corral, located near the city center (6,500 person capacity).
- Speed skating at the enclosed Olympic Oval on the grounds of the University of Calgary (4,000 person capacity).
- Opening and closing ceremonies at McMahon Stadium, located at the University of Calgary (50,000 person capacity).
- Ski jumping, nordic combined, bobsled, luge, and free-style events at Canada Olympic Park, about fifteen minutes from city center.
- All alpine skiing competitions in Nakiska at Mount Allan, about fifty minutes west of the city in Kananaskis country.
- Cross-country skiing, nordic combined, and biathlon events held at Canmore Nordic Centre, located fifty-five minutes west of Calgary and near Banff.
- Olympic Plaza, located in city center adjacent to City Hall, is the venue for the medal award ceremonies and various cultural events held during the Winter Olympic Games.
- Olympic Village I and II: I is the main athletes' village at the University of Calgary campus; II is near the Canmore Nordic Centre.
- Father David Bauer Olympic Arena (formerly the Foothills Arena) is where Canada's national hockey team will practice and demonstrations of speed skating will be held. This venue is named in honor of Father David Bauer, who was coach of Canada's first national hockey team for the 1964 Winter Olympic Games in Innsbruck, Austria.

If you are unable to come to Calgary's 1988 Winter Olympic Games, note that all of the sporting facilities will remain thereafter for use by residents and visitors.

Touring Service

Brewster Transportation and Tours, Calgary, (403) 276–0766; Banff, (403) 762–2241; Jasper, (403) 852–3332. Brewster provides tours of the city of Calgary, Banff and Jasper national parks, Lake Louise, the Athabasca Glacier, helicopter sightseeing, glacier touring on a Snowcoach, gondola rides up steep mountains, and boat trips on Maligne Lake and Lake Minnewanka.

Attractions

Glenbow Museum, 130 9th Avenue, in city center, (403) 264–8300. Closed Mondays. Admission charged. The Glenbow, housed in modern facilities, is one of the best Western museums in North America. Here you can see exceptional exhibitions on the tribes of the Canadian Prairies and those of the American Plains (actually, for the native people themselves theirs was a "land of four directions" without the white man's borders and topographical designations). There are exhibits telling the story of the fur trappers, the explorers, the missionaries, the Northwest Mounted Police, Louis Riel and the métis people, and the building of the transcontinental railroad. If you have time to visit only one attraction in Calgary, see the Glenbow Museum.

Calgary Tower, 101 9th Avenue S.W., in city center, (403) 266–7171. Open daily. Admission charged. The Calgary Tower is the city's landmark. At 190.9 m. (626 ft.) high, it offers a spectacular view of the city and surrounding countryside, including the snow-capped Canadian Rockies themselves, from its top observation deck. The tower has a revolving restaurant where you can see the views while you dine on western or continental cuisines. Call the Panorama Room for reservations, (403) 266–7171.

Centennial Planetarium and Pleiades Theatre, 11th Street at 7th Avenue S.W., (403) 294–1141. Open daily throughout the summer. Admission charged. This is an excellent facility for exploring the wonders of the cosmos: You're a space traveler in the Star Chamber visiting destinations throughout the heavens. A Rock and Roll Laser Show entertains. There are exhibits of space shuttle tiles and the Millarville Meteorite.

Fort Calgary, 750 9th Avenue S.E., (403) 290–1875. Open throughout the year. Admission charged. Here is where the original Fort Calgary (1875) stood and where the city began. Exhibits depict the early history of the city and the role the Northwest Mounted Police played in facilitating and securing civilization in this part of the country. Displays show clothing and tools used by Calgary's early pioneers. From the fort you can walk down to the spot where the Bow and Elbow rivers converge, a nice area for a picnic or a rest in the sun.

Heritage Park, 1900 Heritage Drive S.W., (403) 255–1182. Open daily throughout the summer. Admission charged. One of Canada's most popular heritage parks, this full-scale prairie town is restored as it was in the early 1900s. There are over one hundred buildings, most of which have demonstrations and/or guides. There are antique railroad cars and a train trip through sixty-six acres of the park, or you can ride aboard a vintage stern-wheeler as it plies over Glenmore Lake.

Calgary Zoo, Botanical Gardens, and Historic Park, on St. George's Island near city center, (403) 262–8144. Admission charged. This park contains life-sized exhibits of dinosaurs and other prehistoric animals from the Mesozoic era, an aviary of exotic birds, and beautiful floral displays. The zoo has one of the largest lowland gorilla populations in North America, as well as thousands of other animals, both from foreign lands and from the Western Canadian wilderness.

Devian Gardens, on the fourth level of Toronto Dominion Square, (403) 269–2531. Open daily. Free. Calgary has created two and a half acres of exquisite gardens, waterfalls, and reflecting pools—all enclosed within a modern city-center office complex. Escape winter winds or broiling summer sun in climate-controlled Devian Gardens, a special world of beauty, tranquility, and comfort. On a mini-scale these enclosed gardens, which are connected by enclosed passageways that lead to all parts of city center, demonstrate that it is possible to create a pleasant year-round environment in climates far more rugged than Calgary's. Perhaps the future of northern Canada has its roots here.

Spruce Meadows Equestrian Ranch, via Macleod Trail Highway 2 to Highway 22X west. Open daily. Free. Spruce Meadows is Western Canada's premier equestrian facility, not to be missed if you love any aspect of this multifaceted sport. You can see riders practicing their jumps on magnificent Hanoverians, which are bred at this ranch, or attend a competition.

Every year a series of major equestrian competitions takes place at Spruce Meadows. For example, in early June 1985 the Spruce Meadows National, one of North America's top jumping competitions, was held; The Texaco Invitational attracted leading Canadian and U.S. riders; and The Spruce Meadows Masters drew the finest riders from around the world.

Calaway Park, 9.6 km. (6 mi.) west of Calgary on the Trans-Canada, (403) 240–3822. Open from mid-May to mid-October. Admission charged. Calaway is Calgary's big theme park. Fifteen exciting rides, attractions, live entertainment, food and gift shops, games, and a nice park environment provide fun and relaxation.

Calgary Aerospace Museum, Hangar 10, 64 McTavish Place North, (403) 250–3752. Open Monday through Friday. Free. Here you can see aircraft being restored and displays of engines and aviation memorabilia.

Royal Canadian Regimental Museum (Lord Strathcona's Horse), 4225 Crowchild Trail S.W., Canadian Forces Base Currie Barracks, (403) 242–6610. Open Monday through Friday. Free. Located at a military base; you'll be asked for identification at the gate. Artifacts from cavalry and armored history of the regiment—uniforms, weapons, and a collection of fascinating photos.

Nickle Art Museum, on the University of Calgary campus, main entrance is from 32nd Avenue N.W., (403) 220–7234. Open throughout the year; closed Monday and Tuesday. Free. This museum has a fine collection of ancient coins and exhibitions of contemporary and historical art.

Photography Gallery, 1717 7th Street, (403) 244–4816. Open Tuesday through Friday. Free. Exhibitions of works by local, national, and international photographers.

Princess Patricia's Canadian Light Infantry Regimental Museum, 4225 Crowchild Trail S.W., Canadian Forces Base Currie Barracks, (403) 240–7322. Closed Saturdays and holidays. Free. Exhibits depict the history of this distinguished Canadian military regiment.

Sarcee People's Museum, 3700 Anderson Road S.W. Open Monday through Friday. Free. Displays on the life and culture of the Sarcee people include artifacts, a model teepee, and clothing.

Stockmen's Memorial Foundation, Suite 126, 2116 27th Avenue N.E., (403) 240–7529. Open Monday through Friday. Free. A museum preserving the heritage of ranching and the cattle industry; includes an art gallery.

Accommodations

Calgary has approximately 8,000 hotel and motel rooms. About 2,500 of these are in city center. The following hotels and motels are recommended choices when staying overnight in Calgary:

Leading Hotels

Hotel Palliser, a Canadian Pacific hotel, 133 9th Avenue S.W., (403) 262–1234. Superior accommodations considered by many travelers to be Calgary's finest. Restored to a new grandeur. Central to businesses and attractions in city center; a Calgary landmark in itself. Some rooms with mini-bars, a nonsmokers' floor, exercise facilities. Rimrock Dining Room with large fireplace; Oak

Room Lounge with entertainment; a deli and boulevard café. Expensive.

The Westin Hotel, 320 4th Avenue S.W., (403) 266–1611. Superior accommodations. Top notch in most respects; many travelers consider the Westin to be Calgary's best. Suites, swimming pool, and many services and amenities. Expensive.

Chateau Airport, a Canadian Pacific hotel, within the Calgary International Airport terminal complex, 2001 Airport Road N.E., (403) 291–2600. An excellent quality accommodation with top quality services and amenities. Expensive.

Delta Bow Valley, 209 4th Avenue S.E., (403) 266–1980. City center location. Conservatory Dining Room, two lounges, indoor pool, whirlpool, saunas, and exercise room. Expensive.

Skyline Calgary, 110 9th Avenue S.E., (403) 266–7331; toll-free (800) 268–1332. Excellent accommodations; twenty-four-hour room service; sun deck; swimming pool. Centrally located; limousine service; dining at the Trader's Room and at the Wheatsheaf Café. Expensive.

International Hotel, 220 4th Avenue S.W., (403) 265–9600. An executive-suite hotel (two rooms); swimming pool and other amenities. Moderate to expensive.

Sandman Hotel, 888 7th Avenue S.W., (403) 237–8628. Excellent accommodations; nightclub; swimming pool; many other amenties. Expensive.

Holiday Inn Downtown, 708 8th Avenue S.W., (403) 263–7600. Excellent accommodations; rooms with mini-bars; swimming pool, many other amenities. Moderate.

Other Fine Places to Stay

All of the places listed below offer fine accommodations and many amenities (such as swimming pools, dining rooms, lounges) and some have nightclubs.

Best Western Hospitality Inn, 135 Southland Drive S.E., (403) 278–5050. Moderate.

Best Western Village Park Inn, 1804 Crowchild Trail N.W., (403) 289–0241. Moderate.

Blackfoot Inn, 5940 Blackfoot Trail S.E., (403) 252–2253. Moderate.

Calgary Centre Inn, 202 4th Avenue S.W., in city center, (403) 262–7091. Moderate.

Carriage House Inn, 9030 Macleod Trail S., south of city center, (403) 253–1101. Moderate.

Crossroads Motor Inn, 2120 16th Avenue N.E., (403) 291–4666. Moderate.

Glenmore Inn, 2720 Glenmore Trail S.E., (403) 279–8611. Moderate.

Highlander Motor Hotel, 1818 16th Avenue N.W., (403) 289–1961. Moderate.

Holiday Inn Macleod Trail, 4206 Macleod Trail S., (403) 287–2700. Moderate.

Marlborough Inn, 1316 33rd Street N.E., (403) 248–8888. Moderate.

Port O'Call Inn, 1935 McKnight Blvd. N.E., (403) 291–4600. Moderate.

Tradewinds Hotel, 6606 Macleod Trail S.W., (403) 252–2211. Moderate.

Westward Inn, 119 12th Avenue S.W., (403) 266–4611. Moderate.

University of Calgary, 2500 University Drive N.W. Open during the summer months when the resident population is on vacation, (403) 220–5051. Pleasant accommodations in a campus setting. An excellent value for families, couples, or the single traveler. Inexpensive.

Dining

Calgary has a wide assortment of restaurants serving all kinds of foods in every price category. Below are a few of the best in the city:

Hy's, 316 4th Avenue S.W., (403) 263–2222. Well known in Western Canada for excellent beef dishes in an elegant setting. A fine selection of wines. Expensive.

Traders, at the Skyline Hotel, 9th Avenue and Centre Street, (403) 266–7331. One of the better restaurants in the city; noted for its excellent cuisine, service, and atmosphere. Expensive.

La Chaumière, 121 17th Avenue S.E., (403) 228–5690. French cuisine at its best in an elegant environment. Expensive.

Franzl's Gasthaus, 2417 4th Street S.W., (403) 266–6288. All kinds of schnitzels and other southern German dishes; music and dancing to keep spirits high. Moderate.

Owl's Nest, at the Westin Hotel, 320 4th Avenue S.W., (403)

266–1611. Beautiful interior. High-class Old World service. Continental cuisine and dishes made with Western Canadian prime ingredients—salmon and Alberta beef. Expensive.

Panorama Room, Calgary Tower, 9th Avenue and Centre Street S.W., (403) 266–7171. Revolving restaurant on top of the tower, offering great views and Alberta beef dishes. Moderate to expensive.

Entertainment

The focus of Calgary's cultural life is the new Centre for Performing Arts, in city center. It is home for the Calgary Philharmonic Orchestra and Theatre Calgary. This complex consists of the Jack Singer Concert Hall, the Max Bell Theatre, and the Martha Cohen Theatre. For information on events and tickets, call (403) 264–8840.

For a complete listing of events, places of entertainment, and restaurants, pick up a copy of *Calgary* magazine at the newstand. It will give you the most current information and reviews.

The following clubs offer entertainment, food, and drink:

Manhattan's, 611 11th Avenue S.W., (403) 294–1828; nightclub.

Stage West, 727 42nd Avenue S.E., (403) 243–6642; dinner theater.

The Unicorn, 304 8th Avenue S.W., (403) 233–2666; resembles an Irish pub; meals also served.

Glenmore Dinner Theatre, 2720 Glenmore Trail S.E., (403) 236–2060; fine place for dinner and live shows.

Shopping

City center Calgary, between 9th and 4th avenues, used to be the main shopping district. Now you need to take the LRT or bus to shopping malls where you will find the large department stores—Eaton's, The Bay—and a wide assortment of shops, from those selling local arts and crafts to high-fashion boutiques. If you would

Just over a hundred years ago, Calgary was a small Mountie post on the ▶ prairies not far from the Rockies. There were few humans in this southern area of Alberta, except for Indian bands, roaming mountain men and whiskey traders, and the Mounties. Today Calgary is Dallas and Houston rolled into one sharp-focused city, Western Canadian style.

like to deck yourself out in the cowboy look, you can buy what you need at Western Outfitters, 128 8th Avenue, (403) 266–3656.

Professional Sports

Calgary Flames of the NHL, call (403) 261–0475 for ticket information and home schedule. The Flames play at the Calgary Olympic Saddledrome in Stampede Park.

Calgary Stampeders of the Canadian Football League, call (403) 289–0258 for ticket and schedule information. The Stampeders play at McMahon Stadium, adjacent to the University of Calgary.

Calgary Cannons' Professional Baseball Club, call (403) 233–2255 for ticket and schedule information. The Cannons are a farm club for the Seattle Mariners and play at Foothills Stadium.

Recreation

During the winter, the weather in Calgary can get so brutal that you need several layers of long johns, a set of ear muffs, thick mittens, and a woolen face mask just to venture out. In response to this, the people of Calgary created indoor environments that simulate summertime at the beach. The many leisure centers throughout the city provide warm indoor beaches, swimming, water slides, even bodysurfing, which is possible because of machine-made waves that rival those on a real ocean beach. In additon, these centers contain indoor rinks, weight lifting areas, racquet courts, restaurants, and many other facilities. Check for family fun at the places listed below.

Family Leisure Centers

Family Leisure Centre, 11150 Bonaventure Drive S.E., (403) 271–5906.

Southland Leisure Centre, 19th Street and Southland Drive S.W., (403) 251–3505.

Village Square Leisure Centre, 2623 56th Street, (403) 280–9714.

Lindsay Park Sports Centre, 225 Macleod Trail Highway 2 south, (403) 233–8619. Open throughout the year. Admission charged. This family sports facility has an Olympic-sized swimming pool, diving pools, a 200 m. (655 ft.) running track, and a fully equipped gym. There is professional instruction for all ages and levels of expertise, including tots and athletes who are disabled.

Swimming
City of Calgary Pools, call (403) 269–2531. The city has twelve indoor and ten outdoor swimming pools for the public to use.

Tennis
Call (403) 269–2531 for information on the use of public courts.

Golf
Call the Calgary Tourist and Convention Bureau at (403) 263–8510 for information on playing at a municipal golf course (there are six in the city).

The Canadian Rockies

Waterton Lakes National Park

Waterton Lakes National Park can be reached via highways 2 and 6 south from Calgary; Highway 5 west from Lethbridge; or U.S. Highway 17 from Great Falls, Montana, to Alberta Highway 5. For more information, contact Superintendent, Waterton Lakes National Park, Waterton Lakes, Alberta T0K 2M0; (403) 859–2262.

Located at the extreme southwestern corner of the province on the Alberta–Montana border, Waterton Lakes National Park and Glacier National Park (to the south in Montana) were joined to form Waterton-Glacier International Peace Park, the first of its kind in the world. Watertown itself has been described as the place "where the mountains meet the prairies." The transition between these two topographical zones is abrupt here, as there are no foothills as such (the same can be said for much of the length of the Rockies in Alberta). Ancient glaciers, however, did carve out lakes and valleys, leaving moraines, eskers, and kames. Upper Waterton Lake, the park's deepest (148 m./485 ft.), juts from Alberta into Montana, crossing the international border. Some unique marine species live here—deepwater sculpin, pygmy whitefish, and opossum shrimp. The park also has zones of shortgrass prairie, aspen groves, and alpine meadows lush with wildflowers. There are many species of birds and waterfowl, elk, mule deer, bighorn sheep, black bears, and grizzly bears. The Waterton-Glacier area supports many grizzlies. If you are hiking or camping, please heed the park's warnings and precautions. People have been severely mauled and killed.

The park has 175 km. (105 mi.) of trails for your hiking enjoyment, which lead to lakes, canyons, waterfalls, forested valleys, and alpine meadows. Scenic auto drives, such as the Promenade Akamina Parkway, wind throughout the park. Cruise boats on Upper Waterton Lake provide tours. You can also tour the park on bus or horseback. The park offers an interpretative program and camping facilities at Crandell Mountain and Belly River. There are boat rentals and fishing (get permit at Cameron Lake). An eighteen-hole public golf course, surrounded by magnificent scenery, is near the park.

Accommodations

Prince of Wales Hotel, advance reservations are a must, (406) 226–5551. Whenever pictures of Waterton Lakes National Park are published, the baronial structure of the Prince of Wales is in the foreground, sitting on a bluff overlooking a sparkling lake and surrounded by snow-capped mountains. The building and the setting are superior, although the hotel lacks some of the amenities typical of other equally expensive places. Expensive.

Aspen-Windflower Motels, (403) 859–2255. Excellent accommodations with many amenities. Expensive.

Bayshore Inn, (403) 859–2211. Excellent accommodations with many amenities. Expensive.

Banff–Lake Louise Area

Banff National Park

Banff National Park can be reached from the west (Vancouver) and from the east (Banff is 130 km.[78 mi.] west of Calgary or about a ninety-minute drive) via the Trans-Canada Highway 1; also via Highway 93 from southern B.C. and through the Kootenay region; and from Edmonton via the Yellowhead Highway 16 west and then on Highway 93 south; also from Edmonton via Highway 2 south to 11 west to 93. For more information, contact Superintendent, Banff National Park, Box 900, Banff, Alberta T0L 0C0; (403) 762–3324; and Banff/Lake Louise Chamber of Commerce, Box 1298, Banff, Alberta T0L 0C0; (403) 762–4646/762–3777.

Banff is Canada's most popular national park, not just for its natural beauty but also for its many recreational and cultural offerings throughout the four seasons. The Banff and Lake Louise area was originally developed as a prime resort and recreational area by the Canadian Pacific Railroad, which built the transcontinental railroad in the 1800s. The great resorts of Banff Springs Hotel and Château Lake Louise, among the world's most famous, have attracted the rich, the famous, and the ordinary for generations. The park itself is in the heart of the Canadian Rockies, with awesome, snow-capped mountains in every direction. The mountain scenery is accented by the ultramarine blue waters of lakes, the tan-greenish rush of streams and rivers, and the dark Prussian blue-green shades of deep evergreen forests—habitats for grizzlies, elk, bighorn sheep, and coyotes. Because the mountains often pierce through fast-moving clouds and the temperature varies so greatly at different levels of elevation, the weather is very changeable. One minute it is a marvelous sunny day, perfect in every way; the next, fierce winds blow and rain or hail beats down. However, the effects are stunning: rainbows, mountains emerging from and disappearing into clouds, dark blotches highlighted and revealed in detail as stands of aspen and evergreen. This is a place where you need a loaded camera close at hand at all times. Perhaps one of the most inspiring experiences of the park is to go off by yourself—even if it's off the road a bit—and listen to the wind and view the mountains and clouds. Whether you are just one of the folk or a "big shot," you'll be humbled and elevated in spirit at the same time.

One of the most-photographed scenes in the park is Mount Rundle with Vermilion Lake in the foreground, at the town of Banff; the best view is from the Trans-Canada. The town of Banff is the major tourism center in the park, offering accommodations, dining, shopping, and entertainment.

North of the town, via the Trans-Canada, is Lake Louise, named in honor of Princess Louise Caroline Alberta, fourth daughter of Queen Victoria and wife of the Marquis of Lorne, governor-general of Canada. (The province of Alberta was named in her honor also. Watch for the side road off the Trans-Canada, which takes you through the village, into higher country, and then to the lake itself. VIA Rail trains stop at Lake Louise station. What has made Lake Louise famous for generations is the ethereal atmosphere here: the clear waters, the high surrounding mountains, the Victoria Glacier and Mount Victoria at the western end of the lake, and the hotel Château Lake Louise. The best way to describe Lake Louise is that it is at the bottom of a deep bowl with steep, beautifully decorated, fluted sides. A trip to the Canadian Rockies would not be complete without a visit to Lake Louise; for some it is a pilgrimage of sorts.

Banff National Park has 1,300 km. (780 mi.) of trails, which encourage you to get into the beautiful countryside on foot or horseback, or by rock climbing or cross-country skiing. A number of interpretive programs are given by professional naturalists and guides. The park has thirteen campgrounds (2,323 campsites for those with vehicles).

The Bow Valley Parkway (part of the Trans-Canada Highway) gives access to all attractions and to the town of Banff and Lake Louise. Just north of Lake Louise, as the Trans-Canada turns west toward Vancouver, Icefield Parkway (Highway 93) continues on north to Columbia Icefields, Jasper National Park, and the resort town of Jasper.

Sports and Recreation

Downhill Skiing

These three ski areas are known throughout the world as being among the best in North America:

Mount Norquay, ten minutes from downtown Banff, overlooking the Bow Valley. Well known for challenging, advanced skiing and for novice runs. Season from mid-November to early April. Highest elevation, 2,135 m./7,000 ft.; vertical rise, 396 m./1,300 ft.; longest run, 2.5 km./1.6 mi.; skiing terrain, 50 percent expert and 35 percent novice; lift capacity, 5,100 people per hour; snowmaking, 30 percent terrain coverage. Norquay offers ski schools for alpine beginners as well as lessons in such specialties as telemarking. Rental equipment is available. For more information, contact Mount Norquay, Box 1258, Banff, Alberta T0L 0C0; (403) 762–4421; Calgary snow phone (403) 253–3383.

Sunshine Village, located 22 km. (13.2 mi.) from the town of Banff and at the tree line in a high alpine bowl, is noted for an abundance of powder and the longest ski season in the region—from mid-November to mid-June. Highest elevation, 2,730 m./8,954 ft.; vertical rise, 1,070 m./3,514 ft.; longest run, 8 km./5 mi.; skiing terrain, 60 percent intermediate, 20 percent expert and 20 percent novice; lift capacity, 13,700 people per hour; annual snowfall, 1,000 cm./400 in. A ski school, cross-country skiing, mountain tours, equipment rentals, and restaurants are all here. For more information, write Sunshine Village, Box 1510 Banff, Alberta T0L 0C0; or call (403) 762–4000, toll-free Canada and western United

States (800) 661–1363; Calgary snow report (403) 235–SNOW, Edmonton snow report (403) 481–SNOW.

Lake Louise, via the Trans-Canada Highway, is famous for its beauty, and many travelers have said that it is the most beautiful part of the Canadian Rockies. The ski area has facilities on two mountains—Mount Whitehorn and Mount Lapalian. There are open slopes, bowls, mogul fields, gladed timberline, and a great deal of delightful powder. The season runs from November to early May. Highest elevation, 2,636 m./8,650 ft.; vertical rise, 991 m./ 3,250 ft.; longest run, 8 km./5 mi.; skiing terrain, 45 percent intermediate, 30 percent expert, and 25 percent novice; lift capacity, 8,830 people per hour; annual snowfall, 356 cm./140 in. There are a ski school for various levels of expertise and specialties, equipment rentals, mountain tours, cross-country skiing, ice-skating, and sleigh rides.

Helicopter Hiking/Skiing

Helicopter hiking/skiing has become a popular sport in the Canadian Rockies. A helicopter takes you to the top of a mountain and drops you off with a top-notch guide and supplies. You hike or ski down through a pristine wilderness that seems to belong to you alone. The following companies provide helicopter skiing in the Canadian Rockies, both in the mountains of Alberta and those nearby in British Columbia (also consult your travel agent; several package tour operators do provide helicopter skiing/hiking vacations in the Canadian Rockies):

Canadian Mountain Holidays, (403) 762–4531.
Cariboo Helicopter Skiing, (403) 762–5548.
Mountain Canada, (403) 762–5383.
Banff Helisports, (403) 678–4888.
Assiniboine Helicopters, (403) 762–5459.

Mountaineering

The Canadian School of Mountaineering, at Haus Alpenrose Lodge, Box 723, Canmore, Alberta T0L 0M0; (403) 678–4134. The CSM was founded by Ottmar Setzer, member of the Association of Canadian Mountain Guides and the International Guides Association. Setzer spent his youth in Gamisch-Partenkirchen, Bavaria, where he began his career in mountaineering. Courses are offered in all phases of mountaineering, cross-country skiing, ski touring, telemark skiing, glacier touring, and waterfall ice climbing. Accommodations are in a Bavarian-style lodge for nonsmokers. Located near the Olympic Games cross-country and downhill events, it gives access to Banff, Kootenay, Jasper, and Yoho national parks, also to Kananaskis and Mount Assiniboine provincial parks.

Banff Alpine Guides, Box 1025, Banff, Alberta T0L 0C0; (403) 762–2991. Operates a school and conducts guided hikes in the Canadian Rockies.

The Lac des Arcs Climbing School, 1116 19th Avenue N.W., Calgary, Alberta T2M 0Z9; (403) 289–6795. Courses in rock climbing, mountaineering, bush survival, river kayaking, mountain rescue.

Wild River Rafting

Hunter Valley Recreational Enterprises, Box 1620, Canmore, Alberta T0L 0M0; (403) 678–2000. White-water rafting trips, rafting and trekking packages, canoe and kayak clinics.

Mad Rafter River Tours, 1188 Northmount Drive N.W., Calgary, Alberta T2L 0C7; (403) 282–1324. White-water river rafting adventures of two or seven days' duration.

Mukwah and Associates Adventure Bound Tours, 1216 16th Avenue N.W., Calgary, Alberta T2M 0K9; (403) 282–0509.

Kootenay River Runners, Caribou Street and Banff Avenue in Banff, (403) 762–5385.

Bicycle Tours

Rocky Mountain Cycle Tours, Box 895-T, Banff, Alberta T0L 0C0; (403) 678–6770. Biking/camping tours through Banff and Jasper national parks. Bike rentals are available, but riders must be in shape for these demanding tours.

Spoke 'n Edge, Banff Avenue and Wolf Street, (403) 762–2854. Bike rentals and repairs.

Mountain Moped, 215 Banff Avenue, (403) 762–5611. Rents 49cc Hondas for touring.

Boat Cruises

Minnewanka Tours, located at Lake Minnewanka, just east of downtown Banff, (403) 762–3473. Cruises around this beautiful lake at the foot of Mount Norquay and to various scenic points. They also provide fishing trips. Bus will pick you up in Banff; call (403) 726–2286.

Outdoor Adventure Centre, at Deadman's Flats, (403) 678–2000, provides windsurfing equipment and lessons; you can sail on Lake Minnewanka, Two Jack Lake, Vermilion Lake, and Lac des Arcs.

Helicopter Touring
Banff Heli Sports, (403) 678–4888.

Fishing
Banff Fishing Unlimited, (403) 762–4936. Provide licensed guides, tackle, foul-weather gear, lunch. They clean and pack your catch.

Golf Courses
Kananaskis Country Golf Course, a Robert Trent Jones course of thirty-six holes (the facility has two eighteen-hole courses), clubhouse, restaurant, equipment rentals, and pro shop. For tee times, call (800) 372–9201.

Canmore Golf Course, eighteen holes, clubhouse, lounge, restaurant, pro shop, equipment and cart rentals. In operation from May to mid-October. One-day advance booking is recommended; call (403) 678–4784.

Banff Springs Hotel Golf Course, eighteen holes; 147 sand traps! This course is smack in the middle of some of the most inspiring scenery in the world. It's not unusual to see elk shoot across the fairways. The facility has a driving range, practice green, equipment and cart rentals, restaurant, lounges, pro shop, and clubhouse. Book your game well in advance by calling (403) 762–2962.

Trail Rides
Holiday on Horseback, Box 2280, Banff, Alberta T0L 0C0; toll-free (Canada and United States) (800) 661–8352. From weekend trips to six-day trips into the remote area of the Canadian Rockies.

Timberline Tours, Box 14, Lake Louise, Alberta T0L 1E0; (403) 522–3743.

Hostelling
Southern Alberta Hostelling Association, headquarters in Calgary, (403) 283–5551, has facilities at Ribbon Creek, Spray River, Banff International, Castle Mountain, Corral Creek, Mosquito Creek, Ramparts Creek, and Hilda Creek.

Gondola Lift Sightseeing

Sulphur Mountain Gondola Lift, (403) 762–2523. Admission charged. Takes you to the summit (2,285 m./7,500 ft. high), where on a clear day you can truly see forever. The ride up is fun and thrilling, and there's a restaurant in the observation complex.

Lake Louise Gondola, on the Trans-Canada, (403) 522–3555). In operation from June to Labour Day. Admission charged (pay for going up and hike down free).

Sunshine Village, operates for sightseeing from end of June to September, (403) 762–4000. Admission charged.

Mount Norquay, sightseeing from end of June to Labour Day, (403) 761–4421. Admission charged.

Hot Springs Bathing

Upper Hot Springs Pool, Mountain Avenue, near the Banff Springs Hotel, (403) 662–2056. Massage services, (403) 762–2966. Open throughout the year. Bathing suit and towel rentals. Upper Hot Springs Pool has attracted bathers from all over the world to its therapeutic natural-hot-springs waters. In this pool the ordinary have bathed along with the rich and famous, seeking relaxation and/or cures to the aches and pains. The Banff experience would not be complete without a good hot soaking here.

Cave and Basin Centennial Centre, (403) 762–3324, has been in operation since 1887 and is the granddaddy of natural hot springs bathing pools in Western Canada. You can rent bathing suits and towels here.

Special Events

Banff Festival of the Arts, from the beginning of June to the end of August. Call for schedule and ticket information at (403) 762–6300 in Banff, (403) 236–1938 in Calgary.

This is Western Canada's premier arts festival. It brings together the finest professional talent and the best of young Canadian talent at the Banff Centre School of Fine Arts. During the summer, the public can partake of more than one hundred events in classical music, jazz, ballet, opera, musical theater, drama, and literary readings. These superior performances are held at Margaret Greeham Theatre, Eric Harvie Theatre, Roubakine Auditorium, Max Bell Auditorium, and Donald Cameron Hall. There are workshops in musical theater, dance, and opera. Art exhibitions are held at the Walter Phillips Gallery. The Banff Festival of the Arts makes summer here splendid, and it all happens right in town. Tickets are scarce close to performance dates and must be obtained *in advance*. This festival is as much a part of the Banff experience as the Rockies themselves.

Museums

Natural History Museum, 112 Banff Avenue, (403) 762–4747. Open May to September. Admission charged. Displays and diorama showing the geological history and present structure of the Canadian Rockies.

Banff Park Museum, 93 Banff Avenue. Open daily. Free. Built in 1903 and housed in the park's administrative building, this museum has displays on the diverse natural history of the area. It also has prints of Robert Bateman, a Canadian artist who has become world famous for his wildlife studies.

Luxton Museum, Cave Avenue, (403) 762–2388. Open daily. Admission charged. An excellent collection of Plains Indian artifacts.

Cave and Basin Centennial Centre, (403) 762–3324. Open daily. Free. The Centre has historical and geological exhibits, including the original bathhouse (1887), and the Discovery Trail, a natural history walk.

Whyte Museum of the Canadian Rockies, at the Banff Centre, (403) 762–2291. Open daily. This relatively new museum, part of the Banff Centre complex, downtown/riverside, has exhibition galleries that show the works of Canadian artists and those from other countries. The **Archives of the Canadian Rockies** are also here.

Walter J. Phillips Gallery, also part of the Banff Centre Complex, St. Julien Road, (403) 762–6283. Open daily when there is an exhibition. Named in honor of W. J. Phillips, a famous Canadian landscape artist, this gallery shows works by leading artists as well as students and faculty of the Centre of Fine Arts.

The Town of Banff

Banff, Alberta, has only one reason for being—tourism. When the transcontinental railroad was being built, Banff (named after a town in Scotland) was selected, because of its surrounding beauty and natural hot mineral springs, as a spa for the wealthy to relax and regain their zest for pursuing their various social, political, and commercial interests. The huge, sprawling Banff Springs Hotel was built just to serve such clients. When the late Duke of Windsor was a young Prince of Wales, he vacationed at Banff Springs Hotel, and his presence served as a magnet drawing more of the "carriage set" to the Canadian Rockies. As time went on, many others came here to vacation, and a thriving, lovely community grew on the valley flats. For much of the town's history, the only way to get here from distant points was by the Canadian Pacific Railroad. Banff and Lake Louise have remained the highlights of this world-famous rail trip across Canada, which continues to bring visitors (via Calgary or Vancouver). In the post–World War II period the Trans-Canada Highway was built, and today Banff and Lake Louise are easily accessible to all.

The main street of Banff, running north and south, is Banff Avenue, where you will find many shops, restaurants and services. Going northeast on Banff Avenue will take you to Tunnel Mountain Campground. Both the Trans-Canada, the VIA Rail station, and Mount Norquay are directly north of downtown. West of downtown are the Vermilion Lakes. Banff Avenue will also take you across the Bow River, past the national park administrative building and its lovely floral displays to Spray Avenue, which leads to the Banff Springs Hotel. Even if you are not staying in the hotel, you should go in and see the beautifully decorated public rooms and the fantastic view from the terrace overlooking the golf course (elk come out on the fairways at dusk to feed), Bow Valley, and the surrounding mountains. Once you see this view you'll instantly know why Banff became such a popular vacation paradise and has continued so for so long. The dining and lounge facilities of the hotel are open for use by nonresidential guests. (In previous decades, because of the luminaries who stayed here, the hotel was not as congenial to walk-ins as it is now.)

Tourist Information
Banff/Lake Louise Chamber of Commerce, 93 Banff Avenue, (403) 762–3777.
Banff Information Centre, 224 Banff Avenue, (403) 762–4256.

Touring Services
Brewster Transportation, (403) 762–2241.
Pacific Western Transportation, (403) 762–4558.
Mountain Tours, (403) 762–5652.
Auto Tape Tour, a tape and recorder that you use in your own vehicle; available for rent at the Thunderbird Gift Shop, 215 Banff Avenue, (403) 762–4661.

The Trail Rider, 132 Banff Avenue, (403) 762–4551, provides horse-drawn carriage rides to Banff Springs Hotel and other attractions and horseback trail rides of two to six days.

Accommodations

Banff has many places to stay; the ones listed here are the best in town. If you require lower-priced accommodations, contact the Banff/Lake Louise Chamber of Commerce, (403) 762–3777. Since Banff is one of Canada's most popular resort towns during the high seasons of summer and winter, reservations for accommodations are essential. For camping information, call the Banff Information Centre, (403) 762–4256.

Banff Springs Hotel, Spray Avenue, (403) 762–2211. One of Canada's best-known hotels, this huge baronial castle surrounded by the splendor of the Rockies has undergone extensive renovations that have greatly helped in sprucing up the rooms (those with views of Bow Valley are superior). The hotel has three dining rooms serving excellent cuisine, and the main dining room is one of the most elegant in Western Canada. There are lounges, indoor and outdoor swimming pools, a great eighteen-hole golf course, several tennis courts, hot springs, shops, live entertainment, and many other services and amenities. Expensive.

Rimrock Inn, at Sulphur Mountain, (403) 762–3356. A modern inn with grand views of Bow Valley and surrounding mountains. Eagles Nest dining room and the View Point lounge. Indoor pool, sauna, hot tub, and exercise room. Expensive.

Banff Park Lodge, Lynx Street, toll-free (800) 661–9266. Excellent accommodations, Terrace and Chinook dining rooms, Glacier lounge with nightly entertainment, indoor pool. Close to ski areas, cross-country trails, boating, fishing, and other sports. Expensive.

Banff Rocky Mountain Resort, off the Trans-Canada near Tunnel Mountain Road, (403) 762–5531. Chalet units with fireplaces and various kitchen conveniences. Restaurant, lounge, squash and tennis courts, indoor pool. Expensive.

Inns of Banff Park, (403) 762–4581. Deluxe rooms, Reflections dining room, Belvedere lounge with entertainment, indoor pool, squash court. Expensive.

Lake Louise Accommodations

Château Lake Louise, on the shore of Lake Louise, (403) 522–3511. Lake Louise is not all that large a body of water. What

makes it mystical and beautiful are the high, steep, snow-capped mountains surrounding it, the high Victoria Glacier at the opposite end of the lake from the hotel, the dark green forests all around, and the sky often made moody by fast-moving clouds. All of these facets reflect off the lake and give it a pantheism that other lakes lack. It's a memorable experience to be here just for a few moments, and so much better if you can stay for a few days. The Château itself is not as impressive as its sister hotel in Banff. Taken out of this setting, it would appear as a sprawling ark of a place. Fortunately, renovations have brought it up to contemporary standards; the grounds, interior public places, and rooms are first-class. Its Victoria dining room offers both excellent cuisine and service. There are an indoor pool, steam room, exercise room, and tanning room, as well as canoeing on the lake, ice-skating, fishing, hiking, horseback riding, and other activities, one of the best of which is simply lounging on the lawn lakeside, drink in hand, and meditating on the glories of nature before you. Expensive.

The Lake Louise Inn, in Lake Louise Village, (403) 522–3791. Excellent accommodations and facilities in a superb natural area; restaurant, swimming pool, health club, lounge, and disco. The best all-around choice in Lake Louise, except that it does not front the lake itself as does Château Lake Louise. Moderate to expensive.

Deer Lodge, near the lake, (403) 522–3747. Pleasant inn that has a fine restaurant. Moderate.

Canmore Accommodations

In Kananaskis area at the southern entrance to Banff National Park, the **Rocky Mountain Chalets** are on the Trans-Canada, (403) 678–5564. Moderate.

Dining

For a small resort town, Banff has a broad choice of fine restaurants. The high quality of restaurant offerings makes sense when you consider the large number of sophisticated travelers who come here every year and are not afraid to take local chefs to task for any slip below standards. For the average traveler, this is a bonus;

◀ **The resorts of the Canadian Rockies offer an excellence of hospitality that has made them famous around the world. You also get the added benefit of some of the best scenery anywhere in the world.**

for in Banff you know you can dine very well. The following is but a sampling of fine Banff eateries.

Banff Springs Hotel, Spray Avenue, (403) 762–2211. The Rob Roy Room, continental cuisine and dancing. Expensive. Alhambra Room, continental dishes and music; the price for table d'hôte dinner is moderate. Alberta Room, North American and continental fare, music while dining, excellent buffet at breakfast and lunch. Moderate to expensive.

Guido's Restorante, 116 Banff Avenue, (403) 762–5899. Tender veal dishes, linguine, smoked filet of trout. Inexpensive to moderate.

Balkan Restaurant, 120 Banff Avenue, (403) 762–3454. Greek fare—shrimp and herbs baked with feta, broiled marinated lamb chops, moussaka, and baklava for dessert. Moderate.

Le Beaujolais, corner of Buffalo Street and Banff Avenue, (403) 762–2712. Excellent French restaurant; perhaps the best in the Canadian Rockies. Châteaubriand, lobster soup, filet mignon, and other haute cuisine dishes. Very nice decor and good wine list. Expensive.

The Yard, 206 Wolf Street, (403) 762–5678. Wonderful hamburgers, Tex-Mex stuff, Eggs Louise, fresh baked croissants, barbecued ribs, seafood enchiladas, Cajun blackened red snapper. Indoor and alfresco dining. Inexpensive to moderate.

Rundle Restaurant, 319 Banff Avenue, (403) 762–3223. Hearty food, more than one hundred menu selections, full plates, low prices. North American and Chinese dishes. Inexpensive to moderate.

Mr. C's, 209 Banff Avenue, (403) 762–5899. The mood here is convivial and the menu creative—for example, Quail Canadiana. Superb desserts made in-house. A deliciously fun place in which to dine. Moderate to expensive.

Joshua's, 205 Caribou Avenue, (403) 762–2833. Here's the place to quell basic cravings for prime roast beef, lobster, salads, and strawberry cheesecake. Moderate.

Entertainment

The larger hotels and motels in both Banff and Lake Louise have lounges with live entertainment, and a number of independent lounges in town offer bands, singers, dancers, and comedians. Banff Springs Hotel has both sedate ballroom dancing and a frenetic disco. The Great Divide, on 124 Banff Avenue, features hard rock.

Shopping

What would a resort town be without lots of shops to keep tourists busy and happy? Banff has its share.

The Scottish Shop, 119 Banff Avenue, (403) 762–4048. Tartans and kilts.

Banff Bears, 225 Banff Avenue, (403) 762–3411. Teddy bears to bear T-shirts.

Wedgwood Shop, 107 Banff Avenue, (403) 762–2477. Imported English china and Waterford glass.

Monod Sports, 111 Banff Avenue (also at Château Lake Louise), (403) 762–4571. Climbing and camping gear, clothing for the out-of-doors, swim suits.

Nijinska's, Harmony Lane, (403) 762–5006. Canadian arts and crafts.

Jasper Area

Jasper National Park

Jasper National Park can be reached from the south (Banff) via Highway 93 and via the Yellowhead Highway 16 from Edmonton or Vancouver. For more information, contact Superintendent, Jasper National Park, Box 10, Jasper, Alberta T0E 1E0, (403) 852–4401; and the Jasper Chamber of Commerce, Box 98, Jasper, Alberta T0E 1E0, (403) 852–3858.

Jasper National Park is one of North America's largest natural areas preserved for present and future generations. Within the boundaries of this magnificent park are high mountains, many lakes—including Maligne Lake—forests, alpine meadows, Columbia Icefield, Athabasca Glacier, and Sunwapta Falls. This is the terrain of grizzly bears, elk, bighorn sheep, and elusive mountain goats. Native peoples, trappers, botanists, geologists, prospectors, and mountain men have been through here. Explorers such as David Thompson, Captain John Palliser, Sir Sanford Fleming, and Philadelphian Mary Shaffer trekked through this inspiring country; their records of and enthusiasm for Jasper (named after the fur trader Jasper Hawes) have attracted countless numbers of people since.

At the southern end of Jasper National Park is the Icefield Parkway (Promenade Champs de Glace), actually Highway 93. This 230 km. (138 mi.) scenic high road will take you to the awesome

Columbia Icefield (125 km. [75 mi.] north of Lake Louise, 105 km. [63 mi.] south of Jasper), with its Athabasca and Dome glaciers. This 389-square-kilometer expanse of ice and snow is accessible, at least at its tip, from the edge of the road. If you have never seen a glacier close up, here it is in all its awesome glory. In the distant west on a clear day, you will be able to see Mount Athabasca (3,491 m. high) and its glacier. The best way to experience this icefield is to take a ride over its bumpy surface in a Snowcoach, in operation from the end of May to the end of September; call (403) 762–2241 for reservations and charges. Or better still take a guided ice-walk tour; call (403) 852–4242 for information. An interpretive center here has a model of the entire Columbia Icefield, highlighting its unique features.

The park has 1,000 km./600 mi. of trails for hiking; campgrounds (Whistler's, Wapiti, Pocahontas, Snaring River, Wabasso, Mount Kerkeslin, Honeymoon Lake, Jonas Creek, Columbia Icefield, Wilcox Creek), fishing, boating, trail riding, SCUBA diving, downhill and cross-country skiing, and body soaking at Miette Hot Springs. The resort town of Jasper offers fine accommodations, dining, entertainment, and shopping.

Sports and Recreation

Downhill Skiing

Marmot Basin, located 365 km./225 mi. west of Edmonton on the Yellowhead Highway 16 and 19 km./12 mi. southwest of the town of Jasper on Highway 93A, has a season that lasts from early December to early May. Highest elevation, 2,423 m./7,950 ft.; vertical rise, 701 m./2,300 ft.; longest run, 5.5 km./3.5 mi.; skiing terrain, 30 percent expert, 35 percent intermediate, 35 percent novice; lift capacity, 7,600 people per hour. Marmot Basin offers ski instruction, equipment rentals, and dining facilities.

Other Winter Sports

In addition to downhill skiing, Jasper National Park offers nordic skiing, canyon crawling, dogsledding, helicopter skiing, ice climbing, ice fishing, ice-skating, snow mobiling, and snowshoeing. For more information, contact Jasper Chamber of Commerce at (403) 852–3858 or Parks Canada at (403) 852–6161.

Mountaineering

Camp Apa Chessta, Box 803, Hinton, Alberta T0E 1B0; (403) 865–7877. Winter and summer wilderness touring with native guides.

Jasper Climbing School, Box 452, Jasper, Alberta T0E 1E0; (403) 852–3964. Instruction in mountaineering, alpine ski touring, avalanche safety, ice climbing.

Jasper Wilderness and Tonquin Valley Pack and Ski Trips, Box 550, Jasper, Alberta T0E 1E0; (403) 852–3909. Ski touring and hiking.

Golf

Jasper Park Lodge, call (403) 852–3301 for tee-off reservations. A superior eighteen-hole golf course in the middle of fantastic scenery. Watch out for such hazards as deer or coyotes darting across the fairways.

Trail Riding

Amethyst Lakes Pack Trips, P.O. Box 508, Jasper, Alberta T0E 1E0; (403) 866–3946. Horseback trips into the Tonquin Valley, also to Mount Edith Cavell and along the Astoria River Trail.

Pyramid Riding Stable, on Pyramid Lake Road, (403) 852–3562.

Jasper Park Riding Academy, at Jasper Park Lodge, (403) 852–5794.

Hot Springs Bathing

Miette Hot Springs, 61 km. (37.8 mi.) east of Jasper on Highway 16, then right at Pocahontas Junction. Open during the summer. This large outdoor pool has some of the hottest water coming up from the bowels of the Canadian Rockies.

Gondola Sightseeing

Jasper Tramway, (403) 852–3093. Bus service is available from the town of Jasper and Jasper Park Lodge. The Tramway is in operation from mid-April to Canadian Thanksgiving. It takes you to the top of Whistler's Mountain. Both the ride up and down the views from the summit are spectacular.

Wild River Rafting
White Water Rafting, reservations at Marmot Texaco, (403) 852–4721. Trips down the mighty Athabasca River.

Jasper Raft Tours, reservations at Jasper Park Lodge or the bus depot, (403) 852–3332/852–3613.

Bike Rentals
Freewheel Cycle, downtown Jasper, (403) 852–5380. Bikes for rent or sale; bike repairs.

Sandy's, at Jasper Park Lodge, (403) 852–5708.

Mountain Air Sports, 622 Connaught Drive, (403) 852–3760.

Maligne Lake Boat Tours
Maligne Lake, intensely explored by Mary Schaffer, an affluent Quaker from Philadelphia, is, in terms of its beauty and mystical qualities, close to the natural splendor of Lake Louise. Maligne Tours takes you out in its boats for two hours, and you can experience a bit of what Mary Schaffer did. These boat tours operate from June through September. Call (403) 852–3370 for information. There's also an office in Jasper at 626 Connaught Drive.

Boat Rentals
Canoes, windsurfing equipment, fishing boats are all available for rent.

Sandy's, at Jasper Park Lodge, (403) 852–5708.

Pyramid Lake Bungalows, at Pyramid Lake, (403) 852–3536.

The Boathouse, at Maligne Lake, (403) 852–5650.

Fishing
Curries's Guiding, 622 Connaught Drive in Jasper, (403) 852–5650.

Maligne Tours, at Maligne Lake or 626 Connaught Drive in Jasper, (403) 852–3370.

The Town of Jasper
Jasper is the second most important resort town in the Canadian Rockies. It's the human oasis within Jasper National Park. It's not as large nor as bustling as Banff, so its pace and intimacy make Jasper an excellent choice for travelers staying a time in the Canadian Rockies. The Jasper Park Lodge, a superior resort, is as well known as its sister hotels in the south, Banff Springs and

Château Lake Louise. VIA Rail provides service to Jasper from points east and west in Canada. Greyhound has daily trips to and from the city of Edmonton. It is easy to reach by car via the Yellowhead Highway 16 (east or west) or Highway 93 from the south. Connaught Drive, which parallels the tracks of the railroad and the Yellowhead Highway, is Jasper's main street. Patricia Street also has a number of services for tourists. Most places to stay (except for Jasper Park Lodge), restaurants, and shops are within a few steps of one another. There are many lakes, such as Patricia and Pyramid, and the Athabasca River is the major waterway. For more information, including accommodations, contact the Jasper Chamber of Commerce at (403) 852–3858, Jasper Information Centre at (403) 852–6161, and the Alberta Motor Association at (403) 852–4444.

Accommodations

Reservations are essential during peak summer and winter months. The following places are the best that Jasper has to offer. There are also budget places and campgrounds. Contact the tourism offices listed above.

Jasper Park Lodge, via Lodge Road, (403) 852–3301. The popular image of Jasper Park Lodge that comes to mind is that of waiters riding bikes around the resort while carrying trays of cocktails. The accommodations and facilities here are superior, possibly among the best in the Canadian Rockies. The list of offerings includes an eighteen-hole golf course, swimming pool, tennis, horseback riding, fishing and touring trips, health club, sailboats, bikes, and excellent restaurants. Book well in advance. Expensive.

Alpine Village, junction of Highways 93 and 93A, (403) 852–3285. Moderate.

The Charlton's Château Jasper, corner of Juniper and Geike streets, (403) 852–5644. Fine accommodations and dining room. Moderate to expensive.

Jasper Inn Motor Lodge, at Bonhomme and Geike streets, (403) 852–4461. Moderate to expensive.

Lobstick Lodge, at Juniper and Geike streets, (403) 852–4431. Moderate.

Marmot Lodge, on Connaught Drive, (403) 852–4471. Moderate.

Sawridge Hotel Jasper, on Connaught Drive, (403) 852–5111. Moderate to expensive.

Dining

Jasper Park Lodge, for reservations, call (403) 852–3301. Beauvert Dining Room, overlooking Lac Beauvert, serves continental cuisine. Expensive. Copper Kettle offers Italian dishes. Moderate. Henry House for steak and salmon. Moderate to expensive. Tonquin Dining Room has gourmet food. Expensive. Moose's Nook for dining and dancing. Moderate to expensive. Terrace Lounge serves lunch and English-style afternoon tea. Moderate.

Beauvallon Dining Room at the Château Jasper, (403) 852–5644. Superb French cuisine, great steaks, freshly made desserts. Moderate to expensive.

Tokyo Tom's Place, at Cavell Court, (403) 852–3780. Japanese dishes and sushi. Moderate.

Amethyst Dining Room at the Andrew Motor Lodge, 200 Connaught Drive, (403) 852–3394. Fresh pasta dishes, Alberta steaks, veal piccata milanaise, apple strudel. Moderate to expensive.

Tricia's, 604 Patricia Street, (403) 852–4945. Fresh fruit ice cream and yogurt, terrific milk shakes, cappuccino, hot dogs. Inexpensive.

Entertainment

The lounges at many of the better places of accommodation feature live entertainment and/or dancing. Check with the desk person at the place you are staying to find out what's happening at night when you're there.

Shopping

Malowney's British Woolens, 606 Patricia Street, (403) 852–3278, and at Jasper Park Lodge. Imported woolens and cashmeres.

Jasper Rock & Jade, 620 Connaught Drive, (403) 852–3631. Jewelry from local minerals.

Mountain Air Sports, 622 Connaught Drive, (403) 852–3760. Sportswear and equipment; tickets for white-water rafting trips.

Quarks and Fribbles, 616 Connaught Drive, (403) 852–3834. Canadian arts and crafts.

◀**Mountain resort towns offer fine accommodations, dining, entertainment, and shopping. They are also at the doorstep of the best in outdoor sports— skiing, hiking, skating, golf, white-water rafting, horseback riding, and a lot more.**

Sherriff's of Jasper, 412 Connaught Drive, (403) 852–3658. English china, Italian silver, Bohemian jewelry.

Edmonton: Oil Capital of Canada

What Makes Edmonton Special

To NHL hockey fans, superstar Wayne Gretzky makes Edmonton special; to lovers of malls and theme parks, the West Edmonton Mall and Canada Fantasyland; to business wheelers and dealers, the rich oil and natural gas fields near the city. To those who want the magnificence of the great national parks of the Canadian Rockies, their resorts and many recreational opportunities, Edmonton's proximity to Jasper and Banff makes it special. And to those who want to kick up their heels at a rip-roaring festival, the rooting-tooting Klondike Days do.

Before the white fur traders and explorers arrived, Amerindian cultures inhabited this region of Alberta for more than 5,000 years. Their descendants still live here, both in the city and in rural reserves. In 1795 the North West Company built Fort Augustus near what is now the town of Fort Saskatchewan. That same year William Tomison set up a competing fur-trading post for Hudson's Bay Company, which he called Fort Edmonton, in honor of the birthplace in England of Sir James Winter Lake, deputy governor of Hudson's Bay Company. By 1821 it was the dominant post. In 1830 the fort was moved to where the legislature building now stands; it was demolished in 1915.

In 1897 Edmonton became the gateway for the gold rush to the Yukon. There was no clear route as such, and many with gold fever perished en route; some turned back and went home with empty pockets; others stayed in Edmonton and helped to expand the city's population. Edmonton, with 9,000 residents, was incorporated a city in 1904, and when Alberta itself became a province in 1905, Edmonton was designated its capital. A. C. Rutherford was Alberta's first premier.

In 1941 when construction began on the Alaska Highway, making the country north of Edmonton accessible by car, the city clearly became the gateway to the north. Perhaps the most important date in its history was February 13, 1947, when Leduc #1 well spouted black gold. This discovery made Edmonton the "oil capital of Canada," although Calgary might also apply this sobriquet to itself. Thousands of oil and gas wells were found within a 160 km. (96 mi.) radius of the city.

Today Edmonton is one of Canada's largest metropolitan centers in land area. Its present population is over 750,000. Close to half of the people here are of British background, and other large ethnic groups are German, Ukrainian, French, Scandinavian, Polish, Chinese, and Hungarian.

The thriving economy of the city is based on manufacturing, tourism, food processing, petroleum refining, agriculture, government and professional services, transportation/distribution, retailing, medicine, and education. Edmonton is a city of grace, vitality, culture, and vision.

How to Get to Edmonton

By Plane

Edmonton International Airport is located 29 km./18 mi. south of city center. This facility has restaurants, lounges, newsstands, and a duty-free shop; nearby are accommodations. Grey Goose Lines provides shuttle bus service to and from city center. There are also taxis and limousines. Several major rental car firms have booths at the airport and offices in city center. The following airlines serve Edmonton: Air Canada, Canadian Airlines, Continental Airlines, Northwest Orient, United, Wardair, and Western.

By Car

Edmonton is 294 km./184 mi. north of Calgary, via Calgary Trail Highway 2; 362 km./226 mi. east of Jasper, via the Yellowhead Highway 16. If you are coming from the east, take the Yellowhead west from Saskatoon, Saskatchewan.

By Bus

The Edmonton bus station is located at 102nd Avenue and 103rd Street. Service to Jasper and Calgary is provided by Greyhound, (403) 421–4211.

By Rail

VIA Rail provides service to Jasper and Vancouver in the West, and to Saskatoon, Winnipeg, and major eastern cities. The VIA Rail station is located at 104th and 101st streets; for fare and schedule information, call (800) 555–1212 and ask the operator for the toll-free VIA Rail number serving your area code. VIA Rail toll-free number in Alberta is (800) 665–8630.

How to Get Around Edmonton

Edmonton is spread out in an easy-to-comprehend grid pattern. City center is where 101st Street bisects Jasper Avenue. The Alberta Telephone Tower at 100 Street and 100th Avenue is a landmark you can use in finding your way around. From the top of this tower you get the best overall view of Edmonton; visit its telecommunications museum, (403) 425–3978. Admission charged. Another landmark is Edmonton Centre—with its three black towers—at 101st Street and 102nd Avenue. The city's LRT (Light Rail Transit) and bus systems will take you to most places you want to see, including the West Edmonton Mall.

Business and Convention Services

Business Hours: 8:30 A.M. to 4:30 P.M. for most offices; stores have extended hours during the week.

Bank Hours: 10:00 A.M. to 4:00 P.M.; most banks stay open until 6:00 P.M. on Fridays.

Convention Facilities: The Edmonton Convention Centre offers 82,000 square feet of exhibition space; main hall can accommodate 8,000 persons. Other exhibition and meeting space is available at Edmonton Northlands Park and at the Northern Jubilee Auditorium. Contact Edmonton Convention and Tourism Authority, 9797 Jasper Avenue, Edmonton, Alberta T5J 1N9, (403) 426–4715, for more information.

Chamber of Commerce: 600 Sun Life Place, 10123 99th Street, (403) 426–4620.

Translating Services: Berlitz, 10089 Jasper Avenue, (403) 428–0831; Alberta Association of Translators, (403) 434–8384.

Secretarial Services: Allied Communications, 10548 82nd Avenue, (403) 433–5153; secretarial services are available at most major hotels also.

Messenger Services: Purolator Courier, 11128 158th Street, (403) 451–5303.

Newspapers: The *Edmonton Journal* (evening); the *Edmonton Sun*, (morning).

Limousine Service: Call Yellow Cab for limos at (403) 462–3456.

Useful Information

Local holiday: Heritage Day, first Monday in August.

Time Zone: Mountain.

Area Code: 403.

Sales Tax: none in Alberta.

Emergencies of all kinds: dial 911.

Hospitals: Edmonton General Hospital, 11111 Jasper Avenue, (403) 482–8111; Royal Alexandra Hospital, 10240 Kingsway, (403) 477–4111.

Liquor: Sold only at government stores; ask desk clerk or concierge at your hotel for closest location.

Tourist information: Edmonton Convention and Tourism Authority, 9797 Jasper Avenue, (403) 422–5505.

Touring Services: Royal Tours, (403) 424–8687 (sightseeing of the city and its attractions, tours of rural Alberta; pickup at major hotels in the city).

Taxis: Yellow Cab (403) 462–3456.

Special Events

Jazz City International Festival: late June through early July.

Klondike Days: mid- to late July. Celebrating the heritage of Edmonton and its role as the gateway to the goldfields of the Yukon. There are parades, pancake breakfasts, gambling casinos, gold panning, top star entertainment, the World Championship Sourdough Raft Race, and the Sunday Promenade.

Heritage Festival: early August. Ethnic food, dance, culture, and fun.

Folk Music Festival: early to mid-August. The city comes alive with music—folk, country, bluegrass, stringband—and dancing.

251

Fringe Theatre Event: mid- to late August. Old, new, and experimental plays in the city's Old Strathcona district; more than 650 performances; the largest alternative theater festival in Canada.

Attractions

The West Edmonton Mall and Canada Fantasyland, 170th Street and 87th Avenue, (403) 481–6666. Open every day. Admission charged for nonshopping attractions. Shuttle bus service is provided to and from the mall from major Edmonton hotels. The mall has become one of Western Canada's prime attractions. A visit here is like nothing else you've experienced and should not be missed.

There is no doubt about this fantastic place—it is the world's largest and most pleasurable shopping mall, with more than 800 stores as well as numerous other attractions. Actually, it is a major theme park that has been merged with a mall. Within this sprawling complex is Canada Fantasyland—world's largest indoor amusement park with more than twenty rides, including a triple-loop roller coaster and a thirteen-story free-fall ride; World Waterpark—a five-acre indoor lake with sixteen water slides, surfing on 6-foot waves, a wild river ride, and a suntan pavilion; Deep Sea Adventure—an indoor lake, 400 feet long and 30 feet deep, offering rides and four submarines, a marine theater with trained dolphins, and a replica of the 80-foot Santa Maria galleon; Pebble Beach Miniature Golf—an eighteen-hole miniature golf course; Ice Palace Skating, an NHL-sized skating rink with equipment rentals; and animal displays—bird aviaries, saltwater aquariums, shark tanks, alligators, penguins, monkeys, bears, tigers, and a petting zoo for children. There are thirteen Italian marble fountains throughout the mall. The Europa Boulevard features expensive boutiques with Parisian storefronts. Bourbon Street has nightclubs, jazz, and restaurants. Motorized carts are available for those who want to ride to shops and attractions. The mall cost over $1 billion to build and employs over 15,000 people.

The mall incorporates the Fantasyland Hotel, which has 360 exotically themed suites depicting different cultures and periods in history, such as the Polynesian Room (with a waterfall), the Roman Room (with marble sculptures and an authentic Roman bath), the Truck Room, the Coach Room, the Hollywood Room, and the Arabian Room. Excellent restaurants and lounges are in the hotel;

kosher food is served on request. This is also a convention hotel, one which would delight delegates. Call (403) 436–7966. With accommodations like these, the price is expensive.

Alberta Legislature Building, 109 Street and 97th Avenue, (403) 427–7362. Open daily. Free. This provincial capitol is noted for being constructed out of terra-cotta blocks. The terra-cotta and steel-reinforced dome has never shown a crack. Beautiful gardens surround the building, with a reflecting pool and water displays. Carillon bells sing every day at noon. The cornerstone was laid in 1909 by the Earl Grey, governor-general of Canada, and the building was officially opened in 1912 by another governor-general, the Duke of Connaught.

Alberta Pioneer Railway Museum, 10158 103rd Street, (403) 427–2031. Open daily May to September. Admission charged. Displays of early railroading equipment used in the development of Western Canada—steam and diesel engines, rolling stock, vintage 1877 to 1950.

Canada's Aviation Hall of Fame, 9797 Jasper Avenue, (403) 424–2458. Open throughout the year. Admission charged. Exhibits honoring Canada's aviation aces, from the pioneering days of flight to the jet age.

Edmonton Art Gallery, 2 Sir Winston Churchill Square, (403) 422–6223. Open throughout the year. Free. Exhibitions of classical and contemporary art.

Edmonton Police Museum, 9620 103A Avenue, (403) 421–2274. Open Tuesday to Saturday. Free. Displays telling the story of the history of the law enforcement in Alberta.

Fort Edmonton Park, via Whitemud and Fox Drive, (403) 436–5565. Open mid-May to September. Admission charged. On the banks of the Saskatchewan River and south of city center, Fort Edmonton is a re-creation of an important early Hudson's Bay trading post (circa 1846). Within this park are several of Edmonton's historic homes and re-creations of early street scenes; the Reverend George McDougall Shrine, honoring a pioneering missionary; rides on an old-time street car. Visit Kelly's Saloon for soda and ice cream, the Jasper House for good meals, and the Masonic Hall, where you can relax and sip sarsaparilla. This large historic park is divided into two main sections: the Fort Complex, and the settlement, consisting of streets that re-create their eras—1885 Street, 1905 Street, and 1920 Street. Fort Edmonton Park is an interesting and enjoyable attraction for all ages.

John Janzen Nature Centre, located next to Fort Edmonton Park, (403) 434–7446. Open throughout the year. Free. Exhibits of Edmonton flora and fauna, including bees, ants, snakes, and salamanders. Nature walks with guide on Sunday afternoons.

Edmonton Space Sciences Centre, 111 Avenue and 142nd Street, (403) 451–7722. Open throughout the year. Admission charged. This is Canada's largest planetarium, featuring the Star Theatre; the IMAX theater, which uses special effects; and science exhibits.

John Walker Historic Site, 10627 93rd Avenue. Call for hours, (403) 436–5565. Four historic homes (circa 1874 to 1886) owned by John Walker, one of the city's first settlers. Displays portray the early development of the province.

Muttart Conservatory, 98th Avenue and 96A Street, (403) 428–2939. Open daily during the summer. Admission charged. Four pyramid-shaped glass buildings containing plantings of the arid, tropical, and temperate climatic zones; the fourth structure has changing exhibits.

Provincial Museum and Archives, 12845 102nd Avenue, (403) 427–1750. Open daily. Free. The galleries of the provincial museum tell the story of Alberta's natural and human history—paleontology, zoology, Amerindian cultures, fur traders, and settlers.

Rutherford House, 11153 Saskatchewan Drive on the University of Alberta campus, (403) 427–5708. Open mid-May to September. Admission charged. Home of Alexander Cameron Rutherford, the first premier of Alberta. Restored and furnished to its early-1900s appearance. Costumed interpretive guides. This is an impressive mansion for a "man of means and considerable influence," both of which Rutherford clearly was.

Strathcona Science Park, located west of 17th Street and Highways 16 and 16A. Alberta Natural Resources Science Centre. Open throughout the year. (403) 427–9490. Free. Tells how the province's natural resources are developed and used. Strathcona Archaeological Centre. Open throughout the year. (403) 427–5708. Free. This is an ongoing archaeological dig at a 5,000-year-old native site. Displays and guides to explain the archaeological process.

Ukrainian Canadian Archives Museum, 9543 110th Avenue, (403) 424–7580. Open Monday to Saturday. Donations. Largest Ukrainian museum in Alberta.

Ukrainian Museum of Canada (Alberta Branch), 10611 110th

Avenue, (403) 483–5932. Open July and August. Free. Displays of beautiful, embroidered tablecloths; wood carvings; hand-painted Easter eggs; ceramics; sculptures; and paintings.

Valley Zoo, 134th Street and Buena Vista Road, (403) 483–5511. Open mid-May to September. Admission charged. Many different animals displayed in their natural habitats. Amusement rides for children.

Accommodations

Edmonton has accommodations ranging from deluxe to budget. There are places to stay along all major routes leading to the city. The deluxe hotels at city center are among Canada's finest. For additional suggestions, contact your travel agent or auto club, or call Edmonton Tourism at (403) 426–4715.

Leading Hotels

Four Seasons Hotel, 10235 101st Street, (403) 428–7111. Edmonton's top hotel. Located in city center and adjoining Edmonton Centre shopping mall, this Four Seasons offers fine service and many luxurious amenities, elegant dining, indoor pool, and saunas. Expensive.

The Westin Hotel, 10135 100th Street, (403) 426–3636. City center location, fine service and amenities, gourmet dining, indoor pool, and exercise facilities. Expensive.

Château Lacombe, 101st Street and Bellany Hill, (403) 428–6611. A modern circular tower structure in city center. Dining at La Ronde, revolving restaurant. Expensive.

Fantasyland Hotel, at West Edmonton Mall, (403) 436–7966. See description above in previous section on the West Edmonton Mall. Expensive.

Mayfield Inn, 16615 109th Avenue, (403) 484–0821. Excellent accommodations and service. Indoor pool, health club, seventeen indoor tennis courts, six racquetball courts, dining room, lounge, and live entertainment. Moderate.

Other Fine Places to Stay

All of the places listed below offer fine accommodations and many amenities, such as swimming pools, dining rooms, and lounges; some have nightclubs.

Capiland Motor Inn, 9125 50th Street, (403) 465–3355. Moderate.

Holiday Inn, 107th Street and 100th Avenue, (403) 429–2861. Moderate to expensive.

Nisku Inn, 4th Street and 11th Avenue, near Edmonton International Airport, (403) 955–7744. Moderate.

Ramada Renaissance Hotel, 10155 105 Street, (403) 428–4811. Expensive.

Renford Inn on Whyte, 10620 82nd Street, (403) 433–9411. Moderate.

Sandman Inn, 17635 Stony Plain Road, (403) 483–1385. Moderate.

Terrace Inn, 4440 Calgary Trail N., (403) 437–6010. Moderate to expensive.

Hotel Van Winkle, 5116 Calgary Trail N., (403) 434–7411. Moderate.

Dining

In Edmonton cuisine the emphasis is on Alberta beef, which in my opinion is the best in North America. Fancy continental and hearty ethnic cuisines are also the pride of Edmonton's chefs.

Bruno's Italian Restaurant, 8223 109th Street, (403) 433–8161. Italian and continental cuisine in an elegant setting. Moderate to expensive.

Four Seasons Room, at the Four Seasons Hotel in Edmonton Centre, (403) 428–7111. The account on food is superbly French, and the surroundings are *trés chic.* Their degustation menu is this room's specialty. Expensive.

Japanese Village, 10126 100th Street, (403) 422–6083. Traditional Japanese dishes prepared at your table; also has a sushi bar. Moderate to expensive.

Walden's, 10245 104th Street, (403) 420–6363. Continental dishes and specialty fare, such as Alberta hare. You can dine in the garden or in the congenial dining room. Expensive.

La Ronde Revolving Restaurant at the Château Lacombe, (403) 428–6611. This restaurant gives you views of the city "from the top," while you dine on prime roast beef, steak, or a fancy continental dish. Moderate to expensive.

Oliver's, 11730 Jasper Avenue, (403) 482–4888. Oliver's is considered by many to serve the best Alberta beef and steak dishes in the city. But it's far more than a simple steak house. This is a sophisticated restaurant that can turn out continental cuisine to compare to the best of them. Expensive.

Entertainment

The Citadel Theatre, 101A Avenue; for ticket and schedule information, call (403) 426–4811. This is a beautiful, modern complex of several theaters. Plays are performed in the Shoctor, Rice, and Maclab theaters. The Tucker Amphitheatre showcases new talent, and the Lee Pavilion presents concerts by the Muttart Conservatory. Even if you don't attend a performance, come here to see the indoor gardens, which have 4,000 tropical plants, a reflecting pools, and a thirty-foot waterfall.

Stage West at the Mayfield Inn, 16615 109th Avenue, (403) 483–4051. Dinner theater with well-known performers.

Jubilee Auditorium, 87th Ave. and 114th St., is the home of the Edmonton Symphony Orchestra and the Edmonton Opera; for performance dates and ticket information, call (403) 482–7030.

Rose and Crown in the Four Seasons Hotel, (403) 428–7111. English pub atmosphere; fun.

Cook County Saloon, 8010 103rd Street, (403) 432–0177. Down country–style entertainment and grub.

Shopping

If you want to spend hours of enjoyable shopping, go to the West Edmonton Mall, which not only is the largest in the world but also combines amusements and theme parks—enough diversions to keep you busy for several days. It's one of the city's great attractions (see description in the earlier section on attractions). In city center the Edmonton Centre mall has a large number of shops, from glitzy to budget-busting boutiques.

Professional Sports

Edmonton Oilers, Stanley Cup champs with Wayne Gretzky, play at Northlands Coliseum, 118th Avenue and 73rd Street. For game dates and tickets, call (403) 474–8561.

Edmonton Eskimos, of the Canadian Football League, play at Commonwealth Stadium, 11100 Stadium Road. For game dates and tickets, call (403) 428–5555.

Thoroughbred and Harness Racing, at Northlands Park, 115th Avenue and 79th Street. Call (403) 471–7210 for racing dates.

Rodeos, at Northlands Coliseum, 118th Avenue and 73rd Street. Call (403) 471–7210 for dates.

Recreation

Golf

Riverside Golf Course, Rowland Road and 84th Street, (403) 465–4710.

Public Swimming Pools

Call (403) 428–3559 for locations and hours.

Public Tennis Courts

Call (403) 429–3570 for locations and hours.

Health Clubs

Kinsmen Sports Centre and Aquatic Centre, 9100 Walterdale Road, (403) 428–5350; swimming pool, tennis courts, fitness trail, racquetball and squash courts.

Millwoods Recreation Centre, 7207 28th Avenue, (403) 463–8550; wave pool, ice-skating rinks, racquetball and squash courts.

Traveling from Edmonton To Alaska or Yellowknife

If you are traveling from Edmonton to the Yukon, Northwest Territories, and/or Alaska, take Highway 43, which begins just west of the city, via the Yellowhead Highway 16. Continue on Highway 43 until you reach the town of Valleyview (a more scenic but longer route is Highway 2 from Edmonton via Lesser Slave Lake to Valleyview or Grande Prairie). At Valleyview turn West on Highway 34, which will take you to Grand Prairie. From here take Highway 2 to Dawson Creek, British Columbia. It is at Dawson Creek that the Alaska Highway officially begins. From Dawson Creek follow the Alaska Highway 97 north to Highway 4 and/or 2, via White-horse, in the Yukon and thence to the state of Alaska.

To reach Yellowknife, the capital of the Northwest Territories, from Edmonton, take Highway 43 north to Valleyview, then Highway 35 north, which connects with Northwest Territories Highway 1. Highway 1 west will take you to Highway 3 north (around the southwest shore of Greater Slave Lake), and then on to Yellowknife via Highway 4 east.

CHAPTER 8

Touring Saskatchewan

Regina • Saskatoon

Saskatchewan in Brief

Although wheat is grown in all three prairie provinces (Alberta, Saskatchewan, and Manitoba), Saskatchewan can claim the title of "Bread Basket of Canada." If you are in the province just before harvesting, you can stand in the middle of a field and it will seem as if for countless miles in every direction there is only a seamless, thick carpet of burnished gold. Here is part of the great wealth of Canada. Here is food for the nation itself and food for people all over the world. Just as the Atlantic and Pacific are awesome and inspiring in their particular ways, so too is the vast ocean of Saskatchewan's wheat-laden prairie land.

When traveling east or west across Canada, many tend to rush through Saskatchewan, perhaps spending a night in the cities of Regina or Saskatoon. People say that they get tired of the endless, flat prairies and can't wait until they reach the mountains or the sea. Along the Trans-Canada or the Yellowhead there may seem to be very little of interest between one side of Saskatchewan and the other, but Saskatchewan is full of surprises and delights, and it reveals these only to those who make the effort to discover them. There are two brilliant cities, national parks and historic sites, cowboy rodeos and Indian powwows, lakes and rivers for swimming and fishing, and more varied cultural offerings than you would have time to sample.

Its human history is one of noble men and women from many different backgrounds, who shaped and made productive a land that was not easy to tame. The first inhabitants of Saskatchewan were the native peoples—Chipewyan, Cree, and Assiniboine. In the north their culture developed around hunting such animals as the moose and the caribou; in the south they hunted buffalo.

One of the first white men to come into this region was Henry Kelsey. Kelsey, an employee of the Hudson's Bay Company, explored the Saskatchewan River in 1690. In the decades that followed, other explorers left their footprints on Saskatchewan soil, and their visions motivated others—Pierre Gaultier de Varennes de La Vérendrye, Peter Pond, David Thompson, Peter Fidler, Sir John Franklin, Dr. John Richardson, John Palliser, and Henry Hind.

Several key events in the nineteenth century radically changed the development of Saskatchewan: Canadian Confederation in 1867; Hudson's Bay Company's relinquishing lands in Saskatchewan to the federal government of Canada in 1869; founding of the Northwest Mounted Police in 1873 to establish and maintain law and order in the Canadian west; through treaties, the confinement of the native peoples into reserves; the final defeat in 1885 of the métis; the building of the transcontinental railroad connecting Saskatchewan to the rest of Canada; and the Dominion Lands Act, which opened up the land to homesteading and immigration. And the immigrants came in droves: Doukhobors, Ukrainians, Germans, Hutterites, Mennonites, Scandinavians, French, Americans, Chinese, and many others. They came to this fertile part of Canada fleeing religious and/or political persecution or simply because they saw better opportunities here than those available whence they came. With a great deal of hard work and sacrifice, they put plows to the tough prairie soil and made it bloom with food.

On September 1, 1905, Saskatchewan entered Canadian Confederation (the alliance of provinces that created a self-governing Dominion of Canada) and has been a province of significance ever since. Among the many outstanding men and women Saskatchewan has contributed to the national life of Canada was John George Diefenbaker. Although born in Ontario in 1895 and having lived some of his early years in the Northwest Territories, Diefenbaker (called "Dief" by his friends and foes) was more closely associated with Saskatchewan than any other province. After distinguishing himself in local and provincial politics, he was elected in 1940 to the federal

parliament in Ottawa. As leader of the Progressive Conservative party from 1956 to 1967, "Dief" was constantly a thorn in the side of the ruling Liberals, but he had a high-minded vision for Canada, based on the values of democracy and self-reliance he learned on the prairies and rough country of Saskatchewan. In 1957 he became prime minister of Canada, giving the nation its first Tory government since R. B. Bennett's (1930 to 1935).

Diefenbaker was responsible for the first wheat sales to the People's Republic of China, the momentum that eventually led to the Canadian Bill of Rights, and the granting of the native people's right to vote in federal elections. His stand against apartheid led to South Africa's leaving the Commonwealth of Nations in 1961. In 1963 the Liberals regained control of the federal government, but not by much. John Diefenbaker, "the man from Prince Albert," who was frequently ridiculed by those with different ideas—including President John F. Kennedy—passed away in August of 1979. As his funeral train slowly went from Ottawa to Saskatoon, Canadians and others around the world mourned a giant who did much for others and who remained true to his vision.

Another noteworthy Canadian from Saskatchewan, Jeanne-Methilde Sauvé (née Benoit), born at Prud'homme, is the first woman in the nation's history to be appointed (in May 1984) governor-general. As governor-general, Madame Sauvé, previously a journalist and politician, represents the queen of Canada (Elizabeth II) and as such holds the highest government position in the country, although without the considerable executive powers of the prime minister, who is elected by House of Commons members of the majority party.

Saskatchewan is also a province of many natural wonders. Its Cree name is Kisiskatchewan: the river that flows swiftly, namely the Saskatchewan River. The province—651,900 square kilometers/251,700 square miles—is almost three times the size of the British Isles. To the north, Saskatchewan borders the Northwest Territories; to the south the states of Montana and North Dakota; to the west Alberta; and Manitoba to the east. Prairies dominate much of the landscape in the south; parklands in the center—a transitional zone of farms and rolling terrain with forests; in the northern portion thousands of square miles of Precambrian wilderness, with more lakes and streams than an angler could enjoy in several lifetimes. Winters, even in the southern portion, can be brutally cold. However, summers are typically warm, dry, and pleasant. The hottest

temperature ever recorded in Canada was 45°C/113°F, in the southern part of the province. During July and August the weather is perfect for all kinds of outdoor recreation. Also during the summer just about every town and city has festivals, rodeos, ethnic events, heritage days, or cultural happenings.

The North and South Saskatchewan, the Assiniboine, and the Churchill are the province's major river systems, and they all flow in a northeasterly direction and empty into Hudson's Bay. The largest lakes in northern Saskatchewan are Athabasca, Lac la Ronge, Cree, Wollaston, Reindeer, Churchill, and Peter Pond. There are more than 100,000 lakes in this region, and the many beaches, such as Waskesiu in Prince Albert National Park, are good places to cool off or get a terrific tan. Cypress Hills (1,392 m./4,564 ft.) has the highest elevation.

The province has approximately 1.1 million inhabitants. Regina is the capital and second-largest city; Saskatoon is slightly larger. Canada's only training academy for the Royal Canadian Mounted Police is located in Regina.

The economy is based on agriculture, mining, construction, manufacturing, tourism, education, health care, and services. The province produces 60 percent of all wheat grown in Canada, and more than half of the world's known recoverable potash reserves (used in making fertilizer) are located here.

Tourism Saskatchewan

To get the best out of traveling in Saskatchewan, use the province's information and travel planning assistance services, all of which are available free of charge. The folks at **Tourism Saskatchewan,** the provincial government agency, will answer your questions, make suggestions, and send you free maps and brochures. If you are interested in fishing, hunting, canoeing, white-water rafting, mountain biking or bike touring, houseboat charters, hiking, nature tours, outfitting organizations, or wilderness lodges, ask for the booklet "Saskatchewan Outdoor Adventure," which has everything you need to know (plus maps). "Saskatchewan Winter" describes opportunities for downhill and cross-country skiing, snowmobiling,

◀ **The first people of Western Canada are those who have lived here for thousands of years. Their progeny keep the unique cultures alive, sustaining themselves and teaching us how to live in harmony with nature.**

ice fishing, sleigh rides, as well as lodges, parks, and special events.

The booklet "Saskatchewan Parks" describes the many provincial parks and the facilities they provide to the public. The main provincial parks in Saskatchewan are Cypress Hills, Danielson, Saskatchewan Landing, Douglas, Buffalo Pond, Moose Jaw Wild Animal Park, Echo Valley, Katepwa Point, Rowan's Ravine, Pike Lake, Good Spirit Lake, Duck Mountain, Greenwater, Meadow Lake, the Battlefords, Nipawin, Lac la Ronge, and Moose Mountain. Most of these parks have campgrounds that provide electricity and other conveniences (Katepwa Point has no camping, and Nipawin has no electric sites).

Other Tourism Saskatchewan free booklets you may find useful are "The Great Saskatchewan Vacation Book"; "Saskatchewan Accommodation" (includes camping and farm vacations); "Saskatchewan Anglers' Guide"; "Saskatchewan Hunting Synopsis."

For specialized (topographic) maps and aerial photos, contact Central Survey and Mapping, 2045 Broad Street, Regina, Sask. S4P 3V7; (306) 787–2799.

Tourism Saskatchewan can be reached throughout the year at these numbers: Toll-free from anywhere in Canada and the United States, (800) 667–7191; toll-free within Saskatchewan, (800) 667–7538; Regina area, (306) 787–2300.

Tourism Saskatchewan has Visitor Reception (information) Centres at these locations:

The Manitoba border on the Trans-Canada Highway 1 (seasonal)
Regina: Bank of Montreal Building, 11th Avenue and Scarth Street (open year round)
Maple Creek on the Trans-Canada (seasonal)
Langenburg on the Yellowhead Highway 16 (seasonal)
Lloydminster at the Alberta border on the Yellowhead (seasonal)
Kindersley near the Alberta border on Highway 7 (seasonal)
North Portal at the North Dakota border on Highway 39 (seasonal)
La Ronge on Highway 2 in the northern part of the province (seasonal)

Useful Information

Time Zone: Central

Telephone area code: 306

Saskatchewan Special Events

Saskatchewan has a great variety of festivals and special events. Some, such as rodeos, are familiar. Others, such as chicken chariot races and a gopher festival, are just plain strange but terrific fun. Here's a sampling of some of the best special events taking place in the province during the summer vacation season:

May

International Marching Bands Championships, Regina; mid-May
Cross-Country Hang Gliding Classic, Qu'Appelle Valley; mid-May
(not held every year)
Golden Sheaf Awards, film festival, Yorkton; late May
Annual Fusilier, rodeo, Major; end of May

June

Western Development Museum Days, North Battleford; early June
Mosaic, multicultural celebration, Regina; early June
Kinsmen Rodeo Western Days, Unity; early June
Northwoods All Arabian Horse Show, Saskatoon; early June
Folk Festival, Regina; mid-June
Our Lady of la Salette Pilgrimage, Forget; mid-June
30 Mile Canoe Race, North Battleford; mid-June
International Kite Festival, Regina; mid-June
Yellowhead Arabian Horse Show, Yorkton; mid-June
Model Air Plane Show, Moose Jaw; mid-June
Western Canada Farm Progress Show, Regina; mid- to late June
Spoke Festival, for recreational bicyclists, Qu'Appelle; late June
South Country Round-up, rodeo, Assiniboia; late June
World Championship Chicken Chariot Races, Wynyard; late June
Three-Day Hoedown, pioneer wagon trek, Foam Lake; late June
Sakimay Indian Pow-Wow, Grenfell; late June
Heritage Fiddlers Championships, Saskatoon; late June
Frontier Days/Frontier Rodeo, Swift Current; late June to early July

July

World Championship Gopher Derby, Eston; beginning July
Heritage Trek, pioneer wagon trip and festival, Foam Lake; early July
Exhibition and Summer Spectacular, Humboldt; early July
Trial of Louis Riel, dramatic reenactment, Regina; from early July to late August

267

Shakespeare on the Saskatchewan Festival, Saskatoon; early July to late August

Saskatoon Exhibition, Saskatoon; early to mid-July

Kinsmen Mid-Summer Kurling Klassic, Bonspiel, Wilkie; mid-July

Wood Mountain Stampede, oldest continuous rodeo in Canada, Wood Mountain; mid-July

Saskatchewan Air Show, Moose Jaw; mid-July; one of the largest air shows in North America, featuring the famed Snowbirds precision-flying team

Heritage Day, Doukhobor arts, crafts, food, and choirs, Veregin; mid-July

Thoroughbred Racing, Saskatoon; mid-July to mid-October

Saskatchewan Handcraft Festival, Battleford; mid-July

Big Valley Jamboree, country/western music, Craven; mid-July

Northwest Territorial Days, North Battleford; late July

Chief Poundmaker Memorial Pow-Wow, Cut Knife; late July

Saskatchewan Tractor Pulling Championships, Moosomin; late July

Buffalo Days Exhibition, Regina; late July to early August

August
Standing Buffalo Indian Pow-Wow, Fort Qu'Appelle; early August

Duck Mountain Triathlon, Duck Mountain Provincial Park; early August

Big Valley Roundup, largest chuck-wagon races in the world, Craven; mid-August

Piapot Indian Pow-Wow, Cupar; mid-August

Our Lady of Lourdes Pilgrimage, Rama; mid-August

Threshermans Show and Seniors Festival, Yorkton; mid-August

Interprovincial Horticultural Show, Lloydminster; end of August

Folkfest, large ethnic festival, Saskatoon; end of August

September
Saskatchewan Open Chili Cookoff, Saskatoon; mid-September

Western Canada Amateur Olde Tyme Fiddling Championships, Swift Current; late September

October
Annual Grub Stake Days, Melfort; mid-October

Annual Octoberfest, St. Walburg; mid-October

November
Canadian Western Agribition, Regina; late November

National Parks

Grasslands National Park, located in the south central part of the province, two separate sections on the border of Montana; access to the western section is via Highway 4 through the town of Val Marie. For more information, contact Superintendent, Grasslands National Park, Val Marie, Saskatchewan S0N 2T0. Landowner permission required for access in some areas; call (306) 298–2257. For information on private, guided tours, call (306) 298–2241.

Grasslands National Park was established in 1981 to protect a special ecosystem of rolling terrain covered with spear grass and other vegetation and inhabited by pronghorn antelope, prairie rattlesnake, sage grouse, prairie dog, and the endangered prairie falcon. This is the only preserve of its kind in North America. Before extensive human settlement, this prairie ecosystem covered thousands of square miles of the continent. Within the proposed park boundaries are also the Killdeer Badlands, a sinking fault (dropping 30 cm./11 in. annually), and the site where in 1874 Sir George Mercer Dawson made the first discovery of dinosaur remains in this area. This was once a prime buffalo-hunting area for Plains Indians and the métis. In 1876 Chief Sitting Bull and his Sioux people found temporary refuge here from the U.S. Army after the Battle of Little Bighorn. The area is the former site of the Wood Mountain Northwest Mounted Police post, the Jean-Louis Legaré Trading Post, and the Fort Walsh–Wood Mountain Trail. Today farming and ranching operations surround the park. As yet there are few visitor facilities in the park; its main function is to protect a vastly diminished ecosystem. However, there are tourist services in the town of Val Marie; (306) 298–2257.

Prince Albert National Park, located due north of Saskatoon, can be reached via Highway 2 north from the city of Prince Albert. Highways 263 and 264 lead to the entrance of the park as well as some of the key areas within it. For more information on facilities and services, contact Superintendent, Prince Albert National Park, Waskesiu Lake, Saskatchewan S0J 2Y0; (306) 663–5322.

Located "dead center" in the province, Prince Albert National Park, named in honor of Queen Victoria's beloved consort, is a vast, oblong-shaped ecological bridge between the aspen parkland of central Saskatchewan and its vast northern forest. Prince Albert has many lakes, streams, and bog areas and supports abundant wildlife—badgers, coyotes, black bear, otter, elk, deer, moose, fox, wolf, lynx, caribou, osprey, and eagle. The three largest lakes are Waskesiu, Crean, and Kingsmere, which along with the many other lakes are favorites with anglers; perch, walleye, whitefish, trout, and northern pike are among the species waiting to be caught. The town of Waskesiu Lake, on the shores of the lake bearing the same name, is a resort community catering to anglers, boaters, campers, swimmers, and those seeking the solitude and beauty of the park. One early naturalist, author, and orator who lived in this wilderness was Archibald Stansfield Belaney. Taking the name of Grey Owl and believing himself to be the son of a Scot and an Apache woman, this eccentric Englishman became immortal for his work in the cause of conservation and as author of *The Men of the Last Frontier, Pilgrims of the Wild, The Adventures of Sajo and her Beaver People,* and *Tales of an Empty Cabin.* Grey Owl's writings on the beavers he raised—Jellyroll and Rawhide—became almost as famous as he. To those of us urban and suburban dwellers, Grey Owl said, "You are tired with years of civilization and I come to offer you, what? . . . a single green leaf." Grey Owl's cabin, at Lake Ajawaan (a 19.5 km./12 mi. hike from the end of Highway 264), is preserved. You can visit it and hear his voice in a gentle breeze, "I offer you a single green leaf."

Prince Albert National Park offerings include interpretive programs; campgrounds at Beaver Glen, Narrows, Trapper's Lake, Namekus, Sandy Lake, and Kingsmere Lake; swimming from the park's main beach at Lake Waskesiu, also at all other lakes except Lavalle; eighteen-hole golf course in town; bike rentals; hiking trails; canoe rentals and canoe routes; horseback riding; and fishing with park permit.

In **Waskesiu Lake** take advantage of the following:

Grey Owl Marina, houseboat rentals, (306) 663–5470.
Paddlewheeler Tours, (306) 663–5253.
Nature Centre, open June through September, (306) 663–5322.
Indian Arts and Crafts Centre, (306) 663–5276.

Accommodations include the following:
Lakeview Hotel, open throughout the year, dining room, (306) 663–5311. Moderate.
Skyline Motel, efficiency units, (306) 663–5461. Moderate.
The city of **Prince Albert,** the gateway to the national park, has many attractions of interest.

Diefenbaker House, 246 19th Street W., (306) 922–9641. Open mid-May to September. Free.

Grace Campbell Art Gallery, in John M. Cuelenaere Library, 125 12th Street E., (306) 763–8496. Open throughout the year. Free.

Lund Wildlife Exhibit, 98 River Street W., (306) 764–2860. Open from June to September. Admission charged.

Also visit the Nisbet Church, Prince Albert Forest Nursery, and Prince Albert Historical Museum.

Accommodations are listed below:

Best Western Inn on the Park, 6th Avenue, (306) 922–9595. Moderate.

Imperial 400 Motel, Highways 2 and 3, (306) 764–6881. Moderate.

Marlboro Inn, 67 13th Street, (306) 763–2643. Moderate.

Winn Inns Prince Albert, 3680 2nd Avenue, (306) 922–5000. Moderate.

National Historic Parks

Fort Walsh National Historic Park, open mid-May to mid-October, near the Alberta–Saskatchewan border, can be reached via the Trans-Canada, then south on Highway 271 from Maple Creek (adjacent to Cypress Hills Provincial Park, an important attraction and recreational area in itself). For more information, contact Superintendent, Fort Walsh National Historic Park, P.O. Box 278, Maple Creek, Saskatchewan S0N 1N0.

In 1873 the Cyprus Hills Massacre took place in this region, known as Whoop-up Country, because of the frenetic trading and whiskey drinking that went on here. A group of white wolf hunters got into a drunken brawl with Assiniboine Indians and twenty of the natives, as well as one of the wolf hunters, were killed. With the territory on the verge of anarchy, the Northwest Mounted Police established a base of operations here at Fort Walsh (named after the first superintendent, James Walsh, a flamboyant but popular commander). From Fort Walsh the Mounties chased out the American whiskey traders operating in this region, secured the international border, and protected the Indians. Superintendent Walsh offered Chief Sitting Bull and his people refuge after the Battle of Little Bighorn.

Today Fort Walsh has been re-created and looks as it did in

271

the late 1800s. A high wooden wall encircles and thus protects several buildings. Nearby are Solomon's and Farewell's trading posts. If you let your imagination go, you can almost hear bugles, men's voices, and horses preparing to venture forth and tame a wild land.

There are camping and recreational opportunities at the 45,000-acre **Cypress Hills Provincial Park,** (306) 662–4411. Open throughout the year; park entry fee charged. Supplies and various tourist services can be obtained in the town of Maple Creek.

Fort Battleford National Historic Park is located near the town of Battleford, 153 km. (92 mi.) northeast of Saskatoon. The best access is off Yellowhead Highway 16. For more information, contact Superintendent, Fort Battleford National Historic Park, Box 70, Battleford, Saskatchewan S0M 0E0.

A great tragedy took place here in 1885—one of the battles of the North West Rebellion, led by one of the proudest and noblest leaders of the native peoples of the Plains, Cree Chief Poundmaker, adopted son of a great Blackfoot leader, Chief Crowfoot. This uprising occurred because by the late 1880s the native Cree and Blackfoot peoples felt hemmed in by the white settlements, whose inhabitants believed that the land was for the taking, and by the building of the transcontinental railroad. The Amerindians could no longer move freely across this limitless landscape; their primary food source—the buffalo—was disappearing; and their liberty was increasingly controlled by white men's laws. According to another version, the battle took place because of the traditional, long-standing antagonism between the Cree and the Blackfoot.

At any rate, the Mounties built Fort Battleford to serve as a buffer between the two tribes. From the fort the police could serve the Indians by distributing annuity payments, enforcing the laws, and settling them on reserves. In 1885 Chief Poundmaker and his Cree warriors lay siege to the fort, where 112 men were stationed— the largest mounted police division then in Western Canada. The Mountie Superintendent, Colonel William Otter, pursued Cree warriors from the fort and engaged them in battle at Cut Knife Hill. Eight warriors were found guilty of treason by the Mounties and were hanged within the stockade. Although pleading innocent to treason and felony charges, Chief Poundmaker was sentenced to three years in prison, but was released after one year. He died shortly thereafter on July 4, 1886, and is buried on a hill where the Battle of Cut Knife was fought.

Commanding officer General Frederick Middleton's residence still stands within the stockade and is furnished with decorations and items from the late-nineteenth century. Government House, a two-story building built in 1877, was the seat of the territorial capital. In the late 1870s Battleford was the capital of the North West Territories, as much of Western Canada was then known. In 1882 the capital was moved to Regina, which was right on the line of the transcontinental railroad and thus linked to major urban centers throughout Canada.

Batoche National Historic Park, located 88 km. (53 mi.) northeast of Saskatoon on the east bank of the South Saskatchewan River, can be reached from Saskatoon via Highway 11 north to Highway 312. For more information, contact Area Superintendent, Batoche National Historic Park, Box 719, Rosthern, Saskatchewan S0K 3R0.

Batoche was the site of the epic battle between the métis and the established authority of Canada in 1885. The Riel Rebellion was the closest Canada ever came to civil war, although there were other rebellions in the nineteenth century. The métis considered themselves a distinct people, neither French nor Indian but a merging of cultures and genes from both. They were the sons and daughters of French or Scottish voyageurs (trappers and/or haulers of furs) and Cree, Saulteaux, or Ojibwa women.

Batoche, located on the Carlton Trail, a trade route between Fort Garry, Manitoba, and Fort Edmonton, Alberta, was part of a larger district known as the Saint-Laurent Settlement. In the mid-1880s this territory was embroiled in conflict. There were battles between the Indians and the Northwest Mounted Police, and the métis expressed grievances against encroachments by the Canadian federal government. Some took up arms against the Mounties, who moved in on the métis at Batoche. General Frederick Middleton's force of 800 attacked 100 métis and Indians. His first attack failed, but the Mounties bombarded the métis with their artillery for about three days. On May 12, 1885, General Middleton and 130 of his men drew the métis to an area where a Mountie Gatling gun was firing (a Gatling gun is on display at the park), and then a Mountie force rushed down on the métis, who by this time were firing nails and stones from their rifles. Within a few minutes

273

the battle was finished, and so was the métis cause—at least from a military perspective.

Both Louis Riel, charismatic political leader of the métis cause, and General Gabriel Dumont, its military chief, escaped. Riel surrendered later and was eventually tried and convicted of treason in Regina. He was hanged in this city on November 16, 1885. The trial and the sentence have been controversial in Canada ever since, especially among French-Canadians who believe that the severity of Riel's sentence was due as much to his ethnic background and religion as to the severity of his crime. Gabriel Dumont escaped to the United States where he joined Buffalo Bill Cody's Wild West Show as a trick rifle shooter. General Middleton was found to have illegally confiscated furs from a métis prisoner; he returned to England where Queen Victoria made him Keeper of the Crown Jewels in the Tower of London. The Batoche Park has become a kind of shrine in Canada, expressing the struggle of a people both to retain their liberty and to preserve their culture. The park contains the church and rectory of Saint-Antoine-de-Padoue, the East Village, the battlefield itself, and General Middleton's encampment.

Other locations associated with the North West Rebellion in Saskatchewan are Steele Narrows, Fort Pitt, Frog Lake, Frenchman Butte, Prince Albert, And Fort Carlton.

Motherwell Homestead National Historic Park is reached via the Trans-Canada east from Regina to Highway 10, at Balgonie. For more information, contact Area Superintendent, Motherwell Homestead National Historic Park, Box 247, Abernethy, Saskatchewan S0A 0A0.

William Richard Motherwell, one of many settlers from Ontario who contributed considerably to the development of Saskatchewan, created an oasis of refined civilization on his prairie lands. He named his estate Lanark Place, after Lanark County in Ontario. The Italianate-style mansion he built in 1897 was of cut fieldstone with a double-pitched gambrel roof; this became one of the most popular architectural styles for the *nouveaux riches* on the prairies. Motherwell had a distinguished career as co-founder and president of the Territorial Grain Grower's Association at Indian Head. He was the province's first minister of agriculture and, as member of the House of Commons in Ottawa, served as federal minister of agriculture. The mansion, buildings, and grounds (the "homestead") are being restored to reflect the peak period of Motherwell's career.

Saskatchewan's Ukrainian Connection

Ever since the late nineteenth century when the lands of Saskatchewan were opened for settlement, people from all over the world have come to the province to start new lives. One ethnic group that has contributed much to the development of Saskatchewan, particularly in agriculture, is the Ukrainians. For the most part they came to this part of Canada from the Bukovyna and Halychyna regions of the Western Ukraine. In many ways the terrain and climate of the prairies were not unlike the fertile steppes of the Ukraine. Just as the Ukraine is the "bread basket" of the Soviet Union, so too is Ukrainian Canada.

Along with their commitment to the land, the Ukrainians have contributed aspects of their rich culture to Canada. You can experience this in their beautiful onion-dome churches, Byzantine or Latin rituals and elaborate decorations or icons, their festivals, and most particularly in their exhuberant dancing groups, which have thrilled audiences throughout the world. You can visit Ukrainian places of interest (museums, churches, schools) located along or near the Yellowhead Highway 16 from Lloydminster at the Alberta border to North Battleford, Radisson, Saskatoon, Wynyard, Foam Lake, Sheho, Insinger, Theodore, Yorkton, and Rokeby near the Manitoba border (open hours and admission charges, if any, are individually posted). Even in some small communities don't be surprised to see two Ukrainian churches, one aligned with the Orthodox hierarchy and the other with the Roman Catholic Church. In Saskatoon visit the **Museum of Ukrainian Culture,** 202 Avenue "M" S., (306) 244–4212. Open throughout the year. Donations accepted. This museum has 2,000 artifacts describing the Ukrainian culture in Europe and in Canada.

Saskatchewan's Special Attractions

The treasure chest that is Saskatchewan requires exploring and discovery. You won't be disappointed with the new enjoyments, experiences, and perceptions you'll find. The following is just a sampling of what a few Saskatchewan communities have to offer.

In Gravelbourg (reached via the Trans-Canada and Highway 58), a French-Canadian cultural center on the prairies, visit **Our Lady of Assumption Cathedral,** Main Street, (306) 648–3322. Open

throughout the year. Beautiful interior with paintings by Charles Maillard.

Stop in Maple Creek, on the Trans-Canada near the Saskatchewan–Alberta border, to see the **Old Timer's Museum,** 218 Jasper Street, (306) 662–2474. Open June to October. Admission charged. This is the oldest museum in the province, with a fine collection of pictures.

Moose Jaw is located on the Trans-Canada. During the 1800s a Red River cart (a wagon mounted on two large wheels that was better able to traverse the rough and soggy ground than other vehicles of the times) broke down in this area and was fixed by an Englishman using a moose jaw. Impressed Indians named the place Moose Jaw, and the name has stuck ever since. Today Moose Jaw, on the line of the transcontinental railroad and the Trans-Canada Highway, is one of the province's largest cities, with an economy based on agriculture and industry. Moose Jaw is home to two outstanding events: **Kinsmen International Band Festival** in mid-May, the largest gathering of musical and marching bands in North America, and **Saskatchewan Air Show** in mid-July, featuring the Snowbirds jet-plane precision-flying team. Visit the **Moose Jaw Wild Animal Park,** 7th Avenue S.W., (306) 694–3659. Open May to September. Admission charged. See the **Western Development Museum,** 50 Diefenbaker Drive, (306) 693–6556. Open throughout the year. Admission charged. Exhibits on the history of transportation in the prairie region.

In St. Victor (reached via Highway 2), **St. Victor Petroglyphs Historic Park,** open throughout the year, (306) 787–9573, free, features rock carvings made by ancient native peoples.

Wood Mountain Post Historic Park, in Wood Mountain on Highway 18, is open end of May to September, (306) 787–9573. Free. Reconstructed buildings have displays on the lives of the Amerindians and the Northwest Mounted Police in this area of the province.

Wood Mountain Stampede, in mid-July, is the oldest continual rodeo in Canada.

Last Mountain House Historic Park, in Craven, on Highway 20, is open throughout the year, (306) 787–9573. Free. This

◀ **In many parts of Saskatchewan the second language, after English, is Ukrainian. Here in Western Canada the cultural mosaic shines with ethnic diversity and harmony.**

fur-trading post was used in the mid-1800s. Buildings have been reconstructed, and there is a limited interpretive program.

In Esterhazy (reached via Highways 16, 80, and 22), **Kaposvar Historic Site Museum** is open mid-May to mid-October, (306) 745–2692. Free. Here is the site of the first Hungarian colony in the province, settled more than one hundred years ago. The museum complex contains pioneer homestead, barn, smokehouse, school, and various artifacts.

Fort Qu'Appelle can be reached via Highway 10, east of Regina. Located in the beautiful Qu'Appelle Valley, **Fort Qu'Appelle Museum,** Bay Avenue and 3rd Street, is open mid-May to September, (306) 332–5227. Free. Displays feature articles used in fur-trading days by the Amerindians and Hudson's Bay Company agents.

Visit **Fort Esperance National Historic Site,** in Rocanville (reached via the Trans-Canada and Highway 8), which is open throughout the year, (306) 333–2116. Free. This is the first fur-trading post established on the Qu'Appelle River.

Overlooking Battle River Valley, **Cut Knife Hill National Historic Site,** in Cut Knife (reached via Highway 40), is open throughout the year, (306) 937–2621. Free. Here is where the battle between Chief Poundmaker and Colonel Otter took place. Chief Poundmaker's remains are buried on a hill at this site and marked with a monument.

Duck Lake Historical Museum, in Duck Lake (reached via Highway 11), is open throughout the year, (306) 467–2057. Admission charged. The museum features thousands of items related to the North West Rebellion and to pioneer life in this region. Also visit nearby **Fort Carlton Historic Park,** reached via Highway 212. Open mid-May to September, (306) 787–9573. Free. This reconstructed stockade has buildings of a fur-trading post with furnishings from the 1800s. There are interpretive programs and walking trails. **St. Laurent Shrine,** open June to September, (306) 467–2075, free, was inspired by the shrine at Lourdes. Pilgrimages are held once in July and once in August.

Fort Pitt Historic Park, open throughout the year, (306) 787–9573, is in Frenchman Butte (reached via Highway 3). Free. Interpretive panels tell the story of the fur trade. Nearby is **Frenchman Butte Historic Site,** where you can see gun pits used in the 1885 skirmish.

In Loon Lake (reached via Highways 55 and 26), visit **Steel**

Narrows Historic Park, open throughout the year, (306) 787–9573. Free. The skirmish between the Cree and the Mounties, which was the last military engagement of the North West Rebellion, took place at this site.

North Battleford (reached via the Yellowhead Highway 16) is located in a lovely and historic area of the province. While in the town, be sure to stop at the following:

Battleford Superslide, open from Victoria Day to Labour Day, (306) 445–0000. Admission charged. Eleven water slides, swimming pool, hot tubs, and restaurants.

George Hooey Wildlife Exhibit, open June to the end of August; call ahead (306) 937–2462. Free. More than 400 mounted specimens of birds, fish, and mammals.

North Battleford Arts Centre, 99th Street, open throughout the year, (306) 445–7266. Donations accepted. Exhibitions of paintings, weavings, pottery, macramé, stained glass, and photography.

Western Development Museum, at Highways 16 and 40, open year-round, (306) 445–7211. Admission charged. Exhibits tell the story of settlement and agricultural development, including demonstrations of farming techniques (summer only). Also here you can walk through the re-creation of an early-twentieth-century small town. **Northwest Territorial Days,** at North Battleford Exhibition Grounds near the museum, in late July, features exhibits, a gambling casino, entertainment, horse pulling, chuck-wagon races, chariot races, super stock tractor pull, livestock competition, and fiddlers' "hoe down."

Take in pioneer wagon rides for one hour or up to five days/four nights with **Covered Wagon Treks.** This is one of the great experiences of Saskatchewan; call (306) 445–2999 for details.

All of the following accommodations have restaurants and other amenities:

Towne House Motel, 11212 Railway Avenue, (306) 445–4458. Moderate.

Tropical Inn, on the Yellowhead Highway, (306) 446–4700. Moderate.

Capri Motel, Railway Avenue and 101st Street, (306) 445–9425. Moderate.

Hudson Bay, reached via Highway 3, is called the "Moose Capital of the World." This is also a good place to catch the train to Churchill, Manitoba, nearly 1000 km. (600 mi.) away on Hudson Bay to view the polar bears when they are roaming that area of Hudson

Bay. While in town, visit **Hudson Bay Heritage Park,** a pioneer village—open from Victoria Day to Canadian Thanksgiving—and **Hudson Bay Musem,** displaying pioneer artifacts, open daily June to August.

St. Peter's Cathedral is near Meunster, off Highway 5, (306) 682–5484. Open daily. Free. This ornate cathedral with paintings by German-born Berthold Imhoff has eighty life-sized figures, portraits of saints, and religious scenes decorating the interior.

National Doukhobor Heritage Village, near Veregin off Highway 5, is open throughout the year, (306) 542–4441. Admission charged. This site has early communal homes of the Doukhobors, a Quakerlike religious society originally from Russia. The complex includes brick oven, bathhouse, prayer home, and blacksmith shop. Veregin's **Heritage Day** in mid-July features bread baking, rug weaving, spinning, cloth work, grist mill operations, and Doukhobor vegetarian dishes.

Regina: Regal Center of the Prairies

What Makes Regina Special

The Indian name for Regina was *Wascana,* or "pile of bones." On the bank of Wascana Creek, near the present-day Legislative Building, the early Indians created a huge pile of buffalo bones as a religious landmark and oblation to the diety for successful hunts. The buffalo, or bison, was essential to their way of life and supplied them with nourishing food and materials for clothing, shelter, and weapons.

Fur traders came through the Wascana area and settled for a time, only to move on when the prospect of riches beckoned elsewhere. The development of a permanent settlement at Wascana was made possible by the Northwest Mounted Police, who provided protection to the Indians from American whiskey traders and security for immigrants wanting to develop the land into agricultural productivity. They protected the progress of the transcontinental railroad and checked the military/political aspirations of the métis. There is very little doubt that the expansion of Canadian Confederation across the continent would have been extremely difficult if not impossible without the efforts of the Mounties. Today, although RCMP headquarters is in Ottawa, the primary training facility for this elite force is in Regina.

In 1882 the city became the capital of the province of the Northwest Territories, which at that time encompassed much of Western Canada (later the prairie provinces and the Yukon Territory evolved out of this vast land area and entered Confederation). The city received its present name—Regina—from Princess Louise, a daughter of Queen Victoria who held the title Queen of Canada and was wife of the governor-general of Canada. In Latin, "regina" means queen.

In 1905 Regina became the official capital of the province of Saskatchewan. Today, it is a modern city of 179,000 people, a center for agriculture, manufacturing, government, finance, medicine, tourism, education, transportation, and food processing. Although the dominant ethnic group is British, Regina is a cosmopolitan city in which many different cultures merge and contribute their own unique flavors and perspectives. The "bottom line" here, regardless of one's heritage, is good old-fashioned prairie friendliness.

How to Get to Regina

By Plane

The following major airlines provide daily service to Regina: Air Canada, Canadian Airlines, and Norcanair. The Regina Airport is located in the southwestern part of the city off Regina Avenue. Its terminal has full facilities, including rental cars. Travelers from the United States can reach Regina via connecting flights.

By Car

Regina is located on the Trans-Canada Highway 1 in the southern part of the province. U.S. Highway 16 from Sidney, Montana, and U.S. Highway 52 from Minot, North Dakota, provide direct access to Regina. U.S. Highway 16 connects with Saskatchewan Highway 16 north, and U.S. Highway 52 connects with Saskatchewan Highway 39 to 6. If you are traveling the Yellowhead Highway 16 from Alberta, take Highway 11 south in Saskatoon, which will bring you directly into Regina.

By Rail

VIA Rail provides passenger service to and from Regina to major cities in Western and Eastern Canada. Call (800) 555–1212 for

VIA Rail toll-free number serving your area code or (306) 359–1822 in Regina.

By Bus

Regina Bus Depot, 2041 Hamilton Street. Greyhound has daily service to Regina from many destinations in Western Canada. For information on fares and schedules, call (306) 787–3340.

Saskatchewan Transportation and Moose Mountain Lines connect Saskatchewan communities.

How to Get Around Regina

Regina is laid out in a logical grid pattern. Its two main streets, which bisect each other in city center, are Albert Street and Victoria Avenue. The Wascana area, which comprises the Legislative Building, Museum of Natural History, and other attractions, is located at Albert and College. Many of the better hotels are on or near Victoria.

Regina Transit provides bus service throughout the city: call (306) 569–7777. There are a number of taxi services in the city.

For additional information on the city, visit the Regina Convention and Visitor Bureau, Highway 1 east, (306) 789–5099, or Tourism Saskatchewan at 2103 11th Avenue.

Touring Services

Double Decker Bus Tours, tours of the city and Wascana Centre; (306) 522–3661.

Ferry Boat Tours, thirty-minute cruises on Wascana Lake; (306) 525–2148.

Prairie City Tour Guides, tours of the city and lovely Qu'Appelle Valley; (306) 949–5727.

Regina/Heritage Walking and Bus Tours, several self-guided tours of the city; (306) 569–7759.

Saskatchewan Land-Roamers Tours, tours of the city and other important areas of the province; (306) 586–8410.

Wascana Freewheelers Cycling Club, bike tours to interesting places throughout the province; (306) 565–0615/584–1834.

Attractions

Royal Canadian Mounted Police Museum, Depot Division, Dewdney Avenue W., (306) 780–5838. Open throughout the year. Free. The RCMP museum is Regina's Number One attraction. Here thousands of men and—more recently—women have been trained to be members of Canada's elite police force, highly respected throughout the country and the world. The standards to get in are high, and the training is comparable to that of the U.S. and Royal Marines. Mounties serve on highway patrols, as law officers in remote communities and areas, as security for political leaders, and as the nation's intelligence service.

The RCMP museum contains uniforms, weapons, flags, documents, and many other artifacts relating to the history and heritage of the Mounties. It has the uniform belonging to Superintendent Walsh, who gave refuge to Chief Sitting Bull and his people after the Battle of Little Bighorn; exhibits on the mad trapper of Rat River; and the crucifixes Louis Riel carried to his hanging here in Regina. Within the complex is also the Little Chapel on the Square—the spiritual heart for the RCMP—originally built as a mess hall in 1883. It is decorated with stained-glass windows depicting noble moments in the Mountie heritage; flags from past campaigns, such as the North West and Indian rebellions; and its baptismal font honors a comrade who fell at the Battle of Cut Knife Hill. Outside, in Barracks Square, is a monument to the *St. Roch,* an RCMP boat which was the first to sail through the North West Passage. There are other memorials as well. An old cemetery is nearby.

Wascana Centre, bounded by 23rd Avenue, Albert Street, and College Avenue, is the most beautiful part of Regina. It covers 920 hectares/2,500 acres through which flows Wascana Creek, forming man-made Wascana Lake. Within the park are located some of Regina's most important attractions: the Legislative Building; a band shell and marina; Wascana Place, which features films and exhibits and provides tourist information; Wascana Waterfowl Park; the Saskatchewan Museum of Natural History; the Saskatchewan Centre of the Arts; a new CBC (Canadian Broadcasting Company) facility; and the University of Regina. During the summer live entertainment and boat cruises are offered. Picnic areas are provided, and walks through the beautifully landscaped park lead you past colorful flower beds. You can take a brief ferry ride to Willow Island, where there are picnic areas. Of all of Canada's provincial capitols, Saskatchewan's in Wascana Park is the most beautifully sited in terms of the surrounding landscaping, extensive lawns, flower beds, and promenades, and its axis on Wascana Lake. The modern campus of the University of Regina is also within Wascana Park, and you are welcome to stroll the grounds.

Legislative Building, is Wascana Park, (306) 787–5358. Open throughout the year; tours (free) from Victoria Day to Labour Day. This fine, domed structure, in cruciform shape, imitates the architecture of eighteenth-century England and France, but it is also solidly North American. The rotunda area, jewel of the building, is faced with marble and decorated with statues and murals depicting Indian chiefs painted by Edward Morris. An art gallery here (open daily; free) displays portraits, photographs, and other objects relating to Saskatchewan history.

Saskatchewan Centre of the Arts, Lakeshore Drive in Wascana Park, (306) 584–5050. Open throughout the year with tours from July to September. Free tours. This modern facility is home of the Regina Symphony Orchestra. Other groups also present performances here—ballet, opera, top star talent, and so on.

Diefenbaker Homestead, in Wascana Park, (306) 522–3661. Open mid-May to the first of September. Free. "Dief's" boyhood, three-room pioneer home is furnished with Diefenbaker family artifacts. It was moved to this site from Borden, Saskatchewan.

Saskatchewan Museum of Natural History, in Wascana Park on the corner of College Avenue and Albert Street, (306) 787–2815. Open throughout the year. Free. This fine modern museum has displays on the geology, paleontology, archaeology, human history, and zoology of Saskatchewan. A must-see attraction.

Plains Historical Museum, 1801 Scarth Street, 4th floor of historic Old Post Office downtown, (306) 352–0844. Admission charged. Here are displays on the history of the Indians, métis, and pioneers who lived in the Regina area. There are pioneer artifacts and period rooms, including a sod hut, school room, kitchen, and parlor.

Government House, Dewdney Avenue at Connaught Street, west of Lewvan Drive, (306) 787–5717. Open throughout the year. Free. This was the official residence of Saskatchewan's lieutenant governors from 1891 to 1945. You are allowed to tour the rooms with their elegant period furnishings. During the summer (July 1 to

August 31), the dramatic production *Trial of Louis Riel* takes place in this mansion; it should not be missed for its history and passion.

Saskatchewan Archives, Hillsdale near Saskatchewan Center, (306) 787–4068. Open Monday through Friday. Free. The archives are open to those seeking historical and genealogical information.

Art Galleries

Regina, for its size and distance from art centers such as Montréal, Toronto, and New York, has a large number of galleries that feature outstanding art and crafts works by artists from the province as well as other areas of Canada and the world. Many of these works are for sale—perfect souvenirs that tend to appreciate in value with time.

Dunlop Art Galleries, three galleries that form part of Regina's public library system, are located at 1601 Dewdney Avenue, (306) 569–7774; 2311 12th Avenue, (306) 569–7577; and 6121 Rochdale Boulevard, (306) 569–7611.

Gallery on the Roof, 13th Floor, Saskatchewan Power Building, 2025 Victoria Avenue, (306) 566–3174.

Joe Moran Gallery, 4th Floor at Wascana Place, (306) 522–3661.

Native Heritage Gallery, 2314 11th Avenue, (306) 352–8788.

Neutral Ground, 1651 11th Avenue, (306) 522–7166.

Norman Mackenzie Art Gallery, College Avenue, on the campus of the University of Regina, (306) 352–5801.

Nunavut Gallery, Warehouse Village Mall, 1750 Lorne Street, (306) 757–3819.

Patchworks, Warehouse Village Mall, (306) 522–0664.

Rosemont Art Gallery, at the Neil Balkwill Civic Arts Centre, 2420 Elphinstone Street, (306) 522–5940.

Saskatchewan Indian Arts and Crafts, 2431 8th Avenue, (306) 352–1501.

Susan Whitney Gallery, 1627 Victoria Avenue, (306) 569–9279.

Terry Sagal Pottery, 6 Princess Place, (306) 584–0964.

Accommodations

Leading Hotels

Hotel Saskatchewan, 2125 Victoria Avenue, (306) 522–7691. An older hotel with lots of class and history. Fine accommodations and services. Restaurants include Formerly's, which smacks of upper-crust British, and the Ranch Room, for traditional Western dining. Moderate to expensive.

Sheraton Centre, 1818 Victoria Avenue, (306) 569–1666. The Sheraton Centre, one of Regina's top hotels, has a beautiful lobby, nice rooms, fine restaurants, and many amenities, plus a swimming pool and water slide. Moderate to expensive.

Regina Inn, 1975 Victoria Avenue, (306) 525–6767. A good value hotel, offering fine accommodations, dining, and such facilities as a swimming pool and sauna. Its restaurants and lounges include Courtyard, Reflections, Victoria's, and Ruffles.

Other Fine Places to Stay

Chelton Inn, 1907 11th Avenue, (306) 599–4600. Moderate.

Imperial 400 Motel, 4255 Albert Street, (306) 584–8800. Moderate.

Landmark Inn, 4150 Albert Street, (306) 586–5363. Moderate.

Regina's Westwater Inn, 1717 Victoria Avenue, (306) 757–0663. Moderate.

Sandman Inn Motor Hotel, 4025 Albert Street, (306) 586–2663. Moderate.

Seven Oaks Motor Inn, 777 Albert Street, (306) 757–0121. Moderate.

Sherwood House Motel, 3915 Albert Street, (306) 586–3131. Moderate.

Turgeon International Hostel, 2310 McIntyre Street, (306) 522–4200. Inexpensive.

YMCA, 2400 13th Avenue, (306) 757–9622. Inexpensive.

YWCA, 1940 McIntyre Street, (306) 347–8537. Inexpensive.

Dining

The Cellar Dining Room, at the Sheraton Centre, (306) 569–1666. Continental and North American dishes. Moderate to expensive.

Diplomat Steak House, 2032 Broad Street, (306) 359–3366. Elegant restaurant with steak at its best. Expensive.

L'Habitant, 1711 Victoria Avenue, next to the Westwater Inn, (306) 525–1551. A famous Saskatchewan steak house. Expensive.

Victoria's Regina Inn, Victoria and Broad Street, (306)

525–6767. Good food from an extensive menu; good service, ambience, and entertainment. Expensive.

Roxy's Bistro, 1844 14th Avenue, (306) 352–4737. Freshly made baked goods, cuisine in the French tradition; a fine choice. The chef is also the owner. Moderate.

Harvest Eating House, 379 Albert Street, (306) 545–3777. Housed in a vintage wooden building, Harvest uses an old chuck wagon for its bountiful salad bar. This is a right proper place for a right proper cut of prime roast rib of beef. Moderate.

Chinese Village Restaurant, 229 Victoria Avenue E., (306) 522–2822. This popular Chinese restaurant serves regional dishes from Cantonese to Szechuan. Moderate.

C.C. Lloyd's, 1907 11th Avenue, (306) 569–4650. The atmosphere re-created here is that of New York City in the 1930s. The dishes are traditional gourmet: veal Oscar, roast rack of lamb, chicken en croute, shellfish bisque with champagne, and upper-crust desserts—strawberry savarin and Grand Marnier cream. Expensive.

Entertainment

Call the following performing arts organizations for their schedules and ticket information:

The Saskatchewan Centre of the Arts, Lakeshore Drive in Wascana Park, (306) 584–5555, is home for the Regina Symphony Orchestra which plays in the 2,000-seat Centennial Theatre. Within this complex is Jubilee Theatre, which is used for recitals and dramatic productions.

The Globe Theatre, in Old City Hall, on Scarth Street, (306) 525–9553, is Regina's main stage for plays professionally produced.

Regina Modern Danceworks, 1100 Broad Street, (306) 359–3183.

Saskatchewan Theatre Ballet, 1876 Wallace Street, (306) 525–1464 for schedule.

Elizabethan Singers of Regina, 54 Massey Road, (306) 543–6823.

Regina Jazz Society, 4517 Elgin Road, (306) 525–6767.

Regina Little Theatre, 2731 Saskatchewan Drive, (306) 352–5335.

South Saskatchewan Opera Guild, 1718 Royal Street, (306) 522–7492.

Wheatland Theatre, 1821 Scarth Street, (306) 525–0667.

Nightclubs

Formerly's English Pub, at the Hotel Saskatchewan, (306) 522–7691.

The Elephant and Castle English Pub, 2101 11th Avenue, (306) 757–4405.

Ruffles Disco, at the Regina Inn, (306) 525–6767.

Bartleby's Dining Emporium and Gathering, 1920 Broad Street, (306) 565–0040.

Athens by Night, 1845 Victoria Avenue, (306) 757–3788; belly and Greek folk dancers.

B-Bop Café, 1834B Scarth Street, (306) 352–3991; folk, blues, and reggae music.

Professional Sports

Professional Football, the Saskatchewan Roughriders play at Taylor Field, (306) 525–2181.

Professional Hockey, the Regina Pats play at the Agridome in Exhibition Park, (306) 527–0688.

Thoroughbred and Harness Racing, at Exhibition Park, (306) 757–2674.

Recreation

Tennis

Lakeshore Tennis Club, in Wascana Park, (306) 525–5095.

Racquetball, Badminton, and Squash

The Regina Courts Club, 3615 Pasqua Street, (306) 585–1212.

Curling

Regina Exhibition Curlodrome, (306) 527–0379.

Golf

Regina Golf Club, 11th Avenue, (306) 565–8800, eighteen holes, clubhouse, and equipment rentals.

Ice-Skating

Exhibition Stadium, 1615 Pasqua Street, (306) 569–7736.

Swimming

Lawson Aquatic Centre, 1701 Elphinstone Street, (306) 569–7378.
Most hotels have swimming pools.

Shopping

Regina has eleven major shopping centers. In downtown visit the Cornwall Centre, which has ninety stores, with two large department stores, The Bay, the Midtown Centre, and the Scarth Street Mall. The Warehouse Village, Old City Hall Mall, and Carriage Square are historic areas that have been refurbished with shops, cafés, and services.

Kettle Creek Canvas Co., 1825 Hamilton Street, (306) 352–7868. 100 percent cotton clothing for the entire family.

The Scandinavian Boutique, Golden Mile Centre, 3806 Albert Street, (306) 584–5776. Fine fashions and gifts imported from Norway, Finland, Denmark, Iceland, and Sweden.

The Lingerie Shoppe, 1832 Hamilton Street, (306) 359–3373. Imported and domestic lingerie: Chantelle, Lejaby, Marie Jo, Christian Dior, Olga, and Bleyle.

Saskatoon: Hub City of Saskatchewan

What Makes Saskatoon Special

Saskatoon is a fast-growing, modern city, but also one that has retained traditional prairie friendliness. Saskatoon, considered a "hub city" because of its transportation facilities, moves the province's grain, minerals, and lumber to customers in all parts of the globe. Among the fascinating architectural features surrounding Saskatoon—for that matter, in many places throughout the prairies—are the grain elevators by the side of railroad tracks. These geometrically pleasing structures are the trademarks of the prairies.

Saskatoon was founded in 1882 by John Lake and his congregation of 113 Ontario Methodists. Granted 200,000 acres, the Methodists wanted to create a utopia based on the values of their denomination, which include temperance. They called their new community Minnetonka, after a local lake. The community's name was later changed to Saskatoon, meaning juneberry, in honor of the red berries that grow here. Unfortunately, utopias can survive as such only in isolation. Starting in the late 1800s, the migration into Western Canada of great numbers of people seeking land transformed Saskatoon into a more ethnically diverse community. Ukrainians, for example, who were expert grain farmers in the Old Country, were among the new people who produced food for

millions from the rough prairie land. Meat processing and various kinds of manufacturing became important industries. Large deposits of potash and uranium, as well as reserves of petroleum and natural gas, were discovered and have been exploited. Today, Saskatoon is a city of gleaming office towers, beautiful parks, and clean streets, with a thriving cultural life.

How to Get to and Around Saskatoon

By Plane
Air Canada, Canadian Airlines, and Norcanair provide daily service to Saskatoon. The Saskatoon Airport is located northeast of city center, via Circle Drive. Its terminal has full facilities, including rental cars.

By Car
Saskatoon is located south of the geographic center of the province on the interprovincial Yellowhead Highway 16. From Regina the city can best be reached by taking Highway 11 north or from Prince Albert, Highway 11 south.

By Rail
VIA Rail provides service to and from Saskatoon. Call (800) 555-1212 for VIA Rail's toll-free number in your area code.

By Bus
Greyhound provides bus service to and from Saskatoon and many other Western Canada destinations. Saskatoon Bus Depot, 50-23rd Street, East, (306) 933-5700.

Saskatoon is located on the South Saskatchewan River. The main streets of city center are Spadina Crescent, Queen Street, 1st through 5th avenues, and 20th to 25th streets. The Saskatoon Transportation Company provides bus service throughout the city, and there are taxi services. For information on the city, visit the Saskatoon Convention and Visitors Bureau in downtown Saskatoon, 347 2nd Avenue, South, (306) 242-1206.

◀ Proud Saskatoon is modern, busy, and forward-looking. A warm welcome to Western Canada travelers is an honored part of its traditional prairie heritage.

Touring Services

Northcote River Cruise, along the South Saskatchewan River, depart from dock in Kiwanis Park, (306) 665–1818.

Saskatoon Cycling Club Tours, starting from Mendel Art Gallery, (306) 244–7332.

Heritage Sightseeing Tours, (306) 382–1911, narrated mini-bus tours; full and half-day trips; trips to Prince Albert National Park, the Battlefords, Batoche, Gardiner Dam; city tours; custom tours can be arranged.

Attractions

Mendel Art Gallery, 950 Spadina Crescent, (306) 664–9610. Open throughout the year. Free. The Mendel is one of Western Canada's most important public art galleries. It was given to Saskatoon by Frederick Mendel, a German immigrant who made his fortune from meat packing. The permanent collection has works by Emily Carr, David Milne, Feininger, Utrillo, Chagall, and Pissarro. There are also significant traveling exhibitions throughout the year. The MAG has a conservatory of rare plants and flowers and a gift shop.

Little Stone School House, on the University of Saskatchewan campus, (306) 966–8382. Free. This is Saskatoon's first school and the city's oldest public building. It was called the Old Victoria School.

Museum of Ukrainian Culture, 202 Avenue "M" S., (306) 244–4212. Open throughout the year. Donations accepted. A superior collection of Ukrainian artifacts, arts and crafts.

Saskatoon Western Development Museum, 2610 Lorne Avenue S., on Exhibition grounds, (306) 931–1910. Open throughout the year. Free. Within this museum is a re-creation of a circa 1910 street with an early bank, stores, Chinese laundry, church, school, hotel, railroad station, pool hall, and theater. Walking down this street you really feel as if you're in "Boomtown Saskatchewan." There's also a gallery of Saskatchewan arts and crafts.

St. Thomas More Art Gallery, on the University of Saskatchewan campus, (306) 966–8953. Open from mid-September to mid-April. Free. Exhibits paintings by provincial and regional artists. Be sure to see the stunning Kurelek mural in the St. Thomas More Chapel. The late William Kurelek was one of Canada's most important contemporary artists. His paintings of ordinary life were highly realistic and also highly mystical in a religious sense.

The Right Honourable John G. Diefenbaker Centre, on the campus of the University of Saskatchewan, (306) 966–8384. Open throughout the year. Free. Diefenbaker museum and archives. The "Dief's" grave is next to the building.

Ukrainian Museum of Canada, 910 Spadina Crescent E., (306) 244–3800. Open throughout the year. Admission charged. Displays on Ukrainian culture and family life in Canada.

Accommodations

Leading Hotels

Hotel Bessborough, 601 Spadina Crescent, (306) 244–5521. Saskatoon's "landmark" hotel has the château-style exterior so characteristic of similar places throughout Canada. It has three fine restaurants—Aerial's Cove for seafood, Samurai Japanese Steak House, and Treetops, with its décor of plants and wicker. There are a swimming pool, steam bath, exercise facilities, and many other services. Moderate.

Sheraton Cavalier, 612 Spadina Crescent, (306) 652–6770. This Sheraton has a wonderful complex of swimming pools, water slides, hot tubs, and other recreational facilities. It offers good accommodations, and fine dining, dancing, and entertainment at the Top of the Inn. Moderate to expensive.

Ramada Renaissance, 405 20th Street, (306) 665–3322. This bright, modern hotel offers excellent accommodations and services. It has a swimming pool with a great water slide, a restaurant, and health club. Moderate to expensive.

Holiday Inn, 90 22nd Street, (306) 244–2311. This Holiday Inn, located downtown, across from the Centennial Auditorium, has a special executive section call the Commonwealth Club. Its top restaurant is R. J. Willoughby's. There are a swimming pool and other facilities. Moderate to expensive.

Other Fine Places to Stay

Best Western Yellowhead Inn, 1715 Idylwyld Drive, (306) 244–5552. Moderate.

Confederation Flag Inn, 3330 Fairlight Drive, (306) 384–2882. Moderate.

Holiday House Motor Hotel, 2901 8th Street, (306) 374–9111. Moderate.

Imperial 400 Motel, 610 Idylwyld Drive, (306) 244–2901. Moderate.

Parktown Motor Hotel, 924 Spadina Crescent, (306) 244–5564. Moderate.

Saskatoon Capri Motor Hotel, 304 2nd Avenue, (306) 653–4662. Moderate.

Saskatoon Inn, corner of Circle Drive and Airport Drive, (306) 242–1440. Moderate to expensive.

Travelodge Motor Hotel, 106 Circle Drive, (306) 242–8881. Moderate.

Wills Inns Saskatoon, 806 Idylwyld Drive, (306) 665–6500. Moderate.

YWCA, 510 25th Street, (306) 244–0944. Inexpensive.

Dining

Aerial's Cove, at the Hotel Bessborough, (306) 244–5521. Aerial's is Saskatoon's best restaurant or just about at the apex. Its specialties include curried shrimp Madras, tournedos Rossini, rack of lamb provençal, and veal Madeira. Expensive.

Samurai Japanese Steak House, also at the Hotel Bessborough, (306) 244–5521. Here you can feast on hibachi steak or scallops—a Shogun special that includes steak, chicken, and lobster—or a vegetarian platter of onions, green peppers, Japanese mushroom, and other vegetables. Moderate.

Fuddruckers, 2910 8th Street, (306) 955–7777. Gourmet hamburgers, salads, and more. Inexpensive to moderate.

Saskatoon Station Place, Idylwyld and 23rd Street, (306) 244–7777. In an old railroad station, this is Saskatoon's most colorful restaurant. It features an extensive menu of goodies: ribs, shrimp, stuffed musrooms, Greek salad, French onion soup, pork chops, lobster tails, halibut steak, stuffed sole, omelettes, burgers, pasta, souvlaki, prime roast rib of beef, steaks, lamb, and more. Moderate.

Xanadu, 2508 8th Street E., (306) 374–9550. Chinese and Greek dishes; also live entertainment. Moderate.

Traeger's Tearoom, Cumberland Square, (306) 374–7881. Light meals and delicate pastries. Inexpensive to moderate.

Lucci's, 3rd Avenue, (306) 653–0188. An excellent Saskatoon restaurant serving continental cuisine. Expensive.

Artful Dodger, 119 4th Avenue, (306) 653–2577. Here is Saskatoon's Ye Old English pub serving the grub and ales that satisfy any stiff-upper-lip mood. Moderate.

Entertainment

Saskatchewan Centennial Auditorium, 22nd Street, (306) 664–9778. A venue for the city's performing arts groups and for visiting talent.

The following nightclubs all feature dancing and live entertainment:

Confetti le Club, 710 Idylwyld Drive, (306) 244–6655.

Esmeralda's, at the Saskatoon Inn, 2002 Airport Drive, (306) 242–1440.

Sliders, 301 1st Avenue N., (306) 664–1900.

Sports and Recreation

Kinsmen Park Rides, in Kinsmen Park at corner of Spadina Crescent and 25th Street. (306) 664–9366, has a miniature merry-go-round, ferris wheel, and train for children.

Riverside Rentals, (306) 244–8347, rents bikes.

Thoroughbred and Harness Racing, at Marquis Downs, Saskatoon Prairieland Exhibition Centre, (306) 931–7149, extension 33.

Shopping

Midtown Plaza, located in city center, at 1st Avenue and between 20th and 22nd streets, has many shops and services, including Eaton's department store. The Bay is nearby on 22nd and 1st.

A-A-A-A-A-A-A Antiques, 33rd Street, (306) 653–3936, military and other collectibles.

Clay Studio Three Potters, 918 B Broadway Avenue, (306) 242–1158.

Handmade House in Grosvenor Park Shopping Centre, (306) 477–2639, Saskatchewan arts and crafts.

House of Treasures, 1416 22nd Street, (306) 653–4885, Canadian-made mukluks and parkas.

James Art Studio, 906 Victoria Avenue, (306) 244–5959, features works by Robert Bateman, Audrey Piper, and Cecil James.

Saskatchewan Indian Arts and Crafts, Midtown Plaza, (306) 665–6977.

Wilkie's Antique Clocks, Avenue "L" and 22nd Street, (306) 665–2888.

CHAPTER 9

Touring Manitoba
Winnipeg • Churchill
on Hudson Bay

What Makes Manitoba Special

When you take a look at the map of Canada—that line of huge provinces from the Atlantic to the Pacific—you'll see that Manitoba is smack in the middle. Manitoba is like a keystone that cements the different blocks of an arch into a strong, symmetrical whole. Although Manitoba sits north of Minnesota and North Dakota, states usually associated with the American midwest, in Canada the province is very much within the western region of the country. Manitoba was and still is considered the "gateway" to Western Canada when traveling from the east. Here is where Western Canada began for settlers, entrepreneurs, and developers from Ontario, Québec, and the Maritimes, and for the thousands of immigrants from many foreign countries seeking a new life in the New World.

Manitoba is a very large province—250,946 square miles (403,772 sq. km.) and the only one in Western Canada (excluding the Northwest Territories) that has extensive shoreline on Hudson Bay. In the province you can travel from southern wheat fields to northern wilderness areas where polar bears roam in large numbers. Manitoba has the largest lake—Lake Winnipeg—within its interior of any province in Canada. (The Great Lakes are not within the interior of any province but share shoreline and territorial waters with various American states.) Specifically, Manitoba has both the Hudson Bay and the province of Ontario at its eastern border; the states of Minnesota and North Dakota on its southern edge (the 49th

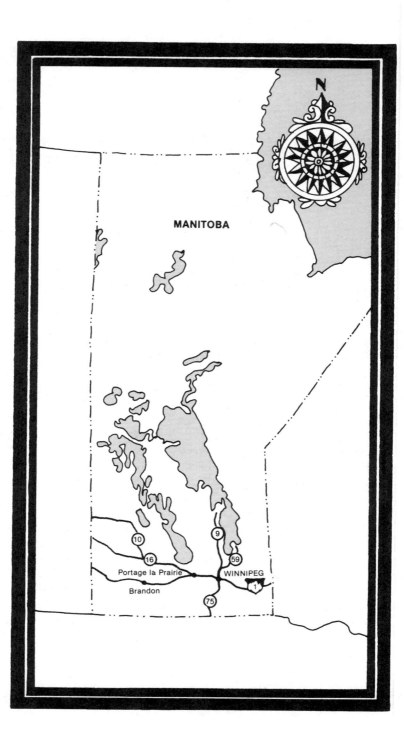

parallel, the straight-line international border between Canada and the United States); Saskatchewan on its western border; and the Northwest Territories to the north.

In the southern portion of the province, where the majority of the 1 million Manitobans live, the climate is similar to that of the other prairie provinces—cold, invigorating winters and warm, pleasant summers. The climate in the south is so congenial, in fact, that agriculture flourishes: wheat and other grains, vegetables, and fruits grow here. In the south, where Winnipeg, the province's capital city, is situated, spring tends to come in sooner than in other places. Topographically, Manitoba is a relatively flat land mass, patterend over by many lakes and rivers. The land in the south has been extensively developed for agriculture; in the midsection it is thick with forests; and in the north the land is subarctic with boreal forests and tundra. The climate in the north during the summer, particularly near Hudson Bay, tends to be cooler than northern sections of Alberta and Saskatchewan, but it is a very attractive area to those interested in experiencing the particular ecology created by this climatic zone.

Human habitation in Manitoba has existed for thousands of years. The first Europeans to arrive and put down stakes were the fur trappers and traders of the Hudson's Bay Company, which established a post and fort at York Factory in 1682. Furs brought into York Factory from countless inland points of origin were placed on ships that sailed up Hudson Bay, through Hudson Strait, into the Atlantic, and on to markets in England (during the summer months Churchill had a direct link with Liverpool, England, 2,936 miles away). For close to 200 years, Manitoba, known as Rupert's Land (an appellation given to most of Western Canada in honor of Prince Rupert, one of the founders of the Hudson's Bay Company), was virtually a "factory" that produced furs for English merchants and European fashions. However, in 1812 the first Selkirk settlers, under the leadership of Thomas Douglas, fifth earl of Selkirk, arrived and, along with fur trading, began a serious effort at expanding agriculture, transforming the rich potential of the grass prairies. With burgeoning agriculture, stable communities were built and grew as more people, seeing potential for themselves in Manitoba, arrived and settled. A habitation of new hope called the Red River Settlement was formed by Lord Selkirk, composed mainly of dispossessed Scottish sharecropping farmers. Rupert's Land was sold by the Hudson's Bay Company to Canada in 1870, and in 1871 the first legislature of Manitoba met, consisting of twelve English-Canadian and twelve French-Canadian members. A year earlier, in 1870, Manitoba actually became the fifth province in Canadian Confederation as a result of the Manitoba Act, which received assent from Queen Victoria.

Although the majority of Manitobans are of British extraction (Scots, English, Irish, Welsh), there are also sizeable groups of French, German, Polish, Icelandic, and Ukrainian. The Mennonites, a German-speaking religious sect, are another large group. Many of the early French fur trappers and a smaller number of Scottish trappers married native Indian women. Their progeny became the métis, who formed a colony at Red River, from which Louis Riel and his people launched a rebellion in 1869 and 1870 when the land was transferred from Hudson's Bay Company to the Canadian government. Métis settlements were in the Red River Valley, in and around Winnipeg, and the métis influence continues to be strong in a number of communities in southern and central Manitoba.

Today Manitoba's economy is based on agriculture, mining (nickel and precious metals), hydroelectric energy, forestry, food processing, manufacturing, transportation, and tourism. Winnipeg is a major transportation hub for all of Canada because of its central location. The city is also well known throughout the world for its cultural life, particularly its Royal Winnipeg Ballet. For the vacation traveler, Manitoba has it all: a sophisticated city, significant history, beautiful scenery, many attractions and recreational opportunities, adventure north to the polar bears and Hudson Bay, and friendly people who say "Welcome!" in many different languages.

Manitoba Tourism

Travel Manitoba, the provincial government's tourism agency, provides this toll-free number for your use: (800) 665–0040, ext. 231, which is operative throughout continental United States and Canada. Their phone number in Winnipeg is (204) 945–3777 (collect). Twenty-four-hour recorded messages on traveling in Manitoba—attractions, events, park vacancy rates, ski conditions—can be obtained by dialing (204) 942–2535. Or you can write to Travel Manitoba, Department 7231, 7th Floor, 155 Carlton Street, Winnipeg, Manitoba, R3C 3H8.

Travel Manitoba will provide free-of-charge maps, brochures, and personal counseling on how you and your party can get the most out of your travels and vacation time in the province. Travel Manitoba has information centers at the following locations, open mid-May through early September:

Manitoba–U.S. border, at Highways 75 and 10
Manitoba–Ontario boundary, at the Trans-Canada Highway 1
Manitoba–Saskatchewan boundary, at the Trans-Canada Highway 1
Manitoba–U.S. border, at Highway 75 (open March to December)
Winnipeg East and West, at the Trans-Canada near Perimeter Highway
Downtown Winnipeg at the Legislative Building (open year-round)
Many local communities also maintain their own tourism information bureaus.

Touring Services

The following companies provide tours to the major attractions in Manitoba.

Churchill Wilderness Encounter, (204) 657–2729; three- to nine-day trips to the Churchill area to see polar bears, wild birds, beluga whales, and local communities on Hudson Bay.

Dymond Lake Air Services, (204) 675–2583; flights to see wildlife in the Churchill area.

Great Canadian Travel Company, (204) 284–1580; sightseeing tours of the province and trips to special events.

Hartwig Wilderness Adventures and Travel, (204) 668–3234; fishing and hunting trips, white-water rafting, guest ranch stays.

M.S. _Lady Chesley_, (204) 738–2250, Netley Marshes to Lake Winnipeg cruises.

M.S. _Lord Selkirk_, (204) 582–2331, cruises on the Red River within the city of Winnipeg; also dinner/dance cruises and dockside lunches.

Manitoba Farm Vacation Association, (204) 475–6624; vacations on family farms.

Mantario Wilderness Skills, (204) 943–9029; canoeing, hiking and fishing trips in Whiteshell Provincial Park.

North Star Tours, (204) 675–2629; trips to Churchill attractions and to Eskimo Point in the Northwest Territories.

Northern Manitoba Native Lodges, (204) 774–4555; fishing packages at Indian-owned-and-operated lodges.

Northern Manitoba Outfitters, (204) 382–2379; trips to Northern Manitoba and Hudson Bay.

Paddlewheel–Grey Line Boat and Bus Tours, (204) 339–1696; vintage boat trips. This paddle wheeler is just like the one you'd expect to see plying the Mississippi during Mark Twain's early years. Only you can ride one right now on the Red River in Manitoba. There's entertainment on board, as well as dining and dancing. You can even book the boat for your wedding. The paddle wheeler *Princess* cruises down to historic Lower Fort Garry.

Prairie Dog Central Steam Train, (204) 284–2690; vintage train trip from Winnipeg to Grosse Isle, 58 km./36 mi.

Riding Mountain Nature Tours, (204) 848–2977; hiking, trail riding, mountain biking, and boat trips in Riding Mountain National Park.

Sea North Tours, (204) 675–2195; boat trips to Fort Prince of Wales on Hudson Bay.

Trailhead Excursions, (204) 848–7649; trail-riding trips in Riding Mountain National Park.

Tundra Buggy Tours, (204) 675–2121; "biophysical" tours of the Churchill area and its polar bears.

VIA Rail Canada Explorer Tour to Churchill, (204) 949–7477; call (800) 555–1212 for toll-free number in your area code. Six-day rail tour to Hudson Bay, one of the most popular trips in Canada; operates from June to September.

River Rouge Cruise Ships and Bus Tours, (204) 669–2824; tours of the city of Winnipeg and its rivers, including dining/dancing cruises; trips to Lower Fort Garry; uses British red double-deck buses in the city.

Northern Expeditions, (204) 675–2793; tours of Churchill, including naturalist, polar bear, birding, and beluga whale tours.

Useful Information

Emergencies: throughout the province dial 911.

Provincial holiday: Civic Holiday, the first Monday in August.

Liquor: The legal age for buying and consuming liquor in Manitoba is eighteen. Bottled liquor is sold in government stores, which are located in cities and large towns.

Sales Tax: Manitoba's sales tax is 7 percent, including meals over $6.00.

Arts and Crafts: Manitoba arts and crafts, including native Indian and Inuit, are sold in stores in cities and large towns. For more information, contact the Manitoba Crafts Council, (204) 942–1816, and/or the Indian Crafts and Arts Manitoba, (204) 943–5276.

Bed and Breakfast: For information on places to stay, contact B&B of Manitoba, 7 Sandale Drive, Winnipeg, Manitoba R2N 1A1, Canada, (204) 256–6151.

Sports Fishing: contact Travel Manitoba toll-free (800) 665–0040, ext. 231.

Provincial parks and camping: Some of Manitoba's provincial parks are open throughout the year. They provide campsides and facilities and various recreational features. For more information, call (204) 945–6784 (collect).

Time Zone: central.

Area Code: 204.

Manitoba Special Events

International Music Camp and Athletic Camp, Peace Gardens, all
  summer
International Festival of the Arts, International Peace Garden, early
  July
Great Northern Pike Festival, Lynn Lake, mid-June
Winnipeg International Children's Festival, Winnipeg, late May
International Festival of Mime, Winnipeg, early June
Provincial Exhibition of Manitoba, Brandon, mid-June
Red River Exhibition, Winnipeg, late June
La Fête de la Saint-Jean Baptiste, La Broquerie, late June
Trout Festival, Flin Flon, late June to July 1
Canadian National Mule Derby, Miami, late June to early July
Strawberry Festival, Portage la Prairie, early July
Winnipeg Folk Festival, Winnipeg, early July
Highland Gathering, Selkirk, early July
Swamp Skimming Championships, Sandy Lake, mid-July

Threshermen's Reunion and Stampede, Austin, late July
Sunflower Festival, Altona, late July
Northwest Round-up, Swan River, late July
Manitoba Stampede and Rodeo, in Morris, mid- to late July
Indian Days: Thompson, late-August
Oktoberfest: Winnipeg, early to mid-September

Some of Manitoba's most entertaining and unusual festivals are held during the month of August:

Canada's **National Ukrainian Festival** is held six miles (9.6 km.) south of Dauphin during the first week in August. (Dauphin is reached from Winnipeg via the Yellowhead Highway 16 west to Highway 10 north—311 km./187 mi.) In Ukrainian *Bitaemo!* means welcome, and it's best expressed here at *Selo Ukraina* in early August. This is Canada's National Ukrainian Festival, where an entire community warmly extends itself to visitors—Ukrainian or not. The festival features the stirring, beautiful and wild Ukrainian dancing and singing (Canada's National Ukrainian Festival Choir and Riding and Dancing Cossacks); Old Country food and plenty of it (succulent *varenyky, holubtsi, kobasa*); parades; traditional arts and crafts. One of the most impressive moments in the festival is *Obzhynky*, the Ukrainian harvest ritual in which an honored guest is presented with bread and salt, an ancient custom symbolizing warmth and hospitality. Another highlight is the enactment of a traditional four-phase Ukrainian wedding—the matchmaking, the engagement, the marriage, and the wedding feast—which in past times went on for several days.

Steinbach Pioneer Days, in Steinbach, early August, is a unique festival celebrating the Mennonite heritage in Manitoba with traditional foods, arts and crafts, demonstrations of pioneer life, and entertainment.

Frog Follies, Canadian national frog-jumping championships, are held in St. Pierre-Jolys, early August.

Folklorama, in Winnipeg, mid-August, is Manitoba's great ethnic festival, where Manitobans representing ethnic, racial, and cultural groups from all over the world celebrate their uniqueness and their contribution to the Canadian cultural "mosaic." You visit pavilions located throughout the city, each one representing a different culture and featuring traditional foods, arts and crafts, and entertainment. In effect, you travel from country to country without ever leaving downtown Winnipeg.

Winnipeg: Where Western Canada Began

What Makes Winnipeg Special

Winnipeg, located where the Assiniboine and Red rivers converge, is nearly equidistant from the Atlantic and Pacific oceans, and 100 km./60 mi. north of the U.S.–Canadian border where the states of Minnesota and North Dakota meet. Ever since the mid-1800s, Winnipeg has been known as the Gateway City to Western Canada, much in the same manner as St. Louis, Missouri, and the American West.

La Vérendrye, the French explorer and entrepreneur, set up a trading post called Fort Rouge here at the "Forks" in 1738. Thomas Douglas, fifth earl of Selkirk, a Scot with big ideas for his beleagured Highlanders, created the Red River Settlement in 1812. Saint-Boniface, one of the métis settlements in this area, is now a part of Greater Winnipeg and is considered the largest center of French culture in Canada outside of Québec. In 1816 the Seven Oaks Massacre took the lives of twenty pioneers in the Red River Settlement. Under Lord Selkirk's leadership the colony again took hold, expanded, and became prosperous. The Red River (along with trails using the famous Red River carts) became the main highway of commerce between Winnipeg and St. Paul, Minnesota. This interchange of business, ideas, and people became so intensive that some in the region were saying that Manitoba would become part of the United States. However, Louis Riel's visions for his country and the creation of Manitoba as a province quashed any prospect of merging with the United States. Today Winnipeg and St. Paul share a sisterly relationship based on a common pioneering heritage.

In 1873 Winnipeg was incorporated as a city. Its growth boomed when in 1881 the transcontinental railroad came in, making Winnipeg the distribution center for almost all of Western Canada. (It still plays that role for the heartland of the country. If you take a VIA Rail trip across Canada—one of the great rail adventures of the world—Winnipeg will be the midpoint in your journey.) The city became the grain market center for the prairies with the establishment of the Winnipeg Grain Exchange in 1887. What oil is to Calgary and cod is to St. John's, grain is to Winnipeg; it's the main commodity of economic prosperity for thousands of people. In 1919 the city went through the Winnipeg General Strike; social upheaval

305

caused basic services to cease operating, stores and factories to close their doors, unemployment to soar, and extreme bitterness between fellow citizens to burst into violence. Just as the wounds from the strike were being soothed, Winnipeg became one of the many North American casualties of the Great Depression of the 1930s. The supply and manpower demands of World War II helped to boost Winnipeg's economy, and it has been on an upswing ever since because of the optimism, hard work, and intelligence of its citizens.

In the sphere of international culture, most people outside of Canada may never have heard of Manitoba, but they surely know of the Royal Winnipeg Ballet, one of the foremost classical dance companies in the world. Sometimes it is difficult to reconcile in one's mind the ethos of the prairies with great cultural institutions, but in Winnipeg the blend works exceedingly well. In addition to dance, there's excellence in visual arts and in dramatic art.

Although the first people of Winnipeg were native Indians, French, Scots, Irish, and English, succeeding waves of immigrants seeking their fortune were Germans, Ukrainians, Poles, Dutch, Italians, Scandinavians, Hungarians, Jews, and Asians. As a result, Winnipeg, although English on the surface, is a merging of many nationalities into one people working together for the common good, yet distinct within their own noble heritages.

Today Winnipeg is a modern city that has been able to blend its historical heritage nicely with gleaming skyscrapers. Its population now numbers more than 602,000 people, who are employed in various industries and services: manufacturing, tourism, food processing, transportation, aerospace, electronics, government, medicine, and education. The standard of living is quite high here, with abundant cultural, educational, shopping, and recreational opportunities for residents and visitors.

When you arrive in Winnipeg, you are where Western Canada begins or ends. This is a significant geographical point, also rich in human history, particularly the development of Canada as a independent nation state. To stay awhile in Winnipeg is not only to absorb this significance but also to enjoy the treasures of a cultural oasis in a vast prairie land.

◀ **Manitoba produces bountiful crops, contributing to the well-being of Canada and providing nourishment to millions of people around the world.**

How to Get to Winnipeg

By Plane

Winnipeg International Airport is located a few miles west of city center Winnipeg; the terminal has full facilities: restaurant, lounge, gift and duty-free shops, and so on. Rental car booths are also here. The following major airlines serve Winnipeg: Air Canada, Canadian Airlines, Nordair, and Northwest Orient, plus several regional carriers.

By Car

Traveling from Calgary and Regina, continue on the Trans-Canada Highway 1; from Edmonton and Saskatoon, stay on the Yellowhead Highway 16. Traveling from Ontario and Eastern Canada, take the Trans-Canada to Winnipeg. Coming north from Minnesota and North Dakota, use Interstate Highway 29 to the border and then Manitoba Highway 75, which will take you straight into Winnipeg.

By Rail

VIA Rail provides train service to and from Winnipeg. The terminal is located on Main Street near the Upper Fort Garry Gate. Call (800) 555–1212 for the toll-free VIA Rail number serving your area code. In Winnipeg, call (204) 944–8780 for schedule information and (204) 949–1830 for fares and reservations. If you are traveling to Western Canada from the East, you have a choice in Winnipeg: to go due west to Regina, Calgary, Banff, Lake Louise, and Vancouver or northwest to Saskatoon, Edmonton, Jasper, and Vancouver.

By Bus

Greyhound provides bus service throughout much of Western Canada. Their terminal is located at 487 Portage Avenue, (204) 775–8301.

How to Get Around Winnipeg

Winnipeg is a very easy city to get around in. City center is laid out in a grid pattern. To the south of city center is the Assiniboine River and to the east is the Red River and the French-speaking community of Saint-Boniface. Portage Avenue and

WINNIPEG

Main Street are among the primary streets. The provincial legislative building is located at Osborne and Broadway. If you require additional information regarding your stay in the city, call the Winnipeg Convention and Visitor's Bureau at (204) 943–1970 or visit them at 226–375 York Avenue.

There are several companies that provide bus and boat tours of the Winnipeg area (see above). Winnipeg Transit operates bus service throughout most of the city; call (204) 284–7190 for information.

The following companies provide taxi service: Duffy's (204) 775–0101, Yellow (204) 942–7555, Preston Limousine (204) 633–6715, Grosvenor (204) 947–6611.

Business and Convention Services

The Winnipeg Convention Centre, 375 York Avenue, (204) 956–1720, offers 6,120 square meters (20,067 sq. ft.) of exhibition space, with seating for 7,200 persons. It also has a councourse of shops and restaurants. A skywalk connects it to a first-class hotel.

Attractions

Manitoba Centennial Centre, opposite City Hall, north of Portage and Main, (204) 956–1360, encompasses the Planetarium, the Museum of Man and Nature, Manitoba Theatre Centre, terraced gardens, and fountains.

Manitoba Museum of Man and Nature, 190 Rupert Avenue at Main Street, (204) 956–2830. Open throughout the year. Admission charged. This exceptional museum, part of the Manitoba Centennial Centre complex, includes the Plantarium—call (204) 943–3142 for Planetarium information. The museum contains fascinating exhibits depicting métis on horseback hunting buffalo, the life of the prairie farmer, the geological history of the province, the role of Hudson's Bay Company in exploration and development of Manitoba, the ecology of the grasslands, and human settlement of the prairies. Its Planetarium presents exciting shows describing the wonders of our cosmos.

The Exchange District, a several-block area in city center; call (204) 943–0783. This visually and architecturally rich district has a fine collection of turn-of-the-century commercial buildings that have been preserved and restored: Massey-Harris Building (1885);

Bate Building (1883); Traveller's Block (1907); Imperial Dry Goods Block (1899); Confederation Life Building (1912); Pantages Playhouse Theatre (1913); J. H. Ashdown Warehouse (1895); the Donald H. Bain Building (1899); Telegram Building (1882); and Canadian Imperial Bank of Commerce (1910). Also in this historic district are many fine shops, restaurants, clubs, and theaters. Among the interesting commercial places are Northern Traditions (Indian, Inuit, and métis art), Canadian Native Handicrafts (handmade mukluks and moccasins), Red River Book Shop, Birt Saddlery (Western and English riding gear and clothes), Marty's Food 'n' Beverage (prime rib and seafood), Old Market Café (salads, soups, and sandwiches), Rorie Street Marble Club (nightclub), Cibo's (good fish dishes), Deeds (a fine deli), Fantasy Theatre for Children, Goof's Bazaar (novelty shop), and Toad Hall Toys.

Also in this area are the Centennial Concert Hall, Warehouse Theatre, Manitoba Theatre Centre, and the Prairie Theatre Exchange. If you'd like a guided walking tour of the district, call (204) 986–5287. Tours start from the Museum of Man and Nature, located at 190 Rupert Avenue.

Winnipeg has a rapidly growing **Chinatown,** in the area of King and Princess streets and James and Rupert avenues, where there are restaurants serving savory Cantonese, Szechuan, and Peking dishes, custom tailors, Oriental gift shops, and herb shops.

Aquatic Hall of Fame, Pan-Am Pool Building, 25 Poseidon Road, open throughout the year, (204) 284–4031. Free. The Hall honors Canadians who have distinguished themselves in aquatic sports.

Legislative Building, at Broadway and Osborne. Open daily, call (204) 945–3700 to arrange a guided tour. Free. The architect of Manitoba's Legislative Building was Frank Worthington Symington from Liverpool, England. Gracing the dome of the building is a 240-foot-high heroic statue known as the *Golden Boy,* who holds a torch. It's one of the best-known symbols of the prairie spirit in Manitoba. The building, constructed of Manitoba's Tyndall stone and Italian marble, is considered one of the finest examples of neoclassical architecture in Canada. It stands on the bank of the Assiniboine River. On the beautiful grounds surrounding the capitol are statues of Queen Victoria, Louis Riel, considered the father of the province, and the great Ukrainian poet Tara Shevchenko. The mansion of the lieutenant governor is also on the grounds, and nearby is Memorial Park, a tranquil place during the summer.

311

Riel House National Historic Site, located on 330 River Road. Open mid-May to end of September, (204) 257–1783; Free. Louis Riel, although tried and hanged for treason, is considered the father of the province of Manitoba (technically he was known as the leader of the Provisional Government of Assiniboia and the North West from 1869 to 1870). This house, which belonged to his family, has been restored and furnished to reflect the lives of the Riel and Lagimodiére families, who lived here in the late 1880s. Riel's grave can be found in the churchyard of Saint-Boniface Basilica. If you are interested in taking a guided walking tour (commentary available in French or English) of the historic points of interest in Saint-Boniface, contact La Société Historique de Saint-Boniface, (204) 233–4888.

Seven Oaks House, Rupertsland Avenue, (204) 339–5627. Open mid-May to mid-June. Admission charged. Oldest habitable home in Manitoba. A two-story log house built by John Inkster in 1851, with furnishings from that period.

Lombard Place, at Portage and Main, (204) 934–5582. Open Monday through Friday. Free. This complex contains the Richardson Building, one of the tallest in the city, which has an observation floor where you can get the best views of the surrounding city and landscape (call ahead for reservation). Also within this complex are the Westin Hotel, the Bank of Canada building, and an underground concourse of many shops and services.

Oseredok (the Ukrainian Cultural and Educational Centre), 184 Alexander Avenue E., (204) 942–0218. Open Tuesday through Sunday. Free. This ethnic museum has a fine collection of Ukrainian folk costumes, embroidery, weaving, decorated Easter eggs (*pysanky*), woodcarving, and ceramics; also coins, stamps, and documents from the Ukrainian National Republic of 1918–1921. There are a library of 40,000 volumes, an art gallery, and archives.

Centre Culturel Franco-Manitobain, 340 boulevard Provencher, (204) 233–8972. Open throughout the year. Home of these performing groups: Foyer (cabaret theater); Cercle Molière (Canada's oldest continual French theater company); Les Danseurs de la Rivière Rouge (folk dance troupe); le 100 Nons (young singers and musicians); and l'Alliance Chorale Manitoba, les Blés au Vent, and les Intrépides (choral groups).

Royal Canadian Mint, 520 Lagimodière Boulevard, (204) 257–3359. Open throughout the year. Free. Tours are offered, and you can see coins being produced for use as Canadian and foreign currency.

Assiniboine Park Zoo, Corydon Avenue W. at Shaftsbury, (204) 888–3634. Open throughout the year. Free. A fine zoo with over 1,000 animals, including North American species, Siberian tiger, and North China leopard. Aunt Sally's Farm has a zoo of baby animals for the enjoyment of youngsters.

Living Prairie Museum, 2795 Ness Avenue, (204) 832–0167. Open daily July to September. Free. A natural prairie preserve of 200 native plants; tours during July and August.

Dalnavert Museum, 61 Carlton Street. (204) 943–2835. Open daily throughout the year. Free. This Victorian mansion belonged to Sir Hugh John Macdonald, the only surviving son of Canada's first prime minister; it is named after his mother's home in Aviemore, Scotland. Dalnavert has been restored to the beauty it had in 1895 and is open as a museum.

Mennonite Genealogy, 790 Wellington Avenue, (204) 772–0747. Open throughout the year. Free. Provides genealogical research for Mennonites with a Prussian/Russian heritage. The Mennonites of Manitoba, a Protestant denomination founded by Menno Simons, are of two different branches: Pennsylvania Deutsch of Ontario and Russian Mennonites of the West. Because of their pacifism, they were persecuted in Europe and fled to North America, settling in Manitoba in 1874. Approximately 60,000 Mennonites now reside in the province and are considered among its most cherished citizens.

Queen's Own Cameron Highlanders of Canada Museum, 969 St. Matthews Avenue, (204) 786–2205. Open Mondays and Wednesdays. Free. Displays of the history of a famous Manitoba Scottish regiment that fought in World Wars I and II.

Royal Winnipeg Rifles Regimental Museum, 969 St. Matthews Avenue, (204) 783–0880. Open Tuesdays and Thursdays. Free. Weapons, uniforms, pictures, and artifacts of the oldest military unit in Western Canada.

Western Canadian Aviation Museum, located in Hangar T2 at the airport, 958 FerryRoad, (204) 786–5503. Open throughout the year. Admission charged. Here is an excellent collection of aircraft: Avro 504K, Vickers Vedette, Canada's first helicopter, Bellanca Aircruiser, Fokker Super Universal, North American Harvard, Vickers Viscount, DeHavilland Tiger Moth, and many others.

Saint-Boniface Museum, on avenue Taché, (204) 237–4500. Open throughout the year. Donations accepted. This museum of French culture in the Red River Valley is housed in the oldest building in Winnipeg. Erected as a convent for the Grey Nuns in 1846, it later served as the first hospital, girl's school, orphanage, and seniors' home in Western Canada.

Ivan Franko Museum, 200 McGregor Street. Open Monday to Friday. Free. A literary museum dedicated to the memory of the Ukrainian poet Ivan Franko.

Winnipeg Art Gallery, 300 Memorial Boulevard, (204) 786–6641, ext. 70. Open daily throughout the year. An excellent example of contemporary architecture and the pride of the city, the WAG has over 14,000 works of art in its permanent collection, including the largest collection of Inuit (Eskimo) sculpture in the world. It also has a fine restaurant and a gift shop. The WAG was officially opened in 1971 by Princess Margaret.

University of Manitoba, off Pembina Highway on University Crescent. Call Information Centre (204) 474–8347. Visitors are welcome to tour the campus of the oldest university in Western Canada. Bookstores, lectures, and exhibitions are open to the public.

Open Air Market. Every Saturday and Sunday during the summer, Old Market Square in the Exchange District comes alive with farmers, vendors, and craftspeople selling their goods. Entertainers delight people with music, dance, and magic tricks. There are antiques for sale and all sorts of finger foods. This market is one of the most joyous places in all of Winnipeg and should not be missed if you are here over the weekend.

Historic Churches

Saint-Boniface Basilica, 190 avenue de la Cathedrale in Saint-Boniface, oldest Roman Catholic cathedral in Western Canada; original structure built in 1818. Here is one of the centers for French-Canadian life and culture in Western Canada. In the churchyard is the grave of Louis Riel, one of the heroes of Western Canadian history.

St. James Church, Portage Avenue and Tylehurst Street, oldest log church in Western Canada (1853).

St. John's Cathedral, 135 Anderson Avenue, oldest Anglican church in Western Canada; original church structures on this site were built in 1820.

St. Nicholas Ukrainian Catholic Church, Main Street and St. John's Avenue, Byzantine architecture and interior decoration.

St. Paul's Anglican Church, Balderstone Road off Main Street, built in 1825.

St. Vladimir and Olga Cathedral, 115 McGregor Street, domed towers and ornate interior are noteworthy of this Ukrainian house of worship.

Ukrainian Greek Orthodox Cathedral, 1175 Main Street, Byzantine domes are a dominant shape on the city's skyline.

St. Andrews, via Highway 9 north to St. Andrews Road, oldest continuously used Protestant church in Western Canada.

Kildonan Presbyterian Church, Black Avenue and Main Street, first Presbyterian church in Western Canada, which still stands (1853).

Knox United Church, 400 Edmonton Street, an attractive church built in 1917 of Manitoba stone.

Parks

Assiniboine Park, Corydon Avenue W. at Shaftsbury. Playgrounds, picnic sites, English garden, zoo, duck pond, miniature railroad.

Assiniboine Forest, Shaftsbury Boulevard and Chalfont Avenue. Trails give you access to view wildflowers, deer, and waterfowl.

Fort Whyte Centre for Environmental Education, 1961 McCreary Road, (204) 895–7001. Open throughout the year. Admission charged. Resident waterfowl, lakes, marshes with floating boardwalks, stands of aspen, self-guiding nature trails, and naturalist-conducted walks.

Stephen Juba Park, west bank of Red River between Alexander Dock and Provencher Bridge. A downtown river park and place where boats depart for tour cruises.

Kildonan Park, 2021 Main Street, on the Red River, has some of the largest trees still standing in the province; also public swimming pool, outdoor theater, and restaurant.

Provincial Parks and Forests Near Winnipeg

Whiteshell Provincial Park, on the Manitoba–Ontario border, via Highways 312 and 44 off the Trans-Canada. Manitoba's first and largest provincial park features a number of hiking and natural history trails, camping facilities, and areas for canoeing, fishing (northern pike, perch, smallmouth bass, walleye, and trout) and hunting. At the Canada goose sanctuary in the park, during May and June, you can get close enough to see hundreds of goslings.

Agassiz Provincial Forest, on the north side of the Trans-Canada, east of Winnipeg. This is mainly a natural preserve, although there are areas where you can picnic.

Sandlands Provincial Forest, on the south side of the Trans-Canada, east of Winnipeg, directly opposite Agassiz Forest. Another forest preserve with picnic sites.

Spruce Woods Provincial Park and Forest, south of Carberry on the Trans-Canada, west of Winnipeg. A forest preserve with picnic sites.

Birds Hill Provincial Park, northeast of Winnipeg via Highway 59. There are an aspen fitness trail, several natural history trails, a bike trail, camping facilities, horseback riding, and hiking.

Accommodations

For travelers who have been to Winnipeg before, the Fort Garry Hotel was both a city landmark and a favorite place to stay. Unfortunately, in early 1987 the hotel declared bankruptcy and closed its doors—hopefully not forever.

Leading Hotels

The Westin, 2 Lombard Place, (204) 957–1350; (800) 228–3000. Winnipeg's Number One deluxe hotel. Beautiful rooms with many amenities, fine service, gourmet cuisine in the Velvet Glove dining room, lounges, rooftop indoor swimming pool, and health club. Expensive.

The Delta Winnipeg, 288 Portage Avenue, (204) 956–0410; (800) 268–1133. Located in city center and connected by walkway to the city's largest downtown shopping complex, this Delta offers excellent accommodations with many amenities, dining, entertainment, and indoor swimming pool with sundeck and view of the city. Its Kennedy's dining room offers good food. Moderate.

Holiday Inn Downtown, good downtown location, close to the convention center, (204) 942–5300; (800) HOLIDAY. Excellent guest rooms with all amenities, fine dining rooms (the Market Grill is superb) and lounges, indoor and outdoor pools, exercise facility, and many other features. Moderate.

Sheraton Winnipeg, 161 Donald Street, (204) 942–5300; (800) 325–3535. Luxury accommodations in city center location. Many rooms have balcony and mini-bar. Fine restaurants and lounges. Twenty-four-hour room service. Indoor pool and sauna. Moderate to expensive.

Other Fine Places to Stay

All of the following have dining rooms and other amenities:

Brittany Inn, 367 Ellice Avenue, (204) 956–0100. Moderate.

Best Western Carlton Inn, 220 Carlton Street, (204) 942–0881; (800) 528–1234. Moderate.

The Marlborough Inn, 331 Smith Street, (204) 942–6411. Moderate.

Holiday Inn South, 1330 Pembina Highway 75 S., (204) 452–4747; (800) 465–4329. Moderate.

Ramada Inn, 1824 Pembina Highway 75 S., (204) 269–7700; (800) 268–8998. Moderate.

Birchwood Inn, on the Trans-Canada east, (204) 885–4478; (800) 665–0352. Moderate.

Dining

Winnipeg has an eclectic array of restaurants—from the elegant continental with a high price tab to match to casual ethnic eateries. The top hotels mentioned earlier also have excellent restaurants. Here's a sampling of what's in town:

Churchill's, at the Marlborough Inn, 331 Smith Street, (204) 947–1526. Elegant and romantic environment, excellent continental cuisine. Expensive.

Trapper John's, 937 St. James Street, (204) 775–2373. Old West décor, basic but tasty grub—prime rib, steaks, seafood, ribs, and salad bar. Moderate.

Mother Tucker's, 335 Donald Street, (204) 942–5538. A chain restaurant that serves great roast beef and other dishes. Inexpensive to moderate.

Homer's Restaurant, 520 Ellice Avenue, (204) 774–9123. A popular Greek dining spot. Moderate.

Restaurant Dubrovnik, 390 Assiniboine at Carlton Street, (204) 944–0594. Fine continental cuisine and Yugoslavian dishes served in an elegant 1897 private home. Moderate to expensive.

Old Swiss Inn, 207 Edmonton, near the Convention Centre, (204) 942–7725. Excellent cheese fondues and chocolate fondue; also fondue bourguignon and bunderfleisch. Moderate.

Tiffani's, 17th Floor, rooftop at 133 Niakwa, (204) 256–7324. An elegant restaurant serving fine gourmet food, with great views of the city. Expensive.

Merteen's, 14th Floor, 210 Oakland Avenue, (204) 334–2106. Another top restaurant with panoramic views of the city. Flambé dishes are a specialty. Expensive.

Alycia's, 559 Cathedral Avenue, (204) 582–8789. Here you can dine like a Cossack on great Ukrainian soul food for a song. Inexpensive.

La Vieille Gare, 630 rue des Meurons in Saint-Boniface, (204) 237–7072. This is one of Winnipeg's best French restaurants—veal dishes in various preparations, rack of lamb, steak with savory sauces, coquille Saint-Jacques are but a few menu selections for a memorable feast. Expensive.

Entertainment

As the cultural center of the prairies, Winnipeg has entertainment galore, from highbrow to wacky fun. Here are some possibilities:

The Royal Winnipeg Ballet, oldest and most famous ballet company in Canada; for information on performance dates and tickets, call (204) 956–0183. Performances are at the Centennial Concert Hall, during the summer at Assiniboine Park.

Contemporary Dancers Canada, performances between September and May, (204) 452–1239, at the Playhouse Theatre, 180 Market Avenue.

Winnipeg Symphony Orchestra, concerts held in the Centennial Concert Hall; call (204) 942–4576.

Manitoba Opera Association, performances between November and May; call (204) 942–7479, at the Centennial Concert Hall.

Rainbow Stage, outdoor theater in Kildonan Park during July and August; (204) 942–2091.

Manitoba Theatre Centre, plays from October to May; (204) 942–6537, 174 Market Avenue.

◀ **Winnipeg is one of North America's important cultural centers. Its Royal Winnipeg Ballet has thrilled audiences in many countries with its superiority in dance arts.**

Gas Station Theatre, contemporary fare, (204) 284–2757, 445 River Avenue.

The Warehouse Theatre, experimental plays, (204) 942–6537, 174 Rupert Street.

Prairie Theatre Exchange, plays for kids and grown-ups, (204) 942–7291, 160 Princess Street.

Le Cercle Molière, plays in French and some bilingual, (204) 233–8972, 340 boulevard Provencher in Saint-Boniface.

Hollow Mug Theatre Cabaret, at the International Inn, 1808 Wellington Street, (204) 786–4801.

Dine and Dance Cruises: Paddle wheeler *Princess,* (204) 339–1696; River Rouge, (204) 669–2826.

Rorie Street Marble Club, 65 Rorie Street, (204) 943–4222, dining and dancing.

Professional Sports

Harness and Thoroughbred Horse Racing at Assiniboia Downs, twenty minutes east of city center, via Portage Avenue and Highway 101 (Selkirk Exit); call (204) 885–3330 for racing schedules.

Professional Football, Winnipeg Blue Bombers, call (204) 786–7071 for schedule and ticket information; games played at Winnipeg Stadium at 1430 Maroons Road.

NHL Hockey, Winnipeg Jets play at the Arena; call (204) 772–9491 for schedule and ticket information.

Recreation

Squash and Racquetball
Court Sports Centre, 1400 Taylor Avenue, (204) 475–7695.

Golf
Kildonan Park Golf Course, eighteen holes, 2021 Main Street, (204) 334–0452.
There are several excellent private courses and six public courses in the city. Check with your club for a reciprocal arrangement.

Tennis
Adsum Park, 434 Adsum Drive; for information on other courts, call (204) 786–5641.

Horseback Riding
Birds Hill Provincial Park, (204) 222–1137; polo is played every
Sunday during the summer.

Water Sports
Fun Mountain Waterslide Park, on Murdock Road, east of the city,
via the Trans-Canada or the Perimeter Highway, (204) 255–3910.
Features several exciting water slides, inner-tube slide, a giant
hot tub holding 150 persons, and much more. A fun place for a
young family.
St. James Civic Centre, 2055 Ness Avenue, (204) 837–9682. Public
swimming pool.
Atlantis Indoor Waterslide, 2077 Pembina Highway, (204)
269–5999.

Shopping

Eaton Place, 234 Donald Street in the heart of city center,
(204) 944–9711. More than 110 shops, services, restaurants, and
Cineplex Theatre under one roof. Eaton Place has just about
everything you need and in an attractive environment.

Osborne Village, on the south side of the Osborne Street
Bridge near the Legislative Building, sixty shops, restaurants,
galleries, and services in restored buildings. Also here is the Gas
Station Theatre.

Crafts Guild of Manitoba, 183 Kennedy Street, (204)
943–1190. Inuit and Indian crafts, handmade quilts, fashions, and
jewelry.

The Upstairs Gallery, 266 Edmonton Street, (204) 943–2734.
Beautiful arts and crafts from the artisans of the Canadian Arctic.

A Hint of Heather, 105 Osborne Street, (204) 453–6583.
Scottish imports and Highland outfitters.

Ukrainian Arts and Crafts, 610 Pasadena Avenue, (204)
269–4887. Hand-painted Easter eggs, cookbooks, records, ceramics.

Manitoba's Special Attractions

Churchill on Hudson Bay
Although a prairie province, Manitoba has extensive shoreline
on Hudson Bay, that immense inland sea that also touches the

borders of Ontario, Québec, and the Northwest Territories. During the summer, when the ice is out, you can sail from Manitoba to Greenland, Iceland, Ireland, and the British Isles. This is just the way the fur-trading entrepreneurs of the Hudson's Bay Company traveled more than 300 years ago. Fort Prince of Wales was built here in the eighteenth century to enforce the territorial sovereignty of the Hudson's Bay Company, and it still stands for the benefit of interested travelers. A plaque at the fort commemorates Samuel Hearne, who reached the Arctic Ocean through the Coppermine River in 1771.

In 1769 **Churchill** was where the first astronomical observations were made in Canada. The displays of aurora borealis (northern lights) here are magnificent; some say the most intense illumination in the world. A railroad was completed in 1931 to connect Churchill with southern cities so that grain could be more economically shipped to international markets via Hudson Bay–Atlantic Ocean routes. This railroad is now also used by VIA Rail to transport tourists to Churchill. In the 1940s the U.S. military had at Fort Churchill a base that was used for air operations during World War II and later as a joint Canadian/American training and experimental facility. The base was closed in 1980.

The best-known Manitoba town on the Hudson Bay coast is Churchill, primarily because of the large number of polar bears that migrate to this area during the fall. *National Geographic* magazine and its television program have featured the polar bears of Churchill, and millions of people have come to know something of this area that way. Churchill was named not for Winston S. but for his equally famous forebear, John Churchill, first duke of Marlborough. In addition to the polar bears, you can see caribou, beluga whales, four species of seals, Canada and snow geese, and close to 200 other species of birds. Wildlife photo opportunities are everywhere. Telephoto lenses are recommended. In the case of polar bears, please heed all safety warnings. Although they look cuddly enough to hug, they've got nasty tempers, sharp teeth and claws, and no hesitation about attacking humans who venture close to their space.

Some of the points of interest are Bird Cove for bird watching; Eskimo Museum, with its excellent collection of carvings and artifacts; Institute of Arctic Ecophysiology, conducting ecological studies; Cape Merry National Historic Site, a defensive counterpart to Fort Prince of Wales and a good place from which to see beluga whales and Fort Prince of Wales; tundra tours on specially designed tracked or rubber-tired vehicles; Dymond Lake Wilderness, at the junction of three ecological zones—boreal forest, tundra, and taiga; polar bear denning area, where cubs are born; and Fort Prince of Wales National Historic Park, a stone, star-shaped bastion built in 1731, with walls forty feet thick. York Factory, an important historic site, where Hudson's Bay Company established a post in 1682, is accessible only by air or boat. Artifacts from centuries of human habitation are in this remote region.

The best way to get to Churchill and experience everything is to use the services of the tour companies listed near the beginning of this chapter. There is no highway to Churchill (it stops at Thompson), and the only way to get here is by VIA Rail or by air. Churchill is also known for sports fishing and waterfowl and ptarmigan hunting. There are outfitters here who will take good care of anglers and hunters. In Churchill itself there are a curling rink, public swimming pool, bowling alley, shops where you can purchase native prints and carvings, restaurants, liquor stores, and churches. While in town orient yourself to the attractions of the area by visiting the **Environment Canada-Parks Interpretive Centre** at Bayport Plaza, (204) 675–8863.

For more information about Churchill, contact Travel Manitoba (800) 665–0040 or the Churchill Chamber of Commerce, (204) 675–2022.

Accommodations are all in the moderate price range.

Arctic Inn, (204) 675–8835.
Beluga Motel, (204) 675–2150.
Churchill Motel, (204) 675–8853.
Polar Motel, (204) 675–8878.
Seaport Hotel, (204) 675–8807.
Tundra Inn, (204) 675–8831; (800) 661–1460.

Western Manitoba

Riding Mountain National Park is located north of the Trans-Canada and the Yellowhead Highways, via Highway 10 north, and approximately halfway between the border of Saskatchewan and Lake Manitoba. If you continue through the park on Highway 10, you will come to the town of **Dauphin** where the famous Ukrainian Festival is held each summer. For more information on the park itself, contact Superintendent, Riding Mountain National Park, Wasagaming, Manitoba R0J 2H0, (204) 848–2811.

Riding Mountain National Park (2,978 square km./1,150

square mi.) has the distinction of being near the geographical center of Canada. The park has three distinct ecological zones: a deciduous forest; aspen and grasslands; and boreal forest with spruce and fir. Each zone has self-guiding nature trails. The deciduous zone has trails named Burls, Bittersweet, Oak Ridge, and Beach Ridge; aspen/grasslands trails take you to Lake Audy, Agassiz Tower, and the Ominik Marsh; and the boreal zone has trails called Brule, Rolling River, and Ma-ee-gun. A Visitor Centre conducting various interpretive programs is located at the town of **Wasagaming.** A campground and other accommodations, as well as supplies and services, can be found in Wasagaming. Within the park are Lake Katherine, Whirlpool, and Moon Lake campgrounds. A beach for swimming is in Wasagaming. There's boating at Clear, Audy, and Moon lakes (boats can be rented at Clear Lake). The park has many other lakes and waterways for canoeing; get details at the Visitor Centre or write the Superintendent. You can fish in all the lakes, but must first obtain a special permit at the Visitor Centre. Wasagaming has an eighteen-hole golf course, horseback riding, and tennis courts.

Valley River can be reached via Highway 362, north of Dauphin. Here is the **Cross of Freedon,** erected in 1897 by Ukrainian settlers to mark their new beginnings in Canada. Also in this area are **St. Michael's,** which claims to be the first Ukrainian church built in Canada, and a museum with a bust of Reverend Nestor Dmytriw, who performed the first church service, as well as a cairn with the names of early settlers.

Selkirk

Lower Fort Garry National Historic Park is twenty minutes north of the city of Winnipeg on Highway 9, (204) 482–6843. Open from mid-May to September 1. Free. Lower Fort Garry was built in the 1830s as a Hudson's Bay Company post. It has been restored to reflect its role in the early days of fur trading and the development of Manitoba. During your visit, you will see people in period costumes moving about and doing chores—baking scones and oatmeal cookies in outdoor ovens, loading carts with grain and produce, making tallow candles, and blacksmithing horses. You can poke around the restored buildings, view the historical exhibits, have a satisfying meal at the restaurant, and buy a gift from the prairies for the folks back home. It's a worthwhile excursion back into the early history of the province.

Visit the **Marine Museum of Manitoba** in Selkirk Park, Eveline and Queen Street, (204) 482–7761. Open from mid-May to August. Admission charged. This museum is dedicated to Manitoba's marine history and the preservation of vessels used on its waterways, such as the S.S. *Keenora*, a beloved passenger steamship, the C.G.S. *Bradbury*, an icebreaker, and *Peguis II*, a dredge tender. Also in the park is a replica of the Red River ox cart, which helped to develop this part of Canada because it could more easily travel through mud. The replica is twenty-two feet high and forty-five feet long. Selkirk has a waterfront area where its maritime heritage has been preserved with period lighting, walkways, and signs.

Lake Winnipeg Area

From Selkirk you might want to explore some of the lower shoreline of Lake Winnipeg, via Highways 8 and 9 on the west side or 59 on the east side. Traveling along the west side of the lake, you will come to **Gimli,** the center of Icelandic heritage in Canada. In Gimli there are an Icelandic heritage museum, a giant statue of a Viking, and the annual *Islendingadagurrinn* (Icelandic Festival of Manitoba), which is held during the first weekend in August. In **Arnes,** just above Gimli, there's a plaque honoring Vilhjalmur Stefansson, the famous Arctic explorer, who was born here in 1879.

Continuing along Highway 8 will take you to **Hecla Provincial Park** (145 km./90 mi. north of Winnipeg), whose islands stretch nearly across the narrows of Lake Winnipeg. This beautiful park features facilities for camping, hiking, tennis, fishing, and sailing. There's a large moose population; thick flocks of waterfowl, bald eagles, great blue herons, and western grebes mass here. The Icelandic influence is expressed in the Gull Harbour Resort and Conference Centre, a luxury accommodation within the park open throughout the year. For more information and reservations, call (204) 475–2354 or toll-free (800) 442–0497. Moderate.

A drive up the eastern shore of Lake Winnipeg, via Highway 59, will bring you to **Grand Beach Provincial Park**. This park has some of the finest sand beaches in North America. Shifting sand dunes here rise close to thirty feet (nine meters) in height. A lagoon behind them is a perfect habitat for pelicans, cranes, orioles, and finches. The park features camping, tennis, windsurfing, fishing, lake swimming, and an amphitheater program. Inexpensive accommodations are available in the nearby town of Grand Marais.

Southern Manitoba

In Steinbach, see the **Mennonite Village Museum,** which can be reached via the Trans-Canada, east of Winnipeg then south on Highway 12, (204) 326–9661. Open from May to end of September. Admission charged. This village museum is an excellent tribute to the heritage and accomplishments of Mennonite pioneers who settled in the Steinbach area in 1874. The village consists of early Mennonite farm buildings; farming machinery; a pristine, unadorned church for meditation and prayer; an obelisk monument to the early settlers; simple homes with period furnishings; and perhaps the most magnificent shingled windmill in all of Canada. There are demonstrations of farming activities, wagon rides, a barn restaurant that serves traditional Mennonite cooking, and a shop where you can buy souvenirs. A visit here is highly recommended.

South of Steinbach, near the Minnesota border, is Gardenton (reached via Highways 59 and 209, south of Winnipeg). Here is **St. Michael's Ukrainian Orthodox church,** the first Ukrainian "orthodox" church built in North America in 1896. There are also a museum and heritage village in town. Admission charged.

International Peace Garden, near Boissevain, is located along the east boundary of Turtle Mountain Provincial Park (reached via Highway 10 south of Brandon on the Trans-Canada). Open Monday through Friday. Admission charged. The International Peace Garden spans the border between Manitoba and North Dakota. It honors the longest unfortified border in the world and is a symbol of the strong, warm, and enduring friendship that exists between the people of Canada and the United States. Within the park there are beautiful flower gardens and extensive landscaped areas, a flower clock (at the entrance), a Peace Chapel, a fountain encircled by stone walls engraved with the writings of famous persons on the theme of peace, a Peace Tower symbolizing the coming together of people from all parts of the world to form two great nations, and the Errick F. Willis Memorial Centre, which has arts and crafts exhibitions. During the summer the park is the site of the International Music Camp and the Royal Legion Athletic Camp.

Chapter 10

Exploring the Yukon and the Northwest Territories

The Yukon: Land of Dreamers

The first people of the Yukon settled here more than 50,000 years ago, perhaps considerably more. The two Amerindian tribes that now live in the Yukon are the Athapaskan and the Inland Tlingit. It is said that the first white man to penetrate the interiors of the Yukon was Robert Campbell, a Hudson's Bay Company fur trader.

There are five places in the Yukon Territory that have become ingrained in North American mythology—the Klondike, Chilkoot Pass, White Pass (both partly in Alaska), Dawson, and Whitehorse. In the late 1800s this was the site of the famous gold strikes, and "gold fever" drew thousands of men here from North America and other parts of the world. George W. Carmack and two Indian friends struck gold at Rabbit "Bonanza" Creek, a tributary of the Klondike River, in 1896. And the dreamers came here in great numbers, about 50,000 of them by 1899, all seeking a great fortune that would turn their lives around and make them as rich as J. P. Morgan. Enough did strike it rich to keep passionate fires burning in the minds of many others who would, after much struggle and hardship, fail. And along with the men of wild dreams came the

327

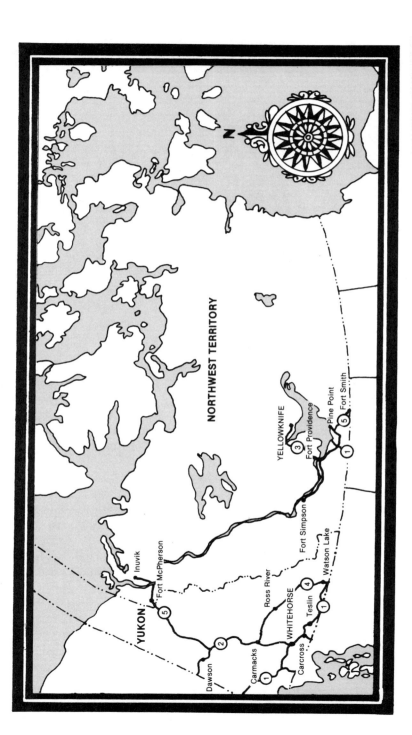

merchants, the bankers, the dance-hall women, and the preachers. Some stole the dreamers' purses, while others tried to save their souls. To survive in this country you had to be handy with your hands—to make your way through an often cruel wilderness and to knock the other guy down before he could do it to you. To say that the heritage of the Yukon was wild, rough, and woolly is about as precise as you can get. This was, after all, where Jack London got his inspiration for novels of life and death in the North. But it was also much more. The Yukon was exerting personal courage and vision against all odds and sometimes winning. It was stranger helping stranger to keep going and to survive. The traditions of fellowship are so strong here that you can't do better than have Yukon people as friends. It was a pioneering spirit that, when the gold fever finally cooled down, produced stable communities of hardy, creative people who took the long view of things, generation after generation. And so it is right now in the Yukon. Gold is still plucked from the ground here but heavy earth-moving equipment and sluice boxes have replaced the gold pan of yesteryear. The Yukon's true future lies with dreamers of a different sort, better educated and seeing more productive possibilities.

The Yukon, comprising an area of 482,500 square kilometers/186,000 square miles, is essentially a magnificent wilderness with gorgeous mountains, lakes, rivers, forests, and tundra. There is an abundance of wildlife here: bear, mountain goats and sheep, moose, caribou, many species of birds and waterfowl, wolves, and salmon. Sports hunters and anglers from all over the world come to the Yukon for prize trophies and for adventure. For such a vast area, though, there are only 26,000 people residing in the Yukon, mostly in the communities of Whitehorse (the capital), Dawson City, Beaver Creek, Faro, Ross River, Mayo, Elsa, Watson Lake, Haines Junction, and Carcross. They also live in tiny pioneering towns, and, in the case of the Ioucheux Indian, in the remote village of Old Crow accessible only by air.

The Yukon borders Alaska to the west and south, the Northwest Territories to the east, and British Columbia to the south along the 60th parallel. The Yukon extends north beyond the Arctic Circle and has well over 200 kilometers (120 mi.) of shoreline on the Beaufort Sea. Herschel Island in the Beaufort Sea is near its most northerly point. Among its many river systems, the Yukon River and the Porcupine River are two of the largest. Mount Logan (6,050 m./19,850 ft.), part of the St. Elias Range, located in Kluane

National Park in the southwest corner of the Yukon and close to the Alaskan border, is Canada's highest mountain and second in height only to Alaska's Mount McKinley, North America's highest peak.

The main highway access into the Yukon is through the town of Watson Lake on the Alaska Highway. Another route, used by cruise ships coming up the Inside Passage, is through Skagway, Alaska, then to Carcross, Yukon, and Whitehorse, along the Klondike Highway. Coming south from Fairbanks, Alaska, the town of Beaver Creek, Yukon, is a gateway at the border. The Alaska and the Klondike are the Yukon's two main highways. Other roads, mostly gravel and with limited services, provide touring into variouis regions; the Dempster Highway will take you all the way to Fort McPherson in the Northwest Territories and beyond to Arctic Red River and Inuvik, all of which are on the Mackenzie Delta (where the Mackenzie, one of Canada's great river, empties into the Beaufort Sea). As in Alaska and the Northwest Territories, much of the transporting of people and goods is accomplished by small regional airlines and independent bush pilots.

Summer days, especially during July, can be quite warm—up to 30°C/86°F (the average is between 10° and 20°C).One of the bonuses of visiting the Yukon during the summer, and for that matter Alaska and the Northwest Territories, are the long days. Dawson City has almost twenty-four hours of sunlight each day in June and twenty hours in July; Whitehorse has twenty hours of light during June and eighteen hours in July. Unfortunately, the reverse is true during the winter: minimal daylight and temperatures that fall to −40°C./−40°F. The very low humidity makes the winter temperatures more tolerable. If you want a wilderness adventure along with your cross-country skiing, skidooing, dogsledding, or ice fishing, the Yukon is the perfect place for you to test your skills and resolve and have some fun in the process. Rock hounds will find prizes in the Yukon—hematite from which the Alaska black diamond is made, in Hunker, Dominion, and Haggart Creeks; agate in its various forms, in the Carmacks area; azurite, malachite, chrysocolla—lapidary materials—in the Whitehorse Copper Belt area; garnet in the Von Wilzon Lake region; jasper, along the Alaska Highway; and rhyolite, in the Wheaton River Valley,

Yukon Facts

The Yukon River begins near the Pacific Ocean and flows for 2,000 miles to the Bering sea.

In the Yukon above the Arctic Circle, the sun never sets on June 21; on December 21, it never rises.

The Yukon is 15 percent larger than the state of California, but it has only one person per seven square miles (11 sq. km.).

Southwest Yukon has the largest concentration of grizzly bears in North America and the largest number of Dall sheep in the world.

More than $250,000,000 worth of gold has been taken out of the Klondike over the years. No wonder people got the itch to get here as fast as possible.

How to Get to the Yukon

By Car

The southern border of the Yukon is 2,200 km./1,367 mi. from Vancouver, British Columbia, via the Trans-Canada Highway 1 east to Cache Creek, then Highway 97 to the Alaska Highway. From Edmonton, Alberta, take the Yellowhead Highway 16 west to Highway 43 to Valleyview and Highway 34 to Dawson Creek and then the Alaska Highway—to the Yukon border, a distance of 1,600 km./994 mi. See pages 31–36 for safety and driving trips on driving the Alaska Highway. Much of the highway is paved with asphalt, although there are gravel sections. Other routes of entry into the Yukon are Highway 2 from Skagway, Alaska; Highway 3 from Haines, Alaska; Highway 2 from Fairbanks, Alaska; the Stewart-Cassiar Highway 37 from southwestern British Columbia (a very scenic route but with few services; see page 192). The highways in this region are well maintained through all seasons, not just for visitors but for the very survival of the people who live here. A number of communities offer full services (fuel, supplies, accommodations) en route to the Yukon and through to Alaska—Siberia it's not. For reports on highway conditions, call Yukon Highways (403) 667–5644 and British Columbia Highways (604) 774–6956.

By Plane

Daily jet plane service is provided to Whitehorse from Vancouver and Edmonton by Canadian Airlines; several regional airlines also provide service in the Yukon and from Alaska. Rental cars are available at the Whitehorse Airport.

By Boat

The following regional ferries provide access to the Yukon via Prince Rupert, British Columbia: British Columbia Ferry, (604) 669–1211, and the Alaska Marine Highway, operating out of Juneau. The Alaska Marine Highway ferries stop at Haines or Skagway, Alaska, and travelers may then travel on to Whitehorse by private vehicle or bus. Costa, Cunard, Exploration, Holland America, Paquet, Princess, Regency, Royal Viking, Sitmar, Sundance, and World Explorer are all cruise lines that bring visitors to the Yukon. Check with your travel agent about the itineraries these cruise lines use for the Inside Passage of coastal British Columbia and Alaska.

Tourist Information

For touring and camping information (brochures—especially helpful if you are driving along any of the routes mentioned earlier—and maps) write or call Tourism Yukon, Box 2703, Whitehorse, Yukon Y1A 2C6, (403) 667–5340; Tourism British Columbia, 802 Hornby Street, Vancouver, B.C. V6Z 2G3, (604) 660–2861; Tourism Alberta, 10065 Jasper Avenue, 14th Floor, Edmonton, Alberta T5J 0H4, (403) 427–4320; North by Northwest Tourism Association of B.C., P.O. Box 1030, Smithers, B.C. V0J 2N0, (604) 847–3847.

Visitor Information Centres, open from mid-May to mid-September, are located in Watson Lake, Carcross, and Whitehorse. Visitor Reception Centres are in Kluane National Park in Haines Junction, Beaver Creek, Faro, and Dawson City.

Useful Information

Climate: Generally, the summers in the Yukon are dry, pleasant, and comfortable.

Area code: 403.

Time zone: Pacific.

◀ The romance and rigor of dogteam racing is both a metaphysical passion and a rabid sport in the Yukon and Northwest Territories.

Touring Services: Adventures, Fishing, and Hunting

These companies—Atlas Tours, (403) 668–3161; Rainbow Adventure Tours, (403) 668–5599; Westours of Seattle, toll-free (800) 544–2206 or (206) 281–0576—provide comprehensive tours of Whitehorse and Dawson City, the 176 km. (110-mi.) scenic Klondike Highway (Whitehorse to Skagway), exciting Yukon River cruises, Yukon-Alaska cruises, and Pleasure Island salmon barbecues (freshly caught and alder-wood smoked and grilled). Rainbow has a trip to the Arctic, from Whitehorse to Inuvik on the Mackenzie River Delta in the Northwest Territories north of the Arctic Circle. On this trip you also fly to Tuktoyaktuk, which is a traditional Inuit (Eskimo) community near the Beaufort Sea as well as a marine base for Arctic oil-drilling. Atlas and Westours have tours from Whitehorse to Juneau and Fairbanks in Alaska. If you are in Juneau, Fairbanks, or Skagway, you can tour the Yukon from these points using Atlas or Westours.

The following companies provide outdoor adventure expeditions in the rugged but magnificent Yukon—canoeing, backpacking, mountaineering, fishing, wildlife photography:

Arctic Edge Canoe, (403) 633–2443
Ecosummer Yukon, (403) 633–5006
Karpes and Pugh Company, (403) 668–4899
Kluane Adventures, (403) 634–2282
Oldsquaw Lodge, (403) 668–6732
Rainbow Adventure Tours, (403) 668–5599
Tatshenshini Expediting, (403) 663–2742
Yukon Mountain and River Expeditions, (403) 399–3131
Yukon Wilderness Unlimited "Gentle Adventures," (403) 668–5244

The following is a listing of fishing lodges; lake trout is the prized catch:

Kluane Lake Tours, (403) 841–4411
Kluane Wilderness Lodge, (403) 668–4365
Peacock's Yukon Camps, (403) 667–2846
Yukon Fishing Safaris, (403) 668–2287

The following are registered hunting outfitters; the species are moose, caribou, Dall sheep, mountain goats, black bear, and grizzlies:

Bonnet Plume Outfitters, (403) 668–2888
Ceaser Lake Outfitters, (403) 536–2174
Belle Desrosiers, (403) 633–5273
Dick Dickson, (403) 633–2228
Bob Hassard, (403) 390–2610
Pete Jensen, (403) 667–2030
Werner Koser, (403) 969–2210
Pelly Mountain Outfitters, (403) 668–2586
MacMillan River Outfitters, (403) 633–4293
Rogue River Outfitters, (403) 969–2250
Teslin Outfitters, (403) 390–2559
David Young, (403) 668–4518
Yukon Outfitting, (403) 667–2721
Kusawa Outfitters, (403) 667–2755

Government Campgrounds

On the Alaska Highway, from Watson Lake to the Alaska Border, there are numerous campgrounds. Their location is indicated by the kilometer mark location on the highway heading north from Watson Lake. Most campsites have drinking water, and some have special features, such as beaches and fishing.

Watson Lake, 1024.9 km. (615 mi.)
Big Creek, 1084.8 km. (651 mi.)
Rancheria, 1143.4 km. (686 mi.)
Morley River, 1251.2 km. (751 mi.)
Teslin Lake, 1307.6 km. (785 mi.)
Squanga Lake, 1368.4 km. (821 mi.)
Marsh Lake, 1429.6 km. (858 mi.)
Wolf Creek, 1458.6 km. (875 mi.)
Takhini River, 1542.6 km. (926 mi.)
Kusawa Lake, 1542.6 km. (926 mi.)
Otter Falls, 1602.2 km. (961 mi.)
Aishihik Lake, 1602.2 km. (961 mi.)
Pine Lake, 1628 km. (1,011 mi.)
Congdon Creek, 1724.8 km. (1,071 mi.)
Lake Creek, 1853.7 km. (1,112 mi.)
Snag Junction, 1912.8 km. (1186 mi.)

There are campsites also on the Haines Road, Atlin Road 7, Tagish Road 8, the Klondike Highway, the Silver Trail 11, South

Canol Road, Robert Campbell Highway, and the Dempster Highway (contact Tourism Yukon, Box 2703, Whitehorse, Yukon Y1A 2C6, for details).

Special Events

January/February

Yukon Championship Dog Race, Whitehorse, mid-January.

Frostbite Folk Festival, Whitehorse, late February.

Sourdough Rendezvous, Whitehorse, late February to early March. If you are in the Yukon this time of year, this is a good one: dog-team races, Mad Trapper competitions (such as leg and arm wrestling), a Chilkoot climb, snowshoeing, beard contest, fiddler competitions, cancan girls, sourdough-pancake breakfasts.

June

Commissioner's Ball, Dawson City, mid-June.

Annual Dog Show, Whitehorse, late June.

Tennis Tournament, Whitehorse, late June.

Yukon Gold Panning Championships, Dawson City, late June.

July

International Moto-Cross Event, Whitehorse, early July.

Horse Show, Whitehorse, mid-July.

International Midnight Dome Race, Dawson City, mid-July.

International Dustball Tournament, Whitehorse, mid-July.

Music Festival, Dawson City, late July.

August

Discovery Days, Dawson City, mid-August. Gold was discovered in the Klondike on August 17, 1896, and is worthy of this annual celebration—parades, raft and canoe races, tournaments, dances, and more.

Kiwanis Horticultural and Hobby Show, Dawson City, mid-August.

Klondike International Outhouse Race, Dawson City, late August, first of September. Another doozy—a race of outhouses on wheels through the streets of Dawson City! Also dances and dinners—away from the outhouses, one hopes.

September/October

Klondike Trail of '98 Road Relay, Skagway to Whitehorse, mid-September. A mixed male and female relay race of 176 km./110 mi. between the two cities.

Octoberfest, Elsa, third week in October.

The Yukon's Special Attractions

Hiking the Chilkoot Trail

If you are the hardy type and are trekking the Yukon, hike the **Chilkoot Trail,** which is actually in a slender slice of British Columbia between Alaska and the Yukon. The trail begins a few miles from Dyea, north of Skagway, a major port of call for Inside Passage ships. If any single place embodies the struggle of hundreds of men trying to reach the goldfields of the Yukon, it is Chilkoot Pass. In old documentary films and photos you can see hundreds of men and pack animals trying to push themselves and their supplies up what seems like a wall. Many were injured and some killed in the attempt to cross over. At the summit the Northwest Mounted Police set up a post where they weighed the supplies of each man. By law each man had to have enough provisions to last one full year (about 2,000 pounds) in order to continue on. Those who were shy of the requirement were sent back down—to go home or start again. It was not unusual for a gold seeker to be transporting a ton of supplies. Some of these dreamers were so insistent on reaching the Yukon that they tried going over Chilkoot Pass in the dead of winter, with often disastrous results. Today you can hike this trek leisurely to enjoy the magnificent scenery and to reflect upon the lives of the dreamers who came this way hungry for gold many decades ago. The trail itself will take you through rain forest, alpine meadow, over talus rock up the pass, and then to the summit, the scene of so many victories or defeats.

Kluane National Park

Kluane National Park is located along Highway 3 and the Alaska Highway 1, in the southwest corner of the territory, bordering British Columbia and Alaska. The key town for the park is Haines Junction, at Highways 1 and 3, 158 km./98 mi. (two-hour drive) west of Whitehorse. For more information, contact Superintendent, Kluane National Park, Haines Junction, Yukon Y0B 1L0, (403) 634-2251.

Kluane National Park is an immense wilderness. It has the highest mountains in Canada; Mount Logan, at 6,050 m./19,850 ft. in the St. Elias Range, is the nationa's highest—and second-highest on the North American continent. Mount St. Elias was the first to be climbed—in 1897 by the Duke of Abruzzi. Mount Logan was climbed in 1925. Scientists from different disciplines and top climbers have been attracted for decades by the park's rugged and splendid ecology, and many come here every year to study and experience its natural wonders. The mountains within the park are among North America's youngest and most active, with faults averaging 1,000 tremors a year. You can see how the earth shifts in this area by watching the seismograph at the Visitor Centre in Haines Junction. This is also a landscape of many glaciers, perhaps as many as 4,000 or more. The snows laid down over thousands of years along the St. Elias Range have made the most extensive icefields outside of the polar regions. The Kaskawulsh Glacier can be reached by a tough two-day hike. Along the Alaska Highway, from where most people see the park, the Front Range Mountains form a 2,400 m./8,000 ft. wall that shields the St. Elias Range and Mount Logan from view. To get into the park and near Mount Logan by trekking takes excellent physical conditioning, much planning, and the right gear (contact the Sierra Club or similar organizations for information on how to take on this adventure so that it's safe and memorable). Another way to see Mount Logan is to fly over it with an air tour service, some of which are listed earlier in this chapter.

Kluane National Park has large populations of grizzly bears, Dall sheep, and other wildlife. If you are camping in the park, keep the grizzlies away from your site by using proper procedures in storing food and garbage (see pages 33–34). There's an Indian village on Klukshu Creek, thought to be the oldest settlement in this part of the territory. Several hiking trails lead off the Alaska Highway: the Rock Glacier Trail, the St. Elias Trail, the Auriol Range Trail, and the Sheep Mountain Trail. Silver City on Kluane Lake is a classic western ghost town, which you should visit. Shells of original buildings remain, as well as a sense of the people who long ago put their hearts and souls into ventures that have drifted away with the winds. South of Haines Junction is Kathleen Lake, the park's major campground, open from mid-June to mid-September, with a maximum stay of two weeks. There are a number of other campgrounds along this eastern edge of the park. Motor boating and fishing are allowed on Kathleen Lake; canoeing is discouraged because of the rough water. Climbing and mountaineering parties who wish to trek to the St. Elias and Icefield ranges must obtain a permit three months in advance from the Warden Service (write to the address given above for Kluane National Park). The Warden Service wants to know the health, physical condition, and skill of each member of your party; you must provide doctors' certificates and information on supplies and communication support. All precautions are essential because Kluane is the very essence of the Yukon wilderness. North of Haines Junction on the Alaska Highway at Destruction Bay and Burwash Landing is Kluane Lake, the largest lake in the Yukon.

Accommodations in the Haines Junction area (both have dining rooms) are **Mountain View Motor Inn,** (403) 634–2646, moderate, and **MacKintosh Lodge,** (403) 634–2301, moderate.

All of the following accommodations in Destruction Bay and Burwash Landing have dining rooms:

Talbot Arms Motel, in Destruction Bay, (403) 841–4461. Moderate.

Burwash Landing Resort, (403) 841–4441. Moderate.

Kluane Wilderness Village, in Burwash Landing, (403) 841–4141. Moderate.

Pine Valley Motel, in Burwash Landing, (403) 862–7407. Moderate.

Koidern River Fishing Lodge, 86 km. (52 mi.) north of Burwash Landing, (403) 862–7402. Moderate.

White River Lodge, 94 km. (56 mi.) north of Burwash Landing, (403) 862–7408. Moderate.

Scenic Highways

See pages 34–36 for safety and driving tips on driving the gravel roads of the Yukon.

Taking the **Alaska Highway 1** from the southern provinces and states to the Yukon and Alaska is one of North America's great road adventures. Driving across the southwest corner of the Yukon from British Columbia to Alaska (Watson Lake to Beaver Creek) is a distance of 912 km./567 mi., a journey that can take several days if you don't rush and enjoy the natural beauty and heritage of the Yukon. There are plenty of services, accommodations, gas stations, and restaurants along the way. Be sure to visit Kluane National Park and to tour the city of Whitehorse.

The **Klondike Highway 2** from Whitehorse will take you to historic Dawson City, a boom town in gold rush days. Both Jack London and the poet Robert Service had cabins here. From Dawson City you can take the **Top of the World Highway 9** into Alaska (border crossing only during the summer), which connects with Alaska Highway 5 south to the Alaska Highway 2 and thence to Fairbanks.

The Haines Road Highway 3 goes from Haines, Alaska, where many Inside Passage cruise ships come in, along the eastern edge of Kluane National Park to Haines Junction in the Yukon. From here you can travel the Alaska Highway north or south or go up to Dawson City.

The Robert Campbell Highway 4 moves in a northwesterly course from Watson Lake on the British Columbia border to the towns of Tuchitua, Ross River, Faro, and Carmacks, which are in the south central part of the territory. When you reach Carmacks, you can take the Klondike Highway 2 north to Dawson City or south to Whitehorse.

The Dempster Highway 5 is a true explorer's road, but you should take it only in mid-summer. If you follow the Dempster from Dawson City to the literal "end of the road," you will have crossed the Arctic Circle, entered the Northwest Territories, passed through Fort McPherson (the largest community in this part of the world) and over the mighty Mackenzie River, and made it to Inuvik, an Inuit (Eskimo) community where the road does end. From Inuvik you can take a flight to visit the remote Inuit village of Tuktoyaktuk. Between Dawson City and Fort McPherson there are few gas stations and services, so plan accordingly. Check at the Visitor Centre in Dawson City for suggestions for the trip, or consult your local auto club and/or environmental society (Audubon or Sierra Club, for instance). Finally, the road all the way is gravel, and a reliable, sturdy RV is your best transportation, although any vehicle will do the trip as long as it is mechanically sound and equipped with at least two spare tires. There are government campgrounds at strategic points. The only commercial lodge facility is at Eagle Plains.

Watson Lake

Watson Lake is the gateway to the Yukon from the provinces and the states. Its major attraction is a forest of posts covered with many signs pointing to cities throughout the world and giving the distance to each one. This tradition was started by a lonely American G.I. working on the construction of the Alaska Highway (25,000 Americans and Canadians worked on the highway). Standing at this signage display, one would think that Watson Lake is the navel of the earth. On the other hand, if you are here, it surely is.

340

Don't leave without having someone take a photo of you by the sign.

Alaska Highway Interpretive Centre, (403) 536–7469. If you are traveling all the way to Fairbanks or on long sections of the highway through the Yukon, this is a good place to get oriented to what's ahead and learn the history of this tremendous engineering and construction effort.

George Johnson Museum, (403) 390–2550, has a fine collection of Inland Tlingit artifacts and more recent arts and crafts.

The following accommodations have dining rooms: **Gateway Motor Inn,** (403) 536–7744. Moderate. **Watson Lake Hotel,** (403) 536–7781. Moderate.

Whitehorse

Whitehorse, capital of the Yukon Territory, is located on the Alaska Highway and on the Yukon River, which meanders for 3,185 km./1,980 mi. north to the Arctic Ocean. This city owes its birth and initial development to the Klondike gold rush of the late 1800s. Both the river, on which plied steamboats, and a railroad, built from Skagway, made Whitehorse a vital transportation and supply center for the rapidly growing population attracted to the region by visions of getting rich quick. When gold mania subsided, enough people remained to make Whitehorse a permanent settlement, although by 1941 the population fell to fewer than 800 persons. Today the city's population is about 18,000. For a short while copper mining pumped new life into the local economy, but that also ended. During World War II, Whitehorse became part of the Northwest Staging Route, a chain of airfields that briefly brought in thousands of Canadian and American construction workers. The Alaska Highway, the major land route linking this region with the provinces and states to the south, made Whitehorse a major transportation center. Whitehorse has fine hotels and restaurants for travelers and a number of interesting attractions. When in town the folks at the **Whitehorse Information Centre,** 302 Steele Street, (403) 667–2915, will answer your questions and assist you in whatever way they can. Students dressed as Northwest Mounted Police patrol the streets to assist travelers with information.

The official season for most Whitehorse attractions listed below is from June to about mid-September:

Whitehorse Library and Art Gallery, located next to the Government Building, (403) 667–5858, exhibits the work of contemporary Yukon artists.

Yukon Government Building Tours, 2nd Avenue and Hanson Street, (403) 667–5811. The history of the territory is displayed in stained-glass windows, wall hangings, paintings, and crafts. The building itself is modern and befits the future potential of the territory, which may one day become Canada's eleventh province.

Yukon Gardens, off the Alaska Highway, (403) 668–7972. The trees, flowers, and other plants of the Yukon are beautifully displayed. There's also a gift shop.

Whitehorse Heritage Walks, (403) 667–4704. A walking tour will show you many of the historic homes and buildings of the city.

Frantic Follies Vaudeville, (403) 668–3161, in the Village Square ballroom of the Sheffield Hotel. A Gay Nineties revue with sexy, high-kicking cancan girls, magic shows, Robert Service humor, and wacky skits. This is the best show in town.

M.V. *Schwatka* **River Tour,** (403) 668–3161, departs from Schwatka Lake moorage. A two-hour cruise on the historic Yukon River through the high-walled Miles Canyon. The canyon was a difficult barrier for the gold rush men to cross. Men and their boats were often crushed by the rapids. A suspension bridge now goes over the rapids so you can see how truly dangerous this crossing was.

MacBride Museum, 1st Avenue and Wood Street, (403) 667–2709. There are artifacts and photos from the gold rush period, including Sam McGee's cabin (McGee was a local character, celebrated in Robert Service's poem—"The Cremation of Sam McGee"); also a display of mounted Yukon animals.

Old Log Church, 3rd Avenue and Elliott Street, (403) 668–2555. Opened in 1900, this Anglican church served Whitehorse for sixty years. It now contains artifacts, photos, and documents telling the story of missionary work in the territory and its development.

Sky High Ranches, on Fish Lake (use services of Reception Centre to make contact). Horseback and pony rides; camping by the lake.

S.S. *Klondike* **Sternwheeler National Historic Site,** in downtown, (403) 667–4511. Launched in 1937, this restored sternwheeler was one of the largest used on the Yukon River. It has been fully fitted and furnished, and it is open for your inspection.

Takhini Hot Springs, located 27.4 km./17 mi. from the city on the Klondike Highway 2, (403) 633–2706. This is the place to soothe your aching body in warm mineral waters. Bathing suits can be rented. If you want more aches along with some pleasure, you can go on guided trail rides from Takhini and then come back for a soaking.

Guided Nature Walks, 302 Hawkins Street, (403) 668–5678. The Conservation Society takes visitors on nature hikes in the Whitehorse area.

Murdoch's Gem Shop, in Sheffield Hotel Mall, (403) 667–7403. Yukon's largest creator of gold-nugget jewelry, just in case you don't find a nugget or two on your own.

Yukon Native Products, 4230 4th Avenue at Baxter Street, (403) 668–5935, and **Northern Images,** 4th Avenue at Jarvis Street, (403) 668–5739. Looking for products made by the native people of the Yukon—beautiful parkas, baskets, snowshoes, soapstone and ivory carvings, mittens, moccasins, mukluks, jewelry? These two stores have everything.

All of the following accommodations have dining rooms and other amenities:

Edgewater Hotel, 101 Main Street, (403) 667–2572. Moderate.

Gold Rush Inn, 411 Main Street, (403) 668–4500. Moderate.

Klondike Inn, 228 2nd Avenue, (403) 668–4747. Moderate.

Regina Hotel, 102 Wood Street, (403) 667–7801. Moderate.

Sheffield Whitehorse, 2nd Avenue and Wood Street, (403) 668–4700. Moderate to expensive.

Whitehorse Centre Motor Inn, 206 Jarvis Street, (403) 668–4567. Moderate.

Yukon Inn Hotel, 4220 4th Avenue, (403) 667–2527. Moderate.

Dining possibilities in Whitehorse are varied:

Cellar Dining Room, at the Edgewater Hotel, (403) 667–2573. A gracious dining room serving excellent beef, steaks, lobster, and the regional specialty—king crab. Moderate.

Golden Garter, 212 Main Street, (403) 667–2626. French cuisine and seafood dishes. Moderate.

Monte Carlo, 404 Wood Street, (403) 667–2116. Food for the family at family prices. Inexpensive.

New Fireside Dining Lounge, 38 Lewes Boulevard, (403) 668–4820. Chinese smorgasbord and Western Canada dishes. Inexpensive to moderate.

The Keg and Cleaver, 3rd Avenue and Jarvis Street, (403) 668–4949. Beef, steaks, and seafood in an early Yukon setting. Moderate.

Talisman Café, 2112 2nd Avenue, (403) 667–2736. European and North American cuisines. Moderate.

Village Garden Dining Room, 2nd Avenue and Wood Street, (403) 668–4700. Prime roast rib of beef, Yukon lake trout, and salmon steaks. Moderate.

Travel services are available at the following:

Rental Cars

Hertz, airport and downtown locations, (403) 667–2505.
Tilden, 2089 Second Avenue, (403) 668–2521.

Camper Rentals

Economy, 304 Jarvis Street, (403) 668–2355.
Globe Camper, 503 Steele Street, (403) 668–4663.

RV Repairs

Second Avenue Chevron, 2240 2nd Avenue, (403) 668–6171.

Air Charter Services

This is a good way to experience the territory—Kluane National Park and northern Inuit settlements near the Beaufort Sea—if you're short on time.
Air North, (403) 668–2228.
Alkan Air, (403) 668–2107.
Glacier Air Tours, (403) 668–7323.
Kluane Airways, (403) 633–4365.
Trans North Air, (403) 668–6616.
Yukon Airways, (403) 668–2354.

Dawson City

Dawson City was called the "City of Gold," the end of the rainbow for thousands of dreamers who flooded here seeking their fortune in the goldfields near the city. In its heyday, when it was a gold-rush boom town, people who knew the place called Dawson the "Paris of North America," meaning that it offered many pleasures (albeit without the beauty and civilization of the real Paris). It was certainly one of the liveliest cities in North America. Among the colorful characters who made Dawson famous were Robert Service, Jack London, Diamond Tooth Gertie, Klondike Kate, and the Northwest Mounted Police. The stereotypical tales of Mounties chasing mad trappers and gold seekers came from here, as did (probably) the slogan "the Mounties always get their man." This was Dawson's exciting, frenetic, crazy, fascinating period. While some dreamers found gold along Bonanza Creek and other gold-rich streams, a large number went bust; but that's the risk dreamers always take, whether in search of gold or Shangri-la.

Today Dawson City is a civilized, proper place of commerce, but with enough gold-rush charm to make it a "must destination" for visitors to the Yukon.

For information on things to see and do in Dawson City, and places to stay and dine, stop in at the **Visitor Reception Centre,** Front Street at King, (403) 993–5566.

Midnight Dome, located 8 km./5 mi. from town via King Street, is an 884 m./2,900 ft. mountain that overlooks Dawson City, the Yukon and Klondike rivers, Bonanza Creek, and many mountain ranges, such as the Ogilvies. This mountain is called the Midnight Dome because at midnight every June 21 the sun shines at the top. (Actually it does so everywhere in this region, but the thrill is to be at the top of the mountain on June 21 at midnight and still be able to see the surrounding scenery because of the daylight.) The road up Midnight Dome is very steep, and extreme caution should be taken in driving. Best bet is to use the services of a Yukon tour company.

Dawson City Museum, 5th Avenue, (403) 993–5291, is the city's heritage museum, featuring exhibits telling the story of the gold mania that took place in this area, the city as a boom town during this exciting period, and its development thereafter. Be sure to see some of the old documentary films that show Dawson and its dreamers during the gold rush days. It also has a genealogy service for you to track down dreamers in your family tree—perhaps one who became wealthy beyond dreams.

Billed as the only gambling casino of its kind in Canada, Gertie's is **Diamond Tooth Gertie's Gambling Hall,** (403) 993–5291, where you make a quick buck or lose a bundle while getting a good meal and being entertained by wildly kicking cancan girls and honky-tonk music. Gertie's is the best show in town and sufficient reason to visit Dawson. Gertie herself was a colorful and now legendary "woman of the flesh," who was also a savvy business entrepreneur catering to the dreamers' needs for female company, strong drink, and games of chance.

Gaslight Follies, (403) 993–5575, provide an evening of good entertainment. Arizona Charlie Meadows built the Palace Grand Theatre at the turn of the century to provide high-class entertain-

345

ment to the dreamers and wheeler-dealers of the Yukon. "Olde Tyme" shows are presented nightly, except Tuesday nights.

Bonanza Creek is located 22 km./14 mi. via the Klondike Highway and Bonanza Creek Road. Along here some men found gold. Claims were based on this measurement: *10 BD*, meaning "10 claims *B*elow the initial *D*iscovery"; *25 AD* was "25 claims *A*bove *D*iscovery." In this area is dredge #4, purported to be the largest gold-recovery dredge in the world.

Visit the **Jack London Cabin**, (403) 993–5575. North America's immortal author Jack London had a cabin in the Dawson City area. His books told of life in the Yukon and Alaska as a mystical struggle, of individual men and women against an unyielding environment and against their own limitations. Readings of London's works— *Call of the Wild* and others—are presented at the cabin.

Robert Service Cabin, (403) 993–5575, is also open to visitors. The poet Robert Service (1874–1958) is called the "bard of the Yukon." He wrote most of his poetry—"Songs of a Sourdough"—in this cabin, and there are daily recitals of his poetry. As you travel through the Yukon, the images Robert Service wrote about will be seen everywhere you go.

Steamer *Keno,* Front Street, (403) 993–5575, was one of the last steamboats to sail the Yukon and Stewart rivers. Now a national historic site, you can visit the *Keno* in its dry dock beside the Yukon River.

The *Yukon Lou* **Stern-Wheeler** is a miniature stern-wheeler that gives visitors rides on the Yukon River. You see the graveyard of old stern-wheelers and feast on a salmon barbecue at Pleasure Island.

Gold Room, located above the Canadian Imperial Bank of Commerce on Front Street, displays assay equipment used in early mining operations.

Harrington's Store, 3rd Avenue and Princess Street, has a photo exhibit showing early boom town days in Dawson City.

M.V. *Klondike,* office on Front Street, (403) 276–8023, provides cruises on the Yukon River on board a modern river cruiser. It has a Gay Nineties interior; meals are served. Also offers trips to Eagle, Alaska, and a historic gold-mining town.

Stamps can be purchased at the historic **1901 Post Office.** It is a favorite stop for stamp collectors.

Claim #33 Below Discovery is 10 km. (6.2 mi.) up the

Bonanza Road, (403) 993–5303. Here you can pan for gold; pans and other gear are supplied, with some gold in every pan.

Early Day Adventures, located 10 km. (6.2 mi.) from town on Bonanza Creek Road, gives an escorted tour of an operating gold mine.

At **Guggieville,** located 2 km. (1.2 mi.) outside of town on Bonanza Creek Road, you can pan for gold at what was Guggenheim's mining camp, which operated in the early 1900s.

Gold City Tours, (403) 993–5175, and **Cheechako Trail Tours,** (403) 993–5460, offer tours of Dawson, Bonanza Creek, and the Midnight Dome.

Yukon River Water Skiing is an adventure, and Chipperfield Enterprises provides everything you need, (403) 993–5230.

Klondike Nugget and Ivory Shop, corner of Front and Queen Street, sells gold-nugget jewelry made in the shop.

All of the accommodations listed below have dining rooms and other amenities:

Downtown Hotel, (403) 993–5346. Moderate.

Eldorado Hotel, 3rd and Princess Street, (403) 993–5451. Moderate.

Klondike Kate's, (403) 993–5491. Moderate.

Midnight Sun Hotel, 3rd and Queen Street, (403) 993–9495. Moderate.

Sheffield Dawson City, (403) 993–5542. Expensive.

Here are two restaurants that you may want to sample:

Nancy's, (403) 993–5633. Homemade soups, sandwiches, pastries, ice cream. Also herbal teas and flavored coffees. Sourdough-pancake breakfasts. Inexpensive.

Pleasure Island Restaurant, reached by *Yukon Lou* boat tour, (403) 993–5482. Salmon barbecues. Moderate.

Beaver Creek

Beaver Creek is the last town of any size on the Alaska Highway at the Yukon–Alaska border. The **ALAS/KON Border Lodge,** (403) 862–7501, has plenty of rooms, a restaurant, and a lounge. Moderate.

The Northwest Territories: An Arctic Adventure

The land mass and water areas comprising the Northwest Territories are so vast that one could place much of Europe inside with plenty of room left over. The Northwest Territories span the North American continent from near Alaska to Greenland. On the southern border, along the 60th parallel, are the provinces of British Columbia, Alberta, Saskatchewan, Manitoba, Ontario, Québec, and Newfoundland-Labrador. Part of Hudson Bay is formed by the Northwest Territories. Within the Northwest Territories are Great Slave Lake, Great Bear Lake, the Mackenzie River, Baffin Island, Ellesmere Island, Victoria Island, Prince of Wales Island, Banks Island, the Parry Islands, and the Sverdrup Islands. About half of the region is above the Arctic Circle. Within this region is the fabled Northwest Passage, from Europe to the Orient. This is the land of the Inuit (Eskimo) and the Déné peoples, and where countless explorers, from Franklin to Byrd, have sought fame. The Northwest Territories is one of the harshest, yet most magnificent, regions on Earth. Much of it defies extensive land touring because of a lack of roads. However, thanks to aviation, many exceptional natural areas and remote communities are accessible within a few hours of such cities as Edmonton, Winnipeg, Toronto, Ottawa, and Montréal. This part of the chapter describes the western portion of the Northwest Territories. A later edition of *Guide to Eastern Canada* will include the eastern portion, including such areas as Baffin Island.

The western portion of the Northwest Territories borders the Yukon in the west; British Columbia, Alberta, and Saskatchewan to the south, the Beaufort Sea and the Amundsen Gulf to the north, the Coppermine River and eastern shores of Great Slave Lake at its East. The high Mackenzie Mountains and the Franklin Mountains rise up in the west; a boreal forest makes a swath across the southern zone; the Mackenzie River, including Great Bear and Great Slave lakes, are among the Earth's great water systems; and the Beaufort Sea, part of the Arctic Ocean, provides many kilometers/miles of shoreline.

Here is an Arctic climate with long, extremely cold winters. On the other hand, midsummer days can have temperatures up to 30°C/86°F, which is bikini weather. Summers tend to be warmer in the Mackenzie River Valley. A tundra environment, during warm weather, does produce mosquitoes, quite large and ravenous ones. If you are trekking and camping, it is a good idea to cover exposed skin areas and use repellent lotions and sprays. Once you overcome this annoyance, you'll love every moment of your stay. July and August are the best months for visiting the Northwest Territories, although many people start coming in mid-May and keep the season going until late September. If you want a real adventure, come here in winter, go dogsledding, and sleep in an igloo you made yourself. When traveling here during the summer, comfortable casual clothes are best, including a sweater or two, windbreaker, good hiking or walking shoes with cushy socks. Cameras with telephoto lenses and binoculars are also important bring-alongs.

Close to 50,000 people live in the Northwest Territories, giving the region one of the lowest population densities per square mile on Earth. The capital of the Northwest Territories is Yellowknife, located on the north shore of Great Slave Lake, with highway access to British Columbia and Alberta (and thence to all major North American centers). Yellowknife became the capital of the Northwest Territories when the office of Federal Commissioner was transferred from Ottawa to this city. Its population is now 12,000 persons. Fort Smith, Hay River, Fort Simpson, and Inuvik are western Northwest Territory communities with populations between two and three thousand persons. There are only sixty-four communities in all of the Northwest Territories. People make their living here from mining, fishing, tourism, arts and crafts, hunting and trapping. The native people of this part of the Northwest Territory are famous for such arts and crafts as moosehair tufting, porcupine quill work, traditional embroidery and beadwork, fine leathercraft, and fur–garment making.

Northwest Territories Facts

The Northwest Territories represent one-third of Canada, or a land area equal to that of the nation of India.

Fort Smith had the highest record temperature in the Northwest Territories—35.4°C/95.7°F; it also had the lowest recorded temperature: − 53.9°C/ − 65°F.

The Mackenzie River is 1,800 km./1,118 mi. long. When considered as including Slave, Peace, and Finlay rivers, it is about 2,635 mi. long, the second longest river in North America.

Great Bear Lake is the ninth-largest lake in the world.

Great Slave Lake is the sixth-deepest lake in the world.

The Northwest Territories entered Confederation on July 15, 1870.

The first white explorers were the Vikings in about A.D. 1000. In 1576 Martin Frobisher was the first of a long stream of explorers who came here searching for the Northwest Passage. Samuel Hearne and Alexander Mackenzie both trekked over much of the uncharted land during the eighteenth century. John Franklin and his expedition in the mid-1800s tried to find the Northwest Passage, but the party disappeared in the Arctic and the search for them was a major *cause célèbre* for many years. In 1984 the frozen, almost perfectly preserved body of one of Franklin's sailors was discovered in the Northwest Territories. Other nineteenth-century explorers included M'Clure, Amundsen, Sverdrup, and Stefansson.

Useful Information

Time zone: mountain (western Northwest Territories).
Area code: 403.
Travel information: TravelArctic, Government of the Northwest Territories, Yellowknife, N.W.T. X1A 2L9, (403) 873–7200 or call the toll-free Arctic Hotline, 1–800–661–0788.

In Yellowknife you can rent cars from Avis, Budget, Hertz, and Tilden. Call your local rental car agency for rates and reservations.

Nahanni National Park

There is no land vehicle access into Nahanni National Park, as it is essentially a wilderness park, but you can experience some of the park's natural wonders, such as Virginia Falls, by using the services of an air charter or an adventure tour organization providing canoe or wild river rafting trips. Wild river tours on the South Nahanni are considered among the top adventure experiences in North America. Some of the companies providing Nahanni trips are listed below. Fort Simpson is the base of operations for air and many other expeditions into the park, and the town can be reached via Highways 7 or 1. Float plane tours can also be booked at Watson

◄ **There is a sense of the eternal about the Inuit living in the northern regions of the Northwest Territories. It seems as if they have always been here and always will be.**

Lake in the Yukon and Fort Nelson, British Columbia. July and August are the best months in which to visit the park. If you are not an experienced wilderness traveler, it is advisable to explore the Nahanni with a guided tour group. The tour and outfitting services are well versed and supply commentary on the park, its features, and history. For more information on the park, contact Superintendent, Nahanni National Park, Box 300, Fort Simpson, N.W.T. X0E 0N0, (403) 369–3151.

An exceptional North American wilderness park, Nahanni was the first such area in the world to be designated by UNESCO in 1979 as a natural site of universal importance. One of the wildest waterways in the park is the South Nahanni River, which charges over 322 km. (193 mi.) before plunging down Virginia Falls, twice the height of Niagara Falls. Downriver from the falls are 8 km. (4.9 mi.) of turbulent rapids and waves. It is not unusual to see wild orchids blooming next to patches of snow near Virginia Falls. The park also has four great canyons, which are up to 1,200 m. (3,935 ft.) deep. Rabbitkettle Hotsprings and Wildmint Hotsprings are other natural features. The waters gushing up from Rabbitkettle are 20°C/68°F and form a terraced mount of tufa rock which is over 27 m. (88.5 ft.) high. The park has 13 species of fish, such as Arctic grayling and Dolly Varden trout; more than 120 species of birds, including the golden eagle and trumpeter swan; and more than 40 species of animals—wolves, grizzly and black bears, caribou, and beaver. Although now a wilderness park, during the gold rush days, Nahanni was combed over by dreamers in search of fortune, mostly to no avail. Their misfortunes gave names to places in the park, such as Deadmen Valley and Headless Creek.

Adventure Touring Services

If you are not bent on planning and executing your own wilderness expedition, the best way to experience this region is through the services of a tour operator who will provide transportation, lodging, meals, outfitters, and knowledgeable commentary. There are both standard packages and those tailored to your interests—hunting and fishing, ski touring, dogsledding, camping, trekking, and so forth. Among the advantages of using these professional services is that the guides usually know where such animals as caribou, reindeer, musk ox, wolves, buffalo, bears (including polar bears), and beavers can be seen. They can take you to remote Déné and Inuit villages, where you can see something of a way of life existing without major change for thousands of years. They know where to go, how to get there, and what to see. These services maximize your vacation experience in an incredibly rich area that, a few years ago, seemed remote and inaccessible.

Arctic Waterways, (416) 382–3882, in Stevensville, Ontario. Rafting the Coppermine and Horton rivers.

Black Feather Wilderness Adventures of Toronto and Ottawa, (416) 862–0881 or (613) 722–9717, has guided canoe trips down the Nahanni.

Canoe Arctic, (403) 872–2308, in Fort Smith, Northwest Territories. Fly-in canoe trips and cross-country skiing.

East Wind Arctic Tours, (403) 873–2170, in Yellowknife. Trophy fishing, wildlife encounters, tundra backpacking.

Dynamic Vacations, (416) 926–0877, in Toronto, Ontario. Specialists in authorized tours of the Western Arctic.

Great Slave Sledging Company, (403) 920–2611, in Yellowknife. Fishing and camping adventures on the remote western shore of Great Slave Lake. Also offer winter experiences: dog-sled trips and skiing expeditions.

Mackenzie River Cruises, (403) 695–2506, in Fort Simpson, Northwest Territories. Tours of the Mackenzie River by boat; accommodations in tents.

Northwest Expeditions, (604) 669–1100, in Vancouver, British Columbia. Coppermine River rafting.

Qaivvik, (403) 873–2074, in Yellowknife. Trips to experience caribou migration.

Sub-Arctic Wilderness Adventures, (403) 872–2467, in Fort Smith, Northwest Territories. Great Slave circle tour, boating the Slave, trip to Wood Buffalo National Park, dogteam wilderness trip, Tazin highlands, subarctic spring experience.

Swiftsure Tours, (604) 388–4227, in Vancouver, British Columbia. Western Arctic birds and mammals.

Nahanni River Adventures, (403) 435–6417, in Edmonton, Alberta. Trips on the Nahanni River by canoe.

Top of the World Tours, (403) 873–2710, in Yellowknife. Tours tailored to the interests of individuals and groups.

Yellowknife

On the north shore of Great Slave Lake, with a population of close to 12,000, Yellowknife is the capital of the Northwest Territories. It was founded in 1934 as a result of a minor gold rush. In the area there are two operating gold mines. Yellowknife is a good base from which to explore remote areas of western Northwest Territories. There are adequate accommodations, restaurants, shops, and services in town. Also visit the **Bush Pilots Monument,** a memorial to the pilots who, in the early days, explored and assisted in the development of the Northwest Territories.

How to Get to Yellowknife

By Car or RV

Yellowknife is the hub city for visiting the western portion of the Northwest Territories. Most roads and air routes lead to and radiate from Yellowknife. If you are interested in driving to the northwest corner of the region (Fort McPherson, Arctic Red River, and Inuvik), use the Dempster Highway from Dawson City, Yukon (see the description of this route in the Yukon section earlier in this chapter).

If you are traveling the Alaska Highway and reach Fort Nelson in British Columbia, you can take Highway 7 north past Nahanni National Park and then to the Mackenzie Highway 1 east, which leads to Highway 3 and then 4 to Yellowknife. If Yellowknife is your primary destination in the north and you are traveling from the east, your best route is the Mackenzie Highway 35 north from Edmonton, Alberta, which connects with Northwest Territories Highways 1, 3, and 4 to the city (see safe driving tips in Chapter 2).

Road distances to the Northwest Territories border using the Mackenzie Highway are listed below:

Edmonton: 990 km./615 mi.
Calgary: 1,276 km./793 mi.
Vancouver: 2,330 km./1,448 mi.
Winnipeg: 2,357 km./1,465 mi.
Toronto: 4,582 km./2,848 mi.
Montréal: 4,734 km./2,942 mi.
Los Angeles: 3,960 km./2,461 mi.

By Plane

Daily air service to Yellowknife from Edmonton and Calgary is provided by Canadian Airlines; Northwest Territorial Airways flew from Edmonton and Winnipeg to Yellowknife. Air service within the NWT is provided by charter and scheduled airlines such as Calm Air, Air Providence, Antler Aviation, Wolverine Air, Latham Island, Kenn Borek Air, Nahanni Air, Ptarmigan Airways. Call TravelArctic at (403) 873–7200, or the toll-free Arctic Hotline (1–800–661–0788), or your travel agent for details.

In addition to jet planes, commonly used aircraft in the region are twin-engine Otters, the workhorse of the North; Piper T 1040; Navajo Chieftain; Aztec; Cheyenne III; Dehavilland Turbo; and Cessna 185. Many of these planes are equipped with floats so that they can land in water in remote areas where there are no airfields. In the winter skis can be used. Flying in the Northwest Territories can be an adventure in itself, and the pilots here are among the finest in the world.

Special Events

Folk on the Rocks, late June, Inuit and Déné performers and folk artists from southern Canada.

Midnight Sun Golf Tournament, late June.

Raven Mad Daze, late June, celebrating the solstice.

Akaitcho-Franklin Reunion, late June, celebrating the meeting between a local chief and Franklin's 1819 overland expedition to the Arctic.

Pettitot Park Entertainment, musical entertainment Saturday evenings in July and August.

Guided Prelude Lake Trail, weekends in July and August, with Déné elder guides along wilderness trails.

Fall Fair, late August, agricultural displays and entertainments.

Attractions

Prince of Wales Northern Heritage Centre, named in honor of HRH Prince Charles, (403) 873–7551. The collection in this museum includes artifacts from Inuit, Déné, and métis cultures, early mining and aviation history, and other aspects of the ecology and human heritage of the Northwest Territories.

Yellowknife Courthouse has the fine Sissons-Morrow collection of Inuit carvings depicting the stories of famous court cases decided in the early days of the Northwest Territories.

Arctic Art Gallery, 5016 50th Street, displays original paintings and prints from northern artists.

Yellowknife Book Cellar, in Panda II center, (403) 920–2220, specializes in books about the North.

Northern Images, (403) 873–5944, sells soapstone sculptures, Inuit prints, parkas, kamiks, wall hangings.

Polar Parkas, (403) 873–3343, sells native handicrafts.

Accommodations and Dining

Discovery Inn, (403) 873–5673. Moderate to expensive.

Explorer Hotel, (403) 873–3531. Moderate to expensive.

Northern Lites Motel, (403) 873–6023. Moderate to expensive.

Twin Pines Motor Inn, (403) 873–8511. Moderate to expensive.

Yellowknife Inn, (403) 873–2600. Moderate to expensive.

YWCA, (403) 920–2777, a good value at a moderate price; efficiency units, no restaurant but close to them.

Lodges Within the General Yellowknife Area

The following lodges are for anglers and those who want to get away from it all. The accommodations are comfortable, and the food is great. Fishing equipment, guides, and boats are provided as needed. Actual services and facilities vary, so call ahead for full details and reservations.

Frontier Fishing Lodge, on Great Slave Lake, (403) 433–4914.

Great Slave Lake Lodge, on Great Slave Lake, (204) 772–8833.

Indian Mountain Fishing Lodge, on Great Slave Lake, (306) 731–3551.

Trophy Lodge, on Great Slave Lake, (403) 873–5420.

Blachford Lake Lodge, (403) 873–3303.

Katimavik Lodge, on Gordon Lake, (403) 920–4141.

MacKay Lodge, on MacKay Lake, (403) 873–2813.

Moraine Point Lodge, (403) 920–4541.

Namushka Lodge, on Harding Lake, (403) 920–2495.

Prelude Lake Lodge, (403) 920–2525.

Stagg Lake Lodge, (403) 371–3226.
Watta Lake Lodge, (403) 873–4036.
Yellowknife Lodge, (403) 873–5669.

Key Communities and Accommodations

All the accommodations listed below have dining rooms and other amenities and are priced in the high moderate to expensive range:

Fort McPherson (reached via Dempster Highway from Dawson City, Yukon) was the northern terminus for Northwest Mounted Police patrols from Dawson City during the early part of this century.

Inuvik means "place of man." Alexander Mackenzie canoed by here in 1789 on his way to the Arctic Ocean. Today the town is the government, commercial, and transportation center for the Western Arctic. It is also a supply base for oil and gas exploration in the Beaufort Sea and headquarters of the Inuvialuit, the first group to receive a land-claim settlement in the Northwest Territories. Accommodations are available at **Eskimo Inn**, (403) 979–2801; **Finto Motor Inn**, (403) 979–2647; and **Mackenzie Hotel**, (403) 979–2861.

Tuktoyaktuk is a remote community on the shores of the Beaufort Sea, only 160 km./99 mi. south of the polar ice cap. From here you can see Canada's famous pingos, hills pushed up by heaving permafrost. Visit *Our Lady of Lourdes* mission boat. Alaskan Inuit and whale-hunting Karngmalit people live the traditional life of hunting, trapping, sealing, fishing, and reindeer herding. **Hotel Tuk Inn**, (403) 977–2381, and **Pingo Park Lodge**, (403) 977–2155, are places to stay here.

Fort Simpson is the center for trips into Nahanni National Park. Established in 1804, it is the oldest continuously occupied community on the Mackenzie River. In 1984 Pope John Paul II was to have visited the people of Fort Simpson, but the trip was canceled because of bad flying weather. He vowed to make that trip one day. In 1987 the Vatican announced that the pope would keep his promise and come to Fort Simpson that year. **Fort Simpson Hotel**, (403) 695–2201, is located here, as is the **Maroda Hotel**, (403) 695–2602.

Fort Smith provides road access to Wood Buffalo National Park (see page 209 for description). Most of the park is in Alberta, but about one-third is in the Northwest Territory. Fort Smith is located on the eastern border parts, on the Northwest Territories/ Alberta border. The town itself was once a part of a chain of fur-trading posts, and Alexander Mackenzie explored this area in his search for the Pacific Ocean. The **Thebacha Campus of Arctic College** is now part of Fort Smith's life. While in Fort Smith visit the **Northern Life Museum,** (403) 872–2859, and **North of 60 Books,** (403) 872–2606, which has a large selection of books, maps, and charts of the North.

Pelican Rapids Inn, (403) 872–2789, has kitchenettes but no restaurant; the **Pinecrest Hotel,** (403) 872–2104, also provides accommodations.

Hay River is the southernmost port on the Mackenzie River system. Visit the Coast Guard headquarters in town. Sandy beaches are on Great Slave Lake, which is good for swimming in the summer, and a golf course is in town. You can drive to here from the south or take a flight from Edmonton, Alberta, on any day of the week. **Hay River Hotel,** (403) 874–2951, and **Ptarmigan Inn,** (403) 874–6781, provide accommodations.

Index

Abbreviations used in this index

B.C. = British Columbia   Sask. = Saskatchewan
N.W.T. = Northwest Territories   Y.T. = Yukon Territory

Abbotsford, B.C., 64–65
accommodations, 20–23
calculating costs, 18–19
Accordion Festival, International Old-
Time, B.C., 84
Agassiz Provincial Forest, Manitoba,
316
Ainsworth, B.C., 82
Air Canada, 28
airport services, 29
Calgary International, 211
Edmonton International, 249
Regina, 281
Saskatoon, 291
Vancouver International, 102
Victoria International, 154
Whitehorse, 331
Winnipeg International, 308
Air Show
Abbotsford International, B.C., 64
Saskatchewan, 277
Vanderhoof International, B.C., 195
Alaska Highway, 339
safety suggestions, 34–36
Alaska Highway Interpretive Centre,
Y.T., 341
Alberni Valley Museum, B.C., 183
Albert, Prince, 197, 269
Alberta, 197–259
accommodations, 202–203
climate, 200
economy, 200–201
geography, 199–200
history, 197, 199
map, 198
population, 200
sales tax, 203
tourism information, 201–203
Alberta Legislature Building, Edmon-
ton, 253

Alberta Pioneer Railway Museum, Ed-
monton, 253
alcohol and drug laws, 23–24
Alert Bay, B.C., 188
Alexander Mackenzie Heritage Trail,
B.C., 89
All Fun Waterslide Park, Victoria, 167
Alpine Slide, B.C., 84
Annual Scottish Gathering, B.C., 86
Aquatic Hall of Fame, Winnipeg, 311
Art Gallery of Greater Victoria, 164
Art Gallery of the South Okanagan,
B.C., 72
Arts and Sciences Technology Center,
Vancouver, 129
Assiniboine Forest, Winnipeg, 315
Assiniboine Park, Winnipeg, 315
Assiniboine Park Zoo, Winnipeg, 313
Ataglass Plant, Alberta, 205
Athabasca Tar Sands region, Alberta,
208
attractions, calculating costs, 20
auto clubs, 33
auto insurance identification, 48
automatic teller machines, 53
Aviation Hall of Fame, Canada's, Ed-
monton, 253
Aviation Museum, Western Canadian,
Winnipeg, 313

Baker, Russ, 195
Bamfield, B.C., 184
Banff, Alberta, 235–37
Banff Festival of the Arts, Alberta,
234–35
Banff National Park, Alberta, 228–41
accommodations, 235
dining, 239–40
entertainment, 240
museums, 235

shopping, 241
special events, 234–35
sports and recreation, 230–34
Banff Springs Hotel, Alberta, 229, 235, 236, 237
Barkerville Historic Park, B.C., 88–89
Bastion Square, Victoria, 164
Bateman, Ralph, 235
Batoche National Historic Park, Sask., 8, 273–74
Battleford, Sask., 273
Battleford Superslide, Sask., 279
Battle of Little Bighorn, 10, 210, 269, 271
Bauer, Father David, 218
Bavaria City Mining Railway, B.C., 84
B.C. Place, Vancouver, 129
B.C. Provincial Museum, Victoria, 161–62
Beacon Hill Park, Victoria, 161
bear safety, 33–34
Beaver Creek, Y.T., 347
bed and breakfast
country home/farm vacations, 22
Manitoba, 303
Reservation Services Victoria, 171
Belaney, Archibald Stansfield, 270
Bella Coola, B.C., 88
Bennett, R.B., 263
bicycling and tours
Banff, 232
Jasper, 244
Regina, 282
Sask., 265
Saskatoon, 292
Vancouver, 147
Big Foot, 65
Billy Barker Rodeo, B.C., 89
Birds Hill Provincial Park, Manitoba, 316
Blackfoot Museum, Alberta, 207
Black Nugget, B.C., 181
Bloedel Conservatory, Vancouver, 122
Blossom Festival, B.C., 82
boat cruises and tours
Banff, 232–33
Dawson City, 346
Jasper, 244
Lake Okanagan, B.C., 72
Manitoba, 301–302
Regina, 282
Saskatoon, 292
Vancouver, 117–18

Victoria, 159
Whitehorse, 342
Bonanza Creek, Dawson City, 346
British Columbia, 56–94
climate, 57
economy, 57, 59
geography, 57
map, 58
population, 56
touring, 60–94
tourist information, 59–60
winter sports, 91–94
British Columbia Forest Museum, B.C., 180
British Columbia Lions, 145
British Columbia World Trade and Convention Centre, Vancouver, 100, 108, 129
British North America Act, 7
Burnaby Village Museum, Vancouver, 129
Bush Pilots Monument, Yellowknife, 354
business hours, 55
Butchart Gardens, Victoria, 160
Butchart, Jennie, 160

Cache Creek, B.C., 87
Calaway Park, Calgary, 220
Calgary, Alberta, 209–26
access, 211–12
accommodations, 221–23
attractions, 218–21
business and convention services, 214
dining, 223–24
entertainment, 224
extra-special events, 216–18
history, 210–11
how to get around, 212
map, 213
professional sports, 226
recreation, 226–27
shopping, 224–26
touring service, 218
tourist information, 214
useful information, 215–16
Calgary Aerospace Museum, 220
Calgary Cannons, 216
Calgary Exhibition and Stampede, Alberta, 216
Calgary Flames, 226
Calgary Stampeders, 226
Calgary Tower, 219

Calgary Zoo, Botanical Gardens, and
Historic Park, 220
Calona Wines, B.C., 69
Campbell River, B.C., 187
Campbell River Museum, B.C., 187
Campbell, Robert, 327
camping, 22
Banff, 230
Harrison Hot Springs, B.C., 65
Jasper, 242
Manitoba, 303
N.W.T., 353
safety suggestions, 33–34
Sask., 266
Vancouver, 136
Victoria/Vancouver Island, 180
Y.T., 335–36, 338
Camrose, Alberta, 206
Canada Customs
clearing, 41–46
passport or visa, 40–41
personal exemptions, 43–46
Canada Fantasyland, Edmonton,
252–53
Canada Pacific Railroad, 6–7, 229
Canada's Aviation Hall of Fame, Ed-
monton, 253
Canadian Airlines, 28
Canadian Confederation, 261
Canadian Consulate General in U.S.
cities, 16–17
Canadian Lacrosse Hall of Fame, B.C.,
64
canoeing
Alberta, 202
Banff, 232
N.W.T., 353
Sask., 265
Cape Merry National Historic Site,
Manitoba, 322
Capilano Suspension Bridge,
Vancouver, 124
Cardston, Alberta, 203
Cariboo Cowboy Adventures, B.C., 87
Carillon, Victoria, 166–67
Carlton Trail, 273
Carmack, George W., 327
Carr, Emily, 163
Casabella Princess, B.C., 72
Casabello Wines, B.C., 69
Castlegar, B.C., 81
Cathedral Grove, B.C., 183
caving, B.C., 187
CBC radio station, 36

Centennial Museum, Alberta, 206
Centennial Museum, B.C., 71
Centennial Planetarium and Pleiades
Theatre, Calgary, 219
Centennial Square, Victoria, 165
Centre Culturel Franco-Manitobain,
Winnipeg, 312
Charles, HRH Prince, 355
Château Lake Louise, Alberta, 229,
237–39
Chemainus, B.C., 181
Cherry Festival, B.C., 80
Children's Zoo, Vancouver, 125–26
Chilkoot Trail, Y.Y., 337
Chinatown
Vancouver, 118–19
Victoria, 165
Winnipeg, 311
Churchill, Manitoba, 322–23
Churchill, John, 322
Churchill, Winston, 86
City of Trail Museum, B.C., 80
City of Vancouver Archives, 126
Claim #33 Below Discovery, Dawson
City, 346–47
Claremont Estate Winery and Vine-
yards, B.C., 69
Classic Car Museum, Victoria, 163
climate and weather
Alberta, 200
B.C., 57
Manitoba, 299
N.T., 348–49
Saskatchewan, 263, 265
Vancouver, 109–10
Victoria, 149
Y.T., 330
Cochrane Ranch, Alberta, 206
Comico Gardens, B.C., 84
Comox, B.C., 186–87
Constitution Act of 1982, 40
Cook, Captain James, 12, 97, 99, 164,
187
Courtenay, B.C., 186–87
Covered Wagon Treks, Sask., 279
Cowichan Valley Museum, B.C.,
180–81
Craigdarroch Castle, Victoria, 164–65
Craigflower Manor, Victoria, 165
Craigflower School, Victoria, 165
Craig Heritage Park, B.C., 182
Cranbrook, B.C., 82–83
Cranbrook Railway Museum, B.C.,
83

credit cards, 53
Creston, B.C., 82
Creston Valley Museum, B.C., 82
Creston Valley Wildlife Management
  Area, B.C., 82
Cross of Freedom, Manitoba, 324
Crowfoot, Chief, 207
Crown Forest Industries Arboretum
  and Museum, B.C., 181
Crowsnest Highway 3, B.C., 79
Crowsnest Pass, Alberta, 203
Crystal Garden, Victoria, 163
curling, Regina, 288
Cut Knife Hill National Historic Site,
  Sask., 272–73, 278
Cypress Hills Massacre, 273
Cypress Hills Provincial Park, Sask.,
  203, 272

Dalnavert Museum, Winnipeg, 313
Dauphin, Manitoba, 323
Dawson, Sir George Mercer, 269
Dawson City, Y.T., 344–47
  accommodations, 347
  attractions, 345–47
  dining, 347
  tourist information, 345
  tours, 347
Dawson City Museum, 345
Deighton, "Gassy Jack," 98, 99,
  119
Dempster Highway 5, Y.T., 340
Devian Gardens, Calgary, 220
Devon, Alberta, 206
Devonian Botanic Gardens, Alberta,
  206
Dewdney Trail, 65
Diamond Tooth Gertie, 344, 345
Diamond Tooth Gertie's Gambling
  Hall, Dawson City, 345
Diefenbaker Centre, The Right Hon-
  ourable John G., Saskatoon, 293
Diefenbaker Homestead, Regina, 284
Diefenbaker House, Sask., 271
Diefenbaker, John George, 261, 263
dining, 23
Dinosaur Provincial Park, Alberta,
  203–204
District Museum, B.C., 186
Divino Estate Winery, B.C., 69
Dmytriw, Reverend Nestor, 324
Dominion Astrophysical Observatory,
  Victoria, 165
Dominion Lands Act, 261

Dominion Radio Astrophysical Observatory, B.C., 72
Douglas, James, 150, 164, 166
Douglas, Thomas (Lord Selkirk), 299,
  305
Doukhobor Heritage Village, National,
  Sask., 280
Doukhobor Historical Museum, B.C.,
  81
Drake, Sir Francis, 12
driving
  auto clubs, 33
  auto insurance identification, 48
  clearing Customs, 41
  on gravel roads, 34–36
  license, 41
  rules of the road, 31
  into Western Canada, 29–31
Drumheller, Alberta, 206–207
Duck Lake Historical Museum, Sask.,
  278
Duke of Abruzzi, 337
Dumont, General Gabriel, 274
Duncan, B.C., 180–81
Dunsmuuir, Robert, 164

Early Day Adventures, Dawson City,
  347
Edmonton, Alberta, 248–59
  access, 249–50
  accommodations, 255–56
  attractions, 252–55
  business and convention services,
    250–51
  dining, 256–57
  entertainment, 257
  history, 248
  how to get around, 250
  professional sports, 257–58
  population, 249
  recreation, 258
  shopping, 257
  special events, 251–52
  useful information, 251
Edmonton Art Gallery, 253
Edmonton Eskimos, 258
Edmonton Oilers, 257
Edmonton Police Museum, 253
Edmonton Space Sciences Centre, 254
electricity use, 55
Elizabeth II, Queen, 40, 99, 164
Elk Falls Provincial Park, B.C., 187
Elk Island National Park, Alberta, 208
Emerald Lake Lodge, B.C., 78–79

emergencies, 31–33
Emily Carr Gallery of the Provincial
    Archives, Victoria, 163
employment in Canada, regulations, 41
Empress, The, Victoria, 167–68
Environment Canada-Parks Interpre-
    tive Centre, Manitoba, 323
Erickson, Arthur, 125, 128, 204
Exchange District, Winnipeg, 310–11
Expo 86, 98, 99, 128–29

Fable Cottage Estate, Victoria, 165
Fairmont Hot Springs Resort, B.C., 85
Fantasy Garden World, Vancouver,
    127–28
Father Pandosy Mission, B.C., 71
ferries to Victoria/Vancouver Island,
    153–54
festivals
    Cariboo, B.C., 87
    Creston blossom, B.C., 82
    Edmonton, 251–52
    International Old-Time Accordion,
        B.C., 84
    Kinsmen International Band, Sask.,
        277
    Manitoba, 303–304
    Okanagan, B.C., 68
    Osoyoos cherry, B.C., 80
    Pysanka, Alberta, 208
    Sask., 267–68
    Vancouver, 110–12
    Victoria, 158–59
    Y.T., 336
Fidler, Peter, 261
Filberg Lodge, B.C., 187
fishing
    Banff, 233
    Jasper, 244
    N.W.T., 353
    Sask., 265
    Victoria, 175
    Y.T., 334
fishing lodges, Yellowknife, 356–57
fishing regulations, 36–37
fishing, salmon
    Campbell River, 187
    Kitimat, B.C., 193
    Port Alberni, B.C., 183
    Vancouver, 146–47
Fleming, Sir Sanford, 241
Folklorama, Winnipeg, 304
forest fire safety, 33–34
Fort Augustus, 248

Fort Battleford National Historic Park,
    Sask., 272–73
Fort Calgary, Calgary, 210, 219
Fort Carlton Historic Park, Sask.,
    278
Fort Churchill, Manitoba, 322
Fort Edmonton Park, Edmonton, 253
Fort Esperance National Historic Site,
    Sask., 278
Fort Fraser, B.C., 194–95
Fort George, B.C., 195
Fort Langley National Historic Park,
    B.C., 64
Fort Macleod, Alberta, 204
Fort McMurray, Alberta, 208
Fort McPherson, N.W.T., 357
Fort Nelson, B.C., 90
Fort Pitt Historic Park, Sask., 278
Fort Prince of Wales, Manitoba, 322,
    323
Fort Qu'Appelle Museum, Sask., 278
Fort Rodd Hill and Fisgard
    Lighthouse, Victoria, 165–66
Fort Rupert, B.C., 189
Fort St. James, B.C., 195
Fort St. John, B.C., 90
Fort Saskatchewan, 248
Fort Simpson, N.W.T., 357
Fort Smith, N.W.T., 357–58
Fort Steele Historic Park, B.C., 83–84
Fort Victoria, Victoria, 150, 164, 166
Fort Walsh National Historic Park,
    Sask., 271–72
Fort Whoop-up, Alberta, 204
Fort Whyte Centre for Environmental
    Education, Winnipeg, 315
Fox, Terry, 66
Franklin, Sir John, 261, 351
Franko, Ivan, 314
Frantic Follies Vaudeville, Whitehorse,
    342
Fraser–Fort George Regional Museum,
    B.C., 196
Fraser River Valley, B.C., 62
Fraser, Simon, 194, 195
Frenchman Butte Historic Site, Sask.,
    278
Frobisher, Martin, 351
Frog Follies, Manitoba, 304

Galbraith, John, 84
Galiano Island, B.C., 115
Gaslight Follies, Dawson City, 345–46
gasoline

costs, 20
Imperial gallon, 50
Gastown, Vancouver, 119–20
George Hooey Wildlife Exhibit, Sask.,
    279
George Johnson Museum, Y.T., 341
Ghost River wilderness area, Alberta,
    207
Gibsons, B.C., 61
Gimli, Manitoba, 325
Glacier National Park, B.C., 75
Glass Castle, B.C., 181
Gleichen, Alberta, 207
Glenbow Museum, Calgary, 218–19
Gold City Auto Museum, B.C., 71
Golden, B.C., 76
"gold fever," 9–10, 327
Gold River, B.C., 187
Gold Room, Dawson City, 346
golf
    Banff, 233
    Calgary, 227
    Edmonton, 258
    Jasper, 243
    Regina, 288
    Vancouver, 145
    Victoria, 174
    Winnipeg, 320
gondola lift sightseeing
    Banff, 234
    Jasper, 243
    Whistler Resort Area, B.C., 116
Gonzales Weather Station, Victoria,
    166
Gordon Southam Observatory, Van-
    couver, 126
government, 38–40
Government House, Regina, 284–85
Government House, Victoria, 164
Grace Campbell Art Gallery, Sask.,
    271
Grand Beach Provincial Park, Mani-
    toba, 325
Grande Cache, Alberta, 207–08
Grand Forks, B.C., 80
Grand Trunk Pacific Railway, 195
Granville Island, Vancouver, 119
Grasslands National Park, Sask., 269
Gray Monk Estate Cellars, B.C., 69
Great Cariboo Ride Society, B.C., 87
Gretsky, Wayne, 248, 257
Grey Owl, 270
Grouse Mountain Recreational Area,
    Vancouver, 123–24

Guggieville, Dawson City, 346
Gulf Islands, B.C., 115–16

Halfmoon Bay, B.C., 61
Hall of Fame
    Aquatic, Winnipeg, 311
    Aviation, Edmonton, 253
    Lacrosse, B.C., 64
    Ski, B.C., 80
Hanceville, B.C., 88
Hardy, Vice Admiral Sir Thomas
    Masterman, 188–89
Harmac Arboretum, B.C., 181
Harrington's Store, Dawson City, 346
Harrison Hot Springs Resort Area,
    B.C., 65
Hatley Castle, Victoria, 166
Hawes, Jasper, 241
Hay River, N.W.T., 358
"Head Smashed In" Buffalo Jump, Al-
    berta, 204
Hearne, Samuel, 322, 351
health insurance, 48
Hecla Provincial Park, Manitoba, 325
Helen Schuler Coulee Centre, Alberta,
    204
helicopter skiing/hiking
    Banff, 231
    B.C., 92–93
    Jasper, 242
    Vancouver, 116
helicopter touring
    Banff, 233
Hell's Canyon Airtram, B.C., 66
Helmcken House, Victoria, 162
Henry, G. W., 68
Heritage Day, Sask., 280
Heritage Park, Calgary, 219
High River, Alberta, 204
Hind, Henry, 261
history of Western Canada, 6–13
holidays, national and provincial, 48–49
home/farm vacations, 22
Hoodoos, Alberta, 207
Hope, B.C., 65–66
hostels, 22
    Banff, 233
    Regina, 286
    Vancouver, 136
hotel chains, major, 22–23
Hotel Vancouver, 131
hot springs
    Ainsworth, B.C., 82
    Banff, 234

Fairmont, B.C., 85
Harrison, B.C., 65
Jasper, 243
Nakusp, B.C., 74
Radium, B.C., 86
Takhini, Whitehorse, 342–43
Hudson Bay, Sask., 279–80
Hudson Bay Heritage Park, Sask., 280
Hudson Bay Museum, Sask., 280
Hudson's Bay Company, 9, 299
Hughes, J. W., 68
hunting
regulations, 36–37
Yukon Territory, 334–35

Indian (Kwakiutl) Museum, B.C., 187
Inkster, John, 312
Inside Passage, 189–91
International Air Show, B.C., 64
International Peace Garden, Manitoba, 326
Inuvik, N.W.T., 357
Invermere, B.C., 85–86
Invermere Museum, B.C., 85
Italian Community Archives, B.C., 80
Ivan Franko Museum, Winnipeg, 314

Jack London Cabin, Dawson City, 346
Jasper, Alberta, 244–45
Jasper National Park, Alberta, 241–48
accommodations, 245
dining, 247
entertainment, 247
shopping, 247–48
sports and recreation, 242–44
Jasper Park Lodge, Alberta, 245
John Janzen Nature Centre, Edmonton, 254
John Paul II, Pope, 357
John Walker Historic Site, Edmonton, 254

Kamloops, B.C., 66–67
Kamloops Museum and Archives, B.C., 66
Kamloops Waterslide and R.V. Park, B.C., 67
Kamloops Wildlife Park, B.C., 67
Kaposvar Historic Site Museum, Sask., 278
Kelowna, B.C., 70–72
Kelowna Centennial Museum and National Exhibit Centre, B.C., 71
Kelsey, Henry, 261

Kicking Horse Pass, B.C., 79
Kildonan Park, Winnipeg, 315
Kildonan Presbyterian Church, Winnipeg, 315
Kimberley, B.C., 84–85
Kimberley Heritage Museum, B.C., 84
King George VI Provincial Park, B.C., 80
Kinsmen International Band Festival, Sask., 277
Kipling, Rudyard, 205
Kitimat, B.C., 193
Kitimat Centennial Museum, B.C., 193
Kitwanga, B.C., 194
Klondike Days, Edmonton, 248, 251
Klondike Highway 2, Y.T., 339
Klondike Kate, 344
Kluane National Park, Y.T., 337–39
accommodations, 339
Knox United Church, Winnipeg, 315
Kootenay Lake, B.C., 82
Kootenay National Park, B.C., 76, 78
'Ksan Village, B.C., 194
Kurelek, William, 292–93
Kwah, Chief, 195

Lacombe, Father Albert, 208
lacrosse
Canadian Hall of Fame, B.C., 64
Ladysmith, B.C., 181
Lake, John, 289
Lake, Sir James Winter, 248
Lake Louise, Alberta
accommodations, 237–39
ski area, 231
Lakelse Provincial Park, B.C., 193
Lake Okanagan Resort, B.C., 71
Lake Winnipeg, Manitoba, 325
Lanark Place, Sask., 274
Last Mountain House Historic Park, Sask., 277–78
La Vérendrye, Pierre Gaultier de Varennes de, 261, 305
Legislative Building, Regina, 284
Legislative Building, Winnipeg, 311
Lethbridge, Alberta, 204–205
Lighthouse Park, Vancouver, 123
Little Stone School House, Saskatoon, 292
Living Prairie Museum, Winnipeg, 313
Lombard Place, Winnipeg, 312
London, Jack, 329, 339, 344, 346
Cabin, Dawson City, 346

Louise Caroline Alberta, Princess, 197, 229, 281
Lower Fort Garry National Historic Park, Manitoba, 324
Lund, B.C., 62
Lund Wildlife Exhibit, Sask., 271

MacBride Museum, Whitehorse, 342
Macdonald, Sir Hugh John, 313
Macdonald, Sir John A., 7
Mackenzie, Sir Alexander, 12, 99, 195, 351, 357, 358
Macleod, Colonel, 199, 207
MacMillan Bloedel Place, Vancouver, 123
MacMillan Planetarium, Vancouver, 126
MacMillan Provincial Park, B.C., 183
Madrona Exposition Centre 900, B.C., 181
Maligne Lake (*See* Jasper National Park)
Maltwood Art Museum and Gallery, Victoria, 166
Manitoba, 297–326
  brief history, 299–300
  climate, 299
  economy, 300
  geography, 297–99
  map, 298
  population, 300
  sales tax, 303
  special attractions, 321–26
  special events, 303–304
  touring services, 301–302
  tourism, 300–301
  useful information, 302–303
Manitoba Centennial Centre, Winnipeg, 310
Manitoba Museum of Man and Nature, Winnipeg, 310
marina services, 36
Marine Drive, Victoria, 160–61
Marine Drives, Vancouver, 114–15
Marine Museum of Manitoba, 325
Maritime Museum, Vancouver, 126
Maritime Museum, Victoria, 164
Markerville, Alberta, 207
Marmot Basin, Jasper, 242
Marquis of Lorne, 197, 229
Martin Mars Water Bombers, B.C., 183
Massey, Geoffrey, 128
Mayne Island, B.C., 115

McGee, Sam, 342
Meadows, Arizona Charlie, 345
Medicine Hat, Alberta, 205
Medicine Hat Museum and Art Gallery, Alberta, 205
Mendel Art Gallery, Saskatoon, 292
Mendel, Frederick, 292
Mennonite Genealogy, Winnipeg, 313
metric system, 49–50
Middleton, General Frederick, 273, 274
Midnight Dome, Dawson City, 345
Mile "0," Victoria, 163
Miniature World, Victoria, 163
Mission/Hatzic area, B.C., 65
money, 50–53
  automatic teller machines, 53
  Canadian dollar, value of, 52
  conversion of currency in Canada, 52–53
  credit cards, 53
Moose Jaw, Sask., 277
Moose Jaw Wild Animal Park, Sask., 277
Morice, Father, 195
Mormon Temple, Alberta, 203
Morris, Edward, 284
Motherwell Homestead National Historic Park, Sask., 274
Motherwell, William Richard, 274
mountaineering
  Banff, 231–32
  Jasper, 243
Mount Assiniboine, B.C., 86
Mounties, 10–12, 280, 344
Mount Logan, Y.T., 337–38
Mount Norquay, Banff, 230
Mount Pope, B.C., 195
Mount Revelstoke National Park, B.C., 74–75
Mount Robson, B.C., 66
Mount St. Elias, 337
Museum of Anthropology, Vancouver, 124–25
Museum of Northern British Columbia, B.C., 191
Museum of the Royal Westminster Regiment, B.C., 64
Museum of Ukrainian Culture, Saskatoon, 275, 292
Muttart Conservatory, Edmonton, 254
M.V. *Klondike*, Dawson City, 346
M.V. *Queen of the North*, 189–90

Nahanni National Park, N.W.T., 351–52
Nakusp Hot Springs, B.C., 74
Nanaimo, B.C., 181–82
Nanaimo Centennial Museum, B.C., 181
National Doukhobor Heritage Village, Sask., 280
National Exhibition Centre West Kootenay, B.C., 81
national historic parks
Batoche, Sask., 273
Fort Battleford, Sask., 272–73
Fort Langley, B.C., 64
Fort Prince of Wales, Manitoba, 323
Fort St. James, B.C., 195
Fort Walsh, Sask., 271
Lower Fort Garry, Manitoba, 324
Motherwell Homestead, Sask., 274
Rocky Mountain House, Alberta, 207
national park
Banff, Alberta, 228–41
Elk Island, Alberta, 208
Fort Rodd Hill and Fisgard Lighthouse, Victoria, 165–66
Glacier, B.C., 75–76
Grasslands, Sask., 269
Jasper, Alberta, 241–48
Kluane, Y.T., 337–39
Kootenay, B.C., 78
Mount Revelstoke, B.C., 74–75
Nahanni, N.W.T., 351–52
Pacific Rim, B.C., 185–86
Prince Albert, Sask., 269–70
Riding Mountain, Manitoba, 323–24
Waterton Lakes National Park, Alberta, 227–28
Wood Buffalo, Alberta, 209, 357–58
Yoho, B.C., 76–78
National Ukrainian Festival, Manitoba, 304
Nechako Bird Sanctuary, B.C., 195
Necoslie Reserve, B.C., 195
New Westminster, B.C., 64
Nickel Art Museum, Calgary, 221
Nikka Yuko Japanese Gardens, Alberta, 204
1901 Post Office, Dawson City, 346
Nitobe, Inazo, 123
Nitobe Memorial Garden, Vancouver, 122–23
North Battleford, Sask., 279
North Battleford Arts Centre, Sask., 279

Northern Life Museum, N.W.T., 358
North Pender Island, B.C., 115
North Vancouver Parks, Vancouver, 124
North West Company, 9
Northwest Mounted Police, formation of, 10, 210
Northwest Rebellion, 8, 272, 279
Northwest Territorial Days, Sask., 279
Northwest Territories, 348–58
adventure touring services, 352–53
basic facts, 349–51
climate, 348–39
geography, 348
population, 349
useful information, 351

Okanagan Game Farm, B.C., 73
Okanagan Indian Project, B.C., 72–73
Okanagan/Similkameen region, B.C., 67–73
festivals, 68
wineries, 68–69
Okanagan Summer School of the Arts, B.C., 72
Okanagan Vineyards, B.C., 69
O'Keefe Ranch, B.C., 69–70
Old Log Church, Whitehorse, 342
Oldtime Fiddlers Contest, B.C., 89
Old Timer's Museum, Sask., 277
Olympic Games, Winter, 1988, 209–10, 216–18
100 Mile House, B.C., 87
Open Air Market, Winnipeg, 314
Oseredok (the Ukrainian Cultural and Education Centre), Winnipeg, 312
Osoyoos, B.C., 79–80
Osoyoos Lake, B.C., 80
Osoyoos Museum, B.C., 80
Otter, Colonel William, 272, 276
Our Lady of Assumption Cathedral, Sask., 275, 277

Pacific National Exhibition, Vancouver, 111–12
Pacific Rim National Park, B.C., 185–86
Pacific Undersea Gardens, Victoria, 162
Palliser, Captain John, 241, 261
Pandosy, Father Charles, 68, 71
Panorama Resort, B.C., 86
Parksville, B.C., 182–83

Parliament Buildings, Victoria, 161
Peachland, B.C., 72
Penticton, B.C., 72–73
Philip, Prince, 99
Phillips, W. J., 235
Photography Gallery, Calgary, 221
Plains Historical Museum, Regina, 284
Point Ellice House, Victoria, 162
Polar Park, Alberta, 207
Pond, Peter, 261
population, 39
Port Alberni, B.C., 183–84
Port Hardy, B.C., 188–89
Port Hardy Museum and Archives,
    B.C., 189
Port Renfrew, B.C., 179–80
postal service (Canadian), 54–55
Poundmaker, Chief, 272–73, 276
Powell River, B.C., 61–62
Prince Albert, Sask., 270–71
Prince Albert National Park, Sask.,
    269–71
Prince George, B.C., 195–96
Prince George Art Gallery, B.C., 196
Prince of Wales Northern Heritage
    Centre, Yellowknife, 355
Prince Rupert, B.C., 191–92
Princess Patricia's Canadian Light In-
    fantry Regimental Museum, Cal-
    gary, 221
Provincial Museum and Archives, Ed-
    monton, 254
Pysanka Festival, Alberta, 208

Qualicum Falls Provincial Park, B.C.,
    182
Queen Charlotte Islands, B.C., 192
Queen Charlotte Islands Museum,
    B.C., 192
Queen Elizabeth Park, Vancouver, 122
Queen's Own Cameron Highlanders of
    Canada Museum, Winnipeg, 313
Quesnel, B.C., 88

radio station, 36
Radium Hot Springs, B.C., 78, 86
ranch
    E.P., Alberta, 204
    O'Keefe, B.C., 69–70
    Sky High, Whitehorse, 342
    Spruce Meadows Equestrian, Cal-
        gary, 220
    Top of the World, B.C., 84–85
Red Mountain Ski Area, B.C., 80

Red River, 300, 305
Red River Settlement, 299, 305
Reg Atkinson Museum, B.C., 73
Regina, Sask., 280–89
    access, 281–82
    accommodations, 285–86
    art galleries, 285
    attractions, 283–85
    dining, 286–87
    entertainment, 287–88
    how to get around, 282
    professional sports, 288
    recreation, 288
    shopping, 289
    touring services, 282
Regina Pats, 288
Remington Collection, Alberta, 203
Revelstoke, B.C., 74
Revelstoke, Lord, 7, 74
restaurants, calculating costs, 19–20
Richardson, Dr. John, 261
Riding Mountain National Park, Mani-
    toba, 323–24
Riel House National Historic Site,
    Winnipeg, 312
Riel, Louis, 8–9, 274, 300, 305, 312,
    314
    statue of, 311
Riel Rebellion, 273, 300
Right Honourable John G. Diefenbaker
    Centre, Saskatoon, 293
Rittich, Dr. Eugene, 68
river rafting
    Banff, 232
    B.C., 86, 193
    Jasper, 244
    N.W.T., 353
    Sask., 265–66
Robert Campbell Highway 4, Y.T., 340
Robert Service Cabin, Dawson City,
    346
Robson Square and Robsonstrasse,
    Vancouver, 120
Rocky Mountain House National His-
    toric Park, Alberta, 207
rodeo
    Calgary, 216
    Edmonton, 258
Rogers, A.B., 75
Rogers Pass, B.C., 75
Rogers Pass Information Centre, B.C.,
    75–76
Rollin Art Centre, B.C., 183
Rossland, B.C., 80–81

Royal Canadian Mint, Winnipeg, 312–13
Royal Canadian Mounted Police (RCMP), 12, 280
museum, Regina, 283
Royal Canadian Regimental Museum (Lord Stratcona's Horse), Calgary, 220
Royal Hudson Steam Train, B.C., 112–14
Royal London Wax Museum, Victoria, 163
Royal Winnipeg Ballet, 300, 307, 319
Royal Winnipeg Rifles Regimental Museum, Winnipeg, 312
Royal Roads Military College, Victoria, 166
Rupert, Prince, 299
Rupert's Land, 299
Rutherford, Alexander Cameron, 248, 254
Rutherford House, Edmonton, 254

Saint Albert, Alberta, 208
St. Andrews, Winnipeg, 315
Saint-Boniface, Manitoba, 305
Saint-Boniface, Basilica, Winnipeg, 312, 314
Saint-Boniface Museum, Winnipeg, 314
St. James Church, Winnipeg, 314
St. John's Cathedral, Winnipeg, 314
Saint-Laurent Settlement, 273
St. Laurent Shrine, Sask., 278
St. Michael's, Manitoba, 324
St. Michael's Ukrainian Orthodox Church, Manitoba, 326
St. Nicholas Ukrainian Catholic Church, Winnipeg, 315
St. Paul's Anglican Church, Winnipeg, 315
St. Peter's Cathedral, Sask., 280
St. Thomas More Art Gallery, Saskatoon, 292–93
St. Victor Petroglyphs Historic Park, Sask., 277
St. Vladimir and Olga Cathedral, 315
sales tax, 24
Saltspring Island, B.C., 115
Samson V Maritime Museum, B.C., 64
Sam Steele Days, B.C., 83
Sandlands Provincial Forest, Manitoba, 316
Sarcee People's Museum, Calgary, 221

Saskatchewan, 260–96
climate, 261, 263
economy, 265
geography, 263, 265
map, 262
national historic parks, 271–74
national parks, 269–71
special attractions, 275–80
special events, 267–68
tourist information, 265–66
Ukrainian connection, 275
useful information, 266
Saskatchewan Air Show, 277
Saskatchewan Archives, Regina, 285
Saskatchewan Centre of the Arts, Regina, 284, 287
Saskatchewan Museum of Natural History, Regina, 284
Saskatchewan Roughriders, 288
Saskatoon, Sask., 289–96
access, 291
accommodations, 293–94
attractions, 292–93
dining, 294–95
entertainment, 295
how to get around, 291
shopping, 295–96
sports and recreation, 295
touring services, 292
Saskatoon Western Development Museum, 292
Sasquatch (Big Foot), 65
Saturna Island, B.C., 115
Sauve, Jeanne-Methilde, 263
SCUBA diving
Ucluelet, B.C., 184, 186
Vancouver, 146
Vancouver Island, 186
Sealand of the Pacific, Victoria, 162
Sechelt, B.C., 61
Selkirk, Manitoba, 324–25
Selkirk, Lord, 299, 305
Service, Robert, 339, 342, 344
Cabin, Dawson City, 346
Seven Oaks House, Winnipeg, 312
Seven Oaks Massacre, 305
Shaffer, Mary, 241, 244
Shevchenko, Tara, statue, 311
Siffleur wilderness area, Alberta, 207
Simon Fraser University Campus, Vancouver, 128
Sir Alexander Galt Museum, Alberta, 204
Sitting Bull, Chief, 10, 210, 269, 271

Ski Hall of Fame, B.C., 80
skiing, downhill
    Banff, 230–31
    B.C., 91–92
    Jasper, 242
    Sask., 265–66
    Vancouver, 116, 124, 145
skiing, Nordic and cross-country
    Banff, 230–31
    B.C., 93–94
    Jasper, 242
    N.W.T., 353
    Sask., 265–66
    Vancouver, 116
skiing, Snow-Cat, B.C., 93
Sky High Ranches, Whitehorse, 342
Smithers, B.C., 194
Sooke, B.C., 179
Sport British Columbia, 145
sports, professional
    Calgary, 226
    Edmonton, 257–58
    Regina, 288
    Vancouver, 144–45
    Winnipeg, 320
Spruce Meadows Equestrian Ranch,
    Calgary, 220
Spruce Woods Provincial Park and
    Forest, Manitoba, 316
S.S. *Klondike* Sternwheeler National
    Historic Site, Whitehorse, 342
Stanley, Governor-General Lord, 121
Stanley Park, Vancouver, 121
Steamer *Keno*, Dawson City, 346
Steele, Samuel B., 84
Steel Narrows Historic Park, Sask.,
    278–279
Stefansson, Vilhjalmur, 325
Steinbach, Manitoba, 326
Steinbach Pioneer Days, Manitoba, 304
Stephansson House, Alberta, 207
Stephansson, Stephan G., 207
Stephen Juba Park, Winnipeg, 315
Stockmen's Memorial Foundation, Cal-
    gary, 221
Strathcona Park, B.C., 187
Strathcona Science Park, Edmonton, 254
Stuart, John, 195
study in Canada, regulations, 41
Sumac Ridge Estate Winery, B.C., 69
Sunshine Coast, B.C., 60–61
Sunshine Village, Banff, 230–31
Swan Lake–Christmas Hill Nature
    Sanctuary, Victoria, 167

Symington, Frank Worthington, 311

Takhini Hot Springs, Whitehorse,
    342–43
telecommunications, 54–55
telephone area codes, 25
Terrace, B.C., 193–94
Terrace Heritage Park, B.C., 192
Thebacha Campus of Arctic College,
    N.W.T., 358
Thompson, David, 85, 241, 261
thoroughbred and harness racing
    Edmonton, 258
    Regina, 288
    Vancouver, 144–45
    Victoria, 175
    Winnipeg, 320
Thunderbird Park, Victoria, 161
time zones, 25
tipping, about, 23
Tofino, B.C., 186
Tomison, William, 248
Topham Brown Art Gallery, B.C., 70
tourism agencies, provincial and city,
    17–18
Tourism Saskatchewan, 265–66
Trail, B.C., 80
trail rides
    Banff, 233
    B.C., 89, 194
    Jasper, 243
    Manitoba, 302
Trans-Canada Highway 1, B.C., 62–64
Mile "0," 163
transportation companies, major, 28–29
travel, 26–31 (*See also* Customs)
    agent, 26
    discount fares, 26
    package tours, cruises, vacations,
        26–28
Travel Alberta, 201–02
Travel Manitoba, 300
Tuktoyaktuk, N.W.T., 357
Turner, John, 97
Turner Valley, Alberta, 205–206
Tweedsmuir Park, B.C., 88
Tyrrell, Joseph Burr, 207
Tyrrell Museum of Paleontology, Al-
    berta, 206–207

Ucluelet, B.C., 184, 185, 186
Ukrainian Canadian Archives Museum,
    Edmonton, 254
Ukrainian connection, Sask., 275

Ukrainian Cultural and Education Centre (Oseredok), Winnipeg, 312
Ukrainian Cultural Heritage Village, Alberta, 208
Ukrainian Culture, Museum of, Saskatoon, 275, 292
Ukrainian Festival, National, Manitoba, 304
Ukrainian Greek Orthodox Cathedral, Winnipeg, 315
Ukrainian Museum of Canada (Alberta Branch), Edmonton, 254–55
Ukrainian Museum of Canada, Saskatoon, 293
U'Mista Cultural Centre, B.C., 188
Uniacke Estate Winery, B.C., 69
University of British Columbia Museums, Vancouver, 127
Anthropology Museum, 124–25
Endowment Lands, 127
Nitobe Memorial Gardens, 122–23
University of Lethbridge, Alberta, 204
University of Manitoba, Winnipeg, 314
U.S. Consulates in Western Canada, 53–54
U.S. Customs (reentry into U.S.A.), 47–48

Valley of a Thousand Faces, B.C., 188
Valley Zoo, Edmonton, 255
Vancouver, B.C., 95–147
access, 100–104
accommodations, 129–36
attractions, 124–29
basic facts, 100
business and convention services, 105, 108–109
dining, 136–41
entertainment, 141–42
history, 97–100
how to get around, 104–105
map, 106–107
neighborhoods, 118–20
parks, gardens, beaches, 120–24
professional sports, 144–45
recreation, 145–47
shopping, 143–44
special events, 110–12
touring services, 117–18
tours outside of city, 112–17
useful information, 109–10
Vancouver Aquarium, 125
Vancouver Art Gallery, 126–27
Vancouver Canucks, 144, 145

Vancouver, Captain George, 12, 97, 99
Vancouver Island, 178–88
camping at provincial parks, 180
Vancouver Millionaires, 99
Vancouver Museum, 126
Vanderhoof, B.C., 195
Vanderhoof International Airshow, B.C., 195
VanDusen Botanical Gardens, Vancouver, 123
Van Horne, Sir William Cornelius, 98
Vernon, B.C., 69–70
Vernon Museum, B.C., 69
Via Rail, 28–29
Victoria, B.C., 148–96
access, 152–55
accommodations, 167–71
attractions, 160–67
basic facts, 152
business and convention services, 157
dining, 171–73
entertainment, 174
history, 150–52
how to get around, 155–57
map, 156
shopping, 176–78
special events, 158–59
sports and recreation, 174–75
touring services, 159–60
useful information, 158
Victoria Heritage Village, 162–63
Victoria, Queen, 197, 229, 274, 300
statue of, 161, 311

Walsh, James, 271
Wardair, 28
Ware, John, 206
Wasagaming, Manitoba, 324
Wascana Centre, Regina, 283–84
Waskesiu Lake, Sask., 270
water for drinking, 55
Waterton-Glacier International Peace Park, 227
Waterton Lakes National Park, Alberta, 227–28
Watson Lake, Yukon Terr., 340–41
Wayside Garden and Arboretum, B.C., 82
West Coast Maritime Museum, B.C., 186
West Coast Trail, B.C., 184
West Edmonton Mall and Canada Fantasyland, Edmonton, 252–53

Western Canada
  geography, 4–6
  great cities, 13–15
  history, 6–13
  map, 2–3
Western Canadian Aviation Museum,
  Winnipeg, 313
Western Cariboo Outfitters, B.C., 89
Western Development Museum, Sask.,
  277, 279
West Kootenay National Exhibition
  Centre, B.C., 81
Whale Town, B.C., 187–88
Whaling Station, B.C., 189
Whippletree Junction, B.C., 181
Whistler Resort Area, B.C., 116–17
White Goat wilderness area, Alberta,
  207
Whitehorse, Y.T., 341–44
  accommodations, 343
  attractions, 341–43
  dining, 343–44
  shopping, 343
  travel services, 341, 344
Whitehorse Heritage Walks, 342
Whitehorse Library and Art Gallery,
  341
Whiteshell Provincial Park, Manitoba,
  315–16
Whoop-up Country, 271
Wickaninnish Centre, B.C., 185
Wild Waters, B.C., 71
Williams Golf and Tennis Club, B.C.,
  88
Williams Lake, B.C., 87–88
Willmore Wilderness Park, Alberta, 208
wineries
  Okanagan/Similkameen region, B.C.,
    68–69
Winnipeg, Manitoba, 305–21
  access, 308
  accommodations, 316–17
  attractions, 310–16
  business and convention services,
    310
  dining, 317, 319
  entertainment, 319–20
  historic churches, 314–15
  how to get around, 308–10
  map, 309
  parks, 315–16
  professional sports, 320

  recreation, 320–21
  shopping, 321
Winnipeg Art Gallery, 314
Winnipeg Blue Bombers, 320
Winnipeg Jets, 320
Wood Buffalo National Park, Alberta,
  209, 357–58
Wood Mountain Post Historic Park,
  Sask., 277
Wood Mountain Stampede, Sask., 277
World Heritage Site
  Burgess, Yoho National Park, 76
  Dinosaur Provincial Park, Alberta,
    203–04
  "Head Smashed In" Buffalo Jump,
    Alberta, 204
Writing on Stone Provincial Park, Al-
  berta, 206

yachting, 36
Yale, B.C., 66
Yellowhead Pass, B.C., 66
Yellowknife, N.W.T., 354–56
  access, 354–55
  accommodations, 356–57
  attractions, 355–56
  dining, 356
  shopping, 356
  special events, 355
Yellowknife Courthouse, 356
Yoho National Park, B.C., 76–78
Yukon Gardens, Whitehorse, 342
Yukon Government Building Tours,
  Whitehorse, 342
Yukon Lou Stern-Wheeler, Dawson
  City, 346
Yukon Territory, 327–47
  access, 331–33
  basic facts, 330–31
  camping, 335–36
  climate, 330
  geography, 329–30
  map, 328
  population, 329
  scenic highways, 339–40
  special attractions, 337–48
  special events, 336
  touring services, 334–35
  tourist information, 333
  useful information, 333

Zalm, Vander, 128